THE WAY, TRUTH, AND LIFE

The Way, the Truth, and the Life

The Teachings and Ministry of Jesus the Messiah

Dr. Frederick Osborn

FREDERICK OSBORN

The Way, the Truth, and the Life:
The Teachings and Ministry of Jesus the Messiah

Frederick Osborn, © 2017

Published in the USA by BfAbooks

Books, U.S.A.

www.bfabooks.com

NOTE:

Portions of Lessons 1, 2, 4 and 10 are from *Exploring the New Testament, A Survey Course for Personal or Group Study,* Frederick Osborn © 2010, (Second Edition, © 2015), Pub. BfA Books, USA

Portions of Lessons 3, 4, 5, 6, and 7 are from *This Gospel of the Kingdom,* Frederick Osborn © 2011, 2014, Pub. BfA Books, USA

Portions of Lesson 7 are from *Our Jehovah Rapha: A Christ Centered, Holistic Approach to Wellness,* Frederick Osborn © 2014, Pub. BfA Books, USA

SPECIAL THANKS:

I would like to give a special thanks to my friend, Maria Clara for generously allowing me to use a number of her paintings to illustrate parts of this book. Maria Clara is a folk artist who lives and works in Hyderabad, India. Her visions are for the glory and majesty of God that are there for everyone to see in His creation. She is a post-graduate in commerce, but also has been trained in art and with the skill that she acquired, she started painting Biblical subjects. Through every work of her art, she wants to glorify God. Married to Chilkuri Sushil Rao, she has a son, Chilkuri Nishan Sampreeth. You can visit her website at: http://artistmariaclara.blogspot.in/

FREDERICK OSBORN

TABLE OF CONTENTS

Introduction	6
1. **"In the Fullness of Time"** The background of the Gospels	9
2. **"Messiah, Son of Man, Son of God, Savior and Lord"** Jesus in Context of the Gospels	48
3. **"Jesus and John the Baptist"** From the birth, of Jesus to the Start of His Earthly Ministry	76
4. **"Jesus the Teacher"** The Public Teachings of Jesus	108
5. **"Jesus Corrects the Distortions of the Law"** Jesus' Conflicts with the Pharisees, Scribes, and Sadducees	136
6. **"The Kingdom Parables of Jesus"** Jesus Teaches the Mysteries of the Kingdom of God	168
7. **"The Miracles of Jesus"** Jesus Authenticates His Ministry by His Authority Over Nature, Sickness, and Demons	188
8. **"The King Enters Jerusalem"**	232

The events of Jesus' Final Week

9. "Jesus on Trial"   260
   The Trials Before the Sanhedrin, Pilate, and Herod

10. "Mission Accomplished"   301
    The Resurrection of Jesus

Final Thoughts

Appendices

Bibliography

FREDERICK OSBORN

Introduction

"Inasmuch as many have undertaken to compile a narrative of the things that have been accomplished among us, just as those who from the beginning were eyewitnesses and ministers of the word have delivered them to us, it seemed good to me also, having followed all things closely for some time past, to write an orderly account for you, most excellent Theophilus, that you may have certainty concerning the things you have been taught." Luke 1:1-4 (ESV)

Beginning with Luke's inspired account numerous books have been written that attempt to describe the words and actions of Jesus of Nazareth in an orderly and chronological fashion. However, one of the great challenges for the modern commentator is the fact that the Gospel writers were not journalists or historians by contemporary standards. Matthew, Mark, Luke, and John were first and foremost, missionaries; and the stories they told had one primary purpose: to convince their readers that what they testified about Jesus Christ was faithful and true. Therefore, they were less concerned with inserting every fact about the man Jesus of Nazareth in chronological order than they were with including those facts that were most relevant to the message they intended to communicate about Jesus the Messiah. Those facts were organized in a way that best fit the particular narrative they presented.

In Lesson One of this study we will examine the background of the gospel narratives – the cultural settings and the primary audiences for each of the authors. How, what, and why they wrote what they did depended a lot upon their target audience. Matthew is the most Jewish of all the Gospels. Mark appears to be intended for a Roman audience. Luke was directed towards those who were immersed in a worldview shaped by the Greeks. And John, believed to be the last Gospel written, was intended for a more universal audience. But in every case the author failed to encompass the entire length and breadth of Jesus' earthly life and ministry. John himself admitted the futility of just such an attempt: "And there are also many other things that Jesus did, which if they were written one by one, I suppose that even the world itself could not contain the books that would be written." John 21:25

Harmonies of the Gospels help to sort and arrange the storylines – especially of the Synoptic Gospels – but it is clear from the discrepancies found in the different harmonies that there are gaps in every narrative. Even after piecing the Gospels together and harmonizing them as best as possible, a single and comprehensive biography of the life of Christ eludes Bible scholars. At best, all we have are four scrapbooks of snapshots and articles portraying Jesus in action or teaching the masses. In each case the author, guided by the unseen hand of the Holy Spirit, carefully selects which scenes best help move his narrative forward and how they ought to be arranged for maximum impact. Matthew, Mark, Luke and John succeed in making convincing arguments for why and how the life of Jesus was unique. In the end, each writer achieves their primary goal: to communicate the idea that through His life, death, and resurrection Jesus of Nazareth is indeed Lord and Christ for all who believe.

This study on the life of Christ will not attempt to lay out every event, person, and place described in the four Gospels onto a tightly arranged timeline – neatly harmonized and tied up with a nice bow. This study will be topical; but it will not completely ignore the Gospels' sequence of events as it moves roughly in chronological order. The topics overlap at times and at times the chronology of a particular topic is close and precise (as in the final hours of Jesus' life). We will at least touch on every major event, but will only go into details when those details are necessary to give greater depth and understanding to the particular topic of that lesson.

After the background of the Gospels is carefully analyzed, the next lesson will highlight the events surrounding the birth of Jesus to the start of His early ministry. The major focus of this lesson will be twofold: (1) to establish the Messianic credentials of Jesus and, (2) to compare and contrast John's ministry with that of Jesus'. Following the lesson on Jesus and John the Baptist will be a lesson discussing the public sermons of Jesus – what He taught to the masses and why. In lesson four Jesus' conflicts with the Pharisees will take center stage. Jesus did not come to destroy the Mosaic Law or replace it with something new; He came to fulfill the law.

No study of Jesus' teachings can be complete unless it includes a study of His parables – and especially those parables intended to reveal the mysteries of the kingdom. A chapter will be devoted to the miracle ministry of Jesus – how it authenticated His teaching ministry and served to confirm His authority to speak to the nation while drawing the crowds to Him so they would hear His message.

The final countdown of events during the last week begins with Lesson seven and continues through the last lesson. Jesus' last major discourses for His disciples are reviewed. The earth shattering events of the Last Days and His final, urgent appeals to His intimate disciples will be studied. Jesus' arrest and trials are studied; His death and resurrection will close the last chapter of this study. Although it is chronological only in a few places and in the general flow of the topics, this study will nevertheless be a comprehensive study of the words and ministry of Jesus of Nazareth. In the end, this study will be thorough and complete.

1.
"In the Fullness of Time"
The Background of the Gospels

FREDERICK OSBORN

LESSON OUTLINE

The purpose of this lesson is to explain the time and place where Jesus was born, lived and ministered in order to gain some understanding of why Jesus was born into the world at that particular time. This lesson will incorporate visual aids (pictures) to help communicate the major ideas and cultures that shaped the world in a unique way, truly making it "the fullness of time."

The picture that introduces this lesson reveals the three major cultural influences that shaped the worldviews of the people Jesus would encounter during His lifetime.

1. GREECE – The Greek letters and philosophers illustrate that although the empire of Alexander the Great was long gone and Greece was now a province in the Roman Empire, the Greek Worldview still dominated civilized culture throughout the West.
   - Humanistic Greek Philosophy and Religion dominated the arts and sciences.
   - Greek was the universal and unifying language

2. ROME – The map of the Roman Empire with the letters "Pax Romana" indicates that when Jesus was born Rome ruled the world around Him, including Palestine.
   - "Pax Romana" was the term used to describe the peace Rome secured by its law and order.
   - Rome unified the Western world through its system of roads, its civil law, and its military might.

3. JUDAISM – Jesus was born and raised a devout Jew. The Hebrew religion was dominated by the Law of Moses and the expectation of the coming of a Messianic Kingdom.

"In the Fullness of Time, God sent His Son…"

"But when the fullness of time had come, God sent forth his Son, born of woman, born under the law, to redeem those who were under the law, so that we might receive adoption as sons." Galatians 4:4-5 (ESV)

The not-so-silent Years – Many historians call the period of history between the Old and New Testaments "The Silent Years" because during that time God had not moved upon any of His servants to add any fresh revelation to the Hebrew Scriptures. The Lord seemed to be silent concerning the destiny of His chosen people, and so it seemed that the people were being held in suspension until the long-awaited Messiah would come and usher in the Golden Age of a new, glorious kingdom. The establishment of this Messianic Kingdom would see all of God's promises to the nation fulfilled.

However, historians of the centuries preceding Christ's birth show that God was far from being silent between the times when the final chapters of the Hebrew Scriptures were written and when John the Baptist appeared on the scene. In fact the Lord was preparing the world stage for the arrival of its Savior, and each of the major events concerning kings and kingdoms in and around the Middle East would lend its own piece to the scene that would form the backdrop for Jesus' life and ministry.

One way or another when Jesus entered upon the world stage, He would have to address those whose lives had been affected to one degree or another by the following defining events of the Silent Years.

- **Rise of the Greek Empire Under Alexander the Great – 300 BC**

King Alexander III of Macedon (356 BC – 323 BC) is commonly known as Alexander the Great. As his name implies, he was and is considered one of the greatest military and political leaders of the ancient world. Born in Pella as a member of the Argead dynasty, he succeeded his father Philip II to the throne of Macedonia at the age of only twenty. He spent almost his entire ruling years on an unparalleled military campaign through Asia and northeast Africa. By

the end of his meteoric career he had created one of the largest empires of the ancient world stretching from Greece to northwestern India.

During his youth, Alexander was tutored by the renowned Greek philosopher, Aristotle. After his father Philip was assassinated in 336 BC, Alexander succeeded him to the throne and inherited a growing kingdom with an experienced, battle-tested army. Once he solidified his power over Macedonia, Alexander united all of Greece and used his authority as supreme commander of the Greeks to launch his conquest of Persia.

In 334 BC, Alexander, at the head of his army invaded the Persian Empire. Vastly outnumbered, nevertheless Alexander began a series of successful campaigns that lasted ten years. Alexander broke the military power of Persia through a series of decisive battles. His victories in battle led to the overthrow of Persian King Darius III, enabling Alexander to completely subdue the Persians. By the age of thirty, Alexander's Empire stretched from the Adriatic Sea to the Indus River. However, Alexander failed to achieve his ultimate goal of reaching the "ends of the world and the Great Outer Sea" because his homesick troops rebelled and demanded that he turn back from his invasion of India.

The article on Alexander in *Wikipedia* states: "Alexander's legacy includes the cultural diffusion which his conquests engendered, such as Greco-Buddhism. He founded some twenty cities that bore his name, most notably Alexandria in Egypt. Alexander's settlement of Greek colonists and the resulting spread of Greek culture in the east resulted in a new Hellenistic civilization, aspects of which were still evident in the traditions of the Byzantine Empire in the mid-15th century AD and the presence of Greek speakers in central and far eastern Anatolia until the 1920s. Alexander became legendary as a classical hero in the mold of Achilles, and he features prominently in the history and mythic traditions of both Greek and non-Greek cultures. He became the measure against which military leaders compared themselves, and military academies throughout the world still teach his tactics. He is often ranked among the most influential people in human history."

- ***Hellenism*: The efforts of the Greeks to make all things Greek**

In its broadest definition, *Hellenism* refers to the period from the death of Alexander the Great in 323 BC to the Romans final defeat of Egypt and its incorporation into the Roman Empire in 30 BC. As it concerns the Jewish people in Palestine and scattered throughout the remnants of Alexander's Empire, the term is used to designate the influences of Greek civilization over non-Greek peoples and cultures of the ancient world.

ONE OF HEROD THE GREAT'S PALACES BUILT AFTER THE GREEK STYLE OF ARCHITECTURE - Large scale animation project for the "Herod The Great: The King's Final Journey" Exhibition, ISRAEL

Alexander was not content to militarily subdue the world. He believed in the superiority of Greek language, science, philosophy, etc. and wanted to spread Greek culture wherever he went. He wanted the Greek language to be a bridge language to unify the various people groups brought into his ever-expanding Empire. Following his army was another army of teachers, scientists, philosophers, architects, doctors, and social engineers assigned the task of remaking the world in the image of the Greeks. The territory of the Jews was one of Alexander's many conquests and was also subject to this program of Hellenism, but with little success. The greatest contribution of the Greeks at that time was the Septuagint, a Greek translation of Jewish writings, including the sacred Scriptures of the Hebrews.

By the time Jesus was born, the major presence of Hellenism in Roman Palestine was in the non-Jewish aristocracy established by

Herod the Great (74 BC – 4 BC). Installed by the Roman government to rule over Palestine, the Herodians were more Hellenistic than Hebrew at heart. They were educated after the Greeks and adopted their language, art, architecture, religion, and philosophy into their administration over the Jewish province.

A great deal of friction existed between the Herodians and the indigenous Jewish population that strictly followed their own religion and spoke Hebrew and Aramean. The Jews resisted those who attempted to impose upon them the Greek cultural influences being imported through Greek literature, philosophy, language, schools and the gymnasia. By the time Jesus was born, the Jews had stubbornly organized themselves in terms of their distinctly religious and traditional beliefs. Although they were politically and culturally under the domination of the Roman State and their Herodian proxies, they maintained their fierce independence in personal and religious matters. "The independence of Jewish intellectual life in the Hellenistic age is partly explained by the fact that while Jews took a great interest in Greek ideas, the outside world took relatively little interest in Hebrew ideas. The translation of the Bible into Greek did not mean that the Greeks read the Bible. The isolation in which the Jews lived, especially in Judea, was conducive to the creation of a style of thought and life which can be (and was) considered competitive with Hellenistic civilization."
(http://www.jewishvirtuallibrary.org/hellenism)

- **The Jewish Revolt under Judas Maccabeus – 166 BC**

Alexander's Empire passed into the hands of his generals. Once the Empire was divided, the generals quickly became involved in numerous conflicts to secure their kingdoms. Power struggles ensued for supremacy over all the territories of the vast empire, but no one was able to unite by political persuasion or force what Alexander had conquered. The Ptolemaic Kingdom was founded in 305 BC to rule Egypt; the Seleucid Empire contained the former territories of Alexander's Persian kingdom; and the Antigonid Dynasty held onto Macedonia including a few of the Greek city states. Eventually, Palestine came under the rule of the Seleucid King Antiochus IV (c. 215 BC – 164 BC). Prior to his reign the Ptolemy and Seleucid kings maintained a benevolent suzerainty over Judea. Although they were pure Hellenists, they respected Jewish culture and religion and did nothing to disturb them. However, this policy was rudely and suddenly reversed by the fanatical Hellenism imposed by Antiochus IV. When the Jews resisted efforts to syncretize their religion with the Greeks, the King ordered severe persecutions to subdue the Jewish territory. This led to the Maccabean Revolt which is written about in the Apocryphal Books of the Maccabees as well as the *Antiquity of the Jews* written by the ancient Jewish historian Flavius Josephus.

After his unsuccessful Egyptian campaign Antiochus IV, returned to Jerusalem to put down a Jewish revolt against him. He attacked the city and subdued it; in the process he brutally executed many of the Jews. Maccabees and Josephus both describe the indiscriminate massacre of young and old, women and children. Approximately eighty thousand souls were destroyed by the brutal King Antiochus IV Epiphanes, and about the same number were sold into slavery, never to see their homes again.

Mina of Antiochus IV Epiphanes

It was only natural for Antiochus to ally himself with the Hellenized Jews in Judea in order to reinforce his rule over the province. With the help of the Greek faction of the Jews, the King outlawed the sacred Jewish rites and traditions and ordered the worship of the Greek supreme god, Zeus (a.k.a. the Roman god Jupiter). The Jews resisted, but Antiochus sent his army back to Jerusalem and the city was destroyed with another great slaughter (168 BC). The continued brutality and forced Hellenization of Judea led to a growing revolt against the Seleucids and their Jewish Hellenistic allies. Similar to the history of the Judges, a series of national heroes arose to lead the anti-Hellenistic party of the Hasidim. Beginning with the village priest Mattathias, followed by his son Judas the Maccabee (Judas the Hammer), Judas' brothers Jonathan, and later Simon, the

Jews fought for their independence on the battlefield and in diplomacy. Under their leadership, the Jews were able to liberate themselves from their Seleucid masters and established the Hasmonean line of succession for the office of the High Priest.

The epic age of the Maccabean struggle for independence came to an abrupt end in 135 BC when Simon and his two sons were assassinated by a power-hungry son-in-law. However, the age did not end in total failure. The Jewish Hellenists had been completely discredited and were fading away; never again would they be able to pressure the people to compromise their religion. The long Maccabean struggle made the Hasidim the dominant faction in the Jewish community. The Pharisees emerged from the ideals of the Hasidim while the party of Sadducees formed around the remnants of the Hellenists. By the time Jesus arrived on the scene, the Sadducees and Pharisees were the two most influential factions in Palestine. The Herodians were non-Jewish Hellenists that gained their power in the region by aligning themselves with Rome and declaring themselves to be loyal subjects.

The politics of Jewish independence had a major impact on the Messianic hopes and dreams of the people. Most believed that when the Messiah came, he would be a military hero – a conquering king from the line of David who would destroy all of Israel's hated enemies and extend Israel's borders to the limits of the Promised Land (Gen. 15:18-20). The Jews believed that when the Messiah came he would establish an exclusively Jewish kingdom and would reign and rule from Mount Zion where a glorious and restored temple would stand.

- **The Rise of the Roman Empire from 215 BC (63 BC Rome conquers Jewish territory)**

The Hasmonean dynasty did not last long; and the independence of Judea would be quickly swept away with the arrival of the Roman legions. Political intrigue and internal struggles left the Jewish state exposed and the venerable Roman General Pompey took advantage of the situation. He invaded Jewish territory on the pretext of wanting to arbitrate a dispute over who was the rightful king to succeed Alexandra.

After the death of Alexander the Great, the Roman State started to expand eastward across the Mediterranean. Before the end of 146 BC, they had conquered Macedonia and North Africa. Egypt came under Roman rule in 30 BC after Antony and Cleopatra's alliance was defeated by Octavian (later known as Caesar Augustus) in a Roman civil war. With Macedonia and Egypt securely in the Roman Empire, it was only a matter of time before Rome would make its move and capture Asia Minor and the all-important lands bordering the eastern Mediterranean Sea.

Rome solidified its power over the Jewish state by installing Antipater as the ruler of Palestine (47 BC). Antipater had backed the right faction in Rome's civil war and was rewarded by being named the governor of the province. Antipater's son Herod (later known as Herod the Great) had Rome's support and he was able to eliminate every rival and deepen his political control over the region. After Antony's defeat, Octavian confirmed Herod as king of the Jews. However, the Jews always resented Herod and his descendants because they were not Jews, but Idumeans. This made the Herodians jealous and suspicious of any Messianic "son of David" who claimed to be the rightful king of the Jews.

- **The Origin of the Major Jewish Sects of Pharisees, Sadducees, Essenes, and Zealots**

"The rise of Jewish sects is traceable to the impact of Hellenism on the life and culture of the Near East. When the new clashes with the old, violent reactions frequently result. This is particularly true when the new ideology has religious and moral overtones." Charles F. Pheiffer, *Between the Testaments,* Baker Book House, Grand Rapids MI, © 1959, p.111

The encroachments of Hellenism into Jewish lives and culture presented a new challenge for those who firmly believed that it was the idolatry of their forefathers that brought God's disfavor and disaster upon nation. As the books of Ezra and Nehemiah confirm, the returning exiles from Babylon arrived in the ruins of Jerusalem more determined than ever not to repeat the mistakes of the past. These pious Jews had no interest in compromise with the new world order of Alexander the Great's Hellenistic vision. Although some Jews had no qualms about embracing a Greek culture that more often than not conflicted with the Torah, other Jews reacted strongly – sometimes violently – against any attempt to syncretize their religion and traditions with what the Hellenizers promoted as a superior culture. The Jews who resisted the temptation to accommodate the Hellenists and who spoke out strongly against Jews that neglected the Torah and their Jewish religious heritage are called the Hasidim of Assidians.

In Jesus' time, those who believed it was acceptable for Jews to embrace the ideology of Hellenism formed around the aristocratic faction of the Sadducees. They were quite willing to compromise with the Gentiles when it profited them. The Sadducees were theological liberals. They discounted the Hebrew Scriptures and limited their authority; they rejected the Pharisees' attempts to define righteousness and maintain religious separation from the Greeks and Romans. Sadducees did not believe in the resurrection, angels, or the existence of a spirit realm. Because their wealth and influence depended upon the Temple and its services, the Sadducees came to an abrupt demise when Jerusalem and the Temple were completely destroyed by the Romans in 70 AD.

The Hasidim formed two groups that strived to preserve the Law of Moses as central to Jewish life, morals, and customs: the Pharisees and the Essenes. The Pharisees gained in power and influence along with Sadducees during the period when the Hasmoneans ruled. The Sadducees solidified their control of the Temple and all the activities related to it. Meanwhile, the scribes and Pharisees emerged from Babylon in control of the synagogue as the primary center of non-sacrificial worship and religious instruction for the Jewish communities. The Pharisees were religious zealots; they were separatists (the name "Pharisee" means "separated ones") which involved maintaining strict separation from the Gentiles and sinners – especially from the Hellenists.

Pharisee

The Pharisees sought to apply the Law to the changing conditions brought on by the influx of Hellenism into their sphere of influence. These fresh applications of Mosaic Law were presented as "oral law" that the Pharisees argued was equal to the written law delivered to Moses at Sinai. It was this "oral law" that Jesus equated with "the traditions of men" that distorted and undermined the true understanding or "fulfillment" of the Mosaic Law. Jesus argued that these traditions kept the Pharisees clean on the outside, but left their souls untouched. It was this external show of religious piety that Jesus fought to unmask in His teachings. "The degeneracy of Pharisaism serves as a warning to those who take a stand for separation from evil. Self-complacency and spiritual pride are temptations to which the pious are particularly susceptible." Charles F. Pheiffer, *Between the Testaments,* Baker Book House, Grand Rapids MI, © 1959, p.115

THE PHARISEES AND SADDUCEES

NAME	POSITIVE CHARACTERISTICS	NEGATIVE CHARACTERISTICS
Pharisees	Were committed to obeying All of God's commands	Behaved as though their own religious rules were just as Important as God's rules for living
	Were admired by the common People for their apparent piety	Their piety was often hypocritical, and their efforts often forced others to try to live up to standards even the Pharisees did not live up to
	Believed in a bodily resurrection and eternal life	Believed that salvation came from perfect obedience to the law and was not based upon forgiveness
	Believed in angels and demons	Became so obsessed with obeying their legal interpretations in every detail that they completely ignored God's message of mercy and grace

		Were more concerned with appearing to be good than obeying God
Sadducees	Believed strongly in the Mosaic Law and in Levitical Purity and were more practically minded than the Pharisees	Relied on logic while placing little importance on faith
		Did not believe all the Old Testament was God's Word. Did not believe in a bodily resurrection or eternal life. Did not believe in angels or demons
		Were often willing to compromise their values with the Romans and others in order to maintain their status and influential positions

(From "Tyndale Handbook of Bible Charts and Maps", Tyndale House Publishers, 2001)

The Essenes were the second important group to emerge from the Hasidim. Josephus fills in some of the details about the Essenes in his history, *The Jewish War* (Book II, Chapter 8). While the Pharisees were actively engaged in the life of the Jewish community, the Essenes were monastic and lived quiet lives of simplicity and uniformity in tight-knit communities away from population centers. Their daily lives were characterized by devotion to the Hebrew Scriptures, religious instruction, and physical labor. The Essenes held all things in common, believed in a life after death, but not in a bodily resurrection. Since the discovery of the Dead Sea Scrolls and other archaeological findings in and around Qumran in the 20th century, the Essenes have become the subject of a large body of New Testament scholarship. Much of what has been written about the Essenes and their connection with early Christianity is highly speculative, but the research done by responsible scholars has been useful to help form a more complete picture of Jewish life and theology at the time Jesus was ministering from Judea to Galilee.

The last important group to mention is the Zealots. The Zealots first appeared in Galilee very early in the Roman occupation of Jewish territory. Some of the religious groups urged the people to accept the Roman presence as just punishment for their sins, but the Zealots refused to accept anyone but the God of Israel to be their King. They considered it a sin to acknowledge Caesar's authority over the Jews and refused to pay taxes to Caesar. Although the Zealots eventually succeeded in winning the majority of the Jews to their side, their fanatical resistance against Rome ended in disaster for the nation.

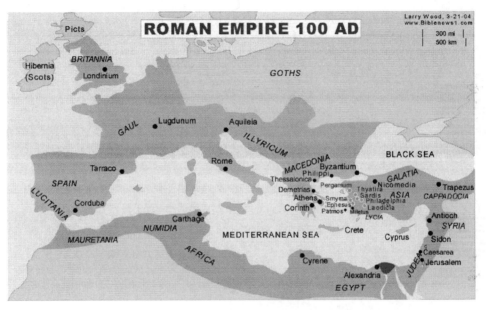

Following the Zealot's call for armed rebellion, the Jews attempted to force Rome to retreat from Jewish lands. Their final rebellion against Roman rule brought the full wrath of Roman legions upon Judea. Exactly as Jesus prophesied in His Olivet Discourse, Jerusalem and the Temple were completely destroyed in 70 AD with the loss of many lives. Most of the surviving Jews were taken captive and scattered throughout the Roman Empire. The Jewish people would not be able to return and rebuild their homeland until the mid-twentieth century.

For the purposes of this study of the life and ministry of Jesus Christ it is only necessary to examine in a general way the impact these historical events had upon Roman Palestine at the time Jesus was born.

Palestine included the territories of Judea, Galilee, and Gaulanitis (the area northeast of Galilee where Caesarea Philippi was located).

There existed in the world of the first century three primary milieus (physical or social settings in which something occurs) which can be easily understood from three separate images. Each image represents one milieu that determined the worldview of the different people Jesus encountered along the way. One way or the other Jesus would have to address these worldviews and offer the kingdom of God as the only viable alternative to each of them. The Three Pictures representing the physical or social settings of first century Roman Palestine are:

1. The picture of Moses on the mountain
2. The picture of the Greek philosophers at the school of Athens
3. The picture of the Roman centurion on horseback

It is important to understand how these pictures represented their times and places and how each shaped the worldviews that existed at the time Jesus was born and carried out His earthly ministry.

A worldview is more than a way of looking at the world; it is the overall perspective from which one sees and interprets the world around them; it is the set of beliefs about life and the universe held by an individual or a group.

- A worldview **Delineates** – outlines and shapes the values and standards of a particular culture

- A worldview **Defines** – explains how people, places, and things are perceived by a particular culture

- A worldview **Determines** – regulates the human behavior of a particular culture (controls how a person responds to the people, places and things all around them).

Each of these worldviews existed in Palestine at the time Jesus was born. And, everyone who encountered Jesus attempted to fit Him into their particular worldview. At one time or another, Jesus responded to each of these worldviews in His teachings and by His actions. His refusal to bend with or accommodate those who would not accept the gospel of the kingdom He preached caused those who were deeply invested in those other worldviews to reject Him as their Lord and Savior. So the more we understand these worldviews, the more we will understand the people, places, and things Jesus encountered. And the more we will understand how and why Jesus responded to them the way He did. Before examining how Jesus responded to each these worldviews, it will be necessary to investigate and understand each one.

1. Moses on the Mountain: Judaic Worldview

For the Jewish people in the time of Jesus, Jerusalem was the center of their world; they believed that the Temple was the dwelling place of God on the earth. All eyes looked to Jerusalem because the Temple was there and the Jews believed that The Temple was the only place to truly worship God. The Pharisees, Scribes, and Sadducees ruled over the religious life of the people from Jerusalem. The Romans may have controlled the streets of Jerusalem, but the Law of Moses controlled the hearts of the people who dwelled there.

All of the Jewish religion is based upon the Law of Moses. The Lord gave the Law to Moses on Mount Sinai, and since that time the Jews learned through trial and error that the fate of the nation depended upon their obedience to the Law. A Jew was someone who was born into the Covenant of Sinai. Every member of the community was taught that being in Covenant relationship with God meant that when they obeyed the Law of Moses, the nation prospered, but when they rebelled and disobeyed, the nation suffered. So they saw a direct relationship between their oppression by the Roman

government and their failure to live in perfect righteousness and obedience before the Lord.

Over the centuries, the changing circumstances of the children of Moses under the Gentiles caused them to become acutely sensitive to any possible infringement of God's commands. For example, exactly how the commandment to "remember the Sabbath Day and keep it holy" was questioned by Jews living under Gentile civil laws. Pharisaic laws amended the Law of Moses and they eventually became the standard of righteousness for all Jews. These oral interpretations of the written Law of Moses were treated by the Jews as equal to the written Law based upon the belief that these interpretations were implied by Mosaic Law. *The Encyclopedia of the Bible* article on the Pharisees states, "The basic issue was the authority of the oral law. The Pharisees accepted along with the Torah, as equally inspired and authoritative, all of the explanatory and supplementary material produced by, and contained within, the oral tradition. This material apparently began to evolve during the Babylonian Exile through the new circumstances thereby brought upon the Jewish people. The Exile was seen as divine punishment for neglect of the law, and accordingly during this period there was an earnest turning to the law. Detailed exposition of the law appeared in the form of innumerable and highly specific injunctions that were designed to 'build a hedge' around the written Torah and thus guard against any possible infringement of the Torah by ignorance or accident. In addition, the new circumstances of the Exile and the post-exilic period involved matters not covered in the written Torah; consequently new legislation had to be produced by analogy to, and inference from, that which already existed. The content of this oral law continued to evolve and to grow in vol. through the intertestamental, NT, and post-NT periods, finally to achieve written form in the Mishnah (A.D. 200). For the Pharisees, the oral law came to be revered so highly that it was said to go back to Moses himself and to have been transmitted over the centuries orally, paralleling the written law that also derived from him."
(https://www.biblegateway.com/resources/encyclopedia-of-the-bible/Pharisees)

Since Palestine was part of the Roman Empire, it was subject to Roman authority, but the Herodians administered the local government. By the time Jesus was born the Pharisees and Sadducees had become the ultimate religious power in Palestine and exercised great authority over the people as part of the Sanhedrin. The Sanhedrin had become the highest Jewish ruling body in Judea. The highest tribunal of 71 members met in Jerusalem. Since it was the supreme court of Jewish Law and Justice, when Jesus was arrested He was brought before this court to be tried for religious sedition. The apostles and other leaders in Jerusalem (including Peter, John, Stephen, and Paul) were also brought before the Sanhedrin to defend themselves (Matthew 26:59; Mark 14:55; Mark 15:1; Luke 22:66; John 11:47; Acts 4:15; Acts 5:21ff; Acts 6:12ff; Acts 22:30; Acts 23:1ff; Acts 24:20). The Great Sanhedrin in Jerusalem was composed of high priests, elders, scribes, Pharisees and Sadducees. The acting high priest was always head and presided over the body.

During the period of Jesus' earthly ministry, the Sanhedrin's power and influence was at its greatest; although it lost to the Roman courts its power to sentence someone to death (John 18:31), the people feared the Sanhedrin because anyone could be tried before that body as a false prophet, idolater, or deceiver of the people, and if found guilty could be punished or excommunicated. As the Pharisees grew in importance, they grew in power in the Sanhedrin. So in the time of Christ, the Sanhedrin was practically ruled by the Pharisees. The civil authority of the Sanhedrin was restricted to Judea proper, and for that reason, it had no judicial authority over our Lord so long as He remained in Galilee. But the Scribes and Pharisees were spiritual watchdogs over the people and made sure no one stepped out of line. The Sanhedrin was abolished after the destruction of Jerusalem (70 AD).

For those who had the Jewish worldview the Law of Moses outlined and shaped their values and standards. The Law of Moses explained how they perceived people, places, and things around them. The Law of Moses regulated their behavior; it controlled how a Jewish person responded to the people, places and things all around them. The Jewish worldview can be summed up in one sentence: THE LAW OF GOD IS THE ANSWER TO EVERY NEED.

2. Greek philosopher: the Hellenistic Worldview

For the Hellenists in the time of Jesus, Athens was the center of their world. For them, Athens was the place where science and philosophy – the systematic studies of nature and human knowledge began. In the time of Alexander the Great, the Greeks began to spread their culture around the world. Because he believed in the superiority of Greek culture, when Alexander conquered a people, he brought in teachers to establish schools and teach them to love and respect all things Greek. This gave the birth to the system known as Hellenism.

School of Athens (Detail)
Fresco Painted by Raphael (1509-11)

Greek language was the primary means the Greeks used to promote and spread their culture. All educated people in Alexander's Empire were taught in Greek. Astronomy, philosophy, medicine, religion, mathematics, architecture, etc. were all transmitted in Greek. The Greek philosophy based upon the idea that human reason was supreme became the scale by which all other ideas were measured. Artists, Scientists, philosophers, intellectuals, and teachers were the most valued people to the Greeks because they were the ones who defined and transmitted their culture around the world.

The Greek worldview was grounded in their humanistic philosophy that placed man as the center of all things; humanism outlined and shaped the values and standards of the Greeks. Their philosophy explained how people, places, and things were perceived by those who believed in the superiority of all human knowledge. Their humanistic worldview determined how the Hellenists responded to the people, places and things all around them. Simply defined, humanism says, "Man is the measure of all things". In essence, self is god because man determines what is and is not true, or right, good, moral, and what is reality itself. The purpose of knowledge was to set man free from the shadowy world of illusions. The Hellenistic worldview can be summed up in one sentence: "HUMAN KNOWLEDGE IS THE ANSWER TO EVERY NEED"

3. The Centurion: The Roman Worldview

The Centurion, on horseback, represents the third worldview that existed at the time of Jesus. He is holding his sword up high and riding into battle to conquer. The Roman worldview states that temporal, earthly power is supreme. For those who had the Roman worldview, Rome was the center of their world. It was said at the time that "All roads lead to Rome"; and in fact the Romans built an advanced system of roads that connected their Empire. The Roman transportation system made travel and trade easy, but most importantly, it allowed their Legions to quickly travel throughout the Empire to enforce Rome's will. Rome's power was established by its military prowess. So the Roman worldview was based upon the idea that "might makes right." Enforcing the Civil laws and social order of *Pax Romana* (Roman peace) were of primary importance to the Romans. A person could live how they wanted, worship whatever gods they chose, or live where they wanted as long as they did not upset the civil or social order or break the laws of Rome. For the Romans, the politician, soldier, statesman, and diplomat were held in highest esteem.

Anyone who exercised power through those offices was considered most valuable to Rome and worthy of the highest respect and honor. Because Caesar held the highest and most powerful position in the Empire, his word was law and no one dared challenge his authority. Romans believed that all power came from above and since there was no one on the earth above Caesar, he was worshiped throughout the Empire as a god.

For those who embraced the Roman worldview it was Roman law and order secured by their vast legions of soldiers that delineated the values and standards of their world. People, places, and things were to be understood or interpreted from the Roman perspective of Roman culture that valued total power and the supremacy of their military might over moral right and absolute truth. Rome alone determined how a person responded to the people, places and things all around them. Roman might is what made them feel superior to anyone subject to Caesar's authority. For the Roman, Caesar was synonymous with Rome; so the Roman worldview can be summed up in the sentence: "ROME IS THE ANSWER TO EVERY NEED."

JESUS CHALLENGED EACH OF THESE WORLDVIEWS

Jesus was born into the world at a time place when everyone around Him lived by one or more of these worldviews. One way or another, Jesus challenged each of these worldviews during His lifetime. And in the end, those who embraced one of these three competing and often conflicting worldviews came together to end His life at Calvary.

Jesus' Response to the Judaic Worldview

"Do not think that I have come to abolish the Law or the Prophets; I have not come to abolish them but to fulfill them. For truly, I say to you, until heaven and earth pass away, not an iota, not a dot, will pass from the Law until all is accomplished. Therefore whoever relaxes one of the least of these commandments and teaches others to do the same will be called least in the kingdom of heaven, but whoever does them and teaches them will be called great in the kingdom of heaven. For I tell you, unless your righteousness exceeds that of the scribes and Pharisees, you will never enter the kingdom of heaven." Matthew 5:17-20 (ESV)

The foundation of the Judaic worldview is based on the belief that after the children of Israel reached Mount Sinai, God gave them the Ten Commandments (Exodus 20) and all other laws that were central to the establishment of Israel as a people in covenant relationship with God (Exodus 21-23). The Ten Commandments consist of broad categorical laws that set forth the absolute principles intended to guide all people into a right relationship with the one, true, living God over all of Creation. The

Ten Commandments do not specify how they are to be enforced or what penalties are to be applied if they are broken, but they do make unconditional commands that place moral obligations on all people who seek to live in right relationship to God. The Jews had to be uncompromising on all of the Mosaic Laws written down by Moses in the Pentateuch because as Deuteronomy 4:1-14 stated, the Sinaitic Law was permanent, unchanging, and the life and prosperity of the Hebrew people depended upon perfect obedience to it.

The long history of the Israelites was an account of their struggles to fulfill the purpose of the Law given through Moses at Mount Sinai. "Hear now, O Israel, the decrees and laws I am about to teach you. Follow them so that you may live and may go in and take possession of the land that the Lord, the God of your fathers, is giving you" Deuteronomy 4:1 (NIV). Contained within the Law of Moses were the importance of and the necessity for keeping its commands and statutes. Israel had learned the hard way that failure to keep those commands would bring only disaster. There was a second purpose for the Law: if they kept the Law it would be a positive sign for the surrounding nations; keeping the Law would show the wisdom and understanding of the nation, "Surely this great nation is a wise and understanding people." Deuteronomy 4:5, 6 (NIV)

Moses stated in that same passage of Deuteronomy (4:13, 14) that the Lord's covenant – specifically the Ten Commandments, "which he commanded you to follow and then wrote them on two stone tablets" were to remain a permanent fixture for the nation. "Do not add to what I command you and do not subtract from it, but keep the commands of the Lord your God that I give you." Deuteronomy 4:2 (NIV)

It took the near annihilation of the twelve tribes of Israel and 70 years of Babylonian exile, but the survivors came back to what was left of the Promised Land more determined than ever to keep the Law. However, after the Exile, the religious leaders considered it their highest duty to make sure every jot and tittle of the Law was kept according to how they perceived what every commandment meant. How the Law of Moses was interpreted was preserved in the oral law of the Jews. And it was this oral law that shaped the Judaic worldview of 1st century Judaism.

Jesus challenged the Judaic worldview by challenging the accepted interpretations of the Law of Moses being taught by the scribes and Pharisees of that day. Although verses 17-20 of Matthew chapter 5 make it clear that the kingdom lifestyle about which He was teaching was in perfect harmony with the Old Testament revelation, what He taught about the meaning and fulfillment of the Law of Moses was totally out of sync with what the established religious leaders were teaching about those same precepts. By the time Jesus started His public teaching ministry, the Pharisees, Sadducees, and other religious leaders who were the self-appointed protectors of the Judaic worldview, were promoting a religious legalism that was only concerned with the outward appearances of conformity to the rules, regulations, and rituals of religious law. But (as we will study in more detail in Chapter Five ("Jesus Corrects the Distortions of the Law") the *kingdom lifestyle* that Jesus promoted fulfilled the Law's requirements by shifting the focus of attention away from the outward appearances of religious legalism and dealt with the inward motives and intents of the heart. Jesus taught that true righteousness "surpasses that of the scribes and Pharisees" and is from the heart. True righteousness cannot be imposed by the strict adherence to any religious system (Read Matt. 12:1, 2; Matt. 15:1, 2; Mark 3:1, 2; Mark 14:55, 56; Luke 11:37, 38; Luke 13:14; John 5:15-18; and John 7:45-49). It is no wonder that Jesus found it necessary to preface His teachings on the Mosaic Law in His Sermon on the Mount with, "Do not think that I came to abolish the Law or the Prophets."

Jesus was a direct threat to those who promoted the Judaic worldview. Contrary to what their leaders were saying, Jesus taught that anyone who believed they could justify themselves before God on the basis of their own acts of righteousness would not enter the kingdom of heaven: *"For I tell you that unless your righteousness surpasses that of the Pharisees and the teachers of the law, you will certainly not enter the kingdom of heaven"* (Matt. 5:20).

Jesus was presenting a concept of obedience to Mosaic Law that was completely contrary to the Judaic worldview; He was teaching that the Law was not intended to bring righteousness, but was intended to expose the sin nature and point sinful men and women back to God (Romans 4:13-18; 5:20, 21; 7:5-7). Without ever nullifying or contradicting the Law, Jesus taught about a righteousness that exceeded what was acceptable to Judaism's elite. Jesus' teachings on the Law almost always shifted the emphasis away from an action or behavior that the Jews understood the Law to be about, to the *inner attitude* or *motivation* of the sinner seeking a righteousness that comes from God by grace through faith. As a result, Jesus Christ was in almost constant conflict with those representatives of the Jewish religion that had their own interpretations of the Law of Moses. Those conflicts centered upon the keeping of Jewish rituals and traditions (washings, prayer, sacrifice, feasts, etc. along with the Jews' obsession with keeping Sabbath rules and regulations). From Jesus' perspective His encounters with the religious authorities went much deeper than external rules and regulations, and went instead to the very heart of what it meant to keep the Law with "all your heart, mind, soul, and strength... and to love your neighbor as yourself":

"But when the Pharisees heard that he had silenced the Sadducees, they gathered together. And one of them, a lawyer, asked him a question to test him. 'Teacher, which is the great commandment in the Law?' And he said to him, 'You shall love the Lord your God with all your heart and with all your soul and with all your mind. This is the great and first commandment. And a second is like it: You shall love your neighbor as yourself. On these two commandments depend all the Law and the Prophets.'" Matthew 22:34-40 (ESV)

Today, Christians often separate the Old Testament – the Hebrew *Tanakh* – from the New Testament Scriptures. They are often under the false impression that Jesus came to supersede the Law of Moses (what they perceive to be a works righteousness of obedience to doing the right "dos" and keeping a list of "do nots") with a New Testament law of love and grace alone for salvation. However, we see in this answer to a question on the Law of Moses that Jesus rightly understood the Law of Moses to be based upon love and grace no less than the New Covenant understanding of righteousness by grace through faith.

Here Jesus answered the question, "what is the greatest commandment" by quoting from the Hebrew Scriptures written by Moses; but He did it in an unexpected way. The Jews would have expected Jesus to answer the question from the Ten Commandments, which were considered to be the supreme expression of God's moral law. However, Jesus answered using two other verses from Moses; and by doing so, He totally turned upside down the Judaic worldview of the Pharisees:

"You shall love the LORD your God with all your heart, with all your soul, and with all your strength." Deuteronomy 6:5

"You shall not take vengeance, nor bear any grudge against the children of your people, but you shall love your neighbor as yourself: I am the LORD." Leviticus 19:18

The clearest example of how Jesus turned the Judaic worldview upside down is illustrated in how He dealt with the Pharisee, Nicodemus when he came to see Him (the story is found in John chapter 3). As a Pharisee, Nicodemus would have been completely immersed in the Judaic worldview shaped by the teachings of the Pharisees. Not only did he believe it, but also he was a teacher and a guide to help others follow it with perfection (v 10). Jesus had stirred something in Nicodemus' soul; he was conflicted because he saw that Jesus was no ordinary man, and yet, Jesus was teaching things that Pharisees like Nicodemus found offensive and subversive.

The Judaic worldview was concerned with the Law of Moses, and no doubt Nicodemus would have wanted to question Jesus about the Law, but Jesus immediately took Nicodemus aside and before the first question came from out of his mouth, lifted him to a different level of understanding by telling him "you must be born again". Nicodemus believed that salvation was the result of a strict adherence to the Jewish religious code, but Jesus told him salvation is "born of the Spirit" (vs. 5-8) and comes by faith in the finished work of the Son of God: *"And as Moses lifted up the serpent in the wilderness, so must the Son of Man be lifted up, that whoever believes in him may have eternal life. For God so loved the world, that he gave his only Son, that whoever believes in him should not perish but have eternal life. For God did not send his Son into the world to condemn the world, but in order that the world might be saved through him."* John 3:14-17 (ESV)

Throughout His earthly ministry, Jesus left no doubt in the minds of those who heard Him that He was presenting a radically new understanding of what it meant to fulfill the Law of Moses. It was an understanding in direct opposition to the established teachings of the Jewish religious leaders of that time:

- When Jesus said, *"I am the bread of life"* (John 6:35), He reminded the Jews of the manna in the wilderness that came through Moses. He was saying in essence, "I am the manna that sustains you spiritually"

- When Jesus identified Himself as *"the light of the world"* (John 8:12), He reminded the Jews of verses like, Isaiah 51:4 "*Listen to me, my people; hear me, my nation: The law will go out from me; my justice will become a light to the nations."*

- When Jesus said, *"I am the gate; whoever enters through me will be saved..."* (John 10:9), He brought to remembrance 2 Chronicles 23:18-19, *"Then Jehoiada placed the oversight of the temple of the Lord in the hands of the priests, who were Levites, to whom David had made assignments in the temple, to present the burnt offerings of the Lord as written in the Law of Moses, with rejoicing and singing, as David had ordered. He also stationed doorkeepers at the gates of the Lord's temple so that no one who was in any way unclean might enter."*

    The Judaic worldview taught that obedience to the Law made one clean so that they might enter the Lord's temple. The priests, Pharisees and other religious leaders of the Jews considered themselves to be the Lord's "gate keepers" and kept the Samaritans, Gentiles, and anyone else they considered "unclean" out of the Temple. *"So Jesus again said to them, 'Truly, truly, I say to you, I am the door of the sheep. All who came before me are thieves and robbers, but the sheep did not listen to them. I am the door. If anyone enters by me, he will be saved and will go in and out and find pasture.'"* (John 10:7-9 ESV)
    The Jews used the Mosaic Law and their religious traditions to exclude Gentiles, Publicans, the infirm, and sinners from the presence of God. But Jesus said, "*Come to me, all you who are weary and burdened, and I will give you rest. Take my yoke upon you and learn from me, for I am gentle and humble in heart, and you will find rest for your souls. For my yoke is easy and my burden is light.*" (Matthew 11:28-30) Jesus offered them healing, forgiveness for their sins, and inclusion in the family of God. The Jews placed the yoke of the Law upon the shoulders of sinners; Jesus removed that yoke and offered them the cross, which permanently removed their sins.

- Moses led the children of Israel to the Promised Land like a shepherd. So the message was not lost upon the Jews who heard

Jesus say, "*I am the good shepherd...*" (John 10:11). And beyond that, Jesus prophetically told them, *"the good shepherd gives His life for the sheep"*, which was something Moses could not do.

- The Jews put their trust in the Law of God to save them and keep them out of the jaws of death – as David so eloquently wrote in Psalms 119:81-96: *My soul faints with longing for your salvation, but I have put my hope in your word. My eyes fail, looking for your promise; I say, "When will you comfort me?" Though I am like a wineskin in the smoke, I do not forget your decrees. How long must your servant wait? When will you punish my persecutors? The arrogant dig pitfalls for me, contrary to your law. All your commands are trustworthy; help me, for men persecute me without cause. They almost wiped me from the earth, but I have not forsaken your precepts. Preserve my life according to your love, and I will obey the statutes of your mouth.*

    Your word, O Lord, is eternal; it stands firm in the heavens. Your faithfulness continues through all generations; you established the earth, and it endures.
    Your laws endure to this day, for all things serve you. If your law had not been my delight, I would have perished in my affliction. I will never forget your precepts, for by them you have preserved my life. Save me, for I am yours; I have sought out your precepts. The wicked are waiting to destroy me, but I will ponder your statutes. To all perfection I see a limit; but your commands are boundless."

    So when Jesus said, "*I am the resurrection and the life. He who believes in me will live, even though he dies; and whoever lives and believes in me will never die. Do you believe this?*" (John 11:25-26), He challenged the Jews to put their trust and hope for deliverance from death in the One who was the living fulfillment of the Law.

- Once again, Jesus' proclamation, "*I am the way and the truth and the life. No one comes to the Father except through me.*" (John 14:6) was another direct challenge to the Judaic worldview that taught the way to the Father is through the Law.

- The Jews understood that they were God's chosen people, and as such, Israel was the Lord's vineyard. Jesus' statement, "*I am the true vine..."* (John 15:5), would have caused them to question that belief. If Jesus is the true vine, then the Jews must attach themselves to HIM to receive the blessings of God. Jesus was saying to them that *Abiding* in Him would produce the fruit of the Spirit that God is seeking, and not obedience to the Law.

So in the end, those who held fast to the Judaic worldview were forced to either embrace a whole new paradigm, with salvation by grace through faith in Jesus Christ as the center and focus of their life, or cling to their belief in salvation by the Law of Moses; which meant they would have to find a way to destroy Jesus and silence His message.

Jesus' Response to the Hellenistic Worldview

Apart from knowing the history of the four centuries prior to Jesus' birth, it would seem from the Gospels that the Greeks had little or nothing to do with 1st century Jewish Palestine. The words "Hellenists" or "Hellenism" do not appear in any of the New Testament writings. Mark records only one encounter Jesus had with a "Greek", the Syrophoenician woman He encountered outside of Palestine in Tyre (7:26). John mentions a time when some Greeks wanted to meet with Jesus, but He refused them an audience (12:20-22). So then, to know who the Hellenists in Palestine were and how Jesus responded to them, it is necessary to know the history of the Herodians and to understand their influence in Palestine in the time Jesus was born.

The Herodian dynasty ruled over Palestine from 40 B.C. – 100 A.D. They were not Jews, but Gentiles. Herod the Great was the first in the line of kings installed by Rome to rule over Palestine. He was appointed procurator of Judea by Julius Caesar in 47 B.C. and because of his loyalty to Rome he was appointed king of the Jews in 40 B.C. The Jews were offended by his rule because Herod was not a member of David's royal family. To eliminate any threat from the Jewish Hasmonean family, whom he had displaced from the throne, Herod systematically had their leaders killed. Even though Herod tried in many ways to placate the Jews, including the restoration of the temple in Jerusalem, they never forgave him for destroying the royal family.

Herod the Great was well-learned, and received the finest education of his day, which meant that he would have learned everything from the Greeks. Herod was a *Philhellene* (a lover of Hellenism). He did not trust the Jews so he hired Greek mercenaries to protect him; he inscribed his coins in Greek as well as in Hebrew; he educated his children after the Greeks; and designed numerous royal and civic building projects in the Greek style of architecture. The Hellenistic worldview reached its peak of influence in Palestine under Herod the Great who ruled Judea 37–4 B.C. Although Herod the Great was skilled in diplomacy and battle, and had undertaken many elaborate building projects, he is best remembered for his cruelty. Any threat, real or imagined, was swiftly dealt with – as is illustrated with the slaughter of the infants of Bethlehem (Mt. 2:16).

Herod Antipas, or Herod the tetrarch, inherited this title along with parts of his father's, kingdom – later, his nephew would be named king of the Jews. He divorced his first wife to marry his niece Herodias, who was his half-brother Philip's wife. After John the Baptist denounced this marriage as unlawful, Antipas had John imprisoned. Then on the occasion of Antipas' birthday Herodias encouraged her daughter, Salome, to "dance naked before the king and his court." In appreciation of this, Antipas promised with an oath any gift Salome desired. Her request, as instructed by her mother, was for the head of John the Baptist (Mt 14:1-11). Antipas is the Herod that Pilate sent Jesus to be tried (Lk 23:6-12).
When Agrippa became king of the Jews, Antipas at his wife's insistence, petitioned the Roman Emperor Caligula to make him king of the Jews instead.

Agrippa accused Antipas of planning a revolt. Caligula sided with Agrippa, stripped Antipas of his title and lands and gave them to Agrippa. Antipas was banished to Gaul (39 A.D.). When his wife, Herodias challenged the Emperor's decision against Antipas, her wealth was also given to Agrippa, and she was banished to Gaul with her husband. Agrippa is best remembered for ordering the death of Jesus' brother James, imprisoning Paul (Acts 12:21), and for his incestuous relationship with his sister Bernice. He died at the age of 54 (44 A.D.).

The Herodians rose to power by aligning themselves with Rome and expanded their power through political means rather than by conquest. They were never able or willing to challenge Rome's authority, but were kept in power as long as they remained loyal to Caesar, maintained the peace of Rome, and collected the taxes for the Roman State. Herod the Great was the first to be named "King of the Jews" by a

Roman Caesar. He was hated and resented by the Jews. So in an attempt to placate them, Herod transformed the temple in Jerusalem into a magnificent structure. It was Herod's temple that Jesus stood in front of and told His disciples, "not one stone would be left upon another" (Lk 21:6). Herod admired the Greeks and surrounded himself with teachers accomplished in Greek art, literature, philosophy and science. He launched massive building projects all over his kingdom inspired by Greek architecture. He educated his children after the Greek culture, and by the time Jesus began His public ministry, two of Herod's sons ruled in Palestine:

- Philip the Tetrarch ruled over the northeastern area
- Herod Antipas ruled over the region where John the Baptist and Jesus ministered. Antipas continued the building pattern of Herod the Great and built Tiberius after the ideal Greek architectural pattern (*polis*).

The *Herodians* mentioned in Scripture were more than the immediate members of the royal family; they were all the influential citizens of Palestine who aligned themselves with Herod's dynasty. Everywhere Jesus went He could see the Greek influence in the architecture, and hear it in the names of people and places He visited (Philip, Andrew, Mary, Tyre, Caesarea, Decapolis, Lake Tiberius, and Galilee all bear Greek names).

The Gospels mention two separate encounters involving Jesus and the Herodians:

- Mark chapter 3 describes a time when Jesus healed a man with a withered hand on the Sabbath (vs. 1-5). The Pharisees were angry with Jesus as usual because according their interpretation of the Law, it was wrong to heal on the Sabbath. However, what was not usual about this story is that after all was said and done, the Pharisees went out and plotted with the Herodians how they might destroy Jesus (v. 6). The Pharisees and Herodians hated each other. As devout Jews and protectors of the Jewish Sabbath laws, they would have deeply resented the non-Jewish, Greek-influenced Herodians who owed their political power and allegiance to the Roman Caesars instead of the Law of Moses. To the Pharisees, their co-operation with the Herodians was equivalent to making a pact with the devil to destroy Jesus.

- In Mark chapter 12, the Pharisees and the Herodians were joined together questioning Jesus about paying taxes to Caesar in an attempt to get Him to say something to incriminate Himself with the Roman authorities (vs. 13-17).

The Pharisees and Sadducees were lined up on one side against Jesus because He threatened their Judaic worldview; their religious power and control over the people depended upon the Mosaic Law being supreme. The Herodians were lined up on the other side against Jesus because He preached about another kingdom (the belief that Jesus was the Messiah and therefore the rightful king of the Jews threatened their political power and status).

Except for His answer concerning paying taxes to Caesar, Jesus never responded directly to the Hellenists. In John 12:20 a group of Greek converts to the Jewish faith were in Jerusalem for the Passover celebration. These Greeks approached Philip who had a Greek name, and asked him to arrange the meeting. However, Jesus was indirect and cryptic in His response to their request (vs. 23-28); included in His response were the words, "The man who loves his life will lose it, while the man who hates his life in this world will keep it for eternal life." Since Greek philosophy was concerned in particular with loving this life and the things of this world, these words of Jesus would have startled the Hellenists.

The **Socratic Method** – named after the Greek philosopher Socrates, is a form of inquiry and debate between individuals with opposing viewpoints based on asking and answering questions to stimulate rational thinking and to illuminate ideas.

The last direct confrontation Jesus had with the Hellenists is recorded in Luke 23:6-11. It was the final hours before Jesus was led away to be crucified. After interrogating Him, Pilate sent Jesus to Herod to be examined. Herod, educated in the Greek Socratic method of learning, "plied him with many questions". But Jesus refused to be pulled into a philosophical debate with Herod. Jesus did not come to this earth to introduce a new philosophy; He did not come to start a new religious movement based upon some new teaching of His. Those who have a

Hellenistic worldview believe human knowledge and wisdom have all the answers, and Herod wanted Jesus to philosophically justify Himself before the intellectuals gathered around him. After Jesus refused to explain His teachings or perform miracles like magic tricks, for him, Herod had nothing left to say to Jesus. So Herod and his soldiers mocked Him, ridiculed Him, and sent Him back to Pilate to be crucified.

On that day, another strange alliance was formed between two men with competing worldviews. *"That day Herod and Pilate became friends – before this they had been enemies"* (Luke 23:12). So now the Pharisees, Herodians, and Romans were all united by one thing: their need to destroy Jesus Christ.

We can gain a deeper insight into Jesus' answer to the Hellenists if we take a close look at Matthew 16:13-17 (Note also Mark 8:27-30): *When Jesus came to the region of Caesarea Philippi, he asked his disciples, "Who do people say the Son of Man is?" They replied, "Some say John the Baptist; others say Elijah; and still others, Jeremiah or one of the prophets."*
"But what about you?" he asked. "Who do you say I am?" Simon Peter answered, "You are the Christ, the Son of the living God." Jesus replied, "Blessed are you, Simon son of Jonah, for this was not revealed to you by man, but by my Father in heaven."

Jesus did nothing coincidentally or in a haphazard way. So when he left Galilee and took His disciples to a place called Caesarea Philippi, there was a specific reason for it. It may seem strange that Jesus would take His disciples all the way to Caesarea Philippi to ask them one specific question: "Who do people say that I, the Son of Man, am?" But that is exactly what Jesus did. The reason Jesus brought them there to ask them that question is understood when we discover the fact that Caesarea Philippi was a center of Hellenism. Philip the Tetrarch revitalized the area and renamed the city for himself and Caesar. The influence of the Greeks could be seen everywhere in the architecture and Philip made it a cultural showcase with theatres and temples built to honor the Greek gods – especially the god Pan. It was a strategic city to Rome also, so there would have been a Roman garrison, civil administration, and a Roman bathhouse there as well. The area was part of Palestine, and therefore a strong Jewish presence and synagogue were there as well. So Caesarea Philippi was an economic, strategic, and cultural crossroads where the Roman, Greek, and Judaic worldviews intersected.

When Jesus asked, "who do men say that I am?" He was very specific in using the term "Son of Man" in reference to Himself. The divine "Son of Man" stood in stark contrast to the humanistic, ideal man of Hellenism. And Peter's confession, *"You are the Christ, the Son of the living God"* came to him not by philosophical reasoning, but as Jesus said, *"...flesh and blood has not revealed this to you, but my Father in heaven..."*

This whole encounter at Caesarea Philippi speaks volumes about Jesus' response to Hellenism. As He led His disciples to a place overlooking a city architecturally and intellectually built upon the Hellenistic ideals of humanism, Jesus was telling His disciples that it was not by the humanistic gods of Hellenism nor by man's wisdom (science, philosophy, art, etc.) that His disciples are enlightened, but it is *only* by divine revelation that Christ is made known.

Jesus' Response to the Roman Worldview

When Jesus was born, the Jewish territories under Roman occupation were called Palestine. Although Jesus rarely mentioned Rome or Caesar by name, Rome's presence was felt by everyone everywhere He went:

- Everyone had to pay their taxes to Rome

- Caesar's image was on the money they used for daily transactions

- Matthew was a tax collector, and therefore, was indirectly working for Rome

- Throughout His earthly ministry, Jesus had many encounters with minor Roman officials

- Roman soldiers would have been in every important town and village where Jesus visited; they would have been watching Jesus and His disciples very closely because everywhere they went, crowds would gather.

- In His Sermon on Mount Jesus mentions a Roman law that allows any civilian to be pressed into service to carry a Roman soldier's baggage one mile (Mt 5:41).

- Jesus praised the faith of a Centurion (Mt 8:5-13) who understood His power and authority.

- Finally, the Jewish leaders responsible for Jesus' arrest would turn to the Roman Governor to issue the death sentence they were seeking.

Nowhere does Jesus denounce Rome or say anything politically subversive against Rome – although many tried to get Him to incriminate Himself by saying something seditious. Jesus never calls for military or political action against Rome, which was particularly frustrating to the Judaic worldview that believed the Messiah would be a conquering king who would overthrow their Gentile oppressors and make Jerusalem the capitol of a restored Davidic Kingdom. At one point the masses were ready to proclaim Him king, but Jesus would not allow it (Jn 6:15). At His arrest Jesus rebuked the disciple who took up his sword against those who came to take Him away (Mt 26:52; Jn 18:11).

The idea proposed in modern Liberation Theologies that Jesus was a zealot or militant revolutionary cannot be supported without serious distortions of Jesus' teachings and actions. Jesus gave His answers to those who say according to the Roman worldview that "might makes right" and who place their security in the civil law and order provided by the State. In His final encounter with Pilate before He is led away to be crucified Jesus answered the Roman's interrogation concerning the accusations that He proclaimed Himself to be King of the Jews:

"Jesus answered, 'My kingdom is not of this world. If my kingdom were of this world, my servants would have been fighting, that I might not be delivered over to

the Jews. But my kingdom is not from the world.' Then Pilate said to him, 'So you are a king?' Jesus answered, 'You say that I am a king. For this purpose I was born and for this purpose I have come into the world – to bear witness to the truth. Everyone who is of the truth listens to my voice.'" John 18:36-37 (ESV)

Later, after hearing the crowd call Jesus the "Son of God", Pilate questioned Him again:

"So Pilate said to him, 'You will not speak to me? Do you not know that I have authority to release you and authority to crucify you?' Jesus answered him, 'You would have no authority over me at all unless it had been given you from above. Therefore he who delivered me over to you has the greater sin.'" John 19:10-11 (ESV)

Jesus' response to Pilate made three things clear about His kingdom that were completely contrary to the Roman worldview:

- 1st – Jesus makes it clear that He is a king, but that His kingdom is not of this world. Therefore, temporal earthly power of Rome cannot have any authority over Him.

- 2nd – His kingdom is established not to subjugate others, but to bring them to the truth. Therefore, the Roman might cannot overpower transcendent truth.

- 3rd – And most stunning to Pilate was Jesus' response to his claim that Rome had power over Him: "You would have no power over Me if it were not given to you from above." Pilate understood the concept of all power coming from above (meaning Caesar). However, implied in Jesus' answer was that a power beyond anything Pilate could understand was truly in control of the fate of the prisoner who stood before him.

Jesus response to the Romans was that He exercised a power and authority that was above and beyond the kingdoms of this world, including Caesar's. And through His life, death, and resurrection, Jesus clearly demonstrated that He operated by a power and authority that was above and beyond anything Rome could comprehend.

CONCLUSION

To those who lived by the Judaic worldview, Jesus taught that it was not obedience to the Law that brought salvation, but they were saved by grace and faith in Him (John 3:16) the Son of God. Everything Jesus taught and did in His lifetime was intended to restore a proper understanding of the Law and the Prophets that had been distorted by the Judaic worldview. Jesus taught that the law was made for man, turning the teachings of the Jewish religious leaders upside down that made the Jews live and die by the Law of Moses. They hated Jesus for it and sought to destroy Him because what He was teaching would set the Jews free from the power and control of those who taught them that man was made for the Law – a Law that the Jewish authorities defined and enforced.

To the Hellenists, Jesus taught that human reason or knowledge cannot save anyone, but it is only by divine revelation that men will come to a saving knowledge of who Jesus is (the Christ, the Son of the living God). The Hellenists believed their knowledge, education and Greek culture made them superior to this unlearned, itinerant village Rabbi who wandered around hills of Judea preaching pastoral messages and performing miracles. The Hellenists would have looked down upon the shepherds, fishermen, and simple village folk who did not have the Greeks' education, and cultural sophistication. The Hellenists hated Jesus because He was truly the salt of the earth, but at the same time, He spoke of a knowledge and wisdom that was beyond any human understanding. Jesus exposed the foolishness of the wise, and in the words of Paul, *"...the foolishness of God is wiser than man's wisdom, and the weakness of God is stronger than man's strength"* (1 Cor 1:25).

To those who believed in the Roman worldview, Jesus taught that the kingdoms of this world have no power to save, but those who put their trust in Him and His kingdom shall know the truth and that truth shall set them free. The Romans believed that there was no power on earth greater than that of Caesar; they were most concerned with maintaining the peace and security of the Empire and resented those who refused to willingly submit to Rome's authority. As long as Jesus and His followers obeyed Roman law on this earth, it mattered little to them what Jesus taught about the kingdom of heaven. Pilate saw no earthly reason to execute Jesus, but he was quite willing to order Him crucified if it kept law and order under Rome's jurisdiction. Rome feared Jesus because they could not control Him; Jesus operated out of a divine power and authority that no Caesar could touch.

How Do We Relate These Worldviews To Our Contemporary World?

The three primary milieus that existed in the ancient world still exist today. In the same way that these three worldviews – represented by the three pictures we examined – encompassed Palestine in Jesus' time, these worldviews also encompass our entire world today.

1. The picture of Moses on the Mountain represents the religious worldview. People who live by the religious worldview live their entire lives based upon religious "dos and don'ts". Where they go, what they do, how they dress, what they eat, where and how they live are all determined by their religion. Their lives are centered on religious rituals, festivals and holy days.

2. The Greek philosopher represents the secular or humanist worldview. People with this "scientific" or "rational" outlook, live their lives based upon what human reason and science tells them is expedient. They are the skeptics, the agnostics, or atheists that believe nothing their human minds cannot comprehend. For them, there are no absolutes because man's knowledge and understanding is constantly changing, learning and growing. They believe that "man is the measure of all things" and not God.

3. The Roman worldview, represented by the Centurion on horseback, says that "might makes right." Those who live by this worldview are modern "statists" (a "statist" is someone who believes the state is the answer to everyone's needs). Those who have this worldview, seek political and economic power as the most important priority. If they cannot control others through political or economic means, they will use their fists, clubs, guns, or bombs – whatever it takes for them to seize control, and stay on top of the world.

Jesus speaks through His word to all of those who hold to the same worldviews today. In His Beatitudes (Matthew 5:3-10) for example Jesus said:

- *"Blessed are the poor in spirit, for theirs is the kingdom of heaven"* (v. 3). This speaks to those who believe human reason and science will lead mankind out of the darkness and into a brave new world with Man at the center. This world is passing away, and however long human medicine extends life expectancy, the fact remains that death and what lies beyond waits for all of us. No amount of time can possibly compare with eternal life. Therefore, eternal life in the kingdom of heaven is the only life that has significance. The kingdom of heaven awaits only those who are humble and broken in spirit because those are the only ones who will trust in God's grace and mercy for salvation.

- *"Blessed are those who mourn, for they will be comforted. Blessed are the meek, for they will inherit the earth... Blessed are the merciful, for they will be shown mercy... Blessed are the peacemakers, for they will be called sons of God."* (vs. 4, 5, 7, & 9). These words speak to those who believe might makes right. Those who push and strive, manipulate, and force their way to the top of the heap believing that money and power over others means success in life will be sadly mistaken in the end. It is not those who bully their way through life – those who use threats and intimidation or the club and the gun against the weak – who are the winners. The meek (humble, gentle, mild, unpretentious, and modest) will inherit the new heavens and the new earth. They may live unassuming lives and not have much wealth by worldly standards, but their names are known in heaven and they know that the Lord has prepared a place for them where He is. They live for His kingdom and not to build their own personal kingdoms.

- *"Blessed are those who hunger and thirst for righteousness, for they will be filled... Blessed are the pure in heart, for they will see God... Blessed are those who are persecuted because of righteousness, for theirs is the kingdom of heaven..."* (vs. 6, 8, & 10). These verses speak volumes to those with the religious worldview. Religion will not save them; only the righteousness, purity and holiness that come by grace through faith in the finished work of Jesus Christ on the cross on their behalf will save them. The kingdom of heaven belongs only to those who hunger and thirst for righteousness.

There is one picture not yet described that best represents the Christian worldview. This picture is of an empty, bloodstained cross on a lonely hill outside of Jerusalem; nearby there is an empty tomb. In the tomb there are some grave cloths folded neatly and lying in a pile where a body once laid. This is the Christian worldview. It is more than how we view the world around us; it is what shapes us; what motivates us and determines where we go and what we do; it determines how we relate and interact with others; it is what identifies us and sets us apart in this world. Finally, it is this worldview that determines our eternal destiny.

The picture represents the message we have been given to communicate to the world; it is the same message that Jesus communicated:

- Religion cannot save anyone. Salvation is not about religion; it is about having an intimate relationship with the Son of the living God. That relationship comes only by humbling ourselves before almighty God and admitting our sinfulness and pride. It is the cross of Christ alone that saves us.

- Human knowledge cannot save this world. Human reason cannot even comprehend the salvation that comes by revelation of grace through faith in Jesus Christ. Those who trust in human knowledge to save them will end up adrift on a sea of moral relativism, existential anguish, and a sham tolerance that excuses everything except moral absolutes. Salvation comes only to those who hunger and thirst for righteousness; it is only the pure in heart who escape the moral relativity of a lost generation, "for they will see God." Those who stand upon moral absolutes without compromise in this age will be persecuted because righteousness will always stand out against the darkness surrounding them – and men love the darkness for their deeds are evil. But those who live as light and salt in this world will obtain the kingdom of heaven in the end.

- The kingdoms of this world cannot save anyone. Kingdoms come and kingdoms go; their power is passing away. It is only the power of love and truth that flows out of the eternal, invisible kingdom of heaven and into the hearts of men that is true power. The power of the indestructible life of Jesus Christ is greater than any army upon the earth.

So, when the fullness of time had come, God sent His Son into this world to redeem those who were lost in these worldviews - ways that could not save them or lead them out of the darkness an into the light of God's grace, mercy and truth. We are still living in this "fullness of time" when salvation comes to all by grace and faith alone. We Christians have been given this same mandate – a commission – to take this vision of salvation to the world and communicate it to whosoever will believe and receive it.

FREDERICK OSBORN

2.
Messiah, Son of Man, Son of God, Savior and Lord
Jesus in Context of the Gospels

LESSON OUTLINE

- The purpose of this lesson is to present the Four Views of Jesus presented by the writers of the Gospels.

    Matthew – the promised King of the Jews
    Mark – the Servant of God
    Luke – the Son of Man
    John – the Son of God

- To understand how each of these views was understood in its original context by its immediate audience:

    Matthew – the Jews
    Mark – the Romans
    Luke – the Greeks
    John – Universal

- To present how each Gospel is understood by Christians today.

"Jesus: Messiah, Son of Man, Son of God, Savior and Lord"

"Each of the four Gospels has its own emphasis. Matthew's book is called, 'the Gospel of the King.' It was written primarily for Jewish readers. Mark's book, the Gospel of the Servant, was written to instruct Roman readers. Luke wrote mainly to the Greeks and presented Christ as the perfect 'Son of Man,' John's appeal is universal, and his message was, 'This is the Son of God.' No one Gospel is able to tell the whole story as God wants us to see it. But when we put these four gospel accounts together, we have a composite picture of the person and work of our Lord."

– Warren Wiersbe
"Be Loyal"

"Matthew, Mark, Luke, and John" stainedglassclassic.com

Before anyone begins a serious study of the life of Christ from the Gospels of Matthew, Mark, Luke and John, it is essential to understand that these writers were not biographers; they were not journalists, nor were they historians. Their intention was not to write comprehensive day-by-day, chronological, or journalistic (event-by-event) accounts of Jesus' life story. In fact, the Apostle John doubted that a complete biography of Jesus could ever be written (John 21:25). Therefore, we must approach the Gospels the way the authors intended them to be read. Matthew, Mark, Luke and John had one thing in common: they were all missionaries and evangelists – Apostles of Jesus Christ. That means they wrote their Gospels with one primary goal in mind: to convince their readers that Jesus Christ was indeed who His followers said He was. Luke best stated the motivations of the Gospel writers in the introduction to his Gospel:

"Inasmuch as many have undertaken to compile a narrative of the things that have been accomplished among us, just as those who from the beginning were eyewitnesses and ministers of the word have delivered them to us, it seemed good to me also, having followed all things closely for some time past, to write an orderly account for you, most excellent Theophilus, that you may have certainty concerning the things you have been taught." Luke 1:1-4 (ESV)

COMPARISON OF THE FOUR GOSPELS

All four Gospels present the life and teachings of Jesus. Each book, however, focuses on a unique facet of Jesus and his character. To understand more about the specific characteristics of Jesus, one must read every one of the four Gospels.

	MATTHEW	**MARK**	**LUKE**	**JOHN**
Jesus is	The promised king	The Servant	The Son Of Man	Son of God
The original Readers were	Jews	Gentiles, Romans	Greeks	All Christians
Significant Themes	Jesus is the Messiah because He fulfilled O.T. Prophecy	Jesus backed up His words with actions	Jesus was God but also fully human	Believe Jesus saves
Character of the writer	Teacher	Storyteller	Historian	Theologian
Greatest emphasis is on	Jesus' sermons and words	Jesus' miracles and actions	Jesus' humanity	The principles of Jesus' Teachings

(From "Tyndale Handbook of Bible Charts & Maps", Tyndale House Publishers, 2001)

Matthew's Portrait of Jesus:
The Promised King and Messiah of the Jews

Author: Matthew – Matthew was the Jewish tax collector who was called by Jesus to become one of His disciples.

Approximate Date Written: A.D. 60-65

Original and Primary Audiences: Jews, and all believers

Purpose: To prove that Jesus is the promised Messiah of the Jews first and the eternal King and Savior of all nations.

Context: This Gospel forms the connecting link between the Old and New Testaments because of its emphasis on the fulfillment of Old Testament messianic prophecy. This Gospel is filled with messianic language that would have been immediately recognizable to a Jewish audience. Terms such as "Son of David" are used frequently in this Gospel. The Old Testament is quoted 53 times with an additional 76 other references. Warren W. Wiersbe in his commentary on Matthew rightly pointed to the fact that if Christians skipped over Matthew and jumped from Malachi directly into Mark, or Acts, or Romans, they would be bewildered. Matthew's Gospel is an important bridge that leads us out of the Old Testament and into the New Testament.

The key to understanding the Gospel of Matthew is that it is the most Jewish of all the Gospels. Too many Christians fail to fully understand the Gospels because they do not fully understand that the roots of their faith are sunk deep into the history of the Jewish people. Matthew's Gospel is the bridge between the Old Testament and the New because it is the gospel written by a Jew to Jews about a Jew: the Rabbi Jesus of Nazareth.

Matthew, once a despised tax collector but nevertheless a Jew, writes to show his own people that Jesus of Nazareth truly was the

Messiah promised by the Old Testament prophets, but rejected by the Jews. Matthew knew that if he was going to convince them, he would have to answer the questions that must have burned in the heart of every first century Jew: if Jesus was the Messiah, why was He rejected by the Jews and what happened to the glorious Messianic kingdom foretold in the Scriptures?

The realization that this was Matthew's primary motivation in writing his Gospel helps us to understand:

- The structure Matthew's Gospel
  And
- The significance Matthew's Gospel

The evidence that Jesus was indeed the long awaited Messiah of the Jews and the answers to the questions about His kingdom come as Matthew's story gradually unfolds. Matthew begins his Gospel by looking back. The genealogy of Jesus in Matthew firmly establishes Him as a descendent of Abraham, and therefore, His story belongs very much to the story of the Jewish people. His genealogy also firmly establishes Jesus as a descendent of David; and every Jew knew that the Messiah would have to be a descendent of David to fulfill the Hebrew prophecy:

"My servant David shall be king over them, and they shall all have one shepherd. They shall walk in my rules and be careful to obey my statutes. They shall dwell in the land that I gave to my servant Jacob, where your fathers lived. They and their children and their children's children shall dwell there forever, and David my servant shall be their prince forever. I will make a covenant of peace with them. It shall be an everlasting covenant with them. And I will set them in their land and multiply them, and will set my sanctuary in their midst forevermore. My dwelling place shall be with them, and I will be their God, and they shall be my people. Then the nations will know that I am the LORD who sanctifies Israel, when my sanctuary is in their midst forevermore." Ezekiel 37:24-28 (ESV)

Matthew follows his genealogy with the story of Jesus' miraculous conception and birth. At the same time Matthew weaves into the text more evidence from the Jewish Scriptures for Jesus' Messianic credentials:

- Christ's birth was the miraculous fulfillment of the prophecy given 300 years earlier in approximately 740-700 BC by Isaiah (Is. 7:14)

- His birth was announced by the Angel of the Lord. This was a divine manifestation of Yahweh's personal involvement in the events that occurred only on rare occasions in Israel's history (Note: Gen. 16:7-14; 22:9-18; Ex. 3:1-4:17)

- The Magi from the East saw and recognized a supernatural sign in the heavens and came seeking the "King of the Jews" (2:1-12)

Matthew 2:2 establishes the royal mission and destiny of Jesus with Jewish prophecy. COMPARE:

- Matt. 2:2 with Jeremiah 23:5

- Matt. 2:6 with Micah 5:2

- Matt. 2:18 with Jer. 31:15

- Matt. 2:23 with Hosea 11:1

The backdrop of prophetic fulfillment in the mysterious workings of God in Matthew's Gospel created an aura of the supernatural that the Jews accepted as part of their history as God's chosen people. The Old Testament prophecies support Matthew's argument that from the very beginning, Jesus was divinely selected and uniquely identified as the One chosen to be God's Messiah. As Matthew's narrative continued, he addressed another question sure to be raised by Jewish leaders: if the Messiah was supposed to be King David's heir, born and raised in David's ancestral home of Bethlehem, why then did Jesus grow up in Nazareth?

The answer is found in Matthew 2:13-23: Jesus' family fled into Egypt to escape the murderous jealousy of Herod – and in so doing, fulfilled God's Word:

"When Israel was a child, I loved him, and out of Egypt I called my son." Hosea 11:1

"This is what the Lord says: 'A voice is heard in Ramah, mourning and great weeping, Rachel weeping for her children and refusing to be comforted, because her children are no more.'" Jeremiah 31:15

Matthew's selection of these prophetic verses helped to cement Jesus' identification as the Jewish Messiah:

- The phrase "out of Egypt" appears numerous times in the Hebrew Scriptures. The Lord reminded Israel time and time again how they were miraculously delivered from bondage in Egypt.

- The image of Israel as "my son" is transferred in a unique and personal way to their Messiah. When Jesus is baptized, Matthew records a voice from heaven, saying, "This is My beloved Son, in whom I am well pleased." (3:17)

- (2:18) Rachel held a special place in the Jewish psyche. She was known among the rabbis as "the mother of all Israel for all time." Her death in childbirth meant life for Benjamin, who was the ancestor of the Messiah. The Jews understood the concept that the way to life, freedom, hope, and blessings often takes us through death, captivity, exile, and bereavement. The Jews would have strongly identified with Matthew's use of Jeremiah 31:15 here to convey the message that out of the evils of this life, can grow the seeds of God's ultimate purpose for our good and blessings.

When the family returned from exile in Egypt, God directed Joseph to settle in Nazareth – and in so doing, Matthew says, it fulfilled another word, which was spoken by the prophets, "He will be called a Nazarene." Since there is no reference to Nazareth in the Old Testament, Matthew's statement seems remarkable to those unfamiliar with the interpretive methods of the Jewish rabbis. But this would have been entirely understood by his Jewish readers who looked for analogy, type and even verbal allusions in the Old Testament. The fact that Matthew speaks of "the prophets" in general indicates that he is not speaking of a particular prophetic verse. It is impossible for us today to be sure which Old

Testament allusions Matthew was thinking about. We can only venture some guesses based upon the low esteem Nazareth of Galilee was held by the Jews who lived in and around Jerusalem and Judea at that time (John 1:46). Another possibility is that Matthew was using a common rabbinic interpretive method of word-play; possibly on the Hebrew for "Branch" (Isaiah 11:1, a notable messianic text), or on "those…have kept" (Isaiah 49:6, part of one of the Servant Songs applied to Jesus by the early church). In any case, Matthew's target audience of Jewish believers would have picked up on the "insider" message he wanted to convey to them.

From the very beginning, Matthew's Gospel is a description of how God was directing the people, places and actions that fulfilled Old Testament prophecies concerning the Jewish Messiah. Verse by verse, the history of God's children is intricately woven into the history of Jesus, God's Son. Jesus' genealogy makes it clear that His story is undeniably linked with Abraham, David, and with the whole history of God's chosen ones. Long ago Israel was led down to Egypt, and so was Jesus; both were called out of Egypt by God to fulfill their destinies. The sufferings of Israel and her children in Egypt, is echoed in the sufferings of the mothers and children slaughtered by Herod.

Matthew uses the Old Testament prophecies to lay the foundation for his argument that Jesus was the Messiah the Jews were waiting for. God had set His own mark upon Jesus, and just as Israel could not be destroyed until it fulfilled God's ultimate purpose, so too Jesus the Messiah could not be stopped. The story Matthew has to tell about Jesus is not the story of an ordinary man, or even of an exceptional Jewish rabbi. His Gospel is above all, the story of Israel's Messiah, God's Son, who also became the Savior of the world. "The name apart, Jesus is often called 'Messiah' in Matthew's Gospel. The Hebrew word, and its Greek equivalent, *Christos*, simply mean 'the anointed one' (1:16, 18). Very soon it became almost a surname of Jesus, but in Matthew it often retains its basic meaning. Israel knew anointed prophets, priests and kings. After their demise the hope persisted that one day there would arise a figure who would recapitulate in his own person those three anointed strands of old. Those hopes were crystallized in the expectation of a messiah…" Michael Green, The Message of Matthew, InterVarsity Press, Downers Grove, IL, © 1988, 2000, p.39

2. Mark's Portrait of Jesus: "The Son of God, and Servant of All"

Author: Mark – John Mark was not one of the original 12 disciples, but he accompanied Paul on his first missionary journey (Acts 13:13). He was the son of a devout woman called Mary, who dwelt at Jerusalem and may have been one of those who believed in Jesus during His earthly ministry. Mark was an early believer, and knew the disciples well because they used to meet at his mother's house.

Approximate Date Written: A.D. 55-65

Original and Primary Audiences: The Christians in Rome, where this Gospel was written, and all believers throughout the Roman world.

Purpose: To present the person, ministry, and teachings of Jesus, the obedient Servant and Son of God to a largely Gentile audience. Mark records more miracles than does any other Gospel.

Context: Mark's gospel is believed by many scholars to be the first Gospel written. The other three Gospels quote all but 31 verses of Mark.

Adam Clarke (1760– 1832) the great theologian and biblical scholar wrote the following about Mark's account: "The Gospel according to Mark, if not an abridgment of the Gospel according to Matthew, contains a neat, perspicuous abridgment of the history of our Lord; and, taken in this point of view, is very satisfactory; and is the most proper of all the four Gospels to be put into the hands of young persons, in order to bring them to an acquaintance with the great facts of evangelical history. But as a substitute for the Gospel by Matthew, it should never be used. It is very likely that it was written originally for the use of the Gentiles, and probably for those of Rome. Of this, there seem to be several evidences in the work itself. Of the other Gospels it is not only a grand corroborating evidence, but contains many valuable hints for completing the history of our Lord, which have been omitted by the others; and thus, in the mouths of four witnesses, all these glorious and interesting facts are established."

The message of Mark's gospel is best captured in two verses:

"The beginning of the gospel about Jesus Christ, the Son of God." Mark 1:1

"For even the Son of Man did not come to be served, but to serve, and to give his life as a ransom for many." Mark 10:45

Chapter by chapter, the book of Mark unfolds the dual focus of Christ's life:

1. He is no ordinary Man; His words and actions reveal His divine authority

2. Great service and sacrifice would be necessary for Jesus to complete the mission he was sent to fulfill

In Mark's gospel, Jesus is a Servant on the move, instantly responsive to the will of the Father. By preaching, teaching, and healing, He ministers to the needs of others even to the point of death. And after His Resurrection, Jesus commissioned His followers to continue His work in His power – servants following in the steps of the perfect Servant Son of God.

The internal evidence of Mark's Gospel indicates that Gentiles, who knew little about Hebrew theology, were his primary audience. "The frequent explanation of Aramaic expressions as well as Jewish laws and customs may well indicate an audience unfamiliar with certain forms of Judaism. To say more goes beyond the limits of the text. Consequently, this generic quality of Mark gives it a universal character that addresses the modern disciple in much the same manner as it did the first readers. It is the 'gospel concerning Jesus Messiah, Son of God' that itself summons one to 'repent and believe the gospel' that God has acted and will act again to effect his sovereign, saving rule in and through Jesus Messiah, God's Son." *Dictionary of Jesus and the Gospels*, Joel B. Green; Scott McKnight; I. Howard Marshall, Editors InterVarsity Press, Downers Grove, ILL, © 1992, p.515

Mark takes the time to explain to his readers the Aramaic expressions he uses – something he would never have to do with Jewish readers:

- Mark 3:17 – *Boanerges,* which means "Sons of Thunder"

- Mark 5:41 – *Talitha koum* which means, "Little girl, I say to you, get up!"

- Mark 7:11 – *Corban,* which means, "a gift devoted to God"

- Mark 7:34 – *Ephphatha,* which means, "Be opened"

- Mark 14:36 – *Abba,* which means, "Father" (or "Daddy")

- Mark 15:34 – *Eloi, Eloi, lama sabachthani?* which means, "My God, my God, why have you forsaken me?"

Scholars, who have studied the language of Mark, have noted that he frequently used Latin grammatical constructions and used expressions that reflected the Latin dialect. For example:

- Mark 15:16 "the palace that is, the Praetorium…"

- Mark 12:42 (NKJV) *"Then one poor widow came and threw in two mites, which make a quadrans."*

Although we recognize those elements of Mark's Gospel that seem to appeal to the Roman Gentile audience, we cannot neglect the fact that Mark was a Jew and his primary source was the Apostle Peter, who was also a Jew. So, it could be said that Mark was being a cross-cultural missionary when he wrote his Gospel: he was a Jewish missionary writing to reach a primarily Roman audience with the "good news" of Jesus Christ, the Jewish Messiah – Savior of the Jews first and the Gentiles. As is true with all of the Gospels, the central theme of the book is the story of Jesus of Nazareth, but Mark relates the story in a way that would appeal to his mostly Roman listeners. He wanted to leave a strong impression of

Jesus that would communicate to those who were steeped in a Roman worldview that valued a civil law and order that flowed from Caesar on down.

So Mark's gospel is marked by rapid movement; gone are the lengthy genealogies of Matthew and Luke because Gentiles would not be particularly interested in the evidence establishing Jesus' Jewish credentials as the Messiah, destined to sit on David's throne in Jerusalem. Instead, Mark shows his Gentile readers that, although His own people rejected the Son of God, He achieved ultimate victory over what appeared to be defeat. Mark just touches on John the Baptist's ministry, Jesus' baptism, His wilderness experience, and the calling of the disciples (all are covered in the first 20 verses of his Gospel). Mark almost immediately launches into his report about the message and ministry of Jesus.

Mark's Gospel sounds more like a military debriefing than a story; he describes Jesus going here and there, making things happen. The people who encounter Jesus on His journey are often amazed by His teachings and awe struck by His miracles. In quick succession, Mark describes Jesus casting out demons, healing diseases, and even forgiving sins. Every movement is intended to portray Jesus as a Man of action exercising divine authority wherever He goes. Christ's healing on the Sabbath demonstrates that as the Son of God, He also holds supreme religious authority – an authority that surpasses those who claimed to be the authentic interpreters of Moses (Mark 2:18-27).

Mark reports a series of incidents that would be significant to those who understood the worldly power and authority that Rome represented. At the same time, through these events, Jesus was demonstrating a power and authority that is above and beyond any earthly power and authority.

- (Mark 3:22-30) The leaders of the Jewish people rejected Jesus. They did not understand or respect His power and authority, and even accused Him of being under Satan's power. However, Christ showed them that not only He was Satan's enemy, but He was greater than the prince of demons and able plunder Him at will. Rome's Legions had conquered the Western World; they invaded cities and looted homes on their way to Supreme power. So they would immediately grasp the kind of power and authority Jesus possessed.

- Caesar's word was law in the Empire, and Roman citizens were expected to obey the will of Caesar or face severe punishment. So Mark stressed Jesus' teaching that only those willing to believe and do the will of God will understand His teachings and enter into His eternal kingdom:

    "I tell you the truth, all the sins and blasphemies of men will be forgiven them. But whoever blasphemes against the Holy Spirit will never be forgiven; he is guilty of an eternal sin." Mark 3:28-29

    "Whoever does God's will is my brother and sister and mother." Mark 3:35

    "The secret of the kingdom of God has been given to you. But to those on the outside everything is said in parables." Mark 4:11

But Mark goes even further to demonstrate Christ's superiority over Caesar:

- He stills the storm, showing His authority over the natural world (4:35-41)

- He drives out a legion of demons, showing His authority over massed supernatural forces (5:1-20)

- He cures a woman suffering from a chronic, incurable disease (5:21-34)

- And even raises the dead (5:35-43)

Mark lets his narrative speak for itself as he tells the story of Jesus, the Servant who constantly ministers to others through preaching, healing, teaching, and, ultimately, His own death and resurrection. The conclusion is inescapable: The Man who did these things is more than a mere man. He is, as Mark announced in the opening verse of his Gospel, the very Son of God!

3. Luke's Portrait of Jesus: "The Son of Man"

"Many have undertaken to draw up an account of the things that have been fulfilled among us, just as they were handed down to us by those who from the first were eyewitnesses and servants of the word. Therefore, since I myself have carefully investigated everything from the beginning, it seemed good also to me to write an orderly account for you, most excellent Theophilus, so that you may know the certainty of the things you have been taught." Luke 1:1-4

Author: Luke—was a Greek physician and believer. He was the only Gentile author of a New Testament book. Luke was a close friend and traveling companion of Paul. He also wrote the book of Acts to compliment his Gospel. Dr. Luke is named three times in the New Testament: Colossians 4:14; 2 Timothy 4:11; Philemon 1:23-24.

Approximate Date Written: A.D. 60

Original and Primary Audiences: Theophilus, "one who loves God", Hellenistic Jews, and all believers

Purpose: To present an accurate, orderly, account of the life of Christ; and present the man Jesus as the perfect "Son of Man" and Savior.

Context: Because Luke's primary audience was those who embraced a Hellenistic worldview, he stresses Jesus' humanity in relationships with people. At the same time, Luke emphasizes the power of Jesus' miracles, and the supernatural. Luke's gospel emphasized Jesus' sacrifice upon the cross for the redemption of mankind as opposed to the Greeks' belief that man's reason and science could save him.

Luke's Gospel is a bridge between Jew and Gentile in the same way that Matthew's Gospel was primarily for Jews. Matthew's Gospel was a bridge between the Jewish worldview rooted and grounded in the Law of Moses and what seemed to be a radical new concept of the messianic kingdom of God that Jesus' followers presented. Conversely, Luke wrote primarily for Gentiles who were looking for a way to reconcile the Greek's humanistic ideal of Man as the measure of all things with the Jewish ideal of the Messianic "Son of Man" that point to God alone as the measure of all things. The Greeks had a man-centered view of history: mighty men of great stature moved the historical narrative where the gods often played a supplemental role. The Jews held to a God-centered view of history where divine interventions directly influenced the course of history. Jesus, the divine Son of Man is God's direct intervention into human history.

Matthew Henry (1662 – 1714) wrote in his introduction to Luke, "Dr. Cave observes that his way and manner of writing are accurate and exact, his style polite and elegant, sublime and lofty, yet perspicuous; and that he expresses himself in a vein of purer Greek than is to be found in the other writers of the holy story. Thus he relates diverse things more copiously than the other evangelists; and thus he especially treats of those things which relate to the priestly office of Christ." Commenting on Luke chapter one, Henry continued, "The narrative which this evangelist gives us (or rather God by him) of the life of Christ begins earlier than either Matthew or Mark. We have reason to thank God for them all, as we have for all the gifts and graces of Christ's ministers, which in one make up what is wanting in the other, while all put together make a harmony."

Luke addressed his gospel to a man named *Theóphilos* (Greek, "loved of God"). We do not know for certain if Theophilus was a Gentile seeker or already a believer, but we can reasonably assume from the text that he had received some instruction about Jesus Christ. But given the tremendous effort that researching and writing this gospel must have been, it also seems clear that Luke did not write for Theophilus alone, but for any "loved of god" that was seeking the truth about Jesus Christ.

Luke's effort to present an orderly and scholarly, historical account of Jesus' earthly ministry would have appealed to the Greek mind. At the same time, the Greeks were a proud race and believed themselves culturally superior to the Hebrews. So they would have questioned whether they really belonged with this culturally inferior and heavily persecuted alien community that was surrounded by a much larger and stronger Gentile world shaped at least in part by Hellenism. At the time this was written, Gentile Christians may have felt out of place in an originally Jewish movement and many would have questioned why there was such a strong opposition from the Jews towards Christians.

Hellenism literally means, "to speak or *make* Greek", but implies a much broader meaning: "to act in a Greek way". Therefore, a Hellenistic Jew would be a Jewish person who spoke, thought, and acted in a Greek way and was less concerned with the strict adherence to Mosaic – and especially Pharisaic – laws.

Modern day theologians are often too quick to point out the obvious differences between Luke's genealogy of Jesus and Matthew's genealogy. They often write as if what is obvious to them was never thought of by the original authors or early theologians. Several theories have emerged to explain the differences and try to reconcile them. However, as Albert Barnes (1798 - 1870) pointed out in his commentary on Jesus' genealogy in Matthew, "The evangelists are not responsible for the correctness of these tables. They are responsible only for what was their real and professed object to do. What was that object? It was to prove to the satisfaction of the Jews that Jesus was descended from David, and therefore that there was no argument from his ancestry that he was not the promised Messiah. Now to make this out, it was not necessary, nor would it have conduced to their argument, to have formed a new table of genealogy. All that could be done was to go to the family records – to the public tables, and copy them as they were actually kept, and show that, according to the records of the nation, Jesus was descended from David. This, among the Jews, would be full and decided testimony in the case. And this was doubtless done. In the same way, the records of a family among us, as they are kept by the family, are proof in courts of justice now of the birth, names, etc., of individuals. Nor is it necessary or proper for a court to call them in question or to attempt to correct them. So, the tables here are good evidence to the only point that the writers wished to establish: that is, to show to the Jews that Jesus of Nazareth was descended from David. The only inquiry which can now be fairly made is whether they copied those tables correctly. It is clear that no one can adduce them as an argument against the correctness of the New Testament."

Luke was written in a time when large numbers of Gentiles were being welcomed into the community of faith apart from Jewish religious traditions and there was no attempt by believers in Jesus to remove faith in Him from Judaism, but history tells us that as time went on the numbers of Gentile believers overwhelmed the numbers of Jewish believers. Eventually, the split between non-believing Jews and the Gentile and Jewish followers of Jesus became irreconcilable. After the church became dominated by Gentile believers, Jewish believers in the Messiah Yeshua (Jesus) were forced out of Judaism while Gentile believers in Jesus Christ gladly divorced themselves from Pharisaic Judaism. This rift exists to this day; and times past, it caused Gentile Christians, whose numbers and power rose rapidly throughout the Roman Empire to ignore or even deny the Jewish roots of the Christian faith for centuries. It has only been in more recent times that Christians in search of the historical Jesus, have returned to serious study of the Jewish context of the Gospels.

We know from various traditional sources that Luke traveled with Paul and wrote the Book of Acts as well as the Gospel that bears his name. Luke's gospel was written at a time when the church was still primarily Jewish, but with a rapidly growing Gentile minority. Luke may have been a Gentile, but because of his training and background he was most likely a Hellenistic Jew. But either way, his training as a doctor would have meant he was most familiar with everything Greek and his long relationship with Paul would have put him in contact with the Apostles and other early church leaders. So Luke, being a Hellenistic, Jewish Christian, would have made him uniquely situated to present a Jewish Messiah to Greeks wanting to know who Jesus Christ was.

In all four Gospels, Jesus uses the term, "Son of Man", to refer to Himself. And there is nothing new or different in the way Luke uses the term. However, the term, "Son of Man" would invoke a totally different meaning to those in Luke's primary audience who were fully immersed in the Hellenistic mindset. The Jews who heard this term "Son of Man" would immediately remember the Messianic prophecy of Daniel 7:13-14: *"In my vision at night I looked, and there before me was one like a son of man, coming with the clouds of heaven. He approached the Ancient of Days and was led into his presence. He was given authority, glory and sovereign power; all peoples, nations and men of every language worshiped him. His dominion is an everlasting dominion that will not pass away, and his kingdom is one that will never be destroyed."*

Daniel's prophecy speaks of a figure like "a son of man" who comes with the clouds of heaven; he appears before God and is given everlasting sovereign power and dominion (Note Revelation 1:7 *"Look, he is coming with the clouds, and every eye will see him, even those who pierced him; and all the peoples of the earth will mourn because of him. So shall it be!"*).

For the Gentiles, the fact that Jesus so clearly identifies Himself with the "son of man" of Jewish prophecy at the same time He is being rejected by the Jews, adds even more drama and mystery to the question. "Why did the Jewish people reject Him as their Messiah?" The Jews were expecting a conquering King to come and deliver them from their Roman oppressors, but Jesus' mission as the "Suffering Servant" of Isaiah 53 was something the Jews looking for the "son of man" from Daniel's prophecy could not comprehend. Luke makes it clear that Jesus knew that His own people would reject him:

"Blessed are you when men hate you, when they exclude you and insult you and reject your name as evil, because of the Son of Man." Luke 6:22

"And he said, 'The Son of Man must suffer many things and be rejected by the elders, chief priests and teachers of the law, and he must be killed and on the third day be raised to life.'" Luke 9:22

"Listen carefully to what I am about to tell you: The Son of Man is going to be betrayed into the hands of men." Luke 9:44

But the Son of Man being rejected by His own people and led away as a Lamb for the slaughter was not something even His disciples were ready to accept:

"From that time Jesus began to show his disciples that he must go to Jerusalem and suffer many things from the elders and chief priests and scribes, and be killed, and on the third day be raised. And Peter took him aside and began to rebuke him, saying, 'Far be it from you, Lord! This shall never happen to you.'" Matthew 16:21-22 (ESV)

The Greeks practically worshiped the human body as a thing of beauty; beauty to them was the very essence of virility. They believed circumcision was nothing less than a gross mutilation of the body, and their image of the glorious human form would have been insulted by the image of Christ mutilated on the cross – for not only did the Greeks make their gods human-like, but actually glorified the human body in their gods. Greek philosophy promoted a perfect balance of mind and body in **meden agan**, ("nothing in excess"), and the pursuit of **Kalos k'agathos** (the 'beautiful and good'). Luke's Jesus said to all of them:

"And he said to all, 'If anyone would come after me, let him deny himself and take up his cross daily and follow me. For whoever would save his life will lose it, but whoever loses his life for my sake will save it. For what does it profit a man if he gains the whole world and loses or forfeits himself?'" Luke 9:23-25 (ESV)

Either consciously or unconsciously, Luke was presenting Jesus, the Son of Man as the measure of all things as opposed to the Greek concept of the ideal Man as the measure of all things. Greek humanism originated with Protagoras, a Greek philosopher and teacher who lived around the 5th century BC. Protagoras' philosophy exhibited two important features which remain opposed to the primary spiritual truths of the New Testament that Luke emphasized in his Gospel account of Jesus Christ. First, Protagoras made human wisdom and scientific observation the starting point for determining all truth when he coined his now-famous statement "Man is the measure of all things." In other words, Protagoras believed it is not the gods that people should look to when establishing morals and standards, but they should look instead to themselves. In Luke's Gospel God is the prime mover and the One who defines and determines everything taking place from the time and place of Jesus' birth, to His death and resurrection: "In that same hour he rejoiced in the Holy Spirit and said, 'I thank you, Father, Lord of heaven and earth, that you have hidden these things from the wise and understanding and revealed them to little children; yes, Father, for such was your gracious will. All things have been handed over to me by my Father, and no one knows who the Son is except the Father, or who the Father is except the Son and anyone to whom the Son chooses to reveal him.'" Luke 10:21-22 (ESV)

Secondly, the humanism of the Hellenist skeptics that followed this line of thinking, doubted traditional religious beliefs and traditional gods. Although most Greeks still believed in their gods, Protagoras claimed that the gods were "...obstacles that impede knowledge, both the obscurity of the question and the shortness of human life." Luke's Gospel challenges

this radical sentiment today, no less than it did 2,000 years ago when he wrote about Jesus. *"And he went down to Capernaum, a city of Galilee. And he was teaching them on the Sabbath, and they were astonished at his teaching, for his word possessed authority."* Luke 4:31-32 (ESV)

Whether it is the individual, or humanity as a collective whole, the Hellenists believed that man is the center of the Universe and that the perfect, ideal man represents divine perfection. Greek artists and sculptors idealized the human form; athletes performed in the nude; their theologians incorporated human attributes such as power, speed and beauty into the gods of Mount Olympus. Greek theatre placed man at center stage; the chorus of Sophocles' *Antigone* sang out again and again, "Many are the awesome and the awful creations of the universe, but there is nothing as awesome and awful as man". Indeed, the sum total of Hellenism cried out, "Man is the measure of all things". The Gospel of Luke has a very different idea to bequeath to the world. Jesus, the Son of Man (as opposed to the Greek humanistic ideal) is the measure of all things and the center of the universe. Jesus' characteristics of compassion, unconditional love, patience, loving kindness and truth are the embodiment of **Kalos k'agathos**. If the Greeks created gods in Man's image, then Luke holds up the Man, Jesus of Nazareth as the perfect human being – the divine Son of God that all human beings must strive to emulate.

Self-knowledge was the motivating force of the Greek humanist philosophers. The essence of the Socratic maxim "Know thyself" means that a man's salvation is by knowledge. The Greeks believed that the highest endeavor of any human being was the cultivation of the mind and the control of the body; this was the aim of the wise man and the philosopher. The mind can apprehend truth, but the bodily senses can hobble the soul from acquiring knowledge. Therefore the mind must be freed as much as possible from the body. The person who succeeds in controlling the body and cultivating the mind will lay hold on truth and partake of immortality so far as that is possible. The Greeks believed that the greatest source of the prevalent confusion, conflict, fear, and darkness in the human soul was ignorance, which includes the failure to realize how little we know about anything, in the true sense of the word "know". The definite meaning, therefore, to be attached to the maxim "know thyself" is not only to lay hold on truth, but also to realize the extent of one's own ignorance or limitations.

Luke presents Jesus as the Divine Teacher, which would have appealed to the Greeks, but His salvation was not in self-knowledge – it comes by grace through faith. Jesus made it clear from His teachings that He did not come to set men free from ignorance, but to forgive them; and through that forgiveness, the confusion, conflict, fear, and darkness of the human soul comes to an end. When the disciples of John asked Jesus if He was the One who came to save the Nation, Jesus answered not with words or arguments, but with actions: *"So He replied to the messengers, 'Go back and report to John what you have seen and heard: The blind receive sight, the lame walk, those who have leprosy are cured, the deaf hear, the dead are raised, and the good news is preached to the poor.'"* (Luke 7:22) And shortly afterwards, Jesus forgave a prostitute of her sins, saying, *"Your faith has saved you. Go in peace."* (Luke 7:50)

The words of the Greek philosophers filled the library shelves and echoed in the corridors of higher learning all around the Roman world, but Luke put all of human wisdom in perspective when he quoted Jesus, saying, *"If anyone is ashamed of me and my words, the Son of Man will be ashamed of him when he comes in his glory and in the glory of the Father and of the holy angels."* Luke 9:26

The philosophies, technologies, and the sciences of men are powerless to save mankind; in fact, they often do as much harm as good. But to know Christ and His word is Luke's prescription for what ails the human soul and keeps it bound in the darkness. Paul said it best, when he wrote: *"I want to know Christ and the power of his resurrection and the fellowship of sharing in his sufferings, becoming like him in his death, and so, somehow, to attain to the resurrection from the dead."* Philippians 3:10-11

Luke records how Jesus proved again and again through His acts of compassion and unconditional love for the lost sheep of humanity all around Him, that *"...the Son of Man came to seek and to save what was lost"* (Luke 19:10).

Luke's gospel continues to challenge the humanist skeptics of the supernatural to this day. Those who are seeking a perfect, rational, and scientific knowledge as a means for mankind's redemption are unable to rationalize the sacrifice of the sinless Son of Man for the salvation of humanity. Paul understood them, and wrote:

"For Jews demand signs and Greeks seek wisdom, but we preach Christ crucified, a stumbling block to Jews and folly to Gentiles, but to those who are called, both Jews and Greeks, Christ the power of God and the wisdom of God. For the foolishness of God is wiser than men, and the weakness of God is stronger than men." 1 Corinthians 1:22-25 (ESV)

Matthew, Mark, and Luke each had a specific audience in mind when they wrote their gospels. Matthew wanted to reach Jews first, and did all he could to prove to them that Jesus was their long-awaited Messiah & King. Mark directed his gospel to Romans, and presented Jesus as the Son of God who was a man of action – a Servant who was submitted to His Father, and yet, He exercised a power, authority, and dominion that was far beyond anything Rome could match. Luke spoke to Greeks submersed in the man-centered, humanistic worldview of Hellenism. Luke's Jesus was the perfect Son of Man who is the measure of all things in this world and in the one beyond. "Luke wanted the readers of his Gospel to know that Jesus is the Son of God, but he used the Son of God role to characterize how Jesus ministers on earth. Jesus is the intimate Son loved by the Father and held in awe by the demons. He is not the miracle-working Son sent to display overpowering divine works that force all observers to recognize him as unearthly." Trent C. Butler, *The Holman New Testament Commentary: Luke*, Broadman & Holman Publishers, Nashville, TN, © 2000, p.22.

Matthew, Mark, and Luke spoke directly to the people they knew best in the world around them, but because of the Holy Spirit's inspiration, each of their messages transcend their immediate audiences and speak to hearts of all people of every tribe and tongue even to this day.

4. John's Portrait of Jesus: "Savior, & Lord"

Author: John the apostle, son of Zebedee, brother of James was called by Jesus a "Son of Thunder." John was one of the original twelve disciples and an eyewitness to every major event in the life of Jesus Christ.

Approximate Date Written: 85-90 A.D.

Original and Primary Audiences: John's Gospel was more universal in scope; it was written for all believers.

Purpose: To prove that Jesus is the Son of God and that by His life, death, and resurrection anyone who believes in Him will have eternal life.

Context: John the apostle, son of Zebedee and brother of James wrote his Gospel after the destruction of Jerusalem in 70 A.D. and before his exile to the island of Patmos where he wrote Revelation. The last of the canonical Gospels to be written, John does not go over much of the same ground covered in the other three Gospels. In fact over 90% of John's content is unique to his Gospel. By the time John wrote his Gospel, Christianity had already penetrated much of the Roman Empire. John countered the Gnostic teachings by presenting Jesus as the eternal Logos (Word), Savior, and Lord of all.

When John chose to write his gospel, he did not elect to cover the same ground as those who wrote before him; he wanted to write from a whole new perspective. In his introduction to his commentary on the Gospel of John, A.W. Pink (1886-1952), considered by many to be one of the most influential evangelical authors in the second half of the twentieth century, wrote, "The viewpoint of this fourth Gospel is more elevated than that of the others; its contents bring into view spiritual relationships rather than human ties; and, higher glories are revealed as touching the peerless Person of the Savior. In each of the first three Gospels, Christ is viewed in human relationships, but not so in John. The purpose of this fourth Gospel is to show that the One who was born in a manger and afterward died on the Cross had higher glories than those of King, that He who humbled Himself to take the Servant place was, previously, 'equal with God,' that the One who became the Son of Man was none other than, and ever remains, the Only Begotten of the Father." By the time John's Gospel was written down, the gospel message had breached the walls of Jerusalem. Evangelists were persistently overtaking the Greco-Roman world and spreading the church beyond its borders. Jesus' commandment to take the "good news" of salvation to the farthest horizons beyond Judea was being taken seriously. But as the gospel message went forward, new questions arose and new challenges came forward from the world around them, making it necessary for the Apostles to refine their message for those audiences unfamiliar with the Hebrew Scriptures while still maintaining the purity of the gospel. John wanted to address some of the theological questions about faith in Christ asked by Jews, Greeks, and Romans, and at the same time, present a Gospel for a universal audience.

At first the Jewish authorities attempted to stop the spread of the gospel and silence the leaders of what they considered a strictly Jewish cult that believed Jesus, an itinerant rabbi from Nazareth, was the Messiah of Jews and Gentiles. The Greek intellectuals for the most part ignored Christians; they dismissed as foolishness the gospel that proclaimed the resurrection from the dead of its leader. Romans resisted the spread of the gospel on political grounds; they were suspicious of any movement that might be a potential threat to the supreme power of Rome or upset the social order. But none of the authorities – Jewish, Greek, or Roman– could stop the dissemination of the gospel that was being carried throughout the world by the divine wind of the Holy Spirit that started from Pentecost.

Soon it became clear to the Jews that they could not stop the spread of the Gospel so Gentile believers in Jesus would have to circumcised or be rooted out of the Jewish faith. Rome was discovering that the more they tried to stamp out the movement, the faster it grew and spread throughout their Empire (before they knew much about this new religion it was already inside the very gates of the city of Rome itself). Greeks could no longer ignore this new faith in a crucified and resurrected Savior that was flourishing all around them, transforming lives and turning their humanistic worldview upside-down. Now it was John's turn to write a response; and as the petals of his Gospel unfolded, his message spoke directly to those from Jerusalem, Athens, and from the heart of Rome to the outermost parts of the world.

John opens his message by describing Jesus Christ as the eternal *Logos*. Volumes have been written about John's use of *logos* in the opening statement of his Gospel and there is no need for me to write in detail about *logos* here. It is enough to say in this short overview of John's Gospel that in Greek philosophical thought, the term *logos* is used to express the *rational principle* or *Mind* that ruled the universe. In Hebrew thought *logos* would relate to "the word of God", which is more than a passive self-expression – it is something that has creative power. Through the word of God a person not only receives the truth about God, but also meets God face-to-face. God's *Logos*, incarnate in Jesus Christ, was sent in order to accomplish a particular purpose, and, after accomplishing that mission, returned to God who sent Him.

"For my thoughts are not your thoughts, neither are your ways my ways, declares the LORD. For as the heavens are higher than the earth, so are my ways higher than your ways and my thoughts than your thoughts. For as the rain and the snow come down from heaven and do not return there but water the earth, making it bring forth and sprout, giving seed to the sower and bread to the eater, so shall my word be that goes out from my mouth; it shall not return to me empty, but it shall accomplish that which I purpose, and shall succeed in the thing for which I sent it." Isaiah 55:8-11 (ESV)

From the beginning, John presents a message that is intended to be universal in scope. He introduces Jesus as the eternal *Logos* from whom all things came into existence. John uses the events of Jesus' earthly life to establish His divine credentials as the Son of God and Savior of all mankind. Soon after His baptism – where John the Baptist declares Jesus, "the Lamb of God who takes away the sins of the world" – He commands His first disciples to leave all to follow Him. John then describes Jesus' absolute power as Son of God when He performs His first sign at the wedding in Cana, transforming the water of legal purification into what some have called the "wine of a new dispensation". Next John takes us to the heart of Jerusalem where Jesus makes a whip out of cords and with divine authority and righteous indignation drives the moneychangers out of the temple. By the end of the second chapter of John, the Romans, Greeks and Jews would have completely understood John's message that Jesus was no ordinary man, but was God's Son, sent to this earth at the perfect time on a mission with divine authority. In the next few chapters of John, Jesus moves from Jerusalem, to Judea and Samaria ministering to the multitudes and to all who come to him seeking divine mercy. John never loses focus on his primary goal of showing that Jesus is the Son of God who is Savior and Lord of all.

The structure of John's gospel (see "The Sevens in John" below) demonstrates a carefully thought out story. John, under the guidance of the Holy Spirit, chooses those words and deeds of Jesus that best described Him as the eternal Word and Son of God who was with the Father from the beginning, and who is in fact, God incarnate.

THE SEVENS IN JOHN

The number seven is a sacred number to God's people; it represents spiritual perfection, for it is the heavenly number in Scripture. Whether by conscious design or by the unconscious leading of the Holy Spirit, John's gospel is formed around three sets of sevens (three, being the number that stands for that which is real, substantial, and complete). So the Gospel of John reveals Jesus Christ in His complete, spiritual perfection.

SEVEN DISCOURSES	SEVEN MIRACLES	SEVEN "I AM" STATEMENTS
1. New Birth (3:1-36)	1. Water Into Wine (2:1-11)	1. Bread of Life (6:35-51)
2. Water of Life (4:1-42)	2. Healing the Official's Son (4:43-54)	2. Light of the World (8:12 – 9:5)
3. Son of Man (5:19-47)	3. Healing the Lame Man (5:1-16)	3. Gate for the Sheep (10:7-9)
4. Bread of Life (6:22-66)	4. Feeding the 5,000 (6:1-14)	4. Good Shepherd (10:11-14)
5. Rivers of Living Water (7:1-52)	5. Walking on Water (6:16-21)	5. Resurrection & Life (11:35)

6. Light of the World (8:12-59)	6. Healing the Blind Man (9:1-12)	6. Way, Truth & Life (14:6)
7. Good Shepherd (10:1-42)	7. Raising Lazarus (11:1-46)	7. True Vine (15:1-5)

    The necessity of Christ's rejection and passion is made known by John who beholds Jesus as the sacrificial Lamb of God who takes away the sins of the world. His resurrection reveals His divine nature as truly being the Son of the living God, and the events leading up to His ascension point His followers to what lies ahead of them as they wait expectantly for His Second Coming. John's Gospel is unique in that chapter 13 beginning in verse 31 through chapter 17 offers the longest personal, private teachings of Jesus for His disciples. The Holy Spirit moved upon John to include this discourse with the disciples for the hope and edification of the church – especially those believers that will face bitter persecution in every era until the Lord's return. John closes his gospel with one final affirming statement that all he wrote was not something he made up, but his testimony about Jesus is real and trustworthy: *"This is the disciple who testifies to these things and who wrote them down. We know that his testimony is true."* (John 21:24)

3.

Jesus & John the Baptist
From the Birth of Jesus to the Start of His Earthly Ministry

Jesus Baptized by John
By Maria Clara (Used by Permission)

LESSON OUTLINE

The purpose of this lesson is to explain the relationship between John the Baptist's ministry as the forerunner and the early ministry of Jesus Christ.

- Circumstances of John the Baptist's Birth Points to Him as the Forerunner

- The Circumstances of Jesus' birth Points to Him as the Messiah

- The Miracles from Jesus' Birth Through His Baptism by John

- John's and Jesus' Messages on Repentance

THE MINISTRY OF JOHN THE BAPTIST

John the Baptist was at once the last great prophet to the covenant nation of Israel and the forerunner of a New Covenant that marked the beginning of the Gentile church. The fact that all four Gospel writers included accounts of John the Baptist's message and ministry to the children of Israel as Christ's forerunner means that we cannot underestimate the great importance of John's mission to the Gospel of salvation presented in the Apostles' teachings.

Luke was the only one of the Gospel writers to include the circumstances surrounding John the Baptist's birth. Although his conception and birth were not miraculous, miraculous events did surround his beginning. John's conception and birth shared some similarities with other important Old Testament figures like Abraham and Sarah, the parents of Samson, and Samuel's parents. Elizabeth and Zechariah experienced unique divine encounters foretelling John's birth and ministry. Like Samson's parents, John's parents were divinely instructed to raise their son as a Nazarite. "It had been appointed (Luke 1:15) that from the beginning of John's life he should not 'drink wine or strong drink,' i.e., should live as a Nazirite, (Nu 6:1-21) implying extraordinary and lifelong consecration to God's service. 'A child of the mountains, and living a temperate life in the open air, he probably became strong in body, as well as 'grew strong in spirit' (Luke 1:80)." John A. Broadus, *Commentary on the Gospel of Matthew*, Database © 2006 WORDsearch Corp

After Mary's visit with her pregnant kinswoman Elizabeth and the prophetic response of her as yet to be born child, we hear nothing of John until his public ministry begins just ahead of Jesus' arrival on the scene.

"In the fifteenth year of the reign of Tiberius Caesar, Pontius Pilate being governor of Judea, and Herod being tetrarch of Galilee, and his brother Philip tetrarch of the region of Ituraea and Trachonitis, and Lysanias tetrarch of Abilene, during the high priesthood of Annas and Caiaphas, the word of God came to John the son of Zechariah in the wilderness. And he went into all the region around the Jordan, proclaiming a baptism of repentance for the forgiveness of sins." Luke 3:1-3 (ESV)

Luke, wanting to be as accurate as possible for his contemporary readers, gave the time of John's appearance with great detail. However, dates from antiquity are not always counted exactly the same and therefore it is difficult for Bible scholars today to be 100% certain of the exact dates. Since Pontius Pilate became Procurator around 25 AD and the

POINTS TO NOTE ABOUT THE BIRTH OF JOHN

- When "the fullness of time" arrived, God selected two unlikely women to give birth. The first woman is to be mother of the one who would be the forerunner of the Messiah, and second woman is to be the mother of the Messiah. Both births are presented in Luke's Gospel as special and unique miracles of God.
- Elizabeth is old and barren; therefore she would not be expected to give birth to anyone (Note Sarah, the wife of Abraham)
- Mary contrasts with Elizabeth: Mary is young and a virgin, and therefore would not be expected to give birth to anyone.

- Elizabeth and Zacharias were from the priestly tribe of Levi (Luke 1:5)
- Elizabeth was related to Mary (1:36) and therefore, Jesus and John were related.
- John was born 6 months before Jesus (1:26).
- Why did John not recognize Jesus at the time of His baptism? It seems that Jesus and John were raised in separate geographical locations (John in wilderness area of Judea and Jesus in Nazareth of Galilee

Matt. 1:-4:12; 11:2-19; 14:1-12; **Mark** 1:1-14; 6:14-29; **Luke** 1:5 – 4:14; 7:18-35; 9:7-9
John 1:19 – 3:36; 4:1-4; 10:40-42

fifteenth year of Tiberius was around that same time, it can be estimated that John probably began his ministry in 26 or 27 AD. Luke states that it was "during the high priesthood of Annas and Caiaphas, the word of God came to John the son of Zechariah in the wilderness" (3:2) and that he was broadcasting "a baptism of repentance for the forgiveness of sins" into the entire region around the Jordon.

"John's dress and habits were strikingly suggestive of Elijah, the old prophet of national judgment. His desert habits have led some to connect him with that strange company of Jews known as the Essenes. There is, however, little foundation for such a connection other than his ascetic habits and the fact that the chief settlement of this sect was near the home of his youth. It was natural that he should continue the manner of his youthful life in the desert, and it is not improbable that he intentionally copied his great prophetic model. It was fitting that the one who called men to repentance and the beginning of a self-denying life should show renunciation and self-denial in his own life. But there is no evidence in his teaching that he required such asceticism of those who accepted his baptism." (*The International Standard Bible Encyclopedia*)

In spite of his importance to the Gospel narratives as the one who announces Jesus the Messiah to the world, very little is known about John. He was considered by the Jews to be a great prophet. He certainly looked and acted the part of an Old Testament prophet, but neither John nor the rest of the nation could have known that his ministry was at once the end of one era and the beginning of a new era that would spread God's message directly to the Gentile nations. Unlike Jesus who foreshadowed the Gentile church in His sermons and parables (Matt.13:47; 22:10; 24:14; 25:32; 28:19; Mk. 11:17; 12:9; 13:10; Lk. 13:19; 14:23; 24:47; Jn. 10:16) there is no evidence that John, in his ministry as the forerunner, ever prophesied beyond his Jewish audience. Mark chose not to detail John's ministry; it includes the bare minimum about John. Matthew chose to include only that information about John that specifically pointed to the Messiahship of Jesus. For the Apostle John, the Baptist's ministry transcended the Jewish nation and bore witness to Jesus as the light of the world. Luke's Gospel included the most information for us about John the Baptist's life and message. Chapter three of Luke's account describes his ministry. Some might wonder why Luke would include a quote from Isaiah (40:3-5), an ancient Jewish prophet in his narrative (Lk. 3:4-6) if he was targeting a gentile, Greek audience. The answer will be quickly found in the particular passage that Luke chose at this point in his narrative. Implied in these verses is the Messianic mission of John's baptism. Isaiah wrote prophetically of the requirement for a national revival ahead of the Messiah's arrival. Straight paths would have to be made – obstacles removed in the hearts of people. John the Baptist's words told the people that if they wanted to see the salvation of God, their hearts would have to be prepared through repentance and faith. John the Baptist used Isaiah's words to challenge the Jews to prepare for the coming of their Messiah (Matthew 3:3). Luke incorporated these verses from Isaiah to remind all people everywhere that repentance and faith are prerequisites for receiving Jesus Christ. As Jesus would later say to the Pharisee Nicodemus, "You must be born again" to see and enter into the kingdom of God.

The passage from Isaiah continues by comparing people to grass and flowers that quickly wither and fade away (40:6-8). The Greeks would have strongly identified with the idea that we are mortal, frail, and cannot stand the tests of time that only the gods can endure. By quoting this passage from Isaiah, Luke is reminding his Greek audience that God's Word is eternal and unfailing. The philosophies of men can change with public opinion; a popular thought or idea can change; and man's knowledge is malleable and unreliable. Even the Greek gods could change their minds on a whim; only God's Word is constant. The Greek audience reading this passage from Isaiah would understand the Hebrew idea that God's Word is eternal and unchanging. Therefore, those who turn to the Word of God for answers instead of the words of men will find lasting explanations to the most fundamental questions about human existence that haunt the souls of men.

"Behold, I will send you Elijah the prophet before the great and awesome day of the LORD comes. And he will turn the hearts of fathers to their children and the hearts of children to their fathers, lest I come and strike the land with a decree of utter destruction." Malachi 4:5-6 (ESV)

"And he will turn many of the children of Israel to the Lord their God, and he will go before him in the spirit and power of Elijah, to turn the hearts of the fathers to the children, and the disobedient to the wisdom of the just, to make ready for the Lord a people prepared." Luke 1:16-17 (ESV)

Malachi had predicted that before the great, final Day of Judgment, God would send a prophet like Elijah to help the Jews prepare for the coming of the Lord. (Note that the Messiah was believed to be that prophet like Moses, promised in Deut. 18:15.) By the time of John's ministry, it had been centuries since any prophet of the stature of an Elijah, Elisha or of any of the writing prophets had appeared. Lessor prophets had come and gone with every generation, but the Jewish nation was longing for the kind of authoritative prophetic utterances of a Moses-like figure that would guide the entire nation. Jewish Messianic traditions were saturated with longings for a prophet who would lead the way:

- **Judas Maccabeus**: After retaking Jerusalem and the Temple, Judas Maccabeus and his followers laid away the stones of the desecrated altar "until a prophet should appear to answer concerning them" (1 Macc. 4:46)

- **The woman of Samaria**, as soon as she perceived that Jesus was a prophet, asked him to settle the long-disputed question between the Jews and Samaritans concerning the proper place to worship God. (John 4:19 f.)

- **The disciples** reported to Jesus that besides the return of Elijah (John 1:21 Luke 9:8 Matthew 16:14, 17:10, 27:49), some of the Jews were still expecting the personal re-appearance of the recently executed John the Baptist (Mk. 6:14), a prophet like Jeremiah (Matt.16:14), or the Prophet like Moses (John 1:21 Deuteronomy 18:15,18)

The Jews were anxiously waiting for the forerunner to be revealed; it would be a sure sign for them of the coming of the Messiah and his Kingdom. Certainly there had been prophets in the land of Israel before John, but John was at last a prophet who in appearance and place of ministry resembled the great Elijah. The people sought out John earnestly believing he might be the Messiah, or at least the forerunner of the Messiah (Lk. 3:15). John's uncompromising preaching was in alignment with what had been spoken by all the great prophets that had come before him; he severely rebuked the Jews for

Jesus Calls Herod a Fox
By Maria Clara (Used by Permission)

taking righteousness for granted and earnestly incited them to revive their evil and unbelieving hearts. John's ministry in the wilderness fueled the hope that the Messianic reign of God was near. He urged them to prepare for the coming of the Messiah by submitting to a rite of baptism that was usually reserved for those needing re-entrance to the community of the righteous after defilement. The Gospels tell us that Jews from all around the country poured forth to see and hear him, confessing their sins and submitting to his baptism. (See Appendix One: John's Baptism) The urgency of John's appeal to the nation was based upon his vision of the imminent arrival of the long-expected Messiah. Like all of the Jews of his day, John was expecting the golden age of the Messianic kingdom to be established at that time. For all Jews the coming king and his messianic reign were undeniably linked. As the Messiah drew near the long-expected kingdom was also believed to be "at hand" (Matthew 4:17, 10:7; 11:3).

What was hidden from John and the rest of the Jews – what they did not foresee – was that there would be a first incarnation of the Suffering Messiah before a second, later incarnation of the Conquering King Messiah who would forever establish David's throne (Rev. 3:7; 5:5; 22:16). God sent another prophet like Elijah in John the Baptist, who prepared the way for Jesus, the sacrificial Lamb of God. The New Testament, which marks the beginning of a new era in human history, begins with this forerunner prophetically calling the people to repent, turn away from their sins and return to God. The prophetic word of Malachi that Elijah the prophet should be sent in advance of the Messiah to prepare the people for his coming, was confirmed by the angel (Luke 1:17) to be John. The baptizer would go before the Lord "in the spirit and power of Elijah." Jesus added another confirmation of John the Baptist as Elijah (Matthew 11:14; Matthew 17:10-13). "John was not a resurrected Elijah, but he took on Elijah's prophetic role—boldly confronting sin and pointing people to God" *Life Application Study Bible*.

It was clear from the Gospel accounts that John's appearance, way of life, his Messianic preaching, and call for national repentance with baptism had caused the people to respond to him in great numbers. A careful study of John's baptism tells us it was more than a mere modification of some existing rite; as a "baptism of repentance" John meant it to be a total renunciation of the past life. The people who responded to John's preaching were baptized by him for spiritual cleansing that symbolized the forgiveness of sins (cleansing the dish inside and outside so to speak). At the same time, they submitted to John's baptism as a spiritual preparation for the coming of the Messiah. Baptism also implied a promise of loyalty to the king and His kingdom once it arrived.

If God sent John to baptize repentant sinners in water (Jn. 1:33) why then did Jesus ask to be baptized by John if it was not for forgiveness of personal sins? By submitting to John's baptism Jesus affirmed that his baptism was "from heaven" (Matt. 21:25). Because Jesus was without sin, He would not feel the need of repentance or forgiveness, but His divinely inspired role as the Messiah led Him to pattern the rite of water baptism for the church and give it a godly stamp of approval. So the baptism of

John was and remains a highly significant and expressive rite for all followers of Jesus Christ and bears the distinct stamp of a divine appointment preceding entrance into the Messianic kingdom of the Lord.

"Now a discussion arose between some of John's disciples and a Jew over purification. And they came to John and said to him, 'Rabbi, he who was with you across the Jordan, to whom you bore witness – look, he is baptizing, and all are going to him.'
John answered, 'A person cannot receive even one thing unless it is given him from heaven. You yourselves bear me witness that I said, "I am not the Christ, but I have been sent before him." The one who has the bride is the bridegroom. The friend of the bridegroom, who stands and hears him, rejoices greatly at the bridegroom's voice. Therefore this joy of mine is now complete. He must increase, but I must decrease.'" John 3:25-30 (ESV)

John's disciples were struggling with his diminished role after Jesus' public ministry took hold, but John had no delusions of grandeur; he spoke of himself only as the one preparing the way for the greater One destined to come after him. As important as his baptism was to the nation, John pointed the way to the higher baptism of the Messiah (Lk. 3:15-17) – the baptism of the Holy Spirit with fire that Jesus was destined to bring (Acts 1:5). John also warned of the Messiah's coming judgment: "His winnowing fork is in his hand, to clear his threshing floor and to gather the wheat into his barn, but the chaff he will burn with unquenchable fire." (Luke 3:17 ESV) And certainly there is an element of that in the ministry of the Holy Spirit: "And when he comes, he will convict the world concerning sin and righteousness and judgment: concerning sin, because they do not believe in me; concerning righteousness, because I go to the Father, and you will see me no longer; concerning judgment, because the ruler of this world is judged. (John 16:8-11 ESV) However, the ultimate fulfillment of this prophecy of the Christ will not come before the end of the age when the Lord returns to judge the nations (Rev. 20:11-15).

THE ADVENT OF THE MESSIAH

Those who study the genealogies of Jesus from Matthew and Luke will note the obvious differences between them. These differences are easily understood by Bible scholars that have researched the names and traced the lineages presented in both Gospels (See Appendix Two: "Why Are There Different Genealogies for Jesus in Matthew 1 and Luke 3?")

First we note that from Abraham to David, their genealogies are identical. Then Luke shifts his emphasis and follows the priestly lineage of Jesus' ancestors, while Matthew follows the royal lineage. We also discover in these genealogies that the royal and priestly families of the tribes of Israel intermarried several times. Their first merging is seen when Aaron, the first High Priest, married into what would become the royal line when he married Elisheba, a daughter of Judah (Ex 6:23). Elisheba's brother, Naashon, would continue the royal lineage in Matthew's genealogy (Matt 1:4). Another example of the uniting of the two families occurred when David married Bathsheba, [Bathsheba was from David's own tribe and the granddaughter of one of David's closest advisors (2 Sam.15:12)]. Luke's account lists several priests. The priestly and royal lineages of Jesus merge again when Joseph who was from Judah's family, married Mary of Aaron's family. Mary was identified with the priestly tribe of Levites along with her much older cousin Elizabeth (Luke 1:5, 36). Because only priests were allowed to minister in the Temple, John the Baptist's father, Zacharias, must have been a Levite and a descendant of Aaron, (there were approx. 20,000 Levites of Aaron's family and only one Temple – thus the need to be chosen by lots to burn incense). Only once each year – on the great Day of Atonement – the High Priest enters behind the veil into the holy of holies, after the burning of incense.

The point to keep in mind when studying these genealogies is that first of all, they were written by missionaries, not historians or biographers. That means these lists had a specific intention that related to the overall message that each Gospel had to present. For Matthew, the fact that Jesus was the long-awaited, Messianic King of the Jews needed to be emphasized in his introduction to his Gospel. The Messiah had to come from Abraham through David to be the rightful King of the Jews. So Jesus' royal line was emphasized by Matthew. Most, but not all scholars argue that Luke traced the priestly line of Jesus through Mary. The priestly line might have been of some interest to Luke's Jewish readers, but it is likely that Luke was primarily appealing to Gentile readers that would have been looking for the legal, biological lineage of Jesus that confirmed His full humanity as the Son of God – thus the need to trace Jesus' roots all the way back to Adam.

THE MIRACLES OF JESUS' BIRTH THROUGH HIS BAPTISM

The Miracle of His Forerunner, John (Luke 1)

"The two preceding evangelists had agreed to begin the gospel with the baptism of John and his ministry, which commenced about six months before our Savior's public ministry (and now, things being near a crisis, six months was a deal of time, which before was but a little), and therefore this evangelist, designing to give a more particular account than had been given of our Savior's conception and birth, determines to do so of John Baptist, who in both was his harbinger and forerunner, the morning-star to the Sun of righteousness. The evangelist determines thus, not only because it is commonly reckoned a satisfaction and entertainment to know something of the original extraction and early days of those who afterwards prove great men, but because in the beginning of these there were many things miraculous, and presages of what they afterwards proved. In these verses our inspired historian begins as early as the conception of John Baptist." Matthew Henry, *Matthew Henry's Commentary on the Whole Bible*, Database © 2014 WORD*search*

Luke's stated desire to write a careful and accurate account of the events of Jesus' life began with his record of John's birth. As the forerunner of the Messiah, John's birth was distinguished by several miracles surrounding it. The time and place of John's birth is clearly established in relationship to Jesus' miraculous birth. John's father, Zechariah was on duty at the temple; the circumstances of Zechariah being chosen by lot for that particular week indicated that it was not an accident, but was part of God's timing (Gal. 4:4). Luke is telling his readers that God was miraculously guiding the events of history to prepare the way for Jesus the Messiah to come to earth. John's barren mother giving birth was another miraculous sign of the coming greater miracle of Jesus' birth to the virgin maiden, Mary. So Elizabeth's barrenness serves to highlight Mary's virginity and the miraculous circumstances of Jesus' birth.

Throughout the Gospels, angels are described as spirit beings with specific assignments in God's service. They are intimately connected with the events surrounding Jesus' life and work from His birth through His resurrection. Zechariah's visitation by the angel came when he was ministering in the Temple. Gabriel appeared to him as he was burning the incense that represented the Jewish people's prayers ascending to the heavens. The angel could have announced the Forerunner anywhere, but chose this time and place to highlight the coming of the messiah as the miraculous answer to centuries of the nation's prayers. The Forerunner would announce that the Jewish nation's hopes and dreams for a Messiah to come and deliver them were about to be fulfilled. The Old Testament established the primary function of angels as bringing divine revelation; that function continued in the intertestamental period and was included in John's Revelation. Therefore, it would only be natural to discover angelic activity surrounding events which would be the beginning of an awesome reawakening of God's redemptive power indicated by the Forerunner's and the Messiah's births.

Because angels have a long history in the Scriptures and in the mythology of the Jewish people, little or no background is provided for the sudden appearances of angels in Luke's Gospel. Gabriel, whose name means 'God is strong' or 'man of God,' is the only angel named in the Gospels (Lk 1:19, 26). He is described in Luke 1:19 and other places as one who stands in God's presence, a ministering angel to God. Daniel identifies Gabriel as the angel who appeared to him in human form to interpret his vision (Dan 8:15-26; 9:21-27). Although the entire Bible calls only two angels by name, Gabriel and Michael, a number of non-canonical Jewish writings name many angels. However, as *The Dictionary of Jesus and the Gospels* notes, "In their angelology the Gospels show marked restraint, not engaging in speculation about angels. Their focus is on Jesus himself." (InterVarsity Press, Downers Grove, ILL, © 1992, p.9)

The Scriptures almost always describe encounters between humans and angels as an upsetting experience. Zechariah was definitely shaken and fearful when he saw the angel (Lk. 1:11, 12). Angels are spiritual beings; they dwell in God's holy presence. When angels are sent on missions to do His will, it is often to deliver special messages from God to humans. Zechariah's encounter with Gabriel is described in such a way to affirm that it was neither a dream nor a vision, but was a physical (visible and audible) encounter with a supernatural being. The angel said, "Don't be afraid, Zechariah! God has heard your prayer. Your wife, Elizabeth, will give you a son, and you are to name him John." This meant that Zechariah's personal prayer was being answered. And as is so often the case, this special prophecy had implications for the nation's prayers as well (Note the prophet Isaiah's pronouncement in 7:10-17 of his book and its messianic implications revealed in Matthew 1:21-23). It is likely that the priest had given up praying for a child long before; so his answered prayer at that moment may have been for the coming of the Messiah to his people. "How odd it must have seemed that the angel would say that his prayer was answered and Zechariah would soon have a son. Yet the greatest desire of Zechariah's heart—to have a son—would come true. At the same time, the answer to the nation's prayer for the Messiah would also come true. Zechariah's son would grow up to prepare the way for the Messiah." *Life Application Study Bible* notes on Luke 1:12.

Both John and Jesus shared another miracle: the miracle of being divinely named. *John* means "the LORD is gracious," and *Jesus* means "the LORD saves." The good news of the Gospel is that God was acting graciously to save not only His chosen people but all the nations. The conclusion of all four Gospels is that the cross of Christ means that God will not withhold salvation from anyone who sincerely comes to Him by faith (John 3:16). Whenever a person, place or thing in the Bible has a special and unique prophetic meaning, they will be named by God. The divinely appointed mission of John (Lk. 1:14-17) was revealed by Gabriel. As the Forerunner, John was set apart for special service to God. In those days a person could take a special Nazirite vow of separation in which they would totally abstain from partaking of any fruit of the vine, including wine (Numbers 6:1-8). John's consecration was special in that like the ancient Judge Samson, he was set apart as a Nazirite before birth (Judges 13).

Luke's Gospel mentions the Holy Spirit's intimate involvement in the miraculous events surrounding the births and early childhoods of John and Jesus Christ. In fact, Luke refers to the Holy Spirit, the third Person of the Trinity, more than any other Gospel writer (Luke 1:15, 35, 41, 67; 2:25-26; 3:16, 22; 4:1; 11:13, 12:10, 12). In his Gospel, Luke acknowledged and emphasized the connection of the Holy Spirit to the beginnings of Christianity. This should not be surprising since Luke's book of Acts also recognized and emphasized the Holy Spirit's miraculous work in inaugurating and guiding the early church. In a similar fashion to God's angels, God's Spirit was often given to faithful men and women in the Old Testament for special tasks. God's chosen people needed the Holy Spirit's help to do God's work effectively. John's role was to be almost identical to that of an Old Testament prophet. He was being sent to prepare the way of the Lord by encouraging people to turn away from sin and back to God. John would be filled with the Holy Spirit "even before his birth" and would be given the authority to baptize with water, but only Jesus, the Son of God, has the authority to baptize with fire and the Holy Spirit (Luke 3:16).

Miracles at the Conception and Birth of Jesus (Matt. 1:18-24; Luke 1; 2)

Luke's investigation into the origin of Jesus' incarnation at some point must have led him to Mary herself or someone intimately knowledgeable with Mary's story. He tells us that in the sixth month of Elizabeth's pregnancy, God sent Gabriel to earth once more – this time to the virgin, Mary. Engaged to be married to the man Joseph, Luke informs us that he was a descendant of King David – an important piece of information for his Jewish audience to note. Gabriel announced to Mary that she had been chosen to bear the long-awaited Messiah of the Jews and was to name Him, Jesus. This no doubt left her with some very important questions that needed to be answered. Least of all was "how could this happen?" since she was a virgin. "The simplicity of Mary's faith is remarkable, given the circumstances. Her simple answer, 'Behold, the bondslave of the Lord; be it done to me according to your word, 'gives us insight into her character. Quietly, modestly, submissively, she saw her role as a simple servant of the Lord. She might have been tempted to either boast or rebel, but she did neither. Luke 2:19 further reveals Mary's godly character, showing her typical response to the extraordinary work of God in her life: 'Mary treasured up all these things, pondering them in her heart.'" John F. MacArthur, Jr., *God with Us: The Miracle of Christmas*, Zondervan Books, Grand Rapids, MI, © 1969, p.55

Divine births of so-called sons of one god or another were not unknown to the ancients at the time of Jesus' incarnation. But what is unique about this story is the pure and holy quality of this birth. The Greeks told tales of gods raping or carrying on illicit sexual relationships with human females; inadvertently producing an offspring that then becomes a source of envy, jealousy, and intrigue among the gods. The Egyptian god Horus had four sons. Geb, the ancient fertility god of Egypt and the one who judges the dead in the afterlife, married his sister Nut, the sky goddess. Set and Nephthys were children of Geb and Nut. The god Ea (whose Sumerian equivalent was Enki) is one of the most powerful gods in the Mesopotamian pantheon. He was often portrayed with an overt, sexually exaggerated feature of his male virility. Enki, said to be the son of the god An, had numerous sexual encounters with other goddesses. In one tale, when Enki became gravely ill one of his lovers, Ninhursanga, gives birth to eight healing deities in order to cure him. Enki then fathered the goddess Ninkurra with his daughter Ninmu, and the goddess Uttu with his granddaughter Ninkurra. All of these various myths gave birth to the modern myth of liberal scholarship that Jesus' birth is equated with the births in these other ancient fables.

However, the facts are obvious: the story of Jesus' birth and parentage contrasts sharply with the myths that were familiar to all in the Greco-Roman world. Luke and Matthew set out from the beginning to establish Jesus' linage from history. His mother was a real human as was His legal father, Joseph. We find nowhere in the events surrounding Jesus' conception and birth the fantastic imagery of ancient myths with their unbelievable characters and otherworldly events. The Gospels all describe Jesus as natural in His humanity, and yet fully divine. The angel Gabriel's declaration of the Messianic prophecies concerning the birth of the Messiah and Elizabeth's conception of the promised forerunner only serve to further separate the circumstances of Jesus' miraculous birth by showing that His birth was planned from the beginning and the Son of God was revealed in the fullness of God's perfect timing (Gal. 4:4-5).

Mary's visit with Elizabeth becomes another miracle in the unfolding story of Jesus' birth. A few days after her encounter with the angel, Mary goes to the hill country of Judea to visit her cousin, Elizabeth. There is little doubt that Mary makes this extraordinary journey to see Elizabeth and confirm the angel's sayings. The encounter between Mary and Elizabeth is overshadowed by the encounter between the fruit of their wombs: John the forerunner, and the One soon to be born as the promised Messiah and Savior of mankind. Mary's song of joy and prophecy (Luke 1:46-55) was preserved in her heart and no doubt was shared verbally for years until Luke recorded it for us.

John's birth was normal and unaccompanied by any angelic visitations. Only Zechariah's by sudden loosening of his tongue with his written pronouncement of the baby's prophetically given name is there any indication of the special purpose for which this baby was born. The news of John's birth was spread with awe and wonder throughout the region. The people who heard the news had no difficulty recognizing that the hand of the Lord was upon John in a special way and that God was about to do something extraordinary. They were wondering "What will this child turn out to be?" In answer to the people's questions, the Holy Spirit came upon John's father Zechariah once more and he prophesied (Luke 1:67-79):

- The Lord had visited His people once again and would redeem them
- At long last, as had been prophesied, the Savior from the line of David had been sent
- That this Messiah would save the Jews from their enemies
- That the Lord had been merciful by remembering His sacred covenantal promises to their ancestors
- Since they have been rescued from their enemies, they can serve God without fear in holiness and righteousness
- That his son, John, would be called the prophet of the Most High because he is destined to prepare the way for the Lord
- That John will tell his people how to find salvation through forgiveness of their sins
- That because of the tender mercy of God, "the sunrise shall visit us from on high to give light to those who sit in darkness and in the shadow of death, to guide our feet into the way of peace."

We do not hear about John again until he is grown up and has become strong in spirit. When we do hear from John again he is living in the wilderness and has already started his public ministry of preparing the people of Israel for the arrival of their Messiah.

The Miracle of the Logos (John 1:1-14)

The Greek word, logos appears 128 times in the Gospels. Logos is the transliteration of the Greek word that means "word," "speech," "account," or "message." By the time the Gospels were written, Greek philosophers used the word to signify that which gives form, shape, or life to the material universe. Matthew, Mark, and Luke use the word in a non-philosophical sense. John's Gospel is unique in that he uses *logos* in his prologue (John 1:1, 14) to signify Jesus' divinity. "There was little good in talking to the Greek about a Messiah or a Son of David; these were terms that meant nothing to the Greeks. Even the term 'Son of God' hardly met the case, for the Greeks knew all about sons of the gods, who were the product of the amours of the gods who had come to hearth and seduced mortal maidens. If Jesus Christ was to be presented to the Greeks, some new way of communication had to be found." William Barclay, *Jesus As They Saw Him*, William B. Eerdmans Publishing, Grand Rapids, MI, © 1962, p. 421

By the time John wrote his Gospel, Christians were seeking new ways to reach their Greek audiences. The book of Acts describes the rapid expansion of the gospel throughout the Roman Empire, which included Athens, the very epicenter of Hellenism in the ancient world. Inspired by the Holy Spirit, John chose a word that would speak powerfully and effectively to both Jew and Greek. For the Jew, *logos* meant more than just a sound or a group of letters that meant something; words actually *did* something – they had to power to move men to action. Words can stir up powerful emotions in the hearts of men and motivate them. In Genesis chapter one, the words of God demonstrated the creative power of God. The Jews understood that God's word is never spoken in an empty and ineffective way, but had power to accomplish the will of God, "For as the rain and the snow come down from heaven and do not return there but water the earth, making it bring forth and sprout, giving seed to the sower and bread to the eater, so shall my word be that goes out from my mouth; it shall not return to me empty, but it shall accomplish that which I purpose, and shall succeed in the thing for which I sent it." Isaiah 55:10-11 (ESV)

The Jewish rabbis taught that the Word (Heb. *Memra*) contained the name and action of God. "So Judaism provided the background of the idea of the Word, and especially the background of the idea of the closeness of the Word to God and the action of the Word in the creation of the world." William Barclay, *Jesus As They Saw Him*, William B. Eerdmans Publisher, Grand Rapids, MI, © 1962, p. 424 The Greek philosophers taught that there were two worlds: an *ideal* world of ideas, thoughts, concepts, and designs in which God and immortality are a part; and another *phenomenal* world experienced by the human senses which is a physical copy of the *ideal*. The Greeks believed that *logos* was the intermediary between the *ideal* and the *phenomenal*; in other words, *logos* symbolized the Divine force from which the *phenomenal* world came into existence from the *ideal*. *Reason* was lifted to the higher plane of the *ideal* by the Greeks. God belonged to the higher plane of the *ideal* – the world of thought and reason which was separate from the lower *phenomenal* world of the senses. God was regarded by the Greek philosophers as the intelligent power by which the world was formed. However the Greeks were not inclined to endow *reason* with personality. The ideas that sprang from Divine mind were merely models or archetypes that fashioned the world of *phenomenon*.

So John's use of *Logos* to describe the pre-incarnate Christ transformed the idea of the Greeks' concept of an intelligent power that formed the world from a higher reality than this world of the senses to describe the Divine Jesus Christ, the Son of the living God who always existed. Jesus Christ was and is the Word who coexists with God in eternity. The *Logos* of John is a Person. It is through Christ the Logos that the world came into being – that the phenomenal world came into existence out of the ideal. When nothing was, the *Logos* was; the eternal preexistence of the Word was made flesh in Jesus Christ the Son of God.

This is truly the miracle John was attempting to communicate in his use of the term *Logos* in the prelude to his Gospel. The miracle of the Incarnation is that the eternal, pre-existent, Person of the godhead was revealed to human kind in the form of the Son of God: "Christ was coexistent. He was and is face-to-face with God forever. The word *with* (pros) has the idea of both *being with* and *acting toward*. Jesus Christ (the Word) was both with God and acting with God. He was 'with God'; by God's side, acting, living, and moving in the closest of relationship. Christ had the ideal and perfect relationship with God the Father. Their life together – their relationship, communion, fellowship, and connection – was a perfect eternal bond." *The Preacher's Outline & Sermon Bible: Volume 1, Matthew – John (The New International Version),* Authentic, Hyderabad, India, © 2000, p.1422

The miracle of the *Logos* inseparably binds everything together – everywhere Jesus went, everything Jesus said, and every encounter with every person He met had an eternal quality about it. In the presence of the divine *Logos*, the kingdom of heaven (the ideal) is manifested on the earth (the phenomenal). The *Logos* means Jesus is fully human and fully God. Although Jesus took upon Himself all the attributes of full humanity He never ceased to be the eternal *Logos* who has always existed. The *Logos* is the Creator and Sustainer of all things, and the source of eternal life. John's introduction to the life of Jesus Christ establishes this truth about

Jesus from the beginning; it is the foundation of all truth. In one way or another, every one of the Apostles expressed the full humanity and divinity of Jesus Christ as the second person of the Trinity of Father, Son, and Holy Spirit. If we cannot or will not believe this basic truth about the *Logos*, where will we find the faith to trust our eternal destiny to Jesus? That is why John and all the others wrote their Gospels. Their intention was far more than telling the story of Jesus' brief life on this earth. Their primary reason for writing down the testimonies concerning Jesus was to build faith and confidence in what they were told about Jesus Christ; and so all who read their stories would believe that Jesus truly was and is the Word of God made real in the person of the Son of God.

The Miracle at the Jordan River (Matt. 3:16-17; Mark 1:9-12; Luke 3:21, 23; John 1:6-34)

"Now when all the people were baptized, and when Jesus also had been baptized and was praying, the heavens were opened, and the Holy Spirit descended on him in bodily form, like a dove; and a voice came from heaven, 'You are my beloved Son; with you I am well pleased.'" Luke 3:21-22 (ESV)

The fact that each of the four Gospel writers mentioned John the Baptist is an indication of the importance of John's ministry in relation to the coming of Jesus Christ. All four Gospels indicate that the promised forerunner to the messiah is none other than John the Baptist. When Jesus arrives on the scene John had been in the wilderness for some time. He had been preaching that the people should be baptized to prepare for the coming of the Messiah. John's baptism was intended to be an outward show that they had turned to God in repentance and faith to receive forgiveness for their sins. Once all of Judea, including the people of Jerusalem, were coming to see and hear John, the time was right for the Messiah to step forward and on to the public stage. The Jews were still coming to John, confessing their sins, and being baptized when Jesus came and stood in front of him. At that moment, John's prophecy that someone was coming soon who would be greater than John was being realized. At the same time there is no indication from any of the Gospel writers that Jesus and John knew each other in person before that encounter – even though they were related to one another by blood. John could only baptize with water, but the One who stood before him at that moment in time was the only one who could baptize with the Holy Spirit.

Matthew, Mark, Luke, and John each describe in their own way the miracle that takes place at the moment of Jesus' baptism. Once again, keeping in mind the fact that these accounts were written by missionaries with a message to proclaim and not by historians concerned with fact checkers, the miracle of the Father, Son, and Holy Spirit converging and being expressed in time, space, and matter is recorded by and for the faithful.

Matthew and Mark indicate that Jesus specifically went from His home in Nazareth of Galilee to be baptized by John in the Jordan River. In Luke's account, Jesus suddenly steps forward from the crowd to be baptized by John. The Gospel of John is much more ambiguous; but we are assured by the Synoptic Gospels that Jesus was indeed baptized by John and that the Baptist's testimony is true that he saw the Holy Spirit descending like a dove from heaven and resting upon Jesus the moment He came up out of the waters of the Jordan River. Matthew and Mark state that Jesus saw the Spirit of God descending like a dove. Matthew adds that the dove not only descended on Him, but also settled on Him. Luke's account does not specify who witnessed the Holy Spirit, and John says that John the Baptist was the one who saw the Holy Spirit descend and rest upon Jesus. John is the only one of the Gospels that does not specifically mention the Father's voice speaking from heaven at that moment and declaring Jesus as His beloved Son.

Both the miracle and the mystery of the Trinity are revealed at the moment of Jesus' baptism. There is a clear typology in the appearance of the Holy Spirit as a dove in the Gospels and the image of the dove that settled on Noah after the ravages of the great flood receded enough for the dry land to appear. "When Noah survived in the ark the rigours of the flood, a dove he had sent out came and settled on him. And Jesus, who offers salvation in himself from the eschatological destruction of which John has been speaking, is marked out by the descent of the dove" Michael Green, *The Message of Matthew*, InterVarsity Press, Downer Grove, IL, © 1988, 2000, p.81. In Jeremiah 48:28 we see another typology: here the dove represents the unrepentant sinner who after trying every other refuge, finally comes to his senses and flies to Christ to hide under His protection and care.

It is essential at this point to note that the image of the Holy Spirit descending as a dove is not intended to be a literal, physical description of the Holy Spirit. The gospel writers used this image to describe only the manner in which the Spirit descended from above (the Holy Spirit looks no look like a dove than Jesus looks like a sheep or a lion). A person can imagine the gentle sweeping spirals as a natural dove slowly descends and rests upon the ground. And so the image of the dove here is indicative of *action* and *manner* not in physical appearance.

It was through His baptism of suffering on the cross that God 'fulfilled all righteousness." Warren W. Wiersbe

The miracle at the Jordan River is a miracle of *identification*. No one would seriously argue that Jesus needed to be baptized for repentance and forgiveness of sins. He is universally described as the sinless Son of God, and the spotless Lamb who takes away the sins of the world. The prophet Isaiah foretold a Messiah that would humble Himself and take the lowest place along with the rest of sinful mankind; and through His baptism, death, burial and resurrection God's Son fulfilled the prophet's words. Jesus Christ carried our griefs and bore our sorrows:

> *Who has believed what he has heard from us? And to whom has the arm of the LORD been revealed?*
> *For he grew up before him like a young plant, and like a root out of dry ground; he had no form or majesty that we should look at him, and no beauty that we should desire him.*
> *He was despised and rejected by men; a man of sorrows, and acquainted with grief; and as one from whom men hide their faces he was despised, and we esteemed him not.*
> *Surely he has borne our griefs and carried our sorrows; yet we esteemed him stricken, smitten by God, and afflicted.*
> *But he was pierced for our transgressions; he was crushed for our iniquities; upon him was the chastisement that brought us peace, and with his wounds we are healed.*
> *All we like sheep have gone astray; we have turned – every one – to his own way; and the LORD has laid on him the iniquity of us all.*
> *He was oppressed, and he was afflicted, yet he opened not his mouth; like a lamb that is led to the slaughter, and like a sheep that before its shearers is silent, so he opened not his mouth.*

> *By oppression and judgment he was taken away; and as for his generation, who considered that he was cut off out of the land of the living, stricken for the transgression of my people?*
> *And they made his grave with the wicked and with a rich man in his death, although he had done no violence, and there was no deceit in his mouth.*
> *Yet it was the will of the LORD to crush him; he has put him to grief; when his soul makes an offering for guilt, he shall see his offspring; he shall prolong his days; the will of the LORD shall prosper in his hand.*
> *Out of the anguish of his soul he shall see and be satisfied; by his knowledge shall the righteous one, my servant, make many to be accounted righteous, and he shall bear their iniquities.*
> *Therefore I will divide him a portion with the many, and he shall divide the spoil with the strong, because he poured out his soul to death and was numbered with the transgressors; yet he bore the sin of many, and makes intercession for the transgressors.*
> *Isaiah 53:1-12 (ESV)*

When Jesus stepped into the waters of John's baptism, He was fully identifying with mankind's sinfulness in order to fully redeem mankind by His blood: "For God so loved the world, that he gave his only Son, that whoever believes in him should not perish but have eternal life. For God did not send his Son into the world to condemn the world, but in order that the world might be saved through him." John 3:16-17 (ESV)

The Miracle in the Wilderness (Matt. 4:1-10; Mark 1:12-13; Luke 4:1-13)

The final miracle before Jesus sets out on His public ministry – a course that will ultimately and inevitably lead to the cross – is the miracle of His trial in the Wilderness. The first Adam failed the test of faith in the Garden of Eden. God's children failed test after test in the Wilderness of Sin. Now it was up to God's only Son to be tested on the anvil of affliction in the Wilderness. Mark's Gospel describes the essential facts of that moment: "The Spirit immediately drove him out into the wilderness. And he was in the wilderness forty days, being tempted by Satan. And he was with the wild animals, and the angels were ministering to him." Mark 1:12-13 (ESV)

The fact that Jesus went through the temptations in the wilderness in His humanity and not in His glorified state, further seals His complete identification with the fallen human race. It would have been no trouble for Jesus to defeat Satan as the glorified Son of God, exalted upon His throne with myriads of angels at His sides. But there is no way we could relate to His trials and temptations at that moment – and there would be no way Jesus could relate to our struggles in this sin-stained world as well. So Jesus not only faced His greatest trial before He reached the cross in the weakness of human flesh, but He did so after being pushed to the very limits of physical endurance by forty days of fasting:

"Therefore he had to be made like his brothers in every respect, so that he might become a merciful and faithful high priest in the service of God, to make propitiation for the sins of the people. For because he himself has suffered when tempted, he is able to help those who are being tempted." Hebrews 2:17-18 (ESV)

"For we do not have a high priest who is unable to sympathize with our weaknesses, but one who in every respect has been tempted as we are, yet without sin. Let us then with confidence draw near to the throne of grace, that we may receive mercy and find grace to help in time of need." Hebrews 4:15-16 (ESV)

It was not until after Jesus refused every Satanic offer to end His human suffering and exalt Himself against His Father's will that ministering angels were sent to Him (Matt. 4:11). The devil's temptation of Jesus is the template for all temptations. At the very root of every temptation of Jesus in the wilderness (and our temptations in this world) is the temptation to compromise and convince ourselves that in some way we **can** serve both God and mammon. In some circles of the church, they have even bought into the lie that prosperity and abundance in the things of this world *is* the kingdom of God. But the things of this world must not be obtained by compromise – they must not be seized by our own hands to be used for our own selfish purposes. James said it plainly: "You adulterous people! Do you not know that friendship with the world is enmity with God? Therefore whoever wishes to be a friend of the world makes himself an enemy of God." James 4:4 (ESV)

What will it profit anyone if they gain the whole world at the expense of their soul? (Matt. 16:26) We are called by God to no longer conform to the pattern of this world, but to be transformed so that we will do God's will in every circumstance (Rom. 12:2). The miracle in the wilderness proves that we who have not endured hardships – that have never faced any real persecution, or have never shed a drop of blood for the cause of Christ – have no excuse for collapsing and compromising our faith for a few more pleasures or to avoid a little pain for the cause of Christ. The miracle in the Wilderness was Jesus' unbending resolve to obey the Father's will at all costs; it inspires us to persevere in every circumstance. "Consider him who endured from sinners such hostility against himself, so that you may not grow weary or fainthearted. In your struggle against sin you have not yet resisted to the point of shedding your blood." Hebrews 12:3-4 (ESV)

THE MINISTRIES OF JOHN THE BAPTIST & JESUS

It had been prophesied long before (Malachi 3:1) that the Lord would send His special messenger to prepare the way for Him. And at that time, the Messiah, the Messenger of the covenant whom they sought for so many years, would suddenly come to His temple. John's mission was to prepare the people of Israel for the arrival of their Messiah and to introduce them to the coming kingdom Christ would bring: "In those days John the Baptist came preaching in the wilderness of Judea, 'Repent, for the kingdom of heaven is at hand.' For this is he who was spoken of by the prophet Isaiah when he said, 'The voice of one crying in the wilderness: "Prepare the way of the Lord; make his paths straight."' Now John wore a garment of camel's hair and a leather belt around his waist, and his food was locusts and wild honey. Then Jerusalem and all Judea and all the region about the Jordan were going out to him, and they were baptized by him in the river Jordan, confessing their sins." Matthew 3:1-6 (ESV)

The Jordan River played a significant part in the life of the nation of Israel. So it was no accident that God called John the Baptist to deliver His message of repentance from dead works and spiritual renewal at this place and time. Matthew 3:1-16; Mark 1:1-9: Luke 3:1-17, 21, 22 & John 1:15-34 describe for us the way John prepared the nation for the coming of the Messiah. John's baptism with water demonstrated the repentance, humility, and cleansing from sin the people needed to prepare themselves for the coming of the Messiah. This was the beginning of the spiritual process. When He emerged from the waters of the Jordan River, Jesus set out on a new phase of His ministry that would involve the public proclamation of the gospel of the kingdom, and the private teaching and training of His disciples. Jesus' mission was to correct the distorted expectations of the Jewish idea of the Messiah and His kingdom. He needed to prepare the nation for His Atonement and the day when He would return to the Father. Finally, Jesus prepared His followers to receive the Holy Spirit who would be sent to His church to lead them and guide them until His return at the end of the age. Jesus' baptism with fire would follow John's baptism. It would be fulfilled on the Day of Pentecost, when the power of the Holy Spirit to all believers to live and to proclaim the gospel of the kingdom.

"They who are baptized with the Holy Ghost are baptized as with fire… is fire enlightening? So the Spirit is a Spirit of illumination. Is it warming? And do not their hearts burn within them? Is it consuming? And does not the Spirit of judgment, as a spirit of burning, consume the dross of their corruptions? Does fire make all it seizes like itself? And does it move upwards? So does the Spirit make the soul holy like itself, and its tendency is heavenward. Christ says I am come to send fire…" Matthew Henry

When we Compare John the Baptist's teaching on true repentance (Matt. 3:8-10; Luke 3:8-16) with Jesus' teachings about entering and living as a citizen of the kingdom from His Sermon on the Mount (Matt. 7:13-27), we clearly see that both John the Baptist and Jesus called people to much more than words or ritual for repentance:

John the Baptist
Produce fruit in keeping with repentance. And do not think you can say to yourselves, 'We have Abraham as our father.' I tell you that out of these stones God can raise up children for Abraham. The ax is already at the root of the trees, and every tree that does not produce good fruit will be cut down and thrown into the fire. Matthew 3:8-10 (NIV)

Produce fruit in keeping with repentance. And do not begin to say to yourselves, 'We have Abraham as our father.' For I tell you that out of these stones God can

raise up children for Abraham. The ax is already at the root of the trees, and every tree that does not produce good fruit will be cut down and thrown into the fire."
"What should we do then?" the crowd asked.
John answered, "The man with two tunics should share with him who has none, and the one who has food should do the same."
Tax collectors also came to be baptized. "Teacher," they asked, "what should we do?"
"Don't collect any more than you are required to," he told them.
Then some soldiers asked him, "And what should we do?" He replied, "Don't extort money and don't accuse people falsely – be content with your pay." The people were waiting expectantly and were all wondering in their hearts if John might possibly be the Christ. 16 John answered them all, "I baptize you with water. But one more powerful than I will come, the thongs of whose sandals I am not worthy to untie. He will baptize you with the Holy Spirit and with fire. Luke 3:8-16 (NIV)

Jesus Christ
"Enter through the narrow gate. For wide is the gate and broad is the road that leads to destruction, and many enter through it.
But small is the gate and narrow the road that leads to life, and only a few find it.
"Watch out for false prophets. They come to you in sheep's clothing, but inwardly they are ferocious wolves.
By their fruit you will recognize them. Do people pick grapes from thornbushes, or figs from thistles?
Likewise every good tree bears good fruit, but a bad tree bears bad fruit. A good tree cannot bear bad fruit, and a bad tree cannot bear good fruit. Every tree that does not bear good fruit is cut down and thrown into the fire.
Thus, by their fruit you will recognize them.
"Not everyone who says to me, 'Lord, Lord,' will enter the kingdom of heaven, but only he who does the will of my Father who is in heaven.
Many will say to me on that day, 'Lord, Lord, did we not prophesy in your name, and in your name drive out demons and perform many miracles?' Then I will tell them plainly, 'I never knew you. Away from me, you evildoers!'
"Therefore everyone who hears these words of mine and puts them into practice is like a wise man who built his house on the rock. The rain came down, the streams rose, and the winds blew and beat against that house; yet it did not fall, because it had its foundation on the rock.

But everyone who hears these words of mine and does not put them into practice is like a foolish man who built his house on sand.
The rain came down, the streams rose, and the winds blew and beat against that house, and it fell with a great crash." Matthew 7:13-27 (NIV)

It is not enough to say a prayer just asking for God to forgive your sins and to go through the rite of baptism to declare yourself "Christian". A citizen of the kingdom of God must also demonstrate the genuineness of their conversion by bearing fruit in keeping with that conversion. Does that mean that salvation is not the free gift of God? No. What it means that salvation if it is genuine will include repentance and a transformed life.

"I am the true vine, and my Father is the vinedresser. Every branch in me that does not bear fruit he takes away, and every branch that does bear fruit he prunes, that it may bear more fruit. Already you are clean because of the word that I have spoken to you. Abide in me, and I in you. As the branch cannot bear fruit by itself, unless it abides in the vine, neither can you, unless you abide in me. I am the vine; you are the branches. Whoever abides in me and I in him, he it is that bears much fruit, for apart from me you can do nothing. If anyone does not abide in me he is thrown away like a branch and withers; and the branches are gathered, thrown into the fire, and burned. John 15:1-6 (ESV)

Likewise, my brothers, you also have died to the law through the body of Christ, so that you may belong to another, to him who has been raised from the dead, in order that we may bear fruit for God. Romans 7:4 (ESV)

The preaching of Jesus and John the Baptist on repentance were very similar at points. But John's exhortations were filled with an urgency that the approach of the long-expected Messiah was near. Jesus' preaching on repentance was filled with a different kind of expectancy: that the kingdom of heaven was already "at hand." Because John's ministry was leading up to the arrival and announcement of the Messiah, he spoke of the Messiah as "the coming one." The Messianic Age was still believed to be in the future. John does not say, "Repent, so that the reign will draw near, but "Repent, for it has drawn near." Jesus' call for repentance is "The time is fulfilled, and the kingdom of God is at hand; repent and believe in the gospel." Mark 1:15 (ESV)

Jesus' public sermons expanded way beyond John's call for repentance and baptism for the forgiveness of sins. Jesus came to introduce a whole new understanding of the kingdom of God. Although the concept of a heavenly kingdom to come at some time in the future was totally familiar to the children of Israel, **Jesus' teachings on the kingdom of heaven were uniquely His.** Jesus spoke of the necessity of being "born again" only once (John 3:3-7), but Jesus is quoted as referring to the kingdom eighty-two times. And in fact, His teaching on being born again is in direct reference to His teaching Nicodemus concerning the prerequisites for entering into the kingdom of God (John 3:3, 5).

The Gospels of Matthew, Mark and Luke leave little doubt of the importance of the Kingdom of God in Jesus' message:

- Matthew 4:23 (NIV) – *"Jesus went throughout Galilee, teaching in their synagogues, preaching the good news of the kingdom, and healing every disease and sickness among the people."*
- Matthew 9:35 (NIV) – *"Jesus went through all the towns and villages, teaching in their synagogues, preaching the good news of the kingdom and healing every disease and sickness."*
- Mark 1:14-15 (NIV) – *"After John was put in prison, Jesus went into Galilee proclaiming the good news of God. 'The time has come," he said. "The kingdom of God is near. Repent and believe the good news!'"*
- Luke 8:1 (NIV) – *"After this, Jesus traveled about from one town and village to another, proclaiming the good news of the kingdom of God. The Twelve were with him…"*
- Luke 9:11 (NIV) – *"…but the crowds learned about it and followed him. He welcomed them and spoke to them about the kingdom of God, and healed those who needed healing.*
- Acts 1:3 (NIV) – *"After his suffering, he showed himself to these men and gave many convincing proofs that he was alive. He appeared to them over a period of forty days and spoke about the kingdom of God."*

Those who came to hear Jesus were immersed in the worldview shaped by the Old Testament; they had come to expect an earthly Messiah who would *immediately* overthrow the Gentile nations that were oppressing the Jewish people and rule over the territories originally conquered by David.

"For to us a child is born, to us a son is given, and the government will be on his shoulders. And he will be called Wonderful Counselor, Mighty God, Everlasting

Father, Prince of Peace. Of the increase of his government and peace there will be no end. He will reign on David's throne and over his kingdom, establishing and upholding it with justice and righteousness from that time on and forever. The zeal of the Lord Almighty will accomplish this." Isaiah 9:6-7 (NIV)

Jerusalem would be the religious and political center of the world and all the kings of the earth would pay homage to the King that sat on David's throne.

It shall come to pass in the latter days that the mountain of the house of the LORD shall be established as the highest of the mountains, and shall be lifted up above the hills; and all the nations shall flow to it, and many peoples shall come, and say: "Come, let us go up to the mountain of the LORD, to the house of the God of Jacob, that he may teach us his ways and that we may walk in his paths." For out of Zion shall go the law, and the word of the LORD from Jerusalem. He shall judge between the nations, and shall decide disputes for many peoples; and they shall beat their swords into plowshares, and their spears into pruning hooks; nation shall not lift up sword against nation, neither shall they learn war anymore. Isaiah 2:2-4 (ESV)

However, it is clear from the Gospels that the kingdom Jesus said was "in the midst" of them was totally different from the one the Jews had come to expect. An incident recorded in Matthew's Gospel reveals the ambivalence of those Jews who thought Jesus might indeed be the "Expected One", but did not understand why He did not make the moves they expected from the one who was destined to sit on David's throne.

"When John heard in prison what Christ was doing, he sent his disciples to ask him, 'Are you the one who was to come, or should we expect someone else?'
Jesus replied, 'Go back and report to John what you hear and see: The blind receive sight, the lame walk, those who have leprosy are cured, the deaf hear, the dead are raised, and the good news is preached to the poor. Blessed is the man who does not fall away on account of me.'" Matthew 11:2-6 (NIV)

John the Baptist was no different than the other Jews that were watching and waiting for the coming King. John, like the other Old Testament prophets before him, knew that when the Messiah came, he would usher in a new age:

THE WAY, TRUTH, AND LIFE

"Behold, the days are coming, declares the LORD, when I will make a new covenant with the house of Israel and the house of Judah, not like the covenant that I made with their fathers on the day when I took them by the hand to bring them out of the land of Egypt, my covenant that they broke, though I was their husband, declares the LORD. For this is the covenant that I will make with the house of Israel after those days, declares the LORD: I will put my law within them, and I will write it on their hearts. And I will be their God, and they shall be my people. And no longer shall each one teach his neighbor and each his brother, saying, 'Know the LORD,' for they shall all know me, from the least of them to the greatest, declares the LORD. For I will forgive their iniquity, and I will remember their sin no more." Jeremiah 31:31-34 (ESV)

As John sat in his prison cell, he saw no evidence of a "Golden Messianic Age" that the Jews were looking for from their Messiah. The wicked King Herod was still on the throne; there was no army of righteous warriors gathering together to overthrow the hated Roman Governor and his legions. The only ones following Jesus were the weak, the humble, the downtrodden and the powerless. John the Baptist must have been wondering at that time if he had got it wrong. Had he missed the Lord? Was Jesus really the Anointed One? Or should the Jews look for yet another to deliver them?

Surely, Jesus' answer to John must have shaken his expectations concerning who and what he thought the Messiah would be. His answer, *"Go back and report to John what you hear and see: The blind receive sight, the lame walk, those who have leprosy are cured, the deaf hear, the dead are raised, and the good news is preached to the poor. Blessed is the man who does not fall away on account of me…"* was designed to challenge John's presuppositions concerning the Messiah and the kingdom of God. But layered in His response to John were clear prophecies that revealed a ministry of the Messiah that the Jews were not looking for:

The stone that the builders rejected has become the cornerstone. This is the LORD's doing; it is marvelous in our eyes. Psalm 118:22-23 (ESV)

Blessed is he whose help is the God of Jacob, whose hope is in the LORD his God, who made heaven and earth, the sea, and all that is in them, who keeps faith forever; who executes justice for the oppressed, who gives food to the hungry. The

LORD sets the prisoners free; the LORD opens the eyes of the blind. The LORD lifts up those who are bowed down; the LORD loves the righteous. The LORD watches over the sojourners; he upholds the widow and the fatherless, but the way of the wicked he brings to ruin. Psalm 146:5-9 (ESV)

In that day the deaf shall hear the words of a book, and out of their gloom and darkness the eyes of the blind shall see. The meek shall obtain fresh joy in the LORD, and the poor among mankind shall exult in the Holy One of Israel. Isaiah 29:18-19 (ESV)

Strengthen the weak hands, and make firm the feeble knees. Say to those who have an anxious heart, "Be strong; fear not! Behold, your God will come with vengeance, with the recompense of God. He will come and save you." Then the eyes of the blind shall be opened, and the ears of the deaf unstopped; then shall the lame man leap like a deer, and the tongue of the mute sing for joy. For waters break forth in the wilderness, and streams in the desert... Isaiah 35:3-6 (ESV)

The Spirit of the Lord GOD is upon me, because the LORD has anointed me to bring good news to the poor; he has sent me to bind up the brokenhearted, to proclaim liberty to the captives, and the opening of the prison to those who are bound; to proclaim the year of the LORD's favor, and the day of vengeance of our God; to comfort all who mourn; to grant to those who mourn in Zion — to give them a beautiful headdress instead of ashes, the oil of gladness instead of mourning, the garment of praise instead of a faint spirit; that they may be called oaks of righteousness, the planting of the LORD, that he may be glorified. Isaiah 61:1-3 (ESV)

It was this *gospel of the kingdom* – the gospel that the builders rejected – that was essential to all of what Jesus did and taught. Matthew, Mark, Luke and John each tell the story of how Jesus went through all the cities and villages, teaching and proclaiming the gospel of the kingdom to those who were captive to sin and death. He began His public ministry by announcing, "The time is fulfilled, and the kingdom of God is at hand" (Mark 1:15). Jesus and His disciples then went from village to village demonstrating the kingdom of God in the midst of them. And in His final days with His disciples, before His Ascension, Jesus was still speaking to His disciples of the things concerning the kingdom (Acts 1:3). And yet it was clear that the kingdom of which He spoke did not fit the Old Testament expressions of that kingdom. Nowhere did Jesus ever suggest that the Old Testament prophets had been in error or that their prophecies should be set aside – He said only that the *time* of fulfillment for all that was written was in the Father's hands (Acts 1:7).

"Salome wants Jesus to accord an important place
to her sons James and John in heaven"
By Maria Clara (Used by Permission)

What then did Jesus mean when he said that the kingdom was at hand? Clearly He was introducing a *new* and *unexpected* reality of God's kingdom here on earth to His disciples – it is also clear that most of Jesus' public teaching described His bold new concept of living as citizens of this invisible kingdom. As we proceed, we will investigate first what Jesus publicly proclaimed about this gospel in His sermons and in His parables, and then what and how He taught His disciples about the kingdom.

FREDERICK OSBORN

4.

Jesus the Teacher
The Public Sermons of Jesus

THE WAY, TRUTH, AND LIFE

LESSON OUTLINE

The purpose of this lesson is to explain the role Jesus played as a teacher to His disciples and to the nation of Israel as a whole.

- The primary focus of Jesus' teaching was the Kingdom of God.

- His teachings about the Kingdom to His disciples were intended to reveal the mysteries and present reality of His kingdom.

- His teachings to the nation of Israel were intended to correct their misunderstandings of the Law of Moses and to correct their misinterpretations of the prophecies regarding the Messiah and His coming kingdom.

Jesus' Kingdom Sermons

"Soon afterwards, He began going around from one city and village to another, proclaiming and preaching the kingdom of God." Luke 8:1 (NIV)

Jesus taught in a day when there was no electronic media to broadcast His message; there were no cassette tapes, CDs, or DVDs to record His sermons and pass on to those who had not heard Him preach; and there were no newspapers or printing presses to print and distribute written copies of His sermons. Like any itinerant preacher of His time, Jesus had to be on the move, personally delivering His message from "one city and village to another." However, sometimes Jesus would send His messengers ahead of Him.

"Calling the Twelve to him, he sent them out two by two and gave them authority over evil spirits. These were his instructions:
'Take nothing for the journey except a staff--no bread, no bag, no money in your belts. Wear sandals but not an extra tunic. Whenever you enter a house, stay

there until you leave that town. And if any place will not welcome you or listen to you, shake the dust off your feet when you leave, as a testimony against them.'
They went out and preached that people should repent. They drove out many demons and anointed many sick people with oil and healed them." Mark 6:7-13 (NIV)

"When Jesus had called the Twelve together, he gave them power and authority to drive out all demons and to cure diseases, and he sent them out to preach the kingdom of God and to heal the sick. He told them: 'Take nothing for the journey-- no staff, no bag, no bread, no money, no extra tunic. Whatever houses you enter, stay there until you leave that town. If people do not welcome you, shake the dust off your feet when you leave their town, as a testimony against them.'
So they set out and went from village to village, preaching the gospel and healing people everywhere." Luke 9:1-6 (NIV)

(Note also, Luke 10:1-17. Pay special attention to verses 1, 8, 9, & 17)

"Do not be afraid, little flock, for your Father has chosen gladly to give you the kingdom." Luke 12:32 (NIV)

At times Jesus gathered His disciples and sent them on ahead to announce His coming. He gave them special instructions about what to do. They were given authority over all kinds of evil and sent out in teams of two for mutual support and protection. Jesus commanded them to travel light so that they might be unencumbered by material possessions, and they were to stay only where they were welcome. Wherever they stopped, they were to preach repentance from sin and the "good news" that Jesus was coming to them. Everywhere they went, they demonstrated the present reality of the kingdom by healing people along the way. "He who listens to you listens to me," Jesus said to His disciples as He sent them out, and "he who rejects you rejects me; but he who rejects me rejects him who sent me" (Luke 10:16). (See Appendix Three "The Seventy Sent Forth")

More often than not, the news that Jesus was in the area would spread by word-of-mouth and the people would flock to wherever Jesus was ministering; the Gospels record several of these instances (Matthew 4:24-25; Mark 10:1; Luke 6:17, 18; John 6:1-2, 24). Once the crowds had gathered, Jesus would heal the sick among them, sit them down, and begin to teach them. The primary focus of Jesus' teaching ministry was the proclamation and demonstration of the reality of the kingdom of God. Much of what He taught was intended to correct the false teachings and misinterpretations of the Jews about the Messiah and His kingdom. The Jews readily accepted the Old Testament's portrait of God as sovereign over the whole world; they embraced those prophecies that spoke of a worldwide messianic kingdom ruled from David's throne in Jerusalem. However, they failed to recognize the "suffering servant": who would come as the "Lamb of God" to take away the sins of the world.

Jesus taught that the kingdom He ushered in was not a political kingdom, established by force of arms and ruled like other earthly kingdoms; His kingdom is the eternal, invisible kingdom that exists within the hearts of all those who truly have been "born again"– born not of the flesh but of the Spirit. The Gospel Jesus preached is the Gospel of the kingdom, which says in essence, "Rejoice for the King and His kingdom has come!" Jesus opened His public ministry in Nazareth where He had been brought up by quoting from the prophet, Isaiah: "The Spirit of the Lord is on me, because he has anointed me to preach good news to the poor. He has sent me to proclaim freedom for the prisoners and recovery of sight for the blind, to release the oppressed, to proclaim the year of the Lord's favor." Luke 4:18-19 (NIV)

Jesus taught with an authority that no one else could have because He was the Son of God. His words were authentic and original because they came directly from the source of all Truth. The kingdom Jesus taught was in perfect alignment with the Law and the Prophets that came from His Father by His Spirit. But Jesus went far beyond the accepted interpretations of the scribes and Pharisees who for centuries added layer upon layer of man-made rules and regulations that had obscured the true meaning of God's words. His teachings also revealed many unexpected attributes of the prophetic kingdom and its King.

Everywhere Jesus went the crowds were amazed at His teaching. He exhibited an authority that no man could bestow and that neither the scribes nor Pharisees could take away. While He taught, He demonstrated the reality of His kingdom and His authority as King of kings through the many miracles He performed (Mark 2:1-11). He promised to give His disciples the same authority to heal the sick and over all the power of the devil, saying, "truly, truly... he who believes in Me, the works that I do, he will also; and greater works than these he will do because I go the Father "John 14:12 (NIV).

Matthew chapters five through seven, and Luke chapters six, eleven and twelve contain the bulk of Jesus' public teachings about the nature of the kingdom of heaven and about the rights, privileges, and responsibilities of citizens of that kingdom. By comparing the different accounts of Jesus' sermons to His disciples and to the masses that followed Him – allowing Scripture to interpret Scripture – we can gain a fuller understanding of this gospel of the kingdom that Jesus emphasized in all of His public sermons.

"Jesus then left that place and went into the region of Judea and across the Jordan. Again crowds of people came to him, and as was his custom, he taught them." Mark 10:1 (NIV)

The Primary Focus of Jesus' Teaching Ministry Was the Proclamation and Demonstration of the Reality of the Kingdom of God.

To accomplish this Jesus did not merely preach the good news of the kingdom; He brought the kingdom with Him. *This is the essence of gospel of the kingdom: that in the presence of the King the rule of God appears on the earth.* The fullness of the gospel is not merely preaching about Jesus and about the kingdom, its fullness is realized with the demonstration of the power of God for salvation (Rom. 1:16-17; 15:18-21; 1 Cor. 1:1-18; 3:2-5; Eph. 3:7; 1 Thess. 1:4-5).

For almost three and one half years Jesus taught His disciples the principles of kingdom living and prepared them for the time when He would ascend to His heavenly throne until His return at the end of the age. Jesus taught His disciples that the time would come when men would reject and crucify Him, but He would rise from the dead – all according to Old Testament prophecy. However, the bulk of His public sermons and teaching ministry was intended to correct their misunderstandings of the Law of Moses and to rectify their misinterpretations of the prophecies regarding the Messiah and His coming kingdom.

The Jews readily accepted the Old Testament's portrait of God as sovereign over the whole world; they embraced those prophecies that spoke of a worldwide messianic kingdom ruled from David's throne in Jerusalem. However, they failed to grasp the prophecies concerning the "suffering servant": who would come as the sacrificial Lamb of God to take away the sins of the world. Jesus taught that the kingdom He ushered in was not a political kingdom, established by force of arms and ruled like other earthly kingdoms. He taught that His kingdom is the eternal, invisible kingdom that exists within the hearts of all those who have been truly "born again", not of the flesh but of the Spirit. This is the Gospel of the kingdom that Jesus preached:

"And this gospel of the kingdom will be preached in the whole world as a testimony to all nations, and then the end will come." Matthew 24:14 (NIV)

"Now after John was put in prison, Jesus came to Galilee, preaching the gospel of the kingdom of God, and saying, 'The time is fulfilled, and the kingdom of God is at hand. Repent, and believe in the gospel.'" Mark 1:14-15 (NKJV)

"And the gospel must first be preached to all nations." Mark 13:10 (NIV)

Although Jesus taught with an authority that no one else could have and His words were authentic and original because He is the source of all Truth, the Gospel of the kingdom that Jesus taught was not "New." Jesus' teachings were not intended to replace the Law and the Prophets. Jesus struggled to correct the distortions of the Sabbath Laws created by the traditions of men and codified through the accepted interpretations of the Hebrew Scriptures by the scribes and Pharisees. His teachings also revealed many unexpected attributes of the prophetic kingdom and its King. In fact, Jesus made it clear that His teachings were not only in perfect alignment with the Law and all of the Prophets, but that He would fulfill them:

"Do not think that I have come to abolish the Law or the Prophets; I have not come to abolish them but to fulfill them. For truly, I say to you, until heaven and earth pass away, not an iota, not a dot, will pass from the Law until all is accomplished. Therefore whoever relaxes one of the least of these commandments and teaches others to do the same will be called least in the kingdom of heaven, but whoever does them and teaches them will be called great in the kingdom of heaven. For I tell you, unless your righteousness exceeds that of the scribes and Pharisees, you will never enter the kingdom of heaven." Matthew 5:17-20 (ESV)

Jesus Fulfilled the Law by Correctly Interpreting the Law in His Teachings

Jesus' Sermon on the Mount is not a radical departure from the Old Testament Mosaic teachings. Jesus' teachings were never intended to replace any of the Law and Prophets handed down from Moses to Malachi. Neither was Jesus establishing a "New Law." As we carefully examine His teachings, we will discover that what Jesus was doing was resetting misplaced priorities. The scribes and Pharisees had lost the true meaning of the Scriptures (John 5:38-40). They emphasized works over righteousness; they chose religion over a childlike faith and love for God the Father; they valued their Jewish birthright over their citizenship in the kingdom of God; and they had no concept of a Spirit filled life. Jesus' public sermons were intended to expose the counterfeit teachings of the scribes and Pharisees and point the way into the kingdom of heaven for all those who were desperately seeking it.

Jesus Taught That Those Who Enter Into His Kingdom Have Certain Rights and Responsibilities.

The world and everything in it is passing away. The picture of decay and of a deep darkness covering the earth is descriptive of a fallen people, living in a fallen world. The good news of the kingdom is that God has not abandoned this world in its fallen condition. Jesus uses the images of salt and light to communicate to His disciples the mission of citizens of His kingdom; the choices of these images were rich with meaning to the people who lived in biblical times.

"Salt is good, but if it loses its saltiness, how can you make it salty again? Have salt in yourselves, and be at peace with each other." Mark 9:49-50 (NIV)

"Salt is good, but if it loses its saltiness, how can it be made salty again? It is fit neither for the soil nor for the manure pile; it is thrown out. He who has ears to hear let him hear." Luke 14:34-35 (NIV)

Salt (*sodium chloride*) was essential to preserve food from corruption. In a time and place where fresh food supplies were scarce and where refrigeration and other methods of food preservation were unavailable, salt was essential to maintain the life of a community. In biblical times salt was most commonly found in the form of the mineral *halite*, or rock salt – found in beds deposited by the dehydration of ancient bodies of salt water. Most commercial salt was produced by steam or direct-heat evaporation of rock-salt brine; once the salt was extracted the remaining minerals were worthless and thrown far away from productive areas of land.

Salt was once an important medium of exchange throughout the Mediterranean world; covenants between individuals or nations were often ratified with the exchange of salt. At one time, Roman soldiers received their pay in the form of salt cakes; the soldier's salt-money allowance, or *salarium*, is where we got our English term *salary*, for a worker's pay. Salt was also commonly used in the religious rites of the Greeks, Romans and Hebrews.

"And on the second day you shall offer a male goat without blemish for a sin offering; and the altar shall be purified, as it was purified with the bull. When you have finished purifying it, you shall offer a bull from the herd without blemish and a ram from the flock without blemish. You shall present them before the LORD, and the priests shall sprinkle salt on them and offer them up as a burnt offering to the LORD." Ezekiel 43:22-24 (ESV)

Salt is necessary to the life of the body. "On the day you were born your cord was not cut, nor were you washed with water to make you clean, nor were you rubbed with salt or wrapped in cloths" (Ezekiel 16:4). The sodium and chloride of salt, along with potassium, help the kidneys regulate the body's fluid levels and balance of acids and bases. Industrially, salt is the source of chlorine, chloroform, bleaching powders, and baking soda; it is used in the manufacture of disparate products like soap and glass. However, by far, the greatest use of salt today is a seasoning, adding flavor to many of our foods.

"The LORD said to Moses, "Take sweet spices, stacte, and onycha, and galbanum, sweet spices with pure frankincense (of each shall there be an equal part), and make an incense blended as by the perfumer, seasoned with salt, pure and holy." Exodus 30:34-35 (ESV)

Salt was required in every grain offering presented to the Lord. *"Season all your grain offerings with salt. Do not leave the salt of the covenant of your God out of your grain offerings; add salt to all your offerings"* (Leviticus 2:13). The altar was the table of the Lord; and therefore, salt being eternally present at His table, represents the preserving and cleansing aspects of God's saving grace. The presence of salt also speaks of God's covenant with mankind. Men confirmed their covenants with each other by sharing a covenant meal together, at which salt was always present.

"Whatever is set aside from the holy offerings the Israelites present to the Lord I give to you and your sons and daughters as your regular share. It is an everlasting covenant of salt before the Lord for both you and your offspring." Numbers 18:19 (NIV)

"Abijah stood on Mount Zemaraim, in the hill country of Ephraim, and said, 'Jeroboam and all Israel, listen to me! Don't you know that the Lord, the God of Israel, has given the kingship of Israel to David and his descendants forever by a covenant of salt?'" 2 Chronicles 13:4-5 (NIV)

"Let your speech always be with grace, seasoned, as it were, with salt, so that you will know how you should respond to each person." Colossians 4:6 (NIV)

Jesus invites us to open the door and let Him come in that we might dine with Him at a table prepared for us – thus confirming His new covenant with us (Psalm 23:5; Revelation 3:20). Among the ancients, salt was also a symbol of friendship. This new, everlasting "covenant of salt", written on our hearts by the Holy Spirit, also speaks of God's desire to be in intimate friendship with us, *"I no longer call you servants, because a servant does not know his master's business. Instead, I have called you friends, for everything that I learned from my Father I have made known to you"* (John 15:15).

"The men of the city said to Elisha, 'Look, our lord, this town is well situated, as you can see, but the water is bad and the land is unproductive.' 'Bring me a new bowl,' he said, 'and put salt in it.' So they brought it to him. Then he went out to the spring and threw the salt into it, saying, 'This is what the Lord says: "I have healed this water. Never again will it cause death or make the land

unproductive." And the water has remained wholesome to this day, according to the word Elisha had spoken." 2 Kings 2:19-22 (NIV)

"He cast the salt into the spring of the waters, and so healed the streams and the ground they watered. Thus the way to reform men's lives is to renew their hearts; let those be seasoned with the salt of grace; for out of them are the issues of life." Matthew Henry

Salt has a healing power that can cleanse and purge out impurities from the body. The image of salt reminds us of the healing power of the blood of Christ that can "cleanse our consciences from acts that lead to death, so that we may serve the living God" (Hebrews 9:14). It is the cleansing presence of Christ within the citizens of the kingdom of heaven that creates a thirst for God in those who are outside of His kingdom (Col. 1:25 – 29). There is nothing more useless in this world than "Christ-less" Christians; they are no longer good for anything, except to be thrown out and trampled underfoot by men.

"'Therefore, as surely as I live,' declares the Lord Almighty, the God of Israel, 'surely Moab will become like Sodom, the Ammonites like Gomorrah – a place of weeds and salt pits, a wasteland forever. The remnant of my people will plunder them; the survivors of my nation will inherit their land.'" Zephaniah 2:9 (Note: Luke 14:34-35)

The picture of *light* communicates a different aspect of the influence the sons of the kingdom are to have in this world.

The primary purpose of light is to make reality or truth visible, thereby giving direction and guidance to those who are searching for the kingdom of God. There are over 200 references to light in the Scriptures, making light an important theme throughout the Bible. Genesis 1:3 records the first words spoken by God, "Let there be light." Exodus 13:21 describes how the children of Israel were led through the darkness of the wilderness by a pillar of light. Leviticus 24:2 contains God's instructions to the priests to keep the light of the tabernacle burning continually. The final chapter of the Bible describes the kingdom of heaven in the new heavens and the new earth to come, and includes these words: "There will be no more night. They will not need the light of a lamp or the light of the sun, for the Lord God will give them light. And they will reign forever and ever" (Revelation 22:5)

"As the first apartment in the tabernacle was illuminated by the sevenfold light of the candlestick, and as the church composed of all genuine believers on earth in every age, is enlightened by the Holy Spirit, so will the church triumphant in heaven, that great temple, not made with hands, be a place of glorious light; and the light will never go out, it will burn always..." William Brown

The Lord strategically positions His citizens that they might shine His light into this world of darkness: *"You, O Lord, keep my lamp burning; my God turns my darkness into light."* Psalms 18:28

Jesus used the image of light to communicate to His followers how they are intended to be the "light of the world." In the same way that a lamp carries light or in the same way that a city on a hill guides the weary sojourners out of the darkness and to a place where they might find rest, believers should so shine the light of Christ into the darkness all around them and lead others to Christ.

"The Lord is my light and my salvation – whom shall I fear? The Lord is the stronghold of my life – of whom shall I be afraid?" Psalm 27:1 (NIV)

Citizens of the kingdom of heaven stand out against the darkness when they follow Jesus, the true Light of the world; they do not generate their own light, but the "Light of life" shines through them (John 8:12). For the Lord is "the fountain of life" and in His light we see the true light of God (Psalms 36:9). Without light, sight is impossible. God created the eye to be the "light of the body" (in this context, the word *body* is interpreted to mean the whole *person*) in the same way a candlestick or lamp – after being lit – illuminates a room. Upon being "born again" into the kingdom of heaven, the Holy Spirit takes up residence within the whole person, and floods the body, soul and spirit with God's light and life.

"Send forth your light and your truth, let them guide me; let them bring me to your holy mountain, to the place where you dwell." Psalms 43:3

"For you have delivered me from death and my feet from stumbling, that I may walk before God in the light of life." Psalms 56:13 (NIV)

The word of God is "lamp" and "light" that shines the light of the Holy Spirit within the soul; it illuminates our path in this dark world of sin (Psalms 119:105); it brings understanding, judgment, and the power to see the truth and expose falsehood (Psalms 119:105). Jesus said, "*Your eye is the lamp of your body. When your eyes are good, your whole body also is full of light. But when they are bad, your body also is full of darkness*" (Luke 11:34). Here, the Greek word *haplous*, "single" or "healthy" is used. He makes the point that whether or not a person sees the kingdom of God depends not on the light's brightness, but on the condition of the person receiving the light. This gospel of the kingdom will come to those people whose hearts are open to receive it; and wherever the reign of God is established, it will bring the light of truth and righteousness with it. Jesus is indeed "the light of the world" (John 8:12 & 9:5) and when he came, the prophecy of Isaiah was fulfilled: *"The people walking in darkness have seen a great light; on those living in the land of the shadow of death a light has dawned."* Isaiah 9:2 (NIV).

"I am the LORD; I have called you in righteousness; I will take you by the hand and keep you; I will give you as a covenant for the people, a light for the nations, to open the eyes that are blind, to bring out the prisoners from the dungeon, from the prison those who sit in darkness." Isaiah 42:6-7 (ESV)

Jesus Taught His Followers the Essentials of Prayer

An important part of Jesus' teaching on the Sermon on the Mount is His teaching on prayer found in Matthew 6:9-13 (NKJV):

"In this manner, therefore, pray:
Our Father in heaven, Hallowed be Your name.
Your kingdom come
Your will be done on earth as it is in heaven.
Give us this day our daily bread.
And forgive us our debts, as we forgive our debtors.
And do not lead us into temptation, but deliver us from the evil one.
For Yours is the kingdom and the power and the glory forever. Amen."

Also known as the Lord's Prayer, Jesus taught that our prayers must be grounded in a one-to-one relationship with our heavenly Father. Outward displays of piety are no substitute for private, intimate and personal prayer in the presence of God. When read in context with Matthew 6:7, the Lord's Prayer is recognized as a pattern that teaches us *how* to pray and is not intended to be formula that tells us *what* words to pray. Since the Lord's Prayer appears in a slightly different form in Luke's Gospel (11:2-4). It is clear from Luke 11:1 that this instruction on prayer is given at a different time and setting than the Sermon on the Mount. The fact that these prayers are not identical reinforces the idea that Jesus was giving His disciples a pattern and not specific words for addressing God in prayer.

Jesus Taught That There Is Only One Entrance Into The Kingdom.

Jesus clearly stated: "I am the way and the truth and the life," that No one comes to the Father except Through Him (John 14:6), and that those who are truly His disciples will both know and do God's will and give Him the glory in all things (John 14:15, 21).

He warned His disciples to watch out for false prophets that would appear in the midst of them like wolves in sheep's clothing (Matthew 7:15). He taught them how to recognize false prophets: they are exposed by the bad fruit they produce. He said, "A bad tree cannot bear good fruit...and by their fruits you will know them" (Matthew 7:16-20). Therefore, those who are truly disciples of Jesus Christ will abide in Him and bear the "good fruit" of the Spirit-filled life.

Everywhere Jesus went the crowds were amazed at His teaching. He exhibited an authority that no man could bestow and that neither the scribes nor Pharisees could take away. But not all of His teachings were understood or welcomed (Matthew 21:23; Mark 3:20-22; John 6:66). Jesus opened the doors of salvation to sinners and Pharisees; and to both Gentiles and Jews. "*For God so loved the world*" Jesus said in John 3:16, "*that he gave his one and only Son, that whoever believes in him shall not perish but have eternal life.*" When Jesus identified Himself as the "Good Shepherd", the Jews immediately recognized that He was speaking to them, but He goes on to reveal that, "*I have other sheep that are not of this sheep pen. I must bring them also. They too will listen to my voice, and there shall be one flock and one shepherd"* (John 10:16), which was speaking of the time about to come when the Gentiles would be brought into His flock.

Jesus' teachings also show that He had a clear sense of His own identity and of the mission He came to complete.

- **Jesus taught He was fulfilling Old Testament Prophecy**
  Matthew 14:33; 16:16, 17; 26:31, 53-56
  Mark 14:21, 61, 62
  Luke 4:16-21; 7:18-23; 18:31; 22:37; 24:44
  John 2:22; 5:45-47; 6:45; 10:34-36; 13:18; 15:25

- **Jesus called Himself the "Son of Man"**
  Matthew 8:20; 12:8; 16:27; 19:28; 20:18, 19; 24:27, 44; 25:31; 26:2, 45, 64
  Mark 8:31, 38; 9:9; 10:45; 14:41
  Luke 6:22; 7:33, 34; 12:8; 17:22; 18:8, 31; 19:10; 21:36
  John 1:51; 3:13, 14; 6:27, 53; 12:23, 34

- **Jesus called Himself the "Son of God"**
  Matthew 11:27; 16:16, 17; 27:43
  Mark 14:61, 62
  Luke 10:22
  John 5:18-26; 6:40; 10:36; 11:4; 17:1; 19:7

- **Jesus called Himself the "Messiah/Christ"**
  Matthew 23:9, 10; 26:63, 64
  Mark 8:29, 30
  Luke 23:1, 2; 24:25-27
  John 4:25, 26; 10:24, 25

- **Jesus called Himself "Teacher/Master"**
  Matthew 26:18
  John 13:13, 14

- **Jesus taught He had the Divine authority to forgive sins**
  Mark 2:1-12
  Luke 7:48, 49

- **Jesus called Himself, Lord**
  Mark 5:19
  John 13:13, 14; 20:28

- **Jesus called Himself Savior**
  Luke 19:10
  John 3:17; 10:9

Jesus did more than teach about the kingdom of God, He demonstrated the reality of the kingdom through the many miracles He performed. When the time was right, He gave His disciples the authority to heal the sick and over all the power of the enemy saying, *"I tell you the truth, anyone who has faith in me will do what I have been doing. He will do even greater things than these, because I am going to the Father. And I will do whatever you ask in my name, so that the Son may bring glory to the Father. You may ask me for anything in my name, and I will do it."* John 14:12-14 (NIV)

THE SERMON ON THE MOUNT

"Now when he saw the crowds, he went up on a mountainside and sat down. His disciples came to him, and he began to teach them, saying: 'Blessed are the poor in spirit, for theirs is the kingdom of heaven…'" Matthew 5:1-3 (NIV)

The word about Jesus had spread from town to town and village to village. Everywhere He went, the crowds were now following Him, and seeking the divine manna from His hand:

"Jesus went throughout Galilee, teaching in their synagogues, preaching the good news of the kingdom, and healing every disease and sickness among the people. News about him spread all over Syria, and people brought to him all who were ill with various diseases, those suffering severe pain, the demon-possessed, those having seizures, and the paralyzed, and he healed them. Large crowds from Galilee, the Decapolis, Jerusalem, Judea and the region across the Jordan followed him." Matthew 4:23-25 (NIV)

At one point, the crowds had grown so large that Jesus had to address them from the natural amphitheater of a mountainside. The scene in Matthew chapters five, six and seven are reminiscent of chapters twenty-seven through thirty in the book of Deuteronomy. In Deuteronomy, Moses gives final instructions to the children of Israel for when they entered the Promised Land (fulfilled in Joshua 8:30-35). He assembled the people and instructed them concerning the blessings of obeying their covenant with God, and the curses sure to visit them if they disobeyed the terms and conditions of the covenant. Also known as the Palestinian Covenant, these blessings and curses were to be recited before the people from Mount Gerizim and Mount Ebal, respectively. It is now centuries later, and God is about to do a new thing – not only for the house of Israel, but also for the nations (Jeremiah 31:31). Once again, the people are assembled on a mountain to hear the Word of God spoken to them, but one greater than Moses, Joshua, and the prophets is about to speak.

It is important to note at this point that the blessings and curses of the Mosaic covenant were pronounced from two mountains. However, Jesus Christ came to only one mountain and announced only the unconditional blessings of the New Covenant to those assembled (Jeremiah 31:31-34; Matthew 5:1-12).

THE BEATITUDES

"Blessed are the poor in spirit, for theirs is the kingdom of heaven.
Blessed are those who mourn, for they will be comforted.
Blessed are the meek, for they will inherit the earth.
Blessed are those who hunger and thirst for righteousness, for they will be filled.
Blessed are the merciful, for they will be shown mercy.
Blessed are the pure in heart, for they will see God.
Blessed are the peacemakers, for they will be called sons of God.
Blessed are those who are persecuted because of righteousness, for theirs is the kingdom of heaven.
Blessed are you when people insult you, persecute you and falsely say all kinds of evil against you because of me.
Rejoice and be glad, because great is your reward in heaven, for in the same way they persecuted the prophets who were before you." Matthew 5:3-12 (NIV)

Matthew chapter five, verses three through ten record Jesus' introductory message of life in the kingdom of God. He characterizes citizens of His kingdom as "blessed." *Makarios*, the Greek term used here for "blessed" means more than a temporary feeling of happiness based upon circumstances. In this context, "blessed" means being approved by God, and rewarded eternally with blessings that cannot be measured by worldly standards. The blessings of God promised in Deuteronomy 28:1-14 are all material blessings: abundant prosperity, "in the fruit of your womb, the young of your livestock and the crops of your ground," etc. These blessings are all dependent upon the people's obedience to the Law. But the kingdom blessings promised in Matthew are intangible: mercy, vision, and relationship with the Father, joy, and inclusion in the kingdom of heaven. These blessings are secured by Jesus Christ on behalf of those who put their faith and trust in Him. He makes it clear from the beginning that the blessings of the kingdom of heaven are assured for the person whose attitudes, values, and commitments are rooted in the eternal things of God. Jesus pointed His listeners towards the inward, spiritual blessings of the kingdom not the external and temporary benefits of this world: (Matthew 6:25-34). This world may bring us many troubles and much sorrow, but those who value their citizenship in the kingdom of heaven will experience the true blessings of God through them all.

"Do not work for the food which perishes, but for the food which endures to eternal life, which the Son of Man will give to you, for on Him the Father, even God, has set His seal." John 6:27 (NIV)

Although Jesus did not specifically address the issue in His Sermon on the Mount, it is clear from His other teachings that His kingdom was not exclusively a Jewish kingdom: *"I have other sheep that are not of this sheep pen. I must bring them also. They too will listen to my voice, and there shall be one flock and one shepherd."* John 10:16 (NIV)

"When the Son of Man comes in his glory, and all the angels with him, he will sit on his throne in heavenly glory. All the nations will be gathered before him, and he will separate the people one from another as a shepherd separates the sheep from the goats." Matthew 25:31-32 (NIV)

"There will be weeping there, and gnashing of teeth, when you see Abraham, Isaac and Jacob and all the prophets in the kingdom of God, but you yourselves thrown out. People will come from east and west and north and south, and will take their places at the feast in the kingdom of God. Indeed there are those who are

last who will be first, and first who will be last.'" Luke 13:28-30 (NIV); NOTE also Matthew 8:10-12

The Jews believed that righteousness was obtained through obedience to the Law and this was the prerequisite for entrance into the kingdom of heaven. The Pharisees were obsessed with keeping every detail of the Mosaic Law and when that was not enough, they began adding layers of religious "dos" and "don'ts" to raise the bar of righteousness ever higher. By the time Jesus began to preach the gospel of the kingdom, only a very few of the religious elites were able to come close to being righteous according to the terms of their religion.

When Jesus arrived on the scene, He began to preach a gospel of repentance from dead works, "Repent for the kingdom of heaven is near" (Matthew 4:17). Jesus taught that the kingdom was not exclusive, but was inclusive. "Do not be afraid, little flock, for your Father has been pleased to give you the kingdom" (Luke 12:32). Greatness in the kingdom of God was not measured by man's standard of righteousness, but God's standard meant that the least of His sheep would by no means be excluded, "I tell you the truth: among those born of woman, there has not risen anyone greater than John the Baptist; yet he who is least in the kingdom of heaven is greater than he" (Matthew 11:11). And, "I tell you the truth, unless you change and become like little children, you will never enter the kingdom of heaven. Therefore, whoever humbles himself like this child is the greatest in the kingdom of heaven" (Matthew 18:3-4; NOTE also Mark 10:14-15).

Jesus was turning the teachings of the scribes and Pharisees upside down and inside out. He taught that a childlike faith and trust in God was all that was required to enter into His Father's kingdom. To fulfill the law, meant to "love the Lord with all your heart, mind, soul and strength; and to love your neighbor as yourself" (Matthew 22:34-40 & Mark 12:28-34). In His Sermon on the Mount, Jesus criticized those who made the Sabbath rules and regulations of the Jews obstructions to obeying the heart and soul of the true commandments of God:

"Anyone who breaks one of the least of these commandments and teaches others to do the same will be called least in the kingdom of heaven, but whoever practices and teaches these commands will be called great in the kingdom of heaven. For I

tell you that unless your righteousness surpasses that of the Pharisees and the teachers of the law, you will certainly not enter the kingdom of heaven." Matthew 5:19-20 (NIV)

Jesus taught that there was only one prerequisite for entrance into the kingdom of God: you must be born again.

"In reply Jesus declared, 'I tell you the truth, no one can see the kingdom of God unless he is born again.'" John 3:3 (NIV)

"Jesus answered, 'I tell you the truth, no one can enter the kingdom of God unless he is born of water and the Spirit. Flesh gives birth to flesh, but the Spirit gives birth to spirit.'" John 3:5-6 (NIV)

"For God so loved the world that he gave his one and only Son, that whoever believes in him shall not perish but have eternal life. For God did not send his Son into the world to condemn the world, but to save the world through him. Whoever believes in him is not condemned, but whoever does not believe stands condemned already because he has not believed in the name of God's one and only Son." John 3:16-18 (NIV)

Nothing that Jesus taught in His sermons was inconsistent with or contradictory to the word of God from the Law and the Prophets. Although Jesus often startled people with the boldness of His confrontations with the scribes, Pharisees and teachers of the law, and He often amazed people with the authority in which He spoke, He was not teaching "new revelation" but was in fact bringing clarity to God's word and bringing back into focus the true meaning and purpose of the Law for the people.

Blessed are the poor in spirit, for theirs is the kingdom of heaven (5:3). The way into the kingdom of heaven is lost to those who strive to enter into it through their own efforts. God will freely give the kingdom to those who recognize their own spiritual bankruptcy and cry out to Him for salvation. Matthew 5:3 means that the kingdom belongs to those who utterly and completely depend upon the finished work of Christ upon the cross for salvation. This same thought – that salvation comes from God alone – is found throughout the Old Testament:

"Yet I am poor and needy; may the Lord think of me. You are my help and my deliverer; O my God, do not delay." Psalms 40:17 (NIV)

"I am in pain and distress; may your salvation, O God, protect me." Psalms 69:29 (NIV)

"The Lord hears the needy and does not despise his captive people." Psalms 69:33 (NIV)

"'Has not my hand made all these things, and so they came into being?' declares the Lord. 'This is the one I esteem: he who is humble and contrite in spirit, and trembles at my word.'" Isaiah 66:2 (NIV)

"Return, O Israel, to the Lord your God. Your sins have been your downfall! Take words with you and return to the Lord. Say to him: 'Forgive all our sins and receive us graciously, that we may offer the fruit of our lips.'" Hosea 14:1-2 (NIV)

Early in His ministry, Jesus returned to His boyhood town of Nazareth and went into the Synagogue. He read the first two verses from the scroll of Isaiah chapter 61: "The Spirit of the Lord is on me, because he has anointed me to preach good news to the poor. He has sent me to proclaim freedom for the prisoners and recovery of sight for the blind, to release the oppressed, to proclaim the year of the Lord's favor" (Luke 4:18-19). These verses set the tone for His ministry; Jesus had come to seek and save the lost (Luke 19:10).

Blessed are those who mourn, for they shall be comforted (5:4). Jesus confirmed the truth that God is close to the brokenhearted of this world. The religious leaders of the day believed that God had abandoned those who were suffering and broken by sin; they only got what they deserved and all that awaited them was God's judgment. Instead, Jesus taught that those who are deeply affected by the sorrows visited upon this fallen world and turn to Him will find God's everlasting comfort, "a crown of beauty instead of ashes, the oil of gladness instead of mourning, and a garment of praise instead of a spirit of despair" (Isaiah 61:2 3).

"The sacrifices of God are a broken spirit; a broken and contrite heart, O God, you will not despise." Psalms 51:17 (NIV)

*"I remember my affliction and my wandering, the bitterness and the gall.
I well remember them, and my soul is downcast within me.
Yet this I call to mind and therefore I have hope: Because of the Lord's great love we are not consumed, for his compassions never fail. They are new every morning; great is your faithfulness."* Lamentations 3:19-23 (NIV)

"And I will pour out on the house of David and the inhabitants of Jerusalem a spirit of grace and supplication. They will look on me, the one they have pierced, and they will mourn for him as one mourns for an only child, and grieve bitterly for him as one grieves for a firstborn son." Zechariah 12:10 (NIV)

Blessed are the meek, for they shall inherit the earth (5:5). Gentleness is not weakness; it takes an enormous strength of character to abandon one's own selfish self-interests and place them at the feet of God. "Not my will, but Thy will be done!" is the heart's cry of anyone who is a citizen in God's kingdom. A person who is boastful, full of pride, and who seeks to "lord over" others is useless to the kingdom: Jesus warned, "all those who take up the sword shall perish by the sword" (Matt. 26:52). Those who humbly submit to the reign of God will experience the blessings of God in their daily lives, and will "inherit the earth" upon Jesus' final triumph over the kings of this earth (Rev. 21:7).

"Here is My Servant, whom I uphold; My chosen one in whom I delight; I will put My Spirit on Him and He will bring justice to the nations. He will not shout or cry out or raise His voice in the streets. A bruised reed He will not break, and a smoldering wick He will not snuff out..." Isaiah 42:1-3 (NIV)

As far as the Jews were concerned, Moses was the model of what a leader should be like. Numbers 12:3 described Moses as "a very humble man, more humble than anyone on the face of the earth." Matthew used Isaiah 42:1-4 to describe Jesus' humility; and to explain why He instructed those He healed and saw His many miracles not to tell anyone who He really was (Matthew 12:15-21). Surely, when Jesus' listeners heard "Blessed are the meek, for they shall inherit the earth" they would have been reminded of the words of another great shepherd, David:

"Be still before the Lord and wait patiently for him; do not fret when men succeed in their ways, when they carry out their wicked schemes. Refrain from anger and turn from wrath; do not fret – it leads only to evil. For evil men will be cut off, but those who hope in the Lord will inherit the land. A little while, and the wicked will be no more; though you look for them, they will not be found. But the meek will inherit the land and enjoy great peace." Psalms 37:7-11 (NIV)

Notice the progression of Jesus' sermon thus far. Citizens of the kingdom of heaven are blessed by God when they:

1. Recognize their spiritual poverty
2. Are grieved over their sins and the sins of others
3. Submit to the reign of God with meekness.

Blessed are those who hunger and thirst for righteousness, for they shall be satisfied (5:6). Jesus reveals yet another characteristic of a person who belongs to the kingdom of heaven: a deep desire to know and do God's will. Those who love this world and the things of this world will never be satisfied. *"For everything in the world – the cravings of sinful man, the lust of the eyes and the boasting of what he has and does - comes not from the Father, but from the world."* 1 John 2:16 (NIV)

Those who hunger and thirst for righteousness know that this world is fading away, and the evil ungodly things of this world will go with it, but those who belong to God's kingdom will live forever and will be forever satisfied. The Pharisees were always shocked and repelled by Jesus' associations with those considered to be unrighteous sinners. At one point, Jesus was having dinner at Matthew's house, and as Matthew tells it (Matthew 9:9-13), "many tax collectors and 'sinners' came and ate with him and his disciples." Jesus overheard the

"Jesus says one has to be like a child to enter the Kingdom of heaven"
By Maria Clara (Used by Permission)

Pharisees interrogating His disciples and asking, "Why does your teacher eat with tax collectors and 'sinners'?" And answered them, "It is not the healthy who need a doctor, but the sick. But go and learn what this means: 'I desire mercy, not sacrifice.' For I have not come to call the righteous, but sinners."

The Pharisees and teachers of the law should have known better; the grace and mercy of God towards sinners were always there before them in the Scriptures they claimed to know and love, and yet they failed to understand the application of the Word when it came to showing mercy towards others.

"Many are the woes of the wicked, but the Lord's unfailing love surrounds the man who trusts in him. Rejoice in the Lord and be glad, you righteous; sing, all you who are upright in heart!" Psalms 32:10-11 (NIV)

"The salvation of the righteous comes from the Lord; he is their stronghold in time of trouble. The Lord helps them and delivers them; he delivers them from the wicked and saves them, because they take refuge in him." Psalms 37:39-40 (NIV)

"He who pursues righteousness and love finds life, prosperity and honor." Proverbs 21:21 (NIV)

"Sow for yourselves righteousness, reap the fruit of unfailing love, and break up your unplowed ground; for it is time to seek the Lord, until he comes and showers righteousness on you." Hosea 10:12 (NIV)

Blessed are the merciful, for they shall receive mercy (5:7). Citizens of the kingdom understand they are objects of God's mercy. This awareness should drive us to show the same mercy towards others. In His parable of "The Unforgiving Servant" (Matthew 18:23-35), Jesus perfectly illustrated this principle of forgiveness. We serve a King who is "rich in mercy, because of His great love with which He loved us" (Eph. 2:4). Therefore, what we have received in abundance, we must give abundantly.

Although there was no specific commandment to forgive one another from the Mosaic Law, the principle of forgiveness was found in the Scriptures first in God's mercy shown towards sinners and second in the instructions of the prophets.

"The Lord is gracious and compassionate, slow to anger and rich in love. The Lord is good to all; he has compassion on all he has made." Psalms 145:8-9 (NIV)

"Your kingdom is an everlasting kingdom, and your dominion endures through all generations. The Lord is faithful to all his promises and loving toward all he has made. The Lord upholds all those who fall and lifts up all who are bowed down." Psalms 145:13-14 (NIV)

"Because of the Lord's great love we are not consumed, for his compassions never fail. They are new every morning; great is your faithfulness." Lamentations 3:22-23 (NIV)

"And the word of the Lord came again to Zechariah: 'This is what the Lord Almighty says: "Administer true justice; show mercy and compassion to one another. Do not oppress the widow or the fatherless, the alien or the poor. In your hearts do not think evil of each other." Zechariah 7:8-10 (NIV)

Blessed are the pure in heart, for they will see God (5:8). Purity of heart is not something manufactured by citizens of the kingdom; it is a gift of God's unmerited favor by the "new and living way" Jesus. When Paul described the armor of God (Ephesians 6:1-18), he said we must "put on the breastplate of righteousness." The breastplate is our "heart protector." The heart is the key to receiving the righteousness of Christ, which is our vindication before God when Satan, the accuser, points his dirty little finger of guilt and self-condemnation at us. It is God's – our King's armor we put on. It is HIS breastplate – HIS righteousness. When our King grants us purity of heart, he gives us:

- *Judicial Purity* or *Justification* – this is the "imputed" righteousness of Christ, credited to us for forgiveness, and absolution from guilt (Romans 3:21-26 & 8:1-4)

- *Holiness* or *Sanctification* – this is the righteousness of God "imparted" (released) to us for the removal of sin (Romans 6:12-14 & Hebrews 10:19-22).

The Pharisees and teachers of the law taught that everyone must live holy because they must fulfill the righteous requirements of the law. The Lord commanded, "be holy because I am holy" (Leviticus 11:25). But the religious leaders defined holiness in a way that was all external, religious ritual, and left the heart untouched: "Then the Lord said to him, 'Now then, you Pharisees clean the outside of the cup and dish, but inside you are full of greed and wickedness. You foolish people! Did not the one who made the outside make the inside also?'" Luke 11:39-40 (NIV)

Jesus knew that it is only the pure in heart that are able to "see" God in this life on earth, and it is only the pure in heart who will see God eternally, in the kingdom of heaven. He never said or did anything that was impure or unholy. Jesus forgave sin, but never excused it. Jesus was clear, "Do not think that I have come to abolish the Law or the Prophets; I have not come to abolish them but to fulfill them. I tell you the truth, until heaven and earth disappear, not the smallest letter, not the least stroke of a pen, will by any means disappear from the Law until everything is accomplished." Matthew 5:17-18 (NIV)

"Who may ascend the hill of the Lord? Who may stand in his holy place? He who has clean hands and a pure heart, who does not lift up his soul to an idol or swear by what is false. He will receive blessing from the Lord and vindication from God his Savior." Psalms 24:3-5 (NIV)

"Surely God is good to Israel, to those who are pure in heart." Psalms 73:1 (NIV)

"I will praise you with an upright heart as I learn your righteous laws. I will obey your decrees; do not utterly forsake me. How can a young man keep his way pure? By living according to your word. I seek you with all my heart; do not let me stray from your commands. I have hidden your word in my heart that I might not sin against you." Psalms 119:7-11 (NIV)

In His Sermon on the Mount, Jesus dealt with the inward motivations of the heart that produce true righteousness. The heart is essential to the spiritual life of the believer, which is why we must keep it pure and holy. Jesus taught that we must live righteously NOT because we must fulfill the righteous requirements of the law, but that we live righteously because we have been made holy.

"I baptize you with water for repentance. But after me will come one who is more powerful than I, whose sandals I am not fit to carry. He will baptize you with the Holy Spirit and with fire." Matthew 3:11 (NIV)

Blessed are the peacemakers, for they shall be called sons of God (5:9). To the kingdoms of this world, "peace" simply means "an interlude between wars". But in the kingdom of heaven, "peace" has a greater significance in that it speaks of health and wholeness that emanates from the innermost being of a person who has been restored to a proper relationship with God. The peace this world has to offer is primarily external, enforced militarily, or maintained politically. Because peace in this world is based upon our immediate circumstances, it is temporary at best.

"Pursue peace with all men, and the sanctification without which no one will see the Lord." Hebrews 12:14 (NIV)

The peace Jesus has to offer is spiritual – from the heart – and originates from within. Lasting peace between nations, between individuals, between man and nature, and between man and his Creator all flow from the hearts of individuals secure in the presence of the supreme peacemaker, Jesus Christ.

"Peace I leave with you; my peace I give you. I do not give to you as the world gives. Do not let your hearts be troubled and do not be afraid." John 14:27 (NIV)

"When you enter a house, first say, 'Peace to this house.' If a man of peace is there, your peace will rest on him; if not, it will return to you." Luke 10:5-6 (NIV)

In Jewish idiom, to be called a "son of" something suggests a strong identity or likeness. A "son of a fisherman" is a fisherman, and a "son of God" is one who bears a likeness to God Himself – in other words, "sons of God" in the context of Matthew 5:9, means "a people who are like God in word and deed." Therefore, citizens of the kingdom are called to be peacemakers, and like Christ, sow seeds of peace wherever they go, producing the fruit of righteousness in the midst of this troubled world (James 3:18).

Blessed are those who are persecuted because of righteousness, for theirs is the kingdom of heaven. Blessed are you when people insult you, persecute you and falsely say all kinds of evil against you because of Me. Rejoice and be glad, for great is your reward in heaven; for in the same way they persecuted the prophets who were before you (5:10 – 12). Persecution comes in many forms in this world; Jesus warned His disciples, "...in the world you have tribulation" (John 16:33). "Persecution is a paradox. It reveals that the true nature of the world is evil. Think about it: the person who lives and speaks for righteousness is opposed and persecuted. The person who cares and works for the true love, justice, and salvation of the world is actually fought against. How deceived is the world and its humanity to rush onward in madness for nothing but to return to dust, to seek life only for some seventy years (*if* nothing happens before then)!" *The Preacher's Outline & Sermon Bible: Volume 1, Matthew – John, New International Version,* © 2000, Apha-Omega Ministries, Inc., p.64

The poor and needy will always be oppressed by the rich and powerful; persecution based upon race, culture, or gender often characterizes even the most "civilized" of nations. However, those who choose to live as citizens of God's kingdom will inevitably find themselves in conflict with the all kingdoms of this world. God's special blessing is reserved for those who are persecuted for the sake of righteousness (5:10) and because of Me (5:11). A person who is truly poor in spirit, who mourns because of sin and is meek, who hungers for righteousness and truth, and who shows mercy to those around him, who is pure in heart and a peacemaker, will unintentionally expose the sinfulness of those who belong to this world. Those who reject the kingdom of heaven for themselves will scorn and persecute those who belong to the kingdom of heaven. Like the prophets of old they may suffer much for the sake of His kingdom, but Jesus encourages His people to rejoice and be glad (5:12) because great will be their reward in heaven.

The Jewish people held the prophets of the Old Testament in the highest regard. Most of those prophets endured persecution and some were put to death for their uncompromising proclamation of the Word of God. A careful study of the Old Testament prophets will show that far from being lonely visionaries, sending proclamations down to the people, these men and women lived and ministered in the midst of the people.

THE WAY, TRUTH, AND LIFE

Though some were set apart as fulltime prophets, most lived and worked in the normal vocations of their day – all but a few married, raised children and had ties to the community. The prophets were individuals chosen by God with a specific mission to their generation. Central to their mission was:

- Pointing the people of Israel back to their destiny to be "a holy people to the Lord" their God and chosen by Him to be "a people for His possession out of all the peoples who are on the face of the earth" (Deut. 7:6).
- And pointing the nations to the God of Israel as the one true and living God over all of creation (Jer. 10:10 – 16).

"I am the Lord, I have called you in righteousness, I will also hold you by the hand and watch over you, And I will appoint you as a covenant to the people, As a light to the nations..." Isaiah 42:6 (NIV)

In the Beatitudes of Matthew 5:3-12, Jesus established the character of the citizens of the kingdom of heaven and what blessings are there for those who choose to enter into it (as well as the expected opposition from those who remain at enmity with God's reign and rule over the earth). The blessings of the kingdom are unconditional and irrevocable because they do not depend upon us to faithfully follow a specific set of instructions to secure them. These heavenly blessings are secured by our position in Christ as "born again" believers by faith in the finished work of Jesus Christ on our behalf. In the verses following the Beatitudes, Jesus continued His Sermon on the Mount by describing the mission of the citizens of the kingdom to the world around them. The blessings of the kingdom bring with them certain responsibilities that we must not ignore. As we have seen, He defines their mission as being "salt" and "light" to a world hungry and thirsting for God.

5.

Jesus Corrects the Distortions of the Law

Jesus' Conflicts with the Pharisees, Scribes, and Sadducees

LESSON OUTLINE

The Purpose of this lesson is to examine the background and nature of the conflicts between Jesus and the religious authorities of the Jews.
- Jesus fulfills the Law of Moses
- The Jewish leaders' failed to fulfill the Law of Moses
- Jesus' Sermon on the Mount and Mosaic teachings
- Jesus rightly interprets the Ten Commandments

Jesus Fulfilled the Law by Correctly Interpreting the Law in His Teachings.

Jesus introduced His teachings on the Law of Moses in His Sermon on the Mount by saying He had come to fulfill the Law, not to destroy it "To fulfill" means "to make full or complete" The whole point of what Jesus taught in His Sermon on the Mount was it is not outward obedience to the demands of the

Law that places man in right standing with God, but it is a healthy inner spiritual life flowing out of a personal relationship with God the Father that leads to righteousness. Jesus taught that the true righteousness of a whole heart given to God surpasses the outward, superficial righteousness of the scribes and Pharisees.

The scene in Matthew chapters five, six and seven is reminiscent of chapters twenty-seven through thirty in the book of Deuteronomy. In Deuteronomy, Moses gives final instructions to the children of Israel for when they entered the Promised Land (fulfilled in Joshua 8:30-35). Moses assembled the people and instructed them concerning the blessings of obeying their covenant with God, and the curses sure to visit them if they did not fulfill the terms and conditions of the covenant.

> To "fulfill" – Gk. *pleroo* "to make full" – Jesus fulfilled the Law by:
>
> 1. Confirming its validity
>
> 2. Bringing out its full, Original, and intended meaning
>
> 3. Expanding its demands beyond mere outward conformity to inward attitudes of the heart
>
> 4. Revealing the true *eschatological* will of God recorded in the Old Testament Scriptures.

Also known as the Palestinian Covenant, these blessings and curses were to be recited before the people from Mount Gerizim and Mount Ebal, respectively. It is now centuries later, and God is about to do a new thing – not only for the house of Israel, but also for the nations (Jeremiah 31:31).

In Matthew's Gospel the people are once again assembled on a mountain to hear the Word of God spoken to them, but one greater than Moses, Joshua, and the prophets is about to speak. It is important to note at this point that the blessings and curses of the Mosaic covenant were pronounced from two mountains. However, Jesus Christ came to only one mountain and announced only the unconditional blessings of the New Covenant to those assembled (Jeremiah 31:31-34; Matthew 5:1-12).

When Moses addressed the people at Moab and Horeb (Sinai), (Deut. 29:1), God was about to establish the nation of Israel in the land He had chosen for them (Deut. 26:9), but the blessings of God and their possession of the Promised Land were conditioned upon their obedience to the Law given at Mount Sinai.

"This day I call heaven and earth as witnesses against you that I have set before you life and death, blessings and curses. Now choose life..." Deuteronomy 30:19 (NIV)

Canaan was never intended to be the kingdom of heaven that the prophets said would be established in the unspecified future. God had a purpose in establishing the nation of Israel in Canaan that by Jesus' day had long ago been lost by them. Deuteronomy 29:22-29 implies that Moses knew that a time would come when a generation of Israelites would fail to keep the conditions for the blessings of God set before the people from Mount Gerizim. This failure would surely bring the curses promised from Mount Ebal upon the nation. The children of Israel would be uprooted from the land by the Lord, and cast into another land where they would be held captives. However, Moses makes it clear that their captivity would not be without hope for the future (Deuteronomy 30). What had been lost to Israel was its mandate to be a light to the Gentiles and the means through which the nations would come to the Lord. Israel readily accepted their privileged position as God's chosen people:

"And the Lord has declared this day that you are his people, his treasured possession as he promised, and that you are to keep all his commands. He has declared that he will set you in praise, fame and honor high above all the nations he has made and that you will be a people holy to the Lord your God, as he promised." Deuteronomy 26:18-19 (NIV)

"If you fully obey the Lord your God and carefully follow all his commands I give you today, the Lord your God will set you high above all the nations on earth." Deuteronomy 28:1 (NIV)

"The Lord will establish you as his holy people, as he promised you on oath, if you keep the commands of the Lord your God and walk in his ways. Then all the

peoples on earth will see that you are called by the name of the Lord, and they will fear you. The Lord will grant you abundant prosperity--in the fruit of your womb, the young of your livestock and the crops of your ground--in the land he swore to your forefathers to give you." Deuteronomy 28:9-11 (NIV)

However, lost to them was the covenant responsibility to be "a kingdom of priests and a holy nation"... to be "blessed to be a blessing" so that "all the nations will be blessed through you."

"I will make you into a great nation and I will bless you; I will make your name great, and you will be a blessing. I will bless those who bless you, and whoever curses you I will curse; and all peoples on earth will be blessed through you." Genesis 12:2-3 (NIV)

"Then Moses went up to God, and the Lord called to him from the mountain and said, 'This is what you are to say to the house of Jacob and what you are to tell the people of Israel: You yourselves have seen what I did to Egypt, and how I carried you on eagles' wings and brought you to myself. Now if you obey me fully and keep my covenant, then out of all nations you will be my treasured possession. Although the whole earth is mine, you will be for me a kingdom of priests and a holy nation.' These are the words you are to speak to the Israelites.'" Exodus 19:3-6 (NIV)

"May God be gracious to us and bless us and make his face shine upon us, that your ways may be known on earth, your salvation among all nations." Psalms 67:1-2 (NIV)

"'You are my witnesses,' declares the Lord, 'and my servant whom I have chosen, so that you may know and believe me and understand that I am he. Before me no god was formed, nor will there be one after me. I, even I, am the Lord, and apart from me there is no savior. I have revealed and saved and proclaimed – I, and not some foreign god among you. You are my witnesses,' declares the Lord, 'that I am God.'" Isaiah 43:10-12 (NIV)

"Before I formed you in the womb I knew you, before you were born I set you apart; I appointed you as a prophet to the nations." Jeremiah 1:5 (NIV)

"As for the foreigner who does not belong to your people Israel but has come from a distant land because of your name – for men will hear of your great name and your mighty hand and your outstretched arm – when he comes and prays toward this temple, then hear from heaven, your dwelling place, and do whatever the foreigner asks of you, so that all the peoples of the earth may know your name and fear you, as do your own people Israel, and may know that this house I have built bears your Name." 1 Kings 8:41-43 (NIV)

After the Jews returned from their exile in Babylon, they were cured of their idolatry. However, in their zeal to keep away from idols and idol worshippers, they unintentionally began to erect walls and barriers to keep others away from God. "But woe to you, scribes and Pharisees, hypocrites! For you shut the kingdom of heaven in people's faces. For you neither enter yourselves nor allow those who would enter to go in." Matthew 23:13 (ESV)

This first Woe against the Pharisees was for their tactless and stupid shutting of the Kingdom of God against men by their opposition to the Christ. This pretentious religious party believed they had the exclusive knowledge of what it took to keep God's covenant and therefore gain entrance into His eternal kingdom. The Pharisees believed only the righteous – as they defined righteous – could enter into God's presence, which automatically excluded the Gentiles and sinners. Those that the Pharisees declared impossible to share in the full blessings of God, are the very ones Jesus came to seek and save. Had the Scribes and Pharisees done what they started out to do and taught the people the Scriptures, they would have shown them the right way. These religious leaders would have been true to their office if they pointed the sinners to Christ where they would find grace and mercy and the way into the kingdom. Jesus declared "woe to them" because in their positions as leaders they not only rejected Jesus and stood with their backs to the door of the Kingdom, but they also prevented the entrance of others by trying to stop them from coming to Christ for salvation.

The commandments of God were always intended to make Israel a distinct and holy nation of priests to the one, true, living God so that the world would know and see who the Lord is and be drawn to Him for salvation. The religious leaders of the Jews used the laws intended to keep the people ceremonially clean and prepared for worship as a means to exclude everyone but the Jews from access to God. As time when on, it even reached the point where the religious leaders were using their own, manmade, religious rules and regulations, and their distorted interpretations of the Mosaic Law to exclude other Jews that they declared outcasts, sinners, and unclean for inclusion in the daily life and worship of the community (lepers, cripples, blind, deaf, demon possessed, lost sheep, etc.).

From this mountain, Jesus would set aright the misinterpretations of the Commandments of God. He exposed the false doctrines of the priests, scribes and Pharisees that excluded people from worshipping their God. Jesus set the terms for accessing the unconditional blessings of the kingdom in this present reality for all people.

Because of His constant conflicts with the Pharisees, Sadducees, and teachers of the Law, Jesus felt it necessary to say at the outset of His sermon that He had not come to abolish the Law or the Prophets. In His words and by His actions as the Lord of the Sabbath, Jesus fulfilled the Law in a way that was totally unexpected by those who had appointed themselves the protectors of the Law for all Jews. But Jesus challenged their authority without challenging the Law itself, "For truly I say to you, until heaven and earth pass away, not the smallest letter or stroke shall pass from the Law until all is accomplished." Matthew 5:17, 18

Jesus' Sermon on the Mount is not a radical departure from the Old Testament Mosaic teachings. Jesus' teachings were never intended to replace any of the Law and Prophets handed down from Moses to Malachi. Neither was Jesus establishing a "New Law." As we carefully examine His teachings, we will discover that what Jesus was doing was resetting misplaced priorities. The scribes and Pharisees had lost the true meaning of the Scriptures. Jesus said to them, "You search the Scriptures because you think that in them you have eternal life; and it is they that bear witness about me, yet you refuse to come to me that you may have life." John 5:39-40 (ESV) These religious leaders emphasized works over righteousness; they chose religion over a childlike faith and love for God the Father; they valued their Jewish birthright over their citizenship in the kingdom of God; and they had no concept of a Spirit filled life. Jesus' public sermons were intended to expose the counterfeit teachings of the scribes and Pharisees and point the way into the kingdom of heaven for all those who were desperately seeking it.

"Then Jesus went about all the cities and villages, teaching in their synagogues, and preaching the gospel of the kingdom, and healing every sickness and every disease among the people." Matthew 9:35

After His "Sermon on the Mount" Jesus continued His public sermons on the Laws of Moses and His proclamations concerning the coming of the kingdom. Jesus offered Himself as the Messiah the nation of Israel was waiting and hoping for. In His kingdom sermons Jesus taught that God's people must acknowledge His authority and accept Him as the One who fulfilled the Old Testament Law and prophetic revelation of the King of the Jews or else they would continue down the wrong pathway marked out for them by the traditions taught by the scribes and the Pharisees. During this period, Christ told very few parables, but instead allowed His miracles to speak for Him.

When we carefully study Matthew chapters 8-11, we discover how Jesus used His miracles as a visible stamp to authenticate Himself as One who spoke to the nation with divine authority. Not everyone who heard Jesus' teachings and witnessed His miracles reacted to Him and to His message in the same way. Those who were in greatest need of God's love and redemption reacted with the greatest love; while those who were wrapped in the robes of religious self-righteousness, often reacted with the greatest hate.

"Therefore, I tell you, her many sins have been forgiven – for she loved much. But he who has been forgiven little loves little." Luke 7:47 (NIV)

A clear example of how Jesus used His miracles to authenticate Himself as the Son of God is found in Matthew 9:1-8 (also Mark 2:5-12; Luke 5:20-26). Everywhere Jesus went there were always three groups of people watching Him. One group was the masses – the curious onlookers who were there to see and hear, but were not committed to Jesus as the Lord. The second group was the disciples – the core group of followers including the twelve who believed Jesus was divine. The third group was composed of the religious leaders – Pharisees and teachers of religious law that were the spiritual watchdogs over the people; they were there to make sure Jesus followed their Sabbath rules and regulations.

As Jesus was teaching, some men came carrying a paralyzed man on his mat. They tried to take him inside to Jesus, but the crowd was too large to get through to Him. So they went up to the roof and removed

THE WAY, TRUTH, AND LIFE

some tiles to make a hole large enough to lower the sick man on his mat right in front of Jesus. Jesus saw their faith, looked at the paralyzed man and said, "Young man, your sins are forgiven." Jesus knew what the Pharisees and teachers of religious law would be thinking to themselves at that moment: "Who does this Jesus think he is? It's blasphemy for any human to forgive sins because only God can forgive sins!"

Jesus responded to their doubting minds and asked them before they could speak, "Why do you question this in your hearts? Is it easier to say 'Your sins are forgiven,' or 'Stand up and walk'? So I will prove to you that the Son of Man has the authority on earth to forgive sins." Then Jesus turned to the paralyzed man and said, 'Stand up, pick up your mat, and go home!' And immediately, as everyone watched, the man jumped up, picked up his mat, and went home praising God." Luke 5:22$_b$ – 25 (NLT) The different groups watching this reacted as expected. The masses were awestruck by what they saw, and they along with Jesus' disciples praised God over what they saw that day, and in particular the authority that had been given to Jesus. The reaction of the religious leaders that day is not recorded by any of the Gospel writers, but if their reaction to Jesus' healing the man with the withered hand (Mark 3:1-6) is any indication, they would have been furious.

Everywhere Jesus went people that were afflicted with every kind of sickness and disease came to Him seeking a healing touch from Him. Along with those who were stricken with physical ailments, came those who were tormented mentally and emotionally by demons and those who were overcome by sin and spiritually paralyzed by the guilt and shame attached to it. Jesus was able to heal any or all that came to Him. As the multitudes continued to come forward, Jesus said to His disciples, "The harvest truly is plentiful, but the laborers are few" (Matt. 9:37. 38; Luke 10:2; & John 4:35-37). The crowds who followed Jesus may have been impressed by His miracles, but they wavered when it came time to totally commit to Him and many fell away not wanting to bear the cost of following Jesus all the way to Calvary (Luke 9:51-62; John 6:60-66).

Those who saw Jesus' healings, yet would not commit themselves to Him, were joined by the scribes, Pharisees and teachers of the law who were the religious "watchdogs" over the people. Also in the crowds were the priests, the keepers of Temple worship in Jerusalem who were the self-appointed "holy men" and the religious police who made sure everyone in Judea knew their place in society and kept it. All but a handful of these religious leaders openly resisted Jesus' influence over the multitudes that came and listened to Him preaching the gospel of the kingdom and to be healed. Jesus' confrontations with these religious leaders over their misinterpretations and outright misrepresentations of Mosaic Law and the Sabbath regulations became increasingly open and hostile. Although they saw His many miracles and knew the Scriptures concerning the coming of the Messiah, they still demanded of Jesus, "Teacher, we want to see a sign from you" (Matthew 12:38). Compounding their unbelief was their blasphemous accusation that Jesus used Satanic power to cast out demons (Matthew 9:33). It was in this context that Jesus began to teach in parables.

Once it became clear that the multitudes and the religious leaders would never respond to His authority and commit themselves to His kingdom, Jesus abandoned the direct approach of His sermons and His authenticating miracles as the means to turn the nation towards Him. It was at this point that Jesus started to present His most important public sayings in parables while reserving the teaching and training of the twelve for private sessions with His most intimate disciples. Jesus already predicted that only a few would choose the "narrow way" and come to Him (Matthew 7:13, 14). Now it was time to speak in parables so that "outsiders" and "the rest" – those who refused to believe – would not be able to hear or understand the mysteries of the kingdom that are only for Jesus' disciples to hear and understand.

Jesus would continue to preach and work miracles almost until the end, but Jesus saw that the increasing unbelief of Israel's leaders and the continuing lack of commitment to their King by the crowds that followed Him was a foreshadowing of the nation's ultimate rejection of Christ. Once He officially presented Himself in Jerusalem as the Messiah, this rejection would culminate in His death on the cross.

Matthew chapter 12 describes a pivotal moment in Jesus' ministry. It opens with another confrontation between Jesus and the Pharisees over the Sabbath. Jesus ends this confrontation, declaring Himself "Lord of the Sabbath." From there Jesus enters a synagogue and heals a man on the Sabbath, once again demonstrating in deed His authority over the Sabbath. But instead of accepting Him, the religious leaders wanted to kill Him, the "Lord of the Sabbath" (Note: Luke 19:14, 15a, 27; & Luke 20:14-16). The offer of the Lord to establish the Davidic form of the Messianic Kingdom at this pivotal moment in Israel's history ends with their rejection of the Messiah.

"But the Pharisees went out and plotted how they might kill Jesus. Aware of this, Jesus withdrew from that place. Many followed him, and he healed all their sick, warning them not to tell who he was. This was to fulfill what was spoken through the prophet Isaiah:
'Here is my servant whom I have chosen, the one I love, in whom I delight; I will put my Spirit on him, and he will proclaim justice to the nations. He will not quarrel or cry out; no one will hear his voice in the streets. A bruised reed he will not break, and a smoldering wick he will not snuff out, till he leads justice to victory. In his name the nations will put their hope.'" Matthew 12:14-21 (NIV)

Matthew turned to the prophetic word of Isaiah to communicate to his Jewish audience these two crucial points:
1. The Lord's offer to establish the Davidic form of the Messianic Kingdom at this time in Israel's history has ended. The King of the Jews has come, but they rejected Him and will eventually kill Him; so Jesus withdraws from them. He will still deal compassionately with all those who come to Him, but the Messianic kingdom will have to wait for some time in the future.
2. The Lord was opening a direct channel to the kingdom of God for the Gentile nations ("In His name, the nations will put their hope")

These same two prophetic promises – one to the Jews and the other to the Gentile nations – concerning the Kingdom were confirmed in the Acts of the Apostles:

"On the next Sabbath almost the whole city gathered to hear the word of the Lord. When the Jews saw the crowds, they were filled with jealousy and talked abusively against what Paul was saying. Then Paul and Barnabas answered them boldly: 'We had to speak the word of God to you first. Since you reject it and do not consider yourselves worthy of eternal life, we now turn to the Gentiles. For this is what the Lord has commanded us: "I have made you a light for the Gentiles, that you may bring salvation to the ends of the earth."' When the Gentiles heard this, they were glad and honored the word of the Lord; and all who were appointed for eternal life believed." Acts 13:44-48 (NIV)

Note also the Holy Spirit's words through the Apostle Paul in Ephesians and 1 Corinthians:

"Therefore, remember that formerly you who are Gentiles by birth and called 'uncircumcised' by those who call themselves 'the circumcision' (that done in the body by the hands of men) – remember that at that time you were separate from Christ, excluded from citizenship in Israel and foreigners to the covenants of the promise, without hope and without God in the world. But now in Christ Jesus you who once were far away have been brought near through the blood of Christ." Ephesians 2:11-13 (NIV)

"However, we speak wisdom among those who are mature, yet not the wisdom of this age, nor of the rulers of this age, who are coming to nothing. But we speak the wisdom of God in a mystery, the hidden wisdom which God ordained before the ages for our glory, which none of the rulers of this age knew; for had they known, they would not have crucified the Lord of glory." 1 Corinthians 2:6-8 (NIV)

The twelfth chapter of Matthew also contains Jesus' rebuke of the leaders of the Jewish nation who first accused Him of being in league with the devil and then demanded another sign from Him before they would accept His authority to speak to the nation. Jesus' words in Matthew 12:22-45 echo those of John the Baptist when John warned the leaders, "even now the axe is laid to the root of the tree" (Matthew 3:7-10). After all that Jesus had said and done in the presence of the multitudes, it was obvious that one more sign would not convince them that He was indeed the promised Messiah. Only one last sign would be offered to the nation of Israel (and to the world):

"He answered, 'A wicked and adulterous generation asks for a miraculous sign! But none will be given it except the sign of the prophet Jonah. For as Jonah was three days and three nights in the belly of a huge fish, so the Son of Man will be three days and three nights in the heart of the earth. The men of Nineveh will stand up at the judgment with this generation and condemn it; for they repented at the preaching of Jonah, and now one greater than Jonah is here. The Queen of the South will rise at the judgment with this generation and condemn it; for she came from the ends of the earth to listen to Solomon's wisdom, and now one greater than Solomon is here.'" Matthew 12:39-42 (NIV)

If they did not believe and receive the Son of Man in His earthly ministry, then why would they believe the sign of the risen Son of God? (John 3:14).

This sad chapter in Israel's history ends with what on the surface seems to be Jesus rejecting His own family, but it is in fact a prophetic utterance that revealed the basis for communal ties with Jesus in the kingdom of heaven: "For whoever does the will of My Father in heaven is My brother and sister and mother." (Matthew 12:50) From this time forward, Jesus would only explain His teachings to His true family. For those on the outside of Jesus' kingdom, the events that were about to unfold in Jerusalem (the death, burial, and resurrection of the Son of God) would remain a mystery, only to be revealed with power on the Day of Pentecost:

"God has raised this Jesus to life, and we are all witnesses of the fact. Exalted to the right hand of God, he has received from the Father the promised Holy Spirit and has poured out what you now see and hear...Therefore let all Israel be assured of this: God has made this Jesus, whom you crucified, both Lord and Christ." Acts 2:32, 33, 36 (NIV)

Note also Matthew 8:10-12 (The healing of the Centurion's servant): *"When Jesus heard it, He marveled, and said to those who followed, 'Assuredly, I say to you, I have not found such great faith, not even in Israel! And I say to you that many will come from east and west, and sit down with Abraham, Isaac, and Jacob in the kingdom of heaven. But the sons of the kingdom will be cast out into outer darkness. There will be weeping and gnashing of teeth.'"* (NIV)

The Jews believed that righteousness was obtained through obedience to the Law and this was the prerequisite for entrance into the kingdom of heaven. The Pharisees were obsessed with keeping every detail of the Mosaic Law and when that was not enough, they began adding layers of religious "dos" and "don'ts" to raise the bar of righteousness ever higher. By the time Jesus began to preach the gospel of the kingdom, only a very few of the religious elites were able to come close to being righteous according to the terms of their religion.

When Jesus arrived on the scene, He began to preach a gospel of repentance from dead works, "Repent for the kingdom of heaven is near"

(Matthew 4:17). Jesus taught that the kingdom was not exclusive, but was inclusive. "Do not be afraid, little flock, for your Father has been pleased to give you the kingdom" (Luke 12:32). Greatness in the kingdom of God was not measured by man's standard of righteousness, but by God's standard. God's standard meant that the least of His sheep would by no means be excluded, "I tell you the truth: among those born of woman, there has not risen anyone greater than John the Baptist; yet he who is least in the kingdom of heaven is greater than he" (Matthew 11:11). And, "I tell you the truth, unless you change and become like little children, you will never enter the kingdom of heaven. Therefore, whoever humbles himself like this child is the greatest in the kingdom of heaven" (Matthew 18:3-4; NOTE also Mark 10:14-15).

Jesus was turning the teachings of the scribes and Pharisees upside down and inside out. He taught that a childlike faith and trust in God was all that was required to enter into His Father's kingdom. To fulfill the law, meant to "love the Lord with all your heart, mind, soul and strength; and to love your neighbor as yourself" (Matthew 22:34-40 & Mark 12:28-34). In His confrontations with the Jewish religious leaders, Jesus criticized those who made the Sabbath rules and regulations of the Jews obstructions to obeying the heart and soul of the true commandments of God:

"Anyone who breaks one of the least of these commandments and teaches others to do the same will be called least in the kingdom of heaven, but whoever practices and teaches these commands will be called great in the kingdom of heaven. For I tell you that unless your righteousness surpasses that of the Pharisees and the teachers of the law, you will certainly not enter the kingdom of heaven." Matthew 5:19-20 (NIV)

Jesus taught that there was only one prerequisite for entrance into the kingdom of God: you must be born again.

"In reply Jesus declared, 'I tell you the truth, no one can see the kingdom of God unless he is born again.'" John 3:3 (NIV)

"Jesus answered, 'I tell you the truth, no one can enter the kingdom of God unless he is born of water and the Spirit. Flesh gives birth to flesh, but the Spirit gives birth to spirit.'" John 3:5-6 (NIV)

Jesus' statement in Matthew 5:17-20 make it clear that He was by no means intending to replace Mosaic Law with His own laws. (Remember that as the eternal "Second Person" of the Godhead, Jesus is also the author and finisher of the Law):

"Do not think that I have come to abolish the Law or the Prophets; I have not come to abolish them but to fulfill them. I tell you the truth, until heaven and earth disappear, not the smallest letter, not the least stroke of a pen, will by any means disappear from the Law until everything is accomplished. Anyone who breaks one of the least of these commandments and teaches others to do the same will be called least in the kingdom of heaven, but whoever practices and teaches these commands will be called great in the kingdom of heaven. For I tell you that unless your righteousness surpasses that of the Pharisees and the teachers of the law, you will certainly not enter the kingdom of heaven." Matthew 5:17-20 (NIV)

After the children of Israel reached Mount Sinai, God gave them the Ten Commandments (Exodus 20) and all the other laws that were central to the establishment of Israel as a people in covenant relationship with God (Exodus 21-23). The Ten Commandments consist of broad categorical laws that set forth the absolute principles intended to guide all people into a right relationship with the one, true living God over all of Creation. The Ten Commandments do not specify how they are to be enforced or what penalties are to be applied if they are broken, but they do make unconditional commands that place moral obligations on all people who seek to live in right relationship to God.

Deuteronomy 4:1-14 is a key passage of Old Testament Scripture because it described for the people of Israel the purpose, permanence and perfection of the Law.

- PURPOSE OF THE LAW

[1] Hear now, O Israel, the decrees and laws I am about to teach you. Follow them so that you may live and may go in and take possession of the land that the Lord, the God of your fathers, is giving you.

⁵ See, I have taught you decrees and laws as the Lord my God commanded me, so that you may follow them in the land you are entering to take possession of it. ⁶ Observe them carefully, for this will show your wisdom and understanding to the nations, who will hear about all these decrees and say, "Surely this great nation is a wise and understanding people." ⁷ What other nation is so great as to have their gods near them the way the Lord our God is near us whenever we pray to him? ⁸ And what other nation is so great as to have such righteous decrees and laws as this body of laws I am setting before you today?

- ## PERMANENCE OF THE LAW

² Do not add to what I command you and do not subtract from it, but keep the commands of the Lord your God that I give you.

⁹ Only be careful, and watch yourselves closely so that you do not forget the things your eyes have seen or let them slip from your heart as long as you live. Teach them to your children and to their children after them.

- ## PERFECTION OF THE LAW

¹¹ You came near and stood at the foot of the mountain while it blazed with fire to the very heavens, with black clouds and deep darkness. ¹² Then the Lord spoke to you out of the fire. You heard the sound of words but saw no form; there was only a voice. ¹³ He declared to you his covenant, the Ten Commandments, which he commanded you to follow and then wrote them on two stone tablets. ¹⁴ And the Lord directed me at that time to teach you the decrees and laws you are to follow in the land that you are crossing the Jordan to possess.

In no way did Jesus ever seek to change the Law of God, but throughout His earthly ministry He boldly challenged the accepted interpretations of the Law of Moses being taught by the scribes and Pharisees of that day. These religious leaders had failed to understand the true meaning and purpose of the Law. They concentrated upon outward, religious ritual purity that left the heart unchanged. Man judges by outward appearances, but God sees what is in the soul. In His confrontations with the Pharisees, Jesus

THE WAY, TRUTH, AND LIFE

warned them to *"Stop judging by mere appearances, and make a right judgment"* (John 7:24).

"Woe to you, teachers of the law and Pharisees, you hypocrites! You clean the outside of the cup and dish, but inside they are full of greed and self-indulgence. Blind Pharisee! First clean the inside of the cup and dish, and then the outside also will be clean." Matthew 23:25-26 (NIV)

"Then the Lord said to him, 'Now then, you Pharisees clean the outside of the cup and dish, but inside you are full of greed and wickedness. You foolish people! Did not the one who made the outside make the inside also? But give what is inside [the dish] to the poor, and everything will be clean for you.'" Luke 11:39-41 (NIV)

Verses 17-20 of Matthew chapter 5 make it clear that the kingdom lifestyle about which He was teaching was different from what the Pharisees and teachers of the law were describing as righteousness. **Jesus was presenting a righteousness that was in perfect harmony with the Old Testament revelation; it went beyond the legalistic, outward "show" of religious purity that the Pharisees had foolishly substituted for true godliness.** *"For I tell you,"* Jesus told His listeners, *"that unless your righteousness surpasses that of the Pharisees and the teachers of the law, you will certainly not enter the kingdom of heaven."*

The "kingdom lifestyle" that Jesus promoted *fulfilled* the Law's requirements by shifting the focus of attention away from the outward appearances of religious legalism and dealt with the inward motives and intents of the heart. The true righteousness that Jesus said surpassed that of the scribes and Pharisees is from the heart, and is not imposed by the strict adherence to any religious system. Once He laid that foundation, then Jesus presented specific examples of how the kingdom lifestyle works in relation to the Law of Moses (Matt. 5:21-48), in relation to God and to others (Matt. 6:1 – 7: 29).

Almost from the beginning of His public ministry, Jesus was in conflict with the religious leaders of the Jews over the Sabbath rules and regulations. The Pharisees in particular felt it was their duty to make sure everyone in Israel was keeping every Sabbath rule and regulation down to the smallest detail. They became the "watchdogs" that would bark and bite anyone who transgressed their traditions, which they believed superseded any contradiction of the Law. At first the Jewish religious leaders expressed surprise and questioned Jesus about His actions, but as time passed and the conflicts intensified, the hostility grew until eventually they sought an opportunity to arrest Jesus and put Him to death for violating their rules.

"At that time Jesus went through the grainfields on the Sabbath. His disciples were hungry and began to pick some heads of grain and eat them. When the Pharisees saw this, they said to him, 'Look! Your disciples are doing what is unlawful on the Sabbath.'" Matthew 12:1-2 (NIV)

"Then some Pharisees and teachers of the law came to Jesus from Jerusalem and asked, 'Why do your disciples break the tradition of the elders? They don't wash their hands before they eat!'" Matthew 15:1-2 (NIV)

"When Jesus had finished speaking, a Pharisee invited him to eat with him; so he went in and reclined at the table. But the Pharisee, noticing that Jesus did not first wash before the meal, was surprised." Luke 11:37-38 (NIV)

"Then he put his hands on her, and immediately she straightened up and praised God. Indignant because Jesus had healed on the Sabbath, the synagogue ruler said to the people, 'There are six days for work. So come and be healed on those days, not on the Sabbath.'" Luke 13-14 (NIV)

"Another time he went into the synagogue, and a man with a shriveled hand was there. Some of them were looking for a reason to accuse Jesus, so they watched him closely to see if he would heal him on the Sabbath.
Jesus said to the man with the shriveled hand, 'Stand up in front of everyone.' Then Jesus asked them, 'Which is lawful on the Sabbath: to do good or to do evil, to save life or to kill?'

But they remained silent. He looked around at them in anger and, deeply distressed at their stubborn hearts, said to the man, 'Stretch out your hand.' He stretched it out, and his hand was completely restored. Then the Pharisees went out and began to plot with the Herodians how they might kill Jesus." Mark 3:1-6 (NIV)

"The chief priests and the whole Sanhedrin were looking for evidence against Jesus so that they could put him to death, but they did not find any. Many testified falsely against him, but their statements did not agree." Mark 14:55-56 (NIV)

"The man went away and told the Jews that it was Jesus who had made him well. So, because Jesus was doing these things on the Sabbath, the Jews persecuted him. Jesus said to them, 'My Father is always at his work to this very day, and I, too, am working.' For this reason the Jews tried all the harder to kill him; not only was he breaking the Sabbath, but he was even calling God his own Father, making himself equal with God." John 5:15-18 (NIV)

"Finally the temple guards went back to the chief priests and Pharisees, who asked them, 'Why didn't you bring him in? "No one ever spoke the way this man does,' the guards declared. 'You mean he has deceived you also?' the Pharisees retorted. 'Has any of the rulers or of the Pharisees believed in him? No! But this mob that knows nothing of the law – there is a curse on them.'" John 7:45-49 (NIV)

Understood in context with His intense battles with the Jewish religious authorities, it is no surprise that Jesus would begin His Sermon on the Mount with the statement, "Do not think that I came to abolish the Law or the Prophets." Jesus wanted to bring correction and break the yoke of religious legalism that was oppressing the people and driving them away from the God of their salvation. In all of His sermons, Jesus taught that those who followed the scribes and Pharisees, and who thought they could justify themselves before God on the basis of their own acts of righteousness, would not enter the kingdom of heaven (Matt. 5:20). The Law was not intended to bring righteousness, but was intended to expose the sin nature and point sinful men and women back to God (Romans 4:13-18; 5:20, 21; 7:5-7).

Without ever nullifying or contradicting the Law, Jesus taught about a righteousness that exceeded what was acceptable to Judaism's elite. Jesus' teachings on the Law almost always shift the emphasis away from an outward action or behavior the scribes understood the Law to be about, and to the *inner attitude* or *motivation* of the sinner seeking a righteousness that transcends a slavish obligation to the traditions of men, but that flows naturally out of a right relationship with God.

JESUS AND THE TEN COMMANDMENTS

"Now, O Israel, listen to the statutes and the judgments which I am teaching you to perform, in order that you may live and go in and take possession of the land which the Lord, the God of your fathers, is giving you." Deut. 4:1 (NIV)

"Now when he saw the crowds, he went up on a mountainside and sat down. His disciples came to him, and he began to teach them..." Matthew 5:1-2 (NIV)

Jesus began His Sermon on the Mount describing the unconditional blessings for citizens of the kingdom of heaven. Now He turns His attention to fulfilling the Commandments of God by confirming their validity in the lives of believers; bringing out their full, original and intended meanings, and by expanding their demands beyond a superficial conformity to the inward attitudes of the heart that produce the good fruit of righteousness.

At one time or another, in His kingdom sermons Jesus addressed each of the Ten Commandments:

1. **You shall have no other gods before me.** (Exodus 20:3; Deuteronomy 5:11). When Jesus faced the temptations of Satan in the Wilderness, He answered each of Satan's challenges with the Word of God. Jesus refused to bow His knee to any other: *"Worship the Lord your God and serve Him only"* (Matthew 4:10). In His Sermon on the Mount, He instructed all those who heard Him to *"seek first his kingdom and his righteousness"* (Matthew 6:33). Jesus sought only one kingdom and when asked "what is the greatest commandment," He answered from the Law, *"The most important one, is this: 'Hear, O Israel, the Lord our God, the Lord is one. Love the Lord your God with all your heart and with all your soul and with all*

your mind and with all your strength'" (Mark 12:28-31). Jesus' earthly life and ministry as the Son of God was set upon bringing glory to His Father in heaven (John 14:11-14).

2. **You shall not make for yourself an idol** (Exodus 20:4-6; Deuteronomy 5:8-10). Unlike idol worshipers that worship images, Jesus instructed His followers to *"pray to your Father, who is unseen."* He also admonished them not to pattern their prayer life after the pagans, who *"keep on babbling... for they think they will be heard because of their many words"* (Matthew 6:6-7). Jesus looked beyond the obvious idolatry of Pagan worship and spoke of the love of money and the pursuit of material possessions that can capture the heart and take the place of God, *"For where your treasure is, there your heart will be also"* (Matthew 6:21). Jesus warned His disciples: *"No one can serve two masters. Either he will hate the one and love the other, or he will be devoted to the one and despise the other. You cannot serve both God and Money."* Matthew 6:24 (Note also Luke 16:13). In answer to the Samaritan woman's question about true worship, Jesus responded that true worshipers must worship the Father spirit and truth, "God is spirit, and his worshipers must worship in spirit and in truth." John 4:24

3. **You shall not misuse the name of the Lord** (Ex. 20:7; Deut. 5:11). Jesus acknowledged and taught others to acknowledge the sacredness of His Father (Matt. 6:9). As with so many other things, pharisaical legal technicalities were used to obscure what was really true. A person's oath should be sacred – especially when the Lord's name is involved: *"Do not swear falsely by my name and so profane the name of your God. I am the Lord"* (Leviticus 19:12).

> *"Again, you have heard that it was said to the people long ago, 'Do not break your oath, but keep the oaths you have made to the Lord.' But I tell you, Do not swear at all: either by heaven, for it is God's throne; or by the earth, for it is his footstool; or by Jerusalem, for it is the city of the Great King. And do not swear by your head, for you cannot make even one hair white or black. Simply let your 'Yes' be 'Yes,' and your 'No,' 'No'; anything beyond this comes from the evil one."* Matthew 5:33-37 (NIV)

"Woe to you, blind guides! You say, 'If anyone swears by the temple, it means nothing; but if anyone swears by the gold of the temple, he is bound by his oath.' You blind fools! Which is greater: the gold, or the temple that makes the gold sacred? You also say, 'If anyone swears by the altar, it means nothing; but if anyone swears by the gift on it, he is bound by his oath.' You blind men! Which is greater: the gift, or the altar that makes the gift sacred? Therefore, he who swears by the altar swears by it and by everything on it. And he who swears by the temple swears by it and by the one who dwells in it. And he who swears by heaven swears by God's throne and by the one who sits on it." Matthew 23:16-22 (NIV)

Jesus saw through the hypocrisy of the Pharisees and teachers of the law who were dishonoring the powerful and holy name of God by appearing to back up their promises with things associated with sacred places and things, but by parsing words and threading loopholes, they were *making* oaths they never intended to keep. However, by dancing around the truth in the name of the Lord, the Pharisees were making the Lord's name seem useless, silly and futile to those who were fooled by such oaths.

4. **Remember the Sabbath day by keeping it holy** (Ex. 20:8-11; Deut. 5:12-15). No issue between the Jewish authorities and Jesus created more conflicts and controversies than the war of words they fought over the Jewish Sabbath. As Jesus' fame and popularity spread throughout the region, He drew greater and greater scrutiny upon His words and actions from the Pharisees and teachers of the Law who were the self-appointed, spiritual watchdogs over the people. As previously stated, Jesus' teachings on the Law almost always shift the emphasis away from an outward action or behavior that the scribes believed the Law was all about, and to the *inner attitude* or *motivation* of person in right relationship with His Father. The religious leaders of Jesus' day were obsessed with keeping up the outward appearances of a self-defined righteousness, but glossed over or completely ignored the inner, spiritual conditions of their hearts. Jesus called out the Pharisees for their obvious hypocrisies:

"Woe to you, teachers of the law and Pharisees, you hypocrites! You give a tenth of your spices--mint, dill and cummin. But you have neglected the

more important matters of the law--justice, mercy and faithfulness. You should have practiced the latter, without neglecting the former. You blind guides! You strain out a gnat but swallow a camel. Woe to you, teachers of the law and Pharisees, you hypocrites! You clean the outside of the cup and dish, but inside they are full of greed and self-indulgence. Blind Pharisee! First clean the inside of the cup and dish, and then the outside also will be clean. Woe to you, teachers of the law and Pharisees, you hypocrites! You are like whitewashed tombs, which look beautiful on the outside but on the inside are full of dead men's bones and everything unclean. In the same way, on the outside you appear to people as righteous but on the inside you are full of hypocrisy and wickedness." Matthew 23:23-28 (NIV)

Jesus' refusal to be frightened or intimidated by the authorities' power to excommunicate from the religious life of the community anyone who challenged their authority drove the Pharisees absolutely crazy (John chapter 9). And yet it seems that to one degree or another, just about every teaching and action of Jesus challenged the power that the religious leaders exercised to keep the people under their control.

"At that time Jesus went through the grainfields on the Sabbath. His disciples were hungry and began to pick some heads of grain and eat them. When the Pharisees saw this, they said to him, 'Look! Your disciples are doing what is unlawful on the Sabbath.'
He answered, 'Haven't you read what David did when he and his companions were hungry? He entered the house of God, and he and his companions ate the consecrated bread--which was not lawful for them to do, but only for the priests. Or haven't you read in the Law that on the Sabbath the priests in the temple desecrate the day and yet are innocent? I tell you that one greater than the temple is here. If you had known what these words mean, "I desire mercy, not sacrifice," you would not have condemned the innocent. For the Son of Man is Lord of the Sabbath.'" Matthew 12:1-8 (NIV) Note also Mark 2:23-28 and Luke 6:1-5.

"Going on from that place, he went into their synagogue, and a man with a shriveled hand was there. Looking for a reason to accuse Jesus, they asked him, 'Is it lawful to heal on the Sabbath?' He said to them, 'If any of

you has a sheep and it falls into a pit on the Sabbath, will you not take hold of it and lift it out? How much more valuable is a man than a sheep! Therefore it is lawful to do good on the Sabbath.' Then he said to the man, 'Stretch out your hand.' So he stretched it out and it was completely restored, just as sound as the other. But the Pharisees went out and plotted how they might kill Jesus." Matthew 12:9-13 (NIV) Note also Mark 3:1-6 and Luke 6:6-11.

The issue for the religious leaders was not if a man should be healed, or the hungry fed; the issue was not whether people like Jesus' disciples kept their hands ceremonially clean before eating. The real issue for the Pharisees and teachers of the law was power. Anything anyone did had to first meet with their approval and had to be done according to the rules and regulations of their traditions. The Pharisees had developed a heavy yoke of traditions and additions to the Torah that they believed protected them from breaking any law of God and therefore, prevented judgment from coming upon themselves and the whole community. They regarded these modifications ("the tradition of the elders" or "the oral law") as of equal authority to the Torah, claiming that both the written and the oral law were derived from Moses on Mount Sinai. Ultimately, the message was clear: "we, by the same authority as Moses, set the rules of our community, and if you don't follow them, you will be killed or cast out." But as the Jewish authorities added layer upon layer of human oral law and traditions on top of the Torah, they found ways to circumvent the letter and spirit of what God first delivered to Moses at Sinai. Matthew gives us a clear example of how Jesus confronted the Pharisees on this very point (which ties into the next commandment, "Honor your father and mother").

5. *Honor your father and mother* **(Ex. 20:12; Deut. 5:16).** Citing Isaiah 29:13 (Matthew 15:7-9), *"...these people draw near with their mouths And honor Me with their lips, But have removed their hearts far from Me, And their fear toward Me is taught by the commandment of men..."*, Jesus gave a perfect example of how these legalists were rejecting God's laws and trampling them under their feet for the sake of their traditions.

> *"Then some Pharisees and teachers of the law came to Jesus from Jerusalem and asked, 'Why do your disciples break the tradition of the elders? They don't wash their hands before they eat!'*
> *Jesus replied, 'And why do you break the command of God for the sake of your tradition? For God said, "Honor your father and mother" and "Anyone who curses his father or mother must be put to death." But you say that if a man says to his father or mother, "Whatever help you might otherwise have received from me is a gift devoted to God," he is not to "honor his father" with it. Thus you nullify the word of God for the sake of your tradition.'"* Matthew 15:1-6

In a method typical of rabbinic method, Jesus does not directly answer the Pharisees' complaint, but instead asks them a counter-question: *"And why do you break the command of God for the sake of your tradition?"* The Pharisees immediately recognized Jesus' question as a direct challenge to the validity of the oral law. Through the commandment, "honor your father and mother", Jesus powerfully and clearly exposed the hypocrisy of the teachers of the law who claimed that the oral law of *korban* (the practice of setting aside money or property for the temple – even though it was understood that what was pledged could be used by the person who pledged it was routinely used to avoid giving it to care for elderly parents) was equal to the law of Moses, which carried with it the death penalty. But in practice, everyone knew that *korban* was being used in a shallow way to override and circumvent a direct command of God for selfish purposes.

Through this encounter with the teachers of the law and the other recorded examples (Matthew 19:16-19; Mark 7:6-13; Luke 18:18-20), Jesus upheld, confirmed, and "fulfilled" the letter and of most importance, the Spirit of the law of God.

6. ***You shall not murder*** **(Ex. 20:13; Deut. 5:17).** Once again, Jesus' teaching affirms the commandment of His Father and at the same time transcends the teachers of the law who saw only the outward restriction on a human action while ignoring the murderous, inward attitude of a heart filled with hate and judgment – and an attitude that is the root cause of man's inhumanity to man:

> *"You have heard that it was said to the people long ago, 'Do not murder, and anyone who murders will be subject to judgment.' But I tell you that anyone who is angry with his brother will be subject to judgment. Again, anyone who says to his brother, 'Raca,' is answerable to the Sanhedrin. But anyone who says, 'You fool!' will be in danger of the fire of hell. Therefore, if you are offering your gift at the altar and there remember that your brother has something against you, leave your gift there in front of the altar. First go and be reconciled to your brother; then come and offer your gift."* Matthew 5:21-24 (NIV)

7. **You shall not commit adultery (Ex. 20:14; Deut. 5:17).** Jesus never quarrels with the Law and the Prophets. Contrary to the accusations of His opponents, His teachings validate them completely as God's perfect revelation that never fails: *"The law of the Lord is perfect, reviving the soul. The statutes of the Lord are trustworthy, making wise the simple"* Psalm 19:7. His quarrels were only with those who substituted a legalistic, legislative superstructure of man-made traditions that obscured the true purpose and intent of the Law, and used everything God intended to reconcile Himself to sinful people – both Jew and Gentile – to build a thick wall, separating those who most needed the "divine Physician" from the One who was longing to heal their spiritual sicknesses: But Jesus said to those who were preventing others from receiving God's forgiveness to *"go and learn what this means: 'I desire mercy, not sacrifice' for I have not come to call the righteous, but sinners"* (Matthew 9:13).

When dealing with the issue of adultery, Jesus was consistent with the Law of Moses and with His other observations upon how that commandment is to be understood:

"You have heard that it was said, 'Do not commit adultery.' But I tell you that anyone who looks at a woman lustfully has already committed adultery with her in his heart. If your right eye causes you to sin, gouge it out and throw it away. It is better for you to lose one part of your body than for your whole body to be thrown into hell. And if your right hand causes you to sin, cut it off and throw it away. It is better for you to lose

one part of your body than for your whole body to go into hell." Matthew 5:27-30 (NIV)

In this, as in every case concerning the commandments of God, Jesus speaks with a greater authority ("You have heard that it was said... But I tell you...") than Moses or the other teachers of the Law. He teaches a "greater righteousness" than the pharisaical traditions while reaffirming the Scriptures and drawing out from them their full, true, intended meanings as only the Son of God could do.

"For while we were in the flesh, the sinful passions, which were aroused by the Law, were at work in the members of our body to bear fruit for death. But now we have been released from the Law, having died to that by which we were bound, so that we serve in newness of the Spirit and not in oldness of the letter." Romans 7:5, 6 (NIV)

8. **You shall not steal (Ex. 20:15; Deut. 5:19).** Jesus affirmed the commandment, "You shall not steal" in His encounter with the rich young ruler recorded in Matthew 19:17, 18 (and also included in Mark 10:19 and Luke 18:20). But in His Sermon on the Mount, Jesus looked farther and deeper into the attitudes of the heart towards material wealth and possessions and how those attitudes – right or wrong – affected the spiritual life of the individual that possessed them: *"For where your treasure is,"* Jesus said, *"there your heart will be also"* (Matthew 6:21). Money and possessions make cruel masters and the ones who find themselves motivated by the love for them will soon discover the truth of Jesus' teaching that *"No one can serve two masters. Either he will hate the one and love the other, or he will be devoted to the one and despise the other. You cannot serve both God and Money"* (Matthew 6:24).

At another point in time, Jesus said, *"It is easier for a camel to go through the eye of a needle than for a rich man to enter the kingdom of God"* (Mark 10:25). His disciples were amazed at this because the Jews had for so long equated material blessings with righteousness. "How then," they reasoned, "could it be so hard for the rich to inherit the kingdom?" However, if we understand Jesus' teachings about wealth and possessions in Matthew 6:19-34, then His later comment in Mark is easier to comprehend. Jesus begins His teachings about money:

"Do not store up for yourselves treasures on earth, where moth and rust destroy, and where thieves break in and steal. But store up for yourselves treasures in heaven, where moth and rust do not destroy, and where thieves do not break in and steal. For where your treasure is, there your heart will be also. The eye is the lamp of the body. If your eyes are good, your whole body will be full of light. But if your eyes are bad, your whole body will be full of darkness. If then the light within you is darkness, how great is that darkness! No one can serve two masters. Either he will hate the one and love the other, or he will be devoted to the one and despise the other. You cannot serve both God and Money." Matthew 6:19-24 (NIV)

Key to having a right attitude about wealth and worldly possessions is having a "good eye." Implied in the language used here is that an eye that is "good" is "single"; you cannot walk straight with one eye on heaven and the other on worldly things. A person who attempts to do this will have double vision and will stagger through this life like a drunkard – first leaning one way, then the other. The only cure for this condition is to focus on one thing or another: the spiritual blessings of "seeking first the kingdom of heaven" or surrendering to a whole-hearted pursuit of mammon. If a person's heart is in the right place, their treasure will be in heaven and not in their bank accounts, jewelry, land, automobiles, and houses.

At the very heart of God's prophetic calling of Abraham (Genesis 12:1-3) is the pronouncement that God will bless Abraham so that he might "be a blessing". God entrusted Abraham and his descendants with tremendous material wealth, and, most importantly, spiritual blessings so that through them "all peoples on earth will be blessed by you." The Hebrew root for "Mammon" means "entrust." Mammon was the wealth people entrusted to another for safekeeping. But as time progressed, Mammon lost that meaning and came to mean that in which people have placed their trust. In other words, instead of recognizing that all they had been given by God was entrusted to them so that they might be a blessing to the world, they turned around and used to bless themselves at others' expense. This should be a strong message to Christians today. It grieves the very heart of God when we prize the gifts above the Giver. In the end we will be held accountable for how we have used that which has been entrusted to us by God to invest in HIS kingdom. Where our heart is, is what we treasure; what we treasure becomes our god. How can we expect God to excuse us if we allow the treasure He entrusted to us to take His place in our life, in effect becoming our god? This generation of Christians is accountable no less than the generation of Abraham's children that Jesus directly addressed in His Sermon on the Mount. His disciples will always be identified clearly by their right attitude toward money and material possessions.

"Jesus replied, 'Man, who appointed me a judge or an arbiter between you?' Then he said to them, 'Watch out! Be on your guard against all kinds of greed; a man's life does not consist in the abundance of his possessions.'" Luke 12:14-15 (NIV)

You don't have to be wealthy to be obsessed with money. The poor can be just as fixated upon obtaining mammon. "Don't worry. Be happy" is easy to say when you have plenty of money in the bank; when your job or business is secure; and when all the bills are paid in full. But unfortunately, that is not the way most of us live. Most of the people in this world live "hand to mouth", not knowing from one day, week, or month to the next if they will be able to feed their family. If there is drought, flood, or famine hunger will surely follow and the farmer may not be able to feed his family until the next year. War, or economic disaster can strike any nation at any time and wipe out a lifetime of savings in a matter of moments. This world is filled with uncertainty and the devil knows how to destroy a heart with worry, doubt and fear. Jesus understood that the only solution to not being overcome with fear is to trust fully in God:

"Therefore I tell you, do not worry about your life, what you will eat or drink; or about your body, what you will wear. Is not life more important

than food, and the body more important than clothes? Look at the birds of the air; they do not sow or reap or store away in barns, and yet your heavenly Father feeds them. Are you not much more valuable than they? Who of you by worrying can add a single hour to his life? And why do you worry about clothes? See how the lilies of the field grow. They do not labor or spin. Yet I tell you that not even Solomon in all his splendor was dressed like one of these. If that is how God clothes the grass of the field, which is here today and tomorrow is thrown into the fire, will he not much more clothe you, O you of little faith? So do not worry, saying, 'What shall we eat?' or 'What shall we drink?' or 'What shall we wear?' For the pagans run after all these things, and your heavenly Father knows that you need them. But seek first his kingdom and his righteousness, and all these things will be given to you as well. Therefore do not worry about tomorrow, for tomorrow will worry about itself. Each day has enough trouble of its own." Matthew 6:25-34 (NIV)

It is the Lord's desire to release us from all worries of this life. At the heart of a greedy person is the lack of faith in God's provision. If we trust God's generosity towards us, and believe His provision will be for us tomorrow, then we are released from the hold money and possessions have over us. Many people who might otherwise give their lives in service to God are prevented from doing so because they are so caught up in the pursuit of worldly wealth that they cannot see a better life of service to God. Still others refuse to give even the smallest amount to help others because they worry, "If I give too generously to others, what shall I eat?" and "How will I pay my bills?" Jesus taught that in the kingdom of heaven, the issue is not self-survival, but self-sacrifice to help others. The only way this is possible is to trust God completely to take care of our every need.

9. *You shall not give false testimony* (Ex. 20:16; Deut. 5:20). God's word is trustworthy and true. If it were not, chaos and confusion would abound in the kingdom of heaven because we would not know from one day to the next if God would contradict or countermand a previous command. One day we might be in God's favor and the next, find ourselves under His curse even though we were following what He had already written. God often bound Himself by an oath, not because He could not be trusted to keep

His word, but in concession to our unbelief. It follows then, that God's people must reflect the character of the God they serve and be faithful and true in word as well as deed.

"Again, you have heard that it was said to the people long ago, 'Do not break your oath, but keep the oaths you have made to the Lord.' But I tell you, Do not swear at all: either by heaven, for it is God's throne; or by the earth, for it is his footstool; or by Jerusalem, for it is the city of the Great King. And do not swear by your head, for you cannot make even one hair white or black. Simply let your 'Yes' be 'Yes,' and your 'No,' 'No'; anything beyond this comes from the evil one." Matthew 5:33-37 (NIV)

Once again, Jesus makes it clear that man may judge by what is on the surface of things, but God looks at the heart. The Pharisees thought they could play tricks with God, and create legal loopholes to slip through a promise or commitment that they felt was too costly to keep, but they were only deceiving themselves. Our God is a God who sees into the heart of every man and nothing escapes the light of His word.

"Peter said, 'Explain the parable to us.'
'Are you still so dull?" Jesus asked them.
'Don't you see that whatever enters the mouth goes into the stomach and then out of the body? But the things that come out of the mouth come from the heart, and these make a man 'unclean.' For out of the heart come evil thoughts, murder, adultery, sexual immorality, theft, false testimony, slander. These are what make a man 'unclean'; but eating with unwashed hands does not make him 'unclean.'" Matthew 15:15-20 (NIV)

10. ***You shall not covet* (Ex. 20:17; Deut. 5:21).** Murder, adultery, divorce, swearing falsely, revenge seeking, and conflicts between nations, races, and families – all have their roots sunk deep into the bitter waters of covetousness. Jesus knew this and addressed each issue in His sermons in the context of the necessity of having a right heart of obedience to God and forgiveness towards others that truly fulfills the letter and spirit of the law (Note Matthew 5:19-48).

Jesus' encounter with a man in the crowd that wanted Jesus to force his brother to divide the inheritance with him (Luke 12:13-34) is indicative of Jesus' teachings concerning the destructiveness of covetousness (compare with Matthew 6:19-34). At that point, Jesus took the opportunity to warn us against covetousness based upon the fact that "one's life does not consist in the abundance of the things he possesses."

Jesus immediately followed His warning with the parable of the rich man who kept building bigger and bigger barns to store his ever increasing yields of crops. The rich man said to himself "Soul, you have many goods laid up for many years; take your ease; eat, drink, and be merry." But God said to him, "Fool! This night your soul will be required of you." The rich man was asked, "whose will those things be which you have provided?" The warning is clear: those who lay up treasures for themselves in this world will have nothing to show for it; in the end it is only those heavenly blessings that are eternal.

Jesus strengthened His teaching on materialism even further when He turned to His disciples and instructed them not to worry about their life, what to eat, or clothes wear because "Life is more than food, and the body is more than clothing." Jesus uses examples from nature about ravens and lilies of the field as examples of how the Father will feed and clothe His people of faith. "And do not seek what you should eat or what you should drink, nor have an anxious mind. For all these things the nations of the world seek after, and your Father knows that you need these things. But seek the kingdom of God, and all these things shall be added to you." Jesus closed this teaching session on materialism assuring His "little flock" that it is the Father's will to give them the kingdom. Citizens of the kingdom are called to a radical lifestyle concerning possession. Rather than accumulate bigger and bigger houses to hold more and more possessions, Jesus urges us to sell what you have in excess and give to the poor. By putting our treasures in heaven, we are in essence providing for ourselves "money bags which do not grow old" and "treasure in the heavens that does not fail, where neither thief approaches nor moth destroys." Jesus' entire teaching covetousness in Luke 12:13-34 can be summed up, "For where your treasure is, there your heart will be also."

A Summary of Jesus' Teachings on the Law in the Kingdom Of God

Jesus' teachings on the Law far exceeded the demands of the scribes and the Pharisees: *"be perfect, as your heavenly Father is perfect"* (Matt. 5:48). Everywhere He went, Jesus taught how the righteousness that the Law called for was of a very different nature than the righteousness exhibited by the religious elite of the day (Matt. 5:20). Jesus rightly taught the Mosaic Law: that its regulations and basic principles were intended to reveal God's moral character and inspire men to be like Him. The Law was not given to bring salvation, but was given to drive men back into a right relationship with God through repentance and faith in God's saving grace where the inner transformation, which only God can work, can take place.

Therefore, in the Kingdom of God the issue in the Old Testament law of murder was not so much the act of violence as the anger that led to it. The issue was not where, when or how to make an offering, but was bringing an offering with the right attitude of heart – a heart that desires reconciliation between sinful men and a holy God. The issue was not so much the act of adultery as it was the lust that can led a husband astray and causes men to treat women as sexual objects rather than persons. The issue in the law of divorce was not when it was permissible, but was one of loyalty and commitment to the marriage covenant under God. The issue in the law concerning oaths was not when an oath might be broken, but was the essential integrity and honesty of the individual making the vow before God and men. The issue in the "eye for an eye" principle was not the right of the individual to receive equal compensation for an injury, but was the unrighteous demand for revenge when forgiveness is called for. In the kingdom of heaven the call to love one's neighbor does not permit someone to hate anyone outside of the kingdom.

Therefore, all of Jesus' teachings on Old Testament law can be best summed up in His answer to the scribe who asked him which is the greatest commandment of the law:

"Jesus replied: 'Love the Lord your God with all your heart and with all your soul and with all your mind.' This is the first and greatest commandment. And the second is like it: 'Love your neighbor as yourself.' All the Law and the Prophets hang on these two commandments." Matthew 22:37-40

FREDERICK OSBORN

6.
"The Kingdom Parables of Jesus"
Jesus Teaches the Mysteries of the Kingdom

LESSON OUTLINE

The purpose of this lesson is to examine Jesus' teachings in parables. To answer why He chose the method of the parable and what were His essential teachings on the kingdom of heaven.

- The mission of the parable
- The Key parable of the sower and the soils
- The Kingdom parables of Matthew 13
- Other important themes from the Parables of Jesus

THE MISSION OF THE PARABLE

"Give ear, O my people, to my teaching; incline your ears to the words of my mouth! I will open my mouth in a parable; I will utter dark sayings from of old, things that we have heard and known, that our fathers have told us. We will not hide them from their children, but tell to the coming generation the glorious deeds of the LORD, and his might, and the wonders that he has done." Psalm 78:1-4 (ESV)

Jesus' parables should be understood in context of the events leading up to Matthew 13. Matthew chapters 10 – 12 give the clearest description of the building tension between Jesus and the religious leaders. This tension reaches a boiling point when the Pharisees accuse Jesus of using satanic power to cast out demons (Matt. 12:24). The direct approach of His sermons and His miracles had failed to move the multitudes in His direction, but His time had not yet come (Matt. 17:22-23; Luke 18:31-22; John 7:8). His disciples had to be made ready for His departure; there were still miraculous signs that needed to be done to seal beyond a doubt that the Messiah had come. It is equally important to understand that Jesus' parables were intended to reveal truth to His disciples while hiding the same truth from those who were unwilling or unable to receive it.

The nation of Israel would not submit to Jesus as their King. They wanted the loaves and fishes, the healings, and the miracles, but they refused to submit to Jesus the Lamb of God. Because they refused to have any part of Jesus (John 6:25-58) He would no longer offer Himself to the nation as their Lord and King. The Scribes, Pharisees, and Sadducees, representing the entire religious system of the Jews, had seen His miracles and had heard His sermons, but still they rejected Jesus as the rightful Messiah. The time had come to speak in parables so that outsiders and "the rest" – those who refused to believe – would not be able to hear or understand the mysteries of the kingdom that are only for Jesus' disciples to hear and understand (Matt. 13:10-15).

So Jesus started down the road that would lead Him to Calvary; the first step was to narrow His message to only those who were willing to listen and obey His teaching on the kingdom of God: "…many people saw the miraculous signs he was doing and believed in his name. But Jesus would not entrust himself to them, for he knew all men. He did not need man's testimony about man, for he knew what was in a man." John 2:23b – 25 (NIV)

Matthew chapter 12 closes with Jesus making a declaration about His true family. From this time forward He would only reveal the mysterious workings of His kingdom to "whoever does God's will" – His "brother and sister and mother" (Matt 12:50). "God keeps secrets in order to reveal them at the proper time to those for whom they are intended. At the right time He unveils them to those whose hearts are seeking after Him. The power of God's Word is such that it can reach those at whom it is aimed and still be hidden from those who are not receptive to it. Parables are designed like this, to reach some and keep others in the dark." Dr. R. T. Kendall, *The Complete Guide to the Parables,* Chosen Books, Grand Rapids, MI, © 2004, p.14. After His resurrection, Jesus commanded His disciples to go into the entire world and preach the Good News, but the mysteries of the kingdom are reserved only for those who have committed themselves fully to the King of kings. Immediately following this declaration, Matthew introduces the first and most important parable about the kingdom that Jesus taught.

Parables in the Bible

The Old and New Testaments contain two hundred and fifty parables, emblems or figures of speech employed by a variety of authors. In each case, the parables of the Bible – especially those used by the Lord Jesus Christ – were intended to communicate or reinforce divine truths. Jesus recognized that the parabolic method of presenting truth was well established in Jewish literature, and He incorporated the parable into His teachings, "and without a parable he did not speak to them." However, Jesus elevated this method of teaching to its highest level, and contributed His unique parables to reinforce the efficacy of this style of spiritual teaching.

A careful study of Christ's parables indicates they are far more than simple pastoral stories designed to help humble and uneducated peasants understand His teachings. The parables of Jesus are powerful word-pictures intended to reveal the mysteries of the kingdom of heaven to those who are open to hear from God, while simultaneously hiding these same truths from those whose hearts are too hard, rocky or thorny to hear and receive the Word of God plainly spoken. A parable has been described as "an outward symbol of an inward reality". And Jesus was the master at drawing the power out of every parable He told. "For since the creation of the world God's invisible qualities--his eternal power and divine nature--have been clearly seen, being understood from what has been made, so that men are without excuse." Romans 1:20

"All things in Nature are prophetic outlines of Divine operations, God not merely speaking parables but doing them." - Tertullian

To be successful, a parable must express the perfect harmony that exists between the natural and the spiritual world in narrative form, and must be true to nature or to human relationships. A parable should also impart meaningful spiritual truth to the mind of the hearer using material objects to express those spiritual truths. Parables reveal that nature is much more than what it seems. Through His parables, Jesus reveals the spiritual reality (hidden from the unspiritual materialists) that this temporal world, which we see, is in fact a reflection of or template for His spiritual, heavenly kingdom that we do not see. Both kingdoms operate according to a particular set of laws. Jesus' parables are not mere mental imagery or window dressing for Divine instruction. The parables are points of comparison between the spiritual kingdom of God and nature – bearing testimony to essential spiritual truths.

Generally speaking, the root word used for "parable" means "to set side by side," and indicates the idea of comparing two distinct objects. A parable of the kingdom is literally placing beside for comparison, earthly truths with heavenly truths – a similitude, or an illustration of one subject to another. Heaven and Earth are the work of the One God; and in this lesson we will discover that The Parables of the Kingdom may in fact be "earthly in form, but in truth they are heavenly in spirit." Parables act like mirrors that superimpose the reflected images of the visible, natural world God created over the invisible, supernatural kingdom of heaven, so that "those who have ears to hear "may discover a deeper spiritual meaning to their existence, increase in intimacy with the Father, and grow in faithful obedience to Jesus Christ who is "the image of the invisible God, the firstborn over all creation" (Colossians 1:15).

"When our Lord appeared among men as a Teacher He took possession of the parable and honored it by making it His own, by using it as the vehicle for the highest truth of all." Herbert Lockyer, All the Parables of the Bible, Zondervan, Grand Rapids, MI, © 1963, p.10 Parables are a unique form of spiritual teaching in that they both attract and sift out those who hear them. Not everyone who came to listen to Jesus' sermons was receptive to His words. Only those who had "eyes to see and ears to hear" – those who were genuinely drawn to God – would diligently dig and seek out the deeper spiritual meaning of a parable. A parable is intended to arouse the hearer to seek out the Lord of the parable, and have Him reveal the hidden meaning to them. Once the parable is fully understood, it is sure to be remembered long after the main body of the sermon is forgotten. The parables Jesus used were designed to hold the attention of those who listened to Him, to excite their consciences, and to inspire them to respond in obedience to what they had heard and understood. Parables are "reservoirs of truth," containing powerful word pictures. Using the language of symbols, Jesus, the Master Painter, composed these pictures, and created enduring images to communicate Divine truths that would be preserved and passed down from generation to generation.

Many Bible scholars have said that there are two extremes to be avoided when interpreting parables: one is to make too much of them – the other is to make too little of them. Although each parable contains valuable lessons of a spiritual nature, not every word of the parable is charged with hidden meaning. All of the parables may be for us, but not everything within a parable is about us. It is essential to understand the parable within the context of the sermon, as well as within the broader, universal context of the present reality of the eternal Kingdom of God that Jesus came to reveal. If we are transparent and sincere in our quest for truth about the kingdom of heaven, we can rely on the Holy Spirit to reveal to us Christ's intended meaning for each of His parables. S.P. Cadman wrote, "In these parables we can discern the unconquerable democracy of Christ's Christianity as a manifestation of redeeming love in which the whole human race is included. By them the peoples of East and West are made aware of god's fatherly love, transcendent grace, everlasting mercy, and inerrant justice." The Parables of Jesus, Testament Books, New York, NY, © 1999, P.18

INTRODUCTION TO JESUS' PARABLES OF THE KINGDOM

"Have you understood all these things?" Jesus asked. "Yes," they replied. He said to them, "Therefore every teacher of the law who has been instructed about the kingdom of heaven is like the owner of a house who brings out of his storeroom new treasures as well as old." Matthew 13:51, 52 (NIV)

The parables, emblems, and figures of speech said to be used by the Lord Jesus during His earthly ministry vary in number from commentary to commentary. Depending upon exactly how a parable is defined, the parables of Jesus number from twenty-five to seventy-five. In the strictest definition of this term used by some Christian theologians, the number is about thirty. (As a point of reference I have listed a total of thirty-one in Appendix Four.) In this lesson we will highlight a few of those parables that will help us address major teachings of Jesus.

In a way, it could be said that every parable Jesus spoke is either directly or indirectly related to the kingdom of God He came to reveal. Some commentaries have taken the words of Matthew 13:34 – "without a parable, He did not speak to them" – quite literally and have attempted to cast His entire oral ministry in parabolic form. However, only those parables that are clearly understood to be speaking directly about the kingdom of God will be examined in this study.

Jesus, the Master Preacher, was wise enough to recognize that men would not easily forget the principles of the kingdom He taught in His sermons if they were couched in the form that is the easiest and most surely remembered – that of the story parable. The kingdom parables have an enduring quality in that they not only relate to the people, places and things of the ancient world of the Old and New Testaments, but they reflect the same world in which men live, suffer, and are tempted today. For centuries, theologians have recognized how these stories lift men's minds above their selfish ambitions; enlighten those who are otherwise ignorant of pure Christianity; teach others to transcend social customs and the traditions of men and live by God's Word; and they serve to turn the sinful back to God. These parables of the kingdom not only reveal the present reality of the kingdom Jesus brought to His disciples, but they reveal His compassion for the lost individuals who are today earnestly seeking God for salvation.

Many who study these parables seek to discover deeper symbolic, prophetic, or eschatological meanings behind each and every word. However, perhaps the most practical way of understanding the parables of Jesus is to read them for their own merits, searching for what may be applied in our personal lives as citizens of God's kingdom. Throughout His earthly ministry, Jesus was concerned for those who came to Him, "like sheep without a shepherd." His teachings were intended to encourage and enlighten those who listened, and revealed principles of the kingdom that were intended to be applied to everyday life. The true worth of Jesus' parables do not depend upon some new and varied truths that we are able to extract from them, but their worth is found in their progressive and practical application of kingdom principles into our daily lives.

"And Jesus, when He came out, saw a great multitude and was moved with compassion for them, because they were like sheep not having a shepherd. So He began to teach them many things." Mark 6:34

The parables Jesus taught demonstrated that He was fully acquainted with the daily lives of the people all around Him. He understood the farmer who sowed the seed, dressed and tilled the earth, and reaped the harvest in its season. Jesus was at home with those who tended the vineyards; He knew their times of reaping the fruit of the vine, and of the fig tree. Jesus' parables showed that He knew what a day's wage would bring, and that He could relate to those who had to work hard for a living. Jesus moved with ease between the rich and poor, royalty and paupers, Pharisees and tax collectors – the words of His parables were designed to communicate the principles of His kingdom to all people. No one is excluded from the kingdom of heaven, except for those who refused to believe and receive His offer of entrance into the kingdom.

Why Jesus Began to Teach in Parables

The Gospels of Matthew, Mark and Luke record for us the beginning of Jesus' parabolic kingdom ministry. In Matthew 13, Mark 4, and Luke 8 & 13 we see a shift in Jesus' public sermons. Throughout His earthly ministry, Jesus greatly emphasized the importance of His words: "I tell you the truth, whoever hears my word and believes him who sent me has eternal life and will not be condemned; he has crossed over from death to life" John 5:24 (NIV). Because Jesus' words were as much an expression of His divine authority as were His many heavenly signs, wonders, and great miracles, it was significant when He changed direction in His teaching ministry and introduced a new and unexpected teaching method to the large crowds that heard Him speak. This change in His public teaching ministry was not lost on His disciples. Mark 4:10, and Luke 8:9 convey the same thought: that the disciples recognized that Jesus was withholding the plain meaning of His words, and that they would have to ask Him privately, what His words truly meant. But Matthew 13:10 adds more significance to the moment by including the specific question asked by His disciples, "Why do you speak to the people in parables?"

The disciples' question implied that they recognized Jesus was introducing a new and unexpected teaching method to the large crowds that came to hear Him speak. By this point in time, Jesus had been preaching and teaching all around the region. He had taught at the Temple, in synagogues, and out in the open for months, but before this time, His sermons were clear and direct. Jesus used symbols, metaphors, and allegories throughout His teaching ministry to illustrate particular points He was making (for example Matthew 7:15-27), but in Matthew 13, Mark 4, and Luke 8 & 13, the Parable becomes the heart of His message and no explanation is given, except in private to His disciples. Jesus' answer to the question, "why parables?" explained His purpose for teaching in parables:

"He replied, 'The knowledge of the secrets of the kingdom of heaven has been given to you, but not to them. Whoever has will be given more, and he will have an abundance. Whoever does not have, even what he has will be taken from him. This is why I speak to them in parables: 'Though seeing, they do not see; though hearing, they do not hear or understand.'" Matthew 13:11-13 (NIV)

"Jesus spoke all these things to the crowd in parables; he did not say anything to them without using a parable. So was fulfilled what was spoken through the prophet: 'I will open my mouth in parables, I will utter things hidden since the creation of the world.'" Matthew 13:34-35 (NIV)

"He told them, 'The secret of the kingdom of God has been given to you. But to those on the outside everything is said in parables so that, "'they may be ever seeing but never perceiving, and ever hearing but never understanding; otherwise they might turn and be forgiven!'"'" Mark 4:11-12 (NIV)

"He said, 'The knowledge of the secrets of the kingdom of God has been given to you, but to others I speak in parables, so that, "'though seeing, they may not see; though hearing, they may not understand.'" Luke 8:10 (NIV)

The fact that three of the gospel writers included Jesus' explanation of why He began to speak in parables highlights the significance and uniqueness of these parables concerning the kingdom of God. There was a prophetic aspect to His use of these parables; the prophets of Israel foretold the Messiah's parabolic teaching ministry, and many of the parables contained prophetic messages for those who would follow Jesus until the end of the age. Jesus explained to His followers that, on the one hand, He used the parables to reveal truth to some people; but on the other hand, He used those same parables to hide truth from others.

"But blessed are your eyes for they see, and your ears for they hear; for assuredly, I say to you that many prophets and righteous men desired to see what you see, and did not see it, and to hear what you hear, an did not hear it."
Matthew 13:16 (NIV)

It is difficult for those who have an evangelistic mindset to grasp the idea that a lot of what Jesus taught was intended to be hidden from "those on the outside", but that is precisely what Jesus said (Matthew 13:11; Mark 4:11; Luke 8:10). Of course, we must never forget that the whole idea of the Gospel is for as many people as possible to hear it, so that those who are on the "outside" of the kingdom will believe and come "inside" where they will discover the same mysteries of the kingdom that have been revealed to the church. Therefore, we must be wise in what we preach to the unsaved because, as Jesus pointed out, not everyone is ready to hear and receive the word of the kingdom.

"I am writing you these instructions so that, if I am delayed, you will know how people ought to conduct themselves in God's household, which is the church of the living God, the pillar and foundation of the truth. Beyond all question, the mystery of godliness is great: He appeared in a body, was vindicated by the Spirit,

was seen by angels, was preached among the nations, was believed on in the world, was taken up in glory." 1 Timothy 3:14-16 (NIV)

Psalm 25:14 says, "The secret of the Lord is with those who fear Him, and He will show them His covenant" (KJV). The Holy Spirit, through the church, reveals the mysteries of the gospel of the kingdom – including the plan of God's redemption for both Jew and Gentile through Jesus Christ. Paul stated it this way:

"...we speak of God's secret wisdom, a wisdom that has been hidden and that God destined for our glory before time began. None of the rulers of this age understood it, for if they had, they would not have crucified the Lord of glory. However, as it is written: 'No eye has seen, no ear has heard, no mind has conceived what God has prepared for those who love him' – but God has revealed it to us by his Spirit. The Spirit searches all things, even the deep things of God." 1 Corinthians 2:7-10

It is important to note at this point that Jesus was not implying that the mysteries of the kingdom are complicated, recondite, and hard to understand. The Greek term used by Mark sheds more light on Jesus' intended meaning. In the Greek, this word mystery has a technical meaning that indicates something which is quite unintelligible to the person who has not been properly initiated and instructed its meaning, but is perfectly clear to the person who has been introduced to the rudiments or principles of what is being communicated. William Barclay in his commentary on Mark 4:10-12, said this: "In New Testament times in the pagan world, one of the great features of popular religion was what were called the mystery religions. These religions promised communion with and even identity with some god, whereby all the terrors of life and of death would be taken away. Nearly all these mystery religions were based on the story of some god who had suffered and died and risen again; they nearly all found their expression in the form of passion plays... As the play was played out, the worshipper felt at one with the god both in suffering and in triumph, and passed through death to immortality by union with the god. The point is that to the uninitiated the whole thing would have been meaningless; but to the initiated the thing was full of meaning which they had been taught to see." Understanding this context of the mysteries helps to explain the difficult meaning of the verse that follows Mark 4:11 (In his account, Matthew specifically references the passage from Isaiah 6:9-10 and repeats more of the passage than in Mark).

By the time Jesus started His earthly ministry, the people had become like Israel in the days of Isaiah, the "people's heart has become calloused; they hardly hear with their ears, and they have closed their eyes". Jesus began his public ministry by preaching, "The time is fulfilled, and the kingdom of God is at hand: repent ye, and believe the gospel." Mark 1:15 (KJV). But He saw that many of the Jews were unable to comprehend the gospel He was telling them to believe in. The expectations were blinding the eyes of the Jews who were looking for a conquering, warrior Messiah who would drive out the hated Roman occupiers; and who would march into Jerusalem and establish an exclusively Jewish, Messianic kingdom ruled by the righteous few. They could not comprehend the Lamb/Messiah who came to seek and save the lost; who opened prison doors to release those in spiritual bondage, and who opened the doors of heaven to all who would lay down their burdens of sin and shame and come to Him for salvation. Jesus' audience would readily embrace the kingdom of their expectations, but Jesus would not allow them to enter the kingdom under false pretenses. Therefore, He chose to hide the reality of the presence and power of the kingdom from those who were not ready to receive it.

The modern application for preachers, teachers, and evangelists of our day might be: make sure that your audience understands the foundational truths of our salvation in Christ before you start telling them of all the promises of God that will come to those whose hearts are fully surrendered to Christ. All too often, Christians are quick to promise unsaved people that all of their prayers will be answered, all their problems will be solved, and that they will have unconditional health and prosperity if only they will say the sinner's prayer and declare themselves "Christian". Who wouldn't come to God that way: "With every eye closed, and every head bowed… now repeat after me"? Matthew 13:11-17; Mark 4:11-12; and Luke 8:10 mean that Jesus would not accept half-baked followers who did not truly know Him (Matthew 7:21-23), or followers who would melt away at the first signs of trials and temptations that must come to every believer.

THE KEY PARABLE OF "THE SOWER AND THE SOILS"

"Then Jesus said to them, 'Don't you understand this parable? How then will you understand any parable?'" Mark 4:13 (NIV)

It bears repeating that most of Jesus' parables should be understood in context of the events leading up to Matthew 13. Matthew chapters 10 – 12 give the clearest description of the building tension between Jesus and the religious leaders. This tension reaches a boiling point when the Pharisees accuse Jesus of using satanic power to cast out demons (Matt. 12:24). The direct approach of His sermons and His miracles had failed to move the multitudes in His direction, but His time had not yet come (Matt. 17:22-23; Luke 18:31-22; John 7:8). His disciples had to be made ready for His departure; there were still miraculous signs that needed to be done to seal beyond a doubt that the Messiah had come.

The nation of Israel would not submit to Jesus as their King; Jesus would no longer offer Himself to the nation as their Lord and Messiah. They had seen His miracles and had listened to His sermons, but still they would not believe. Now was the time to speak in parables so that "outsiders" and "the rest" – those who refused to believe – would not be able to hear or understand the mysteries of the kingdom that are only for Jesus' disciples to hear and understand. So Jesus started down the road that would lead Him to Calvary; the first step was to narrow His message to only those who were willing to listen and obey His teaching on the kingdom of God: "…many people saw the miraculous signs he was doing and believed in his name. But Jesus would not entrust himself to them, for he knew all men. He did not need man's testimony about man, for he knew what was in a man." John 2:23b – 25 (NIV)

Matthew chapter 12 closes with Jesus making a declaration about His true family. From this time forward He would only reveal the mysterious workings of His kingdom to "whoever does God's will" – His "brother and sister and mother" (Matt 12:50). (Jesus commanded His disciples after His resurrection to go into the entire world and preach the Good News, but the mysteries of the kingdom are reserved only for those who have committed themselves fully to the King of kings.) Immediately following this declaration, Matthew introduces the first and most important parable about the kingdom that Jesus taught.

In this opening parable of the sower, Jesus reveals to His disciples and to all spiritual "sowers" who would come after them (the teachers, preachers, missionaries and evangelists) why not everyone who hears this gospel of the kingdom will respond to it. Matthew 13:3-9, & 18-23; Mark 4:3-9, & 13-20; Luke 8:5-8, & 11-15 each record a slight variation of this key parable. It is a great help to study these passages together. Note that there are three key elements in this parable: the sower, the seed and the soils. Note also Jesus' explanation for the meaning of each one.

Before going any further in this study of the parables of Jesus, it is important to emphasize that the immense value of these parables will be lost on anyone who only does a surface reading or quick study of these parables. The literary form of the parable was nothing new in Jesus' day; but what was new was how Jesus infused each of these parables with deep spiritual insights. The Holy Spirit will reveal fresh insights into these parables if we meditate upon their meanings and ask for His guidance. This study of the parables offers only a beginning, but it by no means gives the absolute meaning to any of them. The Holy Spirit will reveal more to you if you ask.

The Sower

"Both in the natural and the spiritual realms, God works majestically alone, and as the Sower, is untiring in His task. He knows full well that although much seed falls by the wayside, ultimately, a great harvest will be His when 'the kingdoms of this world will become the kingdoms of our Lord and Christ.'" Herbert Lockyer, All the Parables of Jesus, Zondervan, Grand Rapids, MI, © 1963, p. 175. Jesus was speaking to an audience that was very well acquainted with the images of the Jewish Scriptures. The prophets of old used the images of sowing and seeds to convey the idea of the Lord as a "sower" (Jeremiah 31:27-28; Hosea 2:23; Zechariah 10:9). So when Jesus revealed to His disciples the hidden meaning, "The one who sowed the good seed is the Son of Man" (Matthew 13:37), it was not hard for them to understand. Every Christian should be a kingdom sower.

The Old and New Testaments speak of the Father and the Son as kingdom sowers. The implication of the Scriptures is that the Holy Spirit works with the divine Sower to accomplish His task. The Holy Spirit is the "Divine Wind" that lifts and scatters the sons of the kingdom throughout the world: "The wind blows wherever it pleases. You hear its sound, but you cannot tell where it comes from or where it is going. So it is with everyone born of the Spirit" (John 3:8)

The Seed

Mark identifies the seed as the "Word"; but Luke tells us that the Word is not just any word, but it is the "Word of God". When we examine Matthew 13:19, we learn that it is not just any Word of God, but it is a specific Word: the word of the kingdom. Peter would later write: "For you have been born again, not of perishable seed, but of imperishable, through the living and enduring word of God... And this is the word that was preached to you." 1 Peter 1:23, 25b (NIV)

This parable reminds us that we are sowers of the kingdom; and like the farmer in his field, we must shamelessly and liberally cast the imperishable Word of this gospel of the kingdom into the hearts of men. As Paul said, "I am not ashamed of the gospel, because it is the power of God for the salvation of everyone who believes..." (Romans 1:16a; note also Romans 10:14-15).

The Soils

"He will be like a tree planted by the water that sends out its roots by the stream. It does not fear when heat comes; its leaves are always green. It has no worries in a year of drought and never fails to bear fruit." Jeremiah 17:8 (NIV)

Matthew 13:3-9; Mark 4:3-8; and Luke 8:5-8 all identify the same four soils that Jesus described in this parable. When we combine all three accounts, we get a richer and fuller understanding of the mystery Jesus wanted to reveal. *The Wayside Soil* represents the ones who hear the word of the kingdom, but do not understand it. *The Rocky Soil* represents the hearts of those who hear the word, they immediately receive it with joy and gladness – yet they have no root in themselves, so endure or believe only for a while. *The Thorny Soil* are the ones who hear the word, and start to grow, but the cares of this world, the deceitfulness of riches, the desires for other things, and the pleasures of life entering in choke the word and it becomes unfruitful, they bring no fruit to maturity, and therefore become unfruitful. The Good Soil represents the good heart that is able to understand the Word, accept it, and keep (obey) it. Those with the hearts produce (bear fruit) with patience; some thirty fold, some sixty, some a hundred.

As we meditate upon the meaning of the Parable of the Sower and the Soils, we should be moved and strive not only to be fruitful, but also to sow generously the seed of the word of the kingdom if we are to expect an abundant harvest to the glory of God. Jesus told this parable to remind His disciples to pay close attention to the conditions and attitudes of the hearts of their hearers. We are not to be discouraged when anyone does not understand God's word plainly spoken to him or her, since their heart may have become too hard to receive the good seed sown upon it. And like seed sown on the path, it will be trampled down, allowing Satan to snatch away the truth before it has chance to be received. It warns us not to take for granted those who immediately receive the "good news" with joy and gladness, since underneath the surface of the heart there may be stony places of rebellion or resistance to the fullness of God's truth; those stony places attract the heat of judgment and/or persecution and if those rocks are left undisturbed they will cause the Holy Spirit to evaporate like moisture in rocky soil. This parable also warns us to watch out for those worldly entanglements that tend to choke out the word of the kingdom before it reaches maturity and our spiritual life becomes fruitless. Finally, through this parable Jesus gives us a vision of encouragement and strength to persevere in our sowing, knowing that the good seed of this gospel of the kingdom sown into a good heart, well-prepared by the work of the Holy Spirit will produce an abundant harvest for the Lord, some thirty, some sixty and some one hundred fold.

PARABLES OF THE KINGDOM IN MATTHEW 13

PARABLES OF THE KINGDOM IN MATTHEW 13 UNEXPECTED CHARACTERISTICS		
PARABLE	EXPECTED FORM	UNEXPECTED FORM
1. Sower 13:3-9	Messiah turns all Israel and all nations to Himself	Individuals respond differently to the Word's invitation. Not all are saved.
2. Wheat/tares 13:24-30 37-43	All sinners are destroyed and righteous rule over the world with their King	The kingdom's citizens are among the men of the world, growing together till God's harvest time.
3. Mustard seed 13:31-32	Kingdom begins in majestic glory.	The kingdom begins in insignificance; its greatness comes as a surprise.
4. Leaven 13:33	Only the righteous can enter the kingdom; the sinners are excluded.	The kingdom is implanted in a different "raw material" and grows to fill the whole person with righteousness.
5. Hidden treasure 13:44	Kingdom is public and evident to all.	Kingdom is hidden and for individual "purchase."
6. Priceless pearl 13:45-46	Kingdom brings all valued things to men.	Kingdom demands abandonment of all other values (cf. 6:33)
7. Dragnet 13:47-50	Kingdom begins with initial separation of righteous and unrighteous.	Kingdom ends with final separation of the unrighteous from the righteous.

In the parable of the Wheat and the Tares Jesus again illustrates a divine principle of the kingdom using the familiar elements of a sower, seed and soil. Central to this parable is the spiritual conflict between good and evil – between God and Satan – and the separation of the evil from the good that must take place at the end of the age. Once again Jesus explains the meaning of this parable only to a select few disciples who came to Him in private and specifically asked Him to explain it to them.

Another important point of this parable and of all the kingdom parables immediately following was to contrast the unexpected and expected forms of the kingdom of heaven. An important element in many of the Lord's kingdom parables was the unexpected quality of the kingdom. The chart above (page 183) lists the parables of the kingdom in Matthew 13 and shows the expected and unexpected forms of the kingdom revealed in each one of them.

"He told them another parable: 'The kingdom of heaven is like a mustard seed, which a man took and planted in his field.'" Matthew 13:31

In the parables of the kingdom recorded in Matthew 13, Jesus presented the kingdom of heaven as a living, growing organism; it is the eternal, invisible, spiritual church, present throughout history but hidden and mysterious until revealed by the Spirit of truth – the Holy Spirit. The kingdom is the priceless pearl and the Hidden treasure that requires all to acquire it. The church in this world is an organization; it is the external, visible, physical church, but its power is derived from the invisible, eternal kingdom of heaven. The kingdom is like that "leaven" hidden in three measures of meal; it is the Holy Spirit working from within to transform those who have been born again. Jesus' parables of the kingdom reveal that the church, established in this world on the day of Pentecost (Acts 2), is expanding to reach every tribe, every tongue and every nation in the world.

A side-by-side comparison of this parable from Matthew 13:31-32; Mark 4:30-32; and Luke 13:18-19 will reveal Jesus' understanding of the strength and power of the kingdom that begins in insignificance, but grows until it extends its reach to the ends of the earth.

The minute size of the mustard seed had become proverbial long before Jesus used it to describe His kingdom. At this time, the mustard seed was considered the smallest discernable weight that could be weighed in a balance. Because of its size, the seed came to symbolize small or humble beginnings, and the smallest measurable particle. Understood in context of His other parables of the kingdom it is easy to discern in this parable that it is "the Son of Man" (and all those laborers in the harvest who follow His footsteps) that sowed the mustard seed, which is the smallest of seeds.

The image of the great tree in this parable reflects Daniel's vision: "These are the visions I saw while lying in my bed: I looked, and there before me stood a tree in the middle of the land. Its height was enormous. The tree grew large and strong and its top touched the sky; it was visible to the ends of the earth. Its leaves were beautiful, its fruit abundant, and on it was food for all. Under it the beasts of the field found shelter, and the birds of the air lived in its branches; from it every creature was fed." Daniel 4:10-12 (NIV). The prophets Ezekiel (17:22-24) and Isaiah (11:1-2) contributed visions of the messianic kingdom to come using the same imagery of a tree, which parallel Jesus' use of images that highlight the living, growing, and expanding organic nature of His kingdom.

Taken collectively, Jesus' parables reinforced the idea of the abundance and expanse of the Messianic kingdom that the Old Testament prophets were trying to communicate. At the same time, when these parables are interpreted within context of all of Jesus' teachings about the present reality of the kingdom of heaven, and the coming kingdom at the end of the age, the images in his parables affirm the Old Testament prophets' pictures of the bounty and expanse of the messianic kingdom that transforms all those who belong to it.

Compared to the power of Rome, the kingdom of heaven that Jesus spoke of in His public sermons and parables seemed weak and insignificant to those who knew the prophecies of old and were awaiting the promised Messiah and His kingdom. How could Jesus' small band followers compare with the mighty armies of the Empires of this world? And yet within a few years those few faithful disciples would be empowered by the Spirit to go forward and preach this gospel of the kingdom everywhere, turning the whole world upside down in the process (Acts 17:6). The tiny seeds of the kingdom sown by the Son of Man in His parables at the dawning of the church age have become a great tree that today provides shelter and rest for people of every nation throughout the world. And still it keeps growing as the citizens of His kingdom continue to obey His commandment and preach the Good News of the kingdom throughout the whole earth.

These parables of the kingdom give hope and solace to millions of Christians today who see the forces of this world arrayed against them. How can so few, with no armies, no weapons of mass destruction, and no earthly wealth or power to speak of, overcome in the end? It is only by the invisible, irreversible, pervasive, persistent, and indestructible life-force of the kingdom that the church will prevail and thrive until the end of this age when God will reconcile all things, judge all things, and restore justice and true peace on earth and goodwill towards men. Until that day, the church is the manifestation of that kingdom. Christians are the sowers in the field, and the fishermen casting the net of the gospel of salvation into the nations to draw to Christ all who will come.

God calls His church to be occupied with preaching and teaching the good news of the Kingdom. Our participation in the work of the Kingdom is to draw all men and women to Christ and "make disciples of all the nations, baptizing them in the name of the Father and of the Son and of the Holy Spirit" (Matt. 28:19). The Lord also commands us to teach those who have entered into His kingdom to obey all of His commands (Matt. 28:20). Disciples of Jesus Christ are not charged with the duty of "casting out" or "weeding out" those we judge as unfit for the Kingdom. The entire purpose of the cross is to demonstrate God's unconditional love for all people and to make a way into the kingdom of heaven for all who will believe and receive His gracious offer. Those who have their minds set on judging who is and who is not fit for entry into the kingdom are out of step with God's will. The Pharisees were obsessed with excluding those they considered unworthy to be included in the community of Abraham's children. Jesus, on the other hand, made it clear in His parables that it is only for God and His angels to judge and that judgment will come at the end of the age and not before.

In His parables, and by His acts of salvation and forgiveness, Jesus affirmed what passages of Scripture like Daniel 12:1-3 and Revelation 20:11-15 said about the Messianic kingdom to come. His parables also describe:

- God's forgiveness, grace, and mercy (Matt. 18:23-25; Matt. 20:1-16; Luke 7:41-43; Luke 10:25-37; Matt. 18:12-14; Luke 15:4-7; Luke 15:8-10; Luke 15:11-32; Luke 18:1-8)

- The need for obedience, good stewardship over earthly affairs, and faithfulness (Matt. 21:28-32; Matt. 25:14-30; Luke 11:5-8; Luke 12:16-21; Luke 16:1-9; Luke 17:1-10; Luke 19:12-27)

- That the kingdom is always rejected by the wicked, but will always be open to all who respond to the Father's invitation (Matt. 21:33-46; Mark 12:1-12; Luke 20:9-19; Matt. 22:1-14; Luke 14:7-11; 12-14;16-24)

- That a time will come when grace will end and judgment will begin (Matt. 25:1-13; Luke 13:6-9; Luke 16:19-31; Luke 18:10-14; Matt. 31:46)

Jesus, the perfect Son of Man and Son of God gives us the assurance that at the End of the Age there will be no mistakes in judgment over who is "good" or "wheat" and who is "bad" or "tare". We should be thankful to God that our eternal destinies are not determined by the imperfect, subjective, and ever-changing judgments of men, but by the saving grace of God. "It has been pointed out that one of Jesus' greatest reasons for using parables was this – He wanted to persuade men to pass a judgment on things with which they were well acquainted, and then to compel them to transfer that judgment to something to whose significance they had been blind. This is exactly what Nathan did with David. He told him a story, whose meaning David saw with crystal clarity. On that situation which he saw so clearly David passed a judgment. 'Now,' said Nathan, 'take that judgment and apply it to yourself.' That was what Jesus was always doing in His parables. He told a story the meaning of which anyone could see, and the hearers could not help passing some kind of judgment even as the story was being told. Then Jesus demanded that they take that judgment and pass it on to something to which they had been blind. If we apply that principle to almost any of the parables, we will see that they are sudden vivid flashes, meant to make men see things which they were well able to see, but which either through deliberate blindness or through dullness of spirit they had never seen." William Barclay, *The Parables of Jesus*, Westminster John Knox Press, Louisville, KY, © 1970, pp.13-14

7.
The Miracles of Jesus
Jesus Authenticates His Ministry to the Nation by His Miracles

"Jesus performs a miracle and feeds 5,000 with five loaves and two fish"
By: Maria Clara (Used by Permission)

LESSON OUTLINE

The purpose of this lesson is to understand Jesus' miracle-working ministry as the Messiah to the Jewish nation.
- Jesus authenticated His ministry to the nation by His power over nature
- Jesus authenticated His ministry to the nation by His healing miracles

- Jesus authenticated His ministry to the nation by His power over demonic forces

"From that time on Jesus began to preach, 'Repent, for the kingdom of heaven is near.'" Matthew 4:17 (NIV)

THE MIRACLES OF JESUS

Through His public proclamation of the coming of the kingdom, Jesus offered Himself as the Messiah the nation of Israel was waiting and hoping for. In His kingdom sermons Jesus taught that God's people must acknowledge His authority and accept Him as the One who fulfilled the Old Testament Law and prophetic revelation of the King of the Jews or else they would continue down the wrong pathway marked out for them by the traditions taught by the scribes and the Pharisees. During this period, Christ told very few parables, but instead allowed His miracles to speak for Him. "Then Jesus went about all the cities and villages, teaching in their synagogues, and preaching the gospel of the kingdom, and healing every sickness and every disease among the people" Matthew 9:35 (NIV).

When we carefully study the miracles in the Gospels, we discover how Jesus used His miracles as a visible stamp to authenticate Himself as One who spoke with divine authority. Of the thirty-seven specific miracles described in the Gospels, twenty-three were healing miracles; nine were miracles over nature (including feeding the multitudes, and miracle catches of fish); three were raising the dead; and two exercised His power over demons. Not everyone who heard Jesus' teachings and witnessed His miracles reacted to Him and to His message in the same way. Those who were in greatest need of God's love and redemption reacted with the greatest love; while those who were wrapped in the robes of religious self-righteousness, often reacted with the greatest hate. The masses for the most part were curious onlookers. They followed Jesus for whatever personal benefit they gained – healing, feeding, cleansing – and they were happy to listen to His teachings, but still refused to commit themselves to Jesus as their Messiah. Their lack of commitment is demonstrated by how quickly they fell away whenever faced with the demands of discipleship. This lack of commitment reached its peak in

John 6, when the masses rejected Jesus' call for them to fully identify with His sacrifice on their behalf in communion with Him. Their hardness of heart (note the Parable of the Sower and Soils in Matthew 13) meant they were unable to hear the Word of truth given at that moment; and so the devil was able to snatch away the Gospel seeds of salvation before they could penetrate the hearts of the masses. The end result was a great falling away and betrayal of the Lord. The same masses that called out "hosanna" when Jesus entered Jerusalem for the last time, were screaming "crucify Him!" only a few days later.

37 Miracles of Jesus

#	Miracle	Matthew	Mark	Luke	John
1	Jesus Turns Water into Wine				2:1-11
2	Jesus Heals an Official's Son				4:43-54
3	Jesus Drives Out an Evil Spirit		1:21-27	4:31-36	
4	Jesus Heals Peter's Mother-in-Law	8:14-15	1:29-31	4:38-39	
5	Jesus Heals Many Sick at Evening	8:16-17	1:32-34	4:40-41	
6	First Miraculous Catch of Fish			5:1-11	
7	Jesus Cleanses a Man With Leprosy	8:1-4	1:40-45	5:12-14	
8	Jesus Heals a Centurion's Servant	8:5-13		7:1-10	
9	Jesus Heals a Paralytic	9:1-8	2:1-12	5:17-26	
10	Jesus Heals a Man's Withered Hand	12:9-14	3:1-6	6:6-11	
11	Jesus Raises a Widow's Son in Nain			7:11-17	
12	Jesus Calms a Storm	8:23-27	4:35-41	8:22-25	
13	Jesus Casts Demons into a Herd of Pigs	8:28-33	5:1-20	8:26-39	
14	Jesus Heals a Woman in the Crowd	9:20-22	5:25-34	8:42-48	
15	Jesus Raises Jairus' Daughter to Life	9:18, 23-26	5:21-24, 35-43	8:40-42, 49-56	
16	Jesus Heals Two Blind Men	9:27-31			
17	Jesus Heals a Man Unable to Speak	9:32-34			
18	Jesus Heals an Invalid at Bethesda				5:1-15
19	Jesus Feeds 5,000	14:13-21	6:30-44	9:10-17	6:1-15

20	Jesus Walks on Water	14:22-33	6:45-52		6:16-21
21	Jesus Heals Many Sick in Gennesaret	14:34-36	6:53-56		
22	Jesus Heals a Gentile Woman's Demon-Possessed Daughter	15:21-28	7:24-30		
23	Jesus Heals a Deaf and Dumb Man		7:31-37		
24	Jesus Feeds 4,000	15:32-39	8:1-13		
25	Jesus Heals a Blind Man at Bethsaida		8:22-26		
26	Jesus Heals a Man Born Blind				9:1-12
27	Jesus Heals a Boy with a Demon	17:14-20	9:14-29	9:37-43	
28	Miraculous Temple Tax in a Fish's Mouth	17:24-27			
29	Jesus Heals a Blind, Mute Demoniac	12:22-23		11:14-23	
30	Jesus Heals a Crippled Woman			13:10-17	
31	Jesus Heals a Man With Dropsy on the Sabbath			14:1-6	
32	Jesus Cleanses Ten Lepers			17:11-19	
33	Jesus Raises Lazarus from the Dead				11:1-45
34	Jesus Restores Sight to Bartimaeus	20:29-34	10:46-52	18:35-43	
35	Jesus Withers the Fig Tree	21:18:22	11:12-14		
36	Jesus Heals a Servant's Severed Ear			22:50-51	
37	Second Miraculous Catch of Fish				21:4-11

http://christianity.about.com/od/biblefactsandlists/a/Miracles-Of-Jesus.htm

    For the purposes of this study it is not necessary to go into details for every one of the 37 miracles performed by Jesus that are recorded in the Gospels. John's Gospel gives a good representation of the miracles of

Jesus within its framework of "sevens" (See page 74). Descriptions of the seven Sabbath-day miracles from John and the other Gospels can give further support to the types of miracles found in the Gospels (healing miracles, miracles over nature, raising the dead; and Jesus' power over demons). It is by these miracles that this lesson will explain the way Jesus authenticated His ministry to the nation.

Miracles Over Nature

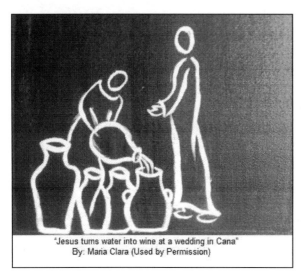
"Jesus turns water into wine at a wedding in Cana"
By: Maria Clara (Used by Permission)

Changing water into wine (Jn. 2:1-11) was the first recorded miracle of Jesus. It would be a prototype for all Jesus' miracles to follow. This miracle was not unlike the Feeding the 5,000 (Mt 14:13-21; Mk 6:30-44; Lk 9:10-17; Jn. 6:1-14) or the feeding of 4,000 (Matt.15:32-39; Mk 8:1-13) in that it concerned man's physical need as well as His spiritual need. The setting was a wedding – a very important social event in the life of the Jews. Jesus and His mother were in attendance. Mary's concern at that moment was a social concern; it would be a disappointment for the guests and an embarrassment for bride and groom if this essential element of the celebration meal ran out.

Two thousand years and a world away from 1st century Palestine of the Jews makes it difficult for us to understand the concern of Mary and the immediate response of Jesus: "why do you involve me? My time has not yet come." In some English translations Jesus' words sound much more abrupt – almost scolding Mary for bothering Jesus at this moment. But from the actions that immediately follow it is clear that Jesus was in essence saying to His mother not to worry and leave things to Him.

Changing water into wine is a model for the miracle ministry of Jesus in that every miracle served to functions. There is the immediate social or physical need or concern that makes supernatural intervention necessary (health, relief, peace, material or physical comfort, social justice, restoration, etc.). Jesus understood the social concern and met the need, but His miracles go beyond the surface to address the deeper inner needs of humanity (life, love, wholeness, acceptance, and self-worth). Mary's concern was typical of the concerns of all who came to Jesus seeking divine help: it was to meet the need of the moment. Jesus' miraculous intervention in every case transcends the moment and gives eternal, everlasting, and universal meaning to His actions. "For *miracle* it is, and will ever remain; not, indeed, magic, nor arbitrary power, but power with a moral purpose, and that the highest. And we believe it, because this 'sign' is the first of all those miracles in which the Miracle of Miracles gave 'a sign,' and manifested forth His glory - the glory of His Person, the glory of His Purpose, and the glory of His Work. Alfred Edersheim, *The Life and Times of Jesus the Messiah*, Database © 2012 WORD*search* Corp.

And so we see this same pattern existing in the first and second miraculous catches of fish (Luke 5:1-11; John 21:4-11) and even in the miraculous Temple Tax drawn out of a Fish's Mouth (Matt 17:24-27). Jesus never used cheap showman's tricks. His miracles were never intended to prove anything to Himself, to put God to the test, or to manipulate the masses (Matt. 4:1-11). Whether walking on water (Matt 14:22-33; Mark 6:45-52; John 6:16-21) or calming the storm (Mt 8:23-27; Mk 4:35-41; Lk 8:22-25) Jesus was always in control of Himself and in control of the situation; His message for His disciples was and is consistent: do to worry and leave things to Him.

In miracles like withering the fig tree (Mt 21:18:22; Mk 11:12-14) the sign is clear and direct. In other miracles, unless Jesus explains the intended purpose, we are left to ponder and seek the wisdom of the Holy Spirit to reveal the transcendent purpose for it. But no miracle of Jesus was ever a "throw away." He did nothing on a whim, but all was calculated by His father to point with absolute certainty that Jesus was, is and forever will be the divine Son of God.

Healing Miracles

The fact that six of the seven Sabbath-day miracles are healing miracles and three of the seven miracles in John are healing miracles indicates the importance of healing in Jesus' ministry. Jesus ministered in a world that is sin-sick and suffering from decay. Therefore, it is only natural that many of those that Jesus encountered along the way were physically hurting, mentally distraught, emotionally troubled, and spiritually in need of restoration. In other words, all were in need of a Savior then no less than the world today is in need of a Savior.

Those believers today who teach that healing miracles are simply a matter of having the right combination of faith and anointing to heal or be healed are hard-pressed to justify that belief from the Scriptures describing Jesus as healer. The backgrounds of those who were healed were as varied as they are today; rich, poor, Jew, Gentile, believing, unbelieving, those who knew who Jesus was, and many who did not know who He was or where He came from were healed. At times Jesus healed all who came to Him and at other times not all were healed. And still, at other times we see incidents where Jesus seemed to pick only one out from a crowd and healed them. There is only one common element in every instance: Jesus Christ. The fact that Jesus never failed to heal anyone He set out to heal should not be surprising since (1) He was given all authority to heal by His father; and (2) in spite of having that authority, Jesus never exercised that authority on His own, but only acted according to the Father's will: "So Jesus said to them, 'Truly, truly, I say to you, the Son can do nothing of his own accord, but only what he sees the Father doing. For whatever the Father does, that the Son does likewise. For the Father loves the Son and shows him all that he himself is doing. And greater works than these will he show him, so that you may marvel.'" John 5:19-20 (ESV)

We will not get into a lengthy theological debate in this lesson over healing in the church today. I deal with the topics of Cessationism and Faith healing in two chapters of my book *Our Jehovah Rapha* ("Does God Heal Today?" And "The Role of Faith in Healing: How Much Faith Does it Take?") In that book I also concentrate on the seven Sabbath-day healing miracles of Jesus recorded in the Scriptures. So in this lesson, I will cover some of the same ground as the Sabbath-day healings, but will also highlight other incidents of healing in order to give a good overview of the scope of Jesus' healing miracles and their importance to His overall ministry as the Messiah.

One of Jesus' early healing miracles is healing the Official's son (John 4:43-54). Jesus had returned to His home place in Galilee after being in Jerusalem for the Passover celebration. As he traveled through Galilee, he came to Cana, where he had performed His first public miracle by turning the water into wine. A government official in nearby Capernaum,

THE WAY, TRUTH, AND LIFE

whose son was very sick, heard that Jesus had come from Judea to Galilee. Jesus' fame as a healer and miracle worker had spread throughout the region, and so this unnamed official went and begged Jesus to come to Capernaum to heal his son, who was about to die. Keeping in mind the fact that in every miracle of Jesus there are two things going on simultaneously (1) the physical, social need of the moment, and (2) the greater spiritual need that transcends the moment; Jesus' immediate response was to address them both at the same time in the same miracle.

The greater spiritual need is addressed in Jesus' mild rebuke "Unless you see signs and wonders you will not believe." At that moment, Jesus was not only addressing this particular individual, but was speaking beyond him to the Jews as a whole who refused to believe Jesus was the promised Messiah unless He proved Himself by working wonders before their very eyes (Matt. 12:38-39). Many people are like that today; for them "seeing is believing" and they will ignore Jesus, never go to church, or never really believe God's word, until they need a miracle for themselves or for a loved one. Then and only then will they believe. Theologically, they are the skeptics and Cessationists. Although God's word clearly shows Jesus as the healer and miracle worker, they refuse to believe God is able to work miracles today because Jesus has not come again. Until or unless Jesus physically shows Himself, they will refuse to believe. But then sickness or some other calamity strikes someone near and dear to them and they suddenly go in search of divine intervention in their prayers for help.

This particular nobleman was like so many of the Jews in His day: he believed that Jesus was a Rabbi – a teacher come from God and that God must somehow be with Him for Him to work wonders – but he would not commit to Jesus as Lord and Christ. Like Nicodemus and so many others, this nobleman still had his doubts about Jesus (John 3:2-3).

"Men's dignity in the world shall not exempt them from the rebukes of the word or providence; for Christ reproves not after the hearing of his ears, but with equity, Isaiah 11:3, 4. Observe, Christ first shows him his sin and weakness, to prepare him for mercy, and then grants his request. Those whom Christ intends to honour with his favours he first humbles with his frowns. The Comforter shall first convince. Herod longed to see some miracle (Luke 23:8), and this courtier was of the same mind, and the generality of the people too." Matthew Henry

Jesus' rebukes often have a greater purpose behind them. In this case, it drew out the man's sincerity of affection for His son over and above his expectations for Jesus to. He may not have been willing to humble himself to God for his own needs, but he would do anything to help his son. On the other hand, Jesus would go to any lengths to save the lost. We see in Jesus' decision not to go with this man a greater purpose being served. By not going with him, Jesus forced the nobleman to be humble and trust in God to heal in the manner of His choosing. The disciple Thomas would learn that same lesson later, when Jesus said to him, "Have you believed because you have seen me? Blessed are those who have not seen and yet have believed." John 20:29 (ESV)

"Jesus calms the wind and the sea"
By: Maria Clara (Used by Permission)

At this critical moment, Jesus told him, "Go back home. Your son will live!" The man put his faith in action, showing he believed what Jesus said by turning and heading home. God had mercy upon this man and did not keep him in suspense for the entire journey home. Some of his servants hurried and met him on the road with the news that his son was alive and well. The final proof that the man's faith in Jesus was not in vain came when he realized that his son was healed the very hour Jesus told him, "Your son will live." The end result was that the nobleman and his entire household believed in Jesus.

A noteworthy contrast exists between this miracle and when Jesus Heals a Centurion's Servant (Mt 8:5-13; Lk 7:1-10). An obvious difference exists between the accounts of Matthew and Luke: Matthew describes the Roman officer as having a face-to-face encounter with Jesus, while Luke tells us that the officer sent a delegation of Jewish elders to present his request to Jesus. Modern-day liberal theologians point to the differences in these passages as a mistake or contradiction. However, these same theologians also believe these Gospels were altered time and again by numerous unknown and unnamed redactors. So an obvious question to ask is "If this is such an obvious contradiction that modern scholars so readily see, then why did none of the ancient editors of the Gospels simply "fix" the mistake and reconcile the two accounts?" A more reasonable explanation is available to us that does not demean the inspiration of the Scriptures and is compatible with what we know about the Gospels and to whom they were originally addressed.

It would not be necessary for Matthew to explain to his primarily Jewish audience that dealing with a person's messengers was considered the same as dealing with the one who had sent them. Since Matthew's primary concern throughout His Gospel is convincing his readers that Jesus was their long-awaited Messiah. Matthew wanted to emphasize the centurion's faith in contrast to the Jews' unbelief. Obviously, Luke had a slightly different primary audience in mind. For his primarily Gentile audience, Luke wanted to emphasize the respectful relationship between the Jewish elders and the Roman officer. The Greeks and Romans felt superior to the Jews in every way, but this Roman soldier was respectful and sensitive to the Jewish customs in Roman Palestine (Note Pilate's concessions to the Jews in John 18:28-32). Throughout the Roman world it was common for someone of the status of this centurion to delegate work and send representatives on important missions; so it is only natural that this was the way he chose to get his message to Jesus. But either way – by direct or indirect means – the extra-ordinary faith of the Centurion is evident.

The nobleman expected Jesus to come to Him (John 4:43-54). He would not believe in Jesus' power to heal simply by His word. Jesus lifted the Jewish nobleman's faith in God by not submitting to his request to come and heal his son. The centurion's faith surpassed that of the Jews. He understood divine authority and believed Jesus possessed it. So the Centurion had no difficulty understanding that all Jesus had to do was speak the Word and it would be done. "Truly, I tell you," Jesus said to the Jews around Him, "with no one in Israel have I found such faith." Luke's account reinforces this idea by filling in the details of the Centurion's indirect interactions with Jesus.

Jesus often used healing miracles as opportunities to reinforce what He was teaching in His public sermons. Everywhere Jesus went in public there were always three groups of people around Him. First there were His chosen Disciples; these twelve men were personally selected by Jesus to leave everything and "come and follow" so that He might teach them all He could about the mysteries of the kingdom of heaven. He said to them, "it has been given to you to know the mysteries of the kingdom of heaven, but to them it has not been given" (Matthew 13:11). The second group was the crowds that followed Him. Some were serious followers and were devoted disciples (Note Luke chapter 10; Matt. 8:21; Luke 6:17; John 4:1; 6:66; & 8:31); but the vast majority were curious onlookers hoping that Jesus was their long-awaited Messiah who would fill their needs (John 6:24-26). The third group was the religious leaders of the Jews. These were the Pharisees and the "teachers of the law" who had been installed as the spiritual gate keepers for the Jewish nation.

To the opposite extreme of the Pharisees were the Herodians. The Herodians were the ruling elites kept in power by the Romans. They were more concerned with threats to their political power than any religious disputes Jesus might have with them. The Herodians knew they were resented by the Jews because they did not have the right of succession from King David's family line. They watched anyone who might threaten their power and were ruthless about protecting it.

In the middle of these two extremes were the Sadducees. They blew with the prevailing winds, but their concerns were purely based upon self-interest. The Sadducees were quite willing to compromise with the Herodians and the Romans if it enriched them. The Sadducees maintained an uneasy peace with the Pharisees. Although the Pharisees' zeal to obey all of God's commands, their dedication to the Mosaic Law, and their desire for Levitical purity were all commendable, they often went too far in practice. Both the Herodians and Sadducees saw the Pharisees as dangerous religious fanatics that might bring down the Roman hammer on Jerusalem if they were not held in check.

In spite of the other factions' restraints, the Pharisees had become the most powerful and influential leaders over the Jews in Jesus' day. They derived their power by controlling access to the places of worship through their rules and regulations for religious purity. The people had to submit to the Pharisees authority if they wanted to be in right standing with God. Although all three groups were often at odds with each other, they united in their opposition to Jesus because each saw His increasing influence over the masses as a threat to their power and control. If Jesus was truly the Messiah and rightful King and High Priest over the nation,

His power and authority would be the end of the established order maintained by the Pharisees, Sadducees, and Herodians. Jesus' miracles were often used by Him as far more than a means to meet some personal need; He often used miracles to expose the corrupt powers that kept the people in fear and bondage:

> *"And he came to Nazareth, where he had been brought up. And as was his custom, he went to the synagogue on the Sabbath day, and he stood up to read. And the scroll of the prophet Isaiah was given to him. He unrolled the scroll and found the place where it was written,*
> > *'The Spirit of the Lord is upon me, because he has anointed me to proclaim good news to the poor. He has sent me to proclaim liberty to the captives and recovering of sight to the blind, to set at liberty those who are oppressed, to proclaim the year of the Lord's favor.'*
>
> *And he rolled up the scroll and gave it back to the attendant and sat down. And the eyes of all in the synagogue were fixed on him. And he began to say to them, 'Today this Scripture has been fulfilled in your hearing.'"* Luke 4:16-21 (ESV)

And so we see in a number of His healings something more happening than what is on the surface. Jesus had a mission to fulfill and a key part of that mission involved setting people free from religious oppression as well as the physical burdens of sin and disease. The Pharisees believed that sickness and disease was the punishment of God upon sinners. So certain diseases – like leprosy – that made a person unfit to enter the Temple for worship were equated with sinful conditions that made men unfit to enter into God's presence. Jesus' pronouncement at the beginning of His public ministry (Luke 4:16-21) made it clear that He had come to set men free from all kinds of oppression. So especially in many of His healing miracles we discover intersecting ministries to the spiritually, physically, and religiously oppressed.

As we saw in Lesson 5, Jesus used the healing of a paralytic (Mt 9:1-8; Mk 2:1-12; Lk 5:17-26) to highlight His conflict with the Pharisees, Scribes, and Sadducees over His divine authority (see pages 142-143). Although Jesus could and did heal any day of the week, there are several times when He healed on the Sabbath to demonstrate His absolute authority over it: "And he said to them, 'The Sabbath was made for man, not man for the Sabbath. So the Son of Man is lord even of the Sabbath.'" Mark 2:27-28 (ESV)

When Jesus healed a man's withered hand on the Sabbath (Mt 12:9-14; Mk 3:1-6; Lk 6:6-11) it only further enraged the religious leaders who witnessed it and deepened the Lord's rift with the Pharisees. The Gospels inform us that after that incident, "The Pharisees went out and immediately held counsel with the Herodians against him, how to destroy him." (Mark 3:6). And again when Jesus healed on a Sabbath an invalid at Bethesda, which was in the very shadow of the Temple Mount in Jerusalem (John 5:1-15), the Pharisees were blind to the power and glorious grace of God to heal a man who had been an invalid for thirty-eight years. Instead, all they could think of was how their Sabbath rules were broken by the man when now walking, carried away his mat. Their objections to this healing followed the same pattern as their objections to all other Sabbath miracles.

Unmoved by the Pharisees' continued resistance to His Messianic authority, Jesus again heals on the Sabbath in Jerusalem when a man born blind is given sight (John 9:1-12). This particular miracle reveals fresh insights into Jesus' teachings. Healing this blind man came at the end of several long heated debates between Jesus and the Jews. At one point Jesus is accused of having a demon (John 7:21); and at another point the Jewish authorities attempted to arrest Jesus on the spot (7:32). John records the considerable division among the people over Jesus. "When they heard these words, some of the people said, 'This really is the Prophet.' Others said, 'This is the Christ.' But some said, 'Is the Christ to come from Galilee? Has not the Scripture said that the Christ comes from the offspring of David, and comes from Bethlehem, the village where David was?' So there was a division among the people over him. Some of them wanted to arrest him, but no one laid hands on him." John 7:40-44 (ESV)

Following the controversies over His identity, Jesus delivers several short public pronouncements concerning His identity and ministry. Jesus declares "I am the light of the world" (John 8:12-20), but still the Jews do not believe. Then He said to them, prophesying His crucifixion, "When you have lifted up the Son of Man, then you will know that I am he, and that I do nothing on my own authority, but speak just as the Father taught me" (John 8:28). Although John says "many" believed Jesus when He spoke these things, still He had done little to persuade the powers in Jerusalem. Those who believed were still unable to understand His words plainly spoken to them; they clung to their Abrahamic heritage and could not accept the possibility that they needed the salvation and freedom from sin that Jesus offered them because the cross was still a mystery to them (John 8:39-47). The intensity of Jesus' verbal war with the Jews reaches its climax as Jesus declares to them: "Truly, truly, I say to you, before Abraham was, I am." That becomes the final words of Jesus to the crowds that day as they had picked up stones to throw at him; so John says, " He hid himself and went out of the temple" (John 8:58-59).

This leads us to the story of Jesus healing the man born blind (John 9:1-12). John tells us that as Jesus "passed by" his adversaries at that moment because He knew that His time had not yet come (Note: John 7:30). And yet, as if He wanted to further provoke those who sought to stone Him for the words He had just spoken, He turned to this man and brought the attention of all those present to what He was about to do. The Jewish authorities were well aware of Jesus' miracles, and had no doubt received reports of His other Sabbath day healings. So when Jesus fixed His eyes upon this blind man, the tension in the air must have been electric. After what had just happened, His disciples must have wondered if He would dare to heal this man on the Sabbath just a stone's throw away from His enemies and in the shadow of the great Temple in the heart of Jerusalem. Jesus' disciples may have felt that by asking a seemingly irrelevant question about the condition at hand, they might diffuse the whole situation and change the subject away from what Jesus might do to who was at fault for this man's blindness. "The light of divine salvation in His face was to overcome the darkness of man's moral and physical blindness. Thus, as the Light, He was to give a blind man sight." Herbert Lockyer, *All the Miracles of the Bible*, Zondervan, Grand Rapids, MI, © 1961, p. 220

The sad and hopeless condition of the blind man did not go unnoticed by Jesus, the Lord of the Sabbath. As He passed by, Jesus saw and took note of the blind man's condition, and therefore could not leave him as He found him. Although the disciples' question was irrelevant concerning whether or not the Lord would heal him, the question was a legitimate one. The Jews saw a direct relationship between sin and misfortune. Therefore, many believed that sickness and disease were the result of sins committed in the flesh. But what about a child that was born with a debilitating condition? Who sinned, this man or his parents that he was born blind? It could hardly be the child's fault for how could he have sinned before he came out of his mother's womb?

When David lamented in Psalm 51, "Behold, I was brought forth in iniquity, and in sin my mother conceived me," he was implying that he could not help but fall into sin and temptation because his condition from birth indicated that he had no control over the fallen state in which he found himself. And so the Jews would debate if being "brought forth in iniquity" meant what many Christians today call "original sin" or if it meant that because of the sinful condition of the parents, humans are born into the midst of their parents' iniquity. Either way – directly or indirectly – it could be argued that this man's blindness was in fact the sins of the parents being visited upon their child. [A careful study of the story of David's sin with Bathsheba that led to his writing Psalm 51, reveals in that story how David's sin was visited upon the child conceived in adultery and led to its death. (2 Sam. 12:13-19)]

Every major religion in the world deals with the issue of sin on some level. Prevalent among some of the world's ancient religions is the idea of a previous existence. Some sort of transmigration of souls from one physical body into another was included in many of the ancient West Asian mystery religions as well. Because the Jews had come into contact with some of these teachings from other religions, they may have been influenced by some of those ideas. There is no indication that the disciples may have been implying by their question that sin in some former state of existence caused him to come into this world blind.

Although the idea that this man's blindness could have had its cause in a previous existence was alien to Jewish theology, it was a common Jewish belief that the good or bad actions of parents would manifest in their children. The Jewish belief that certain diseases are visited upon children by the iniquity of their parents was written into the Torah. The second commandment specifically speaks of iniquities of the father being inflicted upon the children (Exodus 29:5). Although the Scriptures may indicate that a general law exists under the government of God that makes suffering the result of sin, Jesus' answer to the question that day revealed that the relationship between human suffering and sin is not as simple as a karmic law that states every action has an equal but opposite spiritual reaction.

In both the Old and New Testaments, a clear connection is made between sin and physical suffering. The history of the Jews tells how the total destruction of the northern kingdom was a result of their unrepentant rebellion against God (2 Kings 17:7); as was the terrible destruction of Jerusalem, and the Babylonian exile (2 Chronicles 36:15-20). The Jews knew very well the blessings of obedience and curses of disobedience laid out in Deuteronomy chapters 27 and 28. Therefore the curse of blindness must have been the result of sin, and so the disciples were asking Jesus, "whose sin was it... if this blind beggar had not somehow sinned, then was it his parents?" No matter which way Jesus answered, from the disciples' point of view, the blind man was suffering a just punishment for iniquity, and there was nothing for the poor blind man to do but sit and beg because "...since the world began, no one has opened the eyes of a man born blind" (John 9:32). So Jesus' answer, "Neither this man nor his parents sinned, but that the works of God should be revealed in him" was stunning to them, and was designed to turn their perceptions of the relationship between sin and suffering on its head.

Then what did Jesus mean when He answered, "Neither this man nor his parents sinned, but that the works of God should be revealed in him"? A misunderstanding of the word "sin" can lead to misinterpreting this passage and leave one with a wrong impression of God's justice and mercy. If this verse was not intended to mean that Jesus denied that infirmities are often the punishment for sin (Note also 1 Corinthians 11:30-32; 1 Peter 2:20; and 2 Peter 2:4-9), then what was Jesus trying to say? What did Jesus mean when he said that this blind beggar's horrible condition was intended so that "the works of God should be revealed in him"? Does God really permit people to be born with physical or mental abnormalities simply to show His glory by healing them at some point in time? And what do we say about those who never receive a healing? It hardly seems just or loving for God to have allowed this man to be born blind, stumble through his life in blindness, and be reduced to begging on the street for a few alms just to keep himself alive so that one day Jesus would come along and show God's power by healing him. It is a morally vacant theology that concludes that God allowed this man to be born blind so that at some point in time by the exercise of divine power, he might be made to see – not only physically, but spiritually.

Is it necessary for someone to be born blind, lame, dumb, or diseased "for the sake of his or her own spiritual and eternal good" so that in the end they might be led to Jesus as the Son of God? Is it valid, as some have argued, that this man was made blind and then healed so that he in turn, by sharing that experience, would become a channel of divine grace to others? Did Jesus allow Lazarus to enter into the crucible of death, permitting the deep grief and sorrow of Martha, Mary, and his other friends and family just so the Son of God would be glorified when He raised Lazarus from the dead? It would be cruel, capricious, and morally reprehensible for God to use in such a way those He created in His image.

Before anyone can rightly answer such questions, they must have a clearer understanding of sin and sickness and how they relate to the healing ministry of Jesus Christ. It is very important to realize that when the word "sin" appears in the Bible, it is not always talking about the same thing – even when used in the same passage. The Greek helps to clarify the different Biblical concepts of "sin" and how they relate to sickness and disease. Both the Greek and Hebrew languages distinguish between (1) "sin" as in The Fallen condition of Adam's race; (2) the power of "sin" in the world in which we live; and (3) a personal act of sin (Gr. hamartia & Heb. hata) "missing the mark."

According to Vines Expository Dictionary, the New Testament uses "sin" to denote:
(1) a principle or source of action; an inward element producing sinful acts
(2) a governing principle or power that exists in the world
(3) wrong doing or sinful actions

There are those who teach that sin is the source of all sickness and disease, and that can be accurate depending upon which of the three meanings above they are referring to in each individual case. But if the person who hears that statement does not distinguish in their mind the different biblical concepts of "sin" and how they relate to specific issues, it can lead to confusion and unnecessary guilt or self-condemnation because those who are suffering may be led to believe that all sicknesses and diseases are the result of personal sins (wrong doing or sinful actions). When Jesus' answer to the disciples' question about who sinned is analyzed, it can be understood to mean that no matter what the source of the sin might be that produced the malady, the remedy is still the same: the finished, complete work of Salvation that comes from the blood of Jesus. So in the end, the exact cause of the sin is irrelevant because, whenever a person encounters the living God healing will result. Jesus was not looking for whom to blame for the tragedy, but He wanted only for His Father to be glorified. Once again, there was no request from anyone for Jesus to heal at this moment. The blind man and all those who encountered him had accepted that for whatever the reason, his situation was hopeless. If this man would be healed, the Lord would have to take it upon Himself to initiate the miracle. But as is typical with Jesus, He never misses the opportunity to exploit a teaching moment. All those present watched this act of compassion unfold before their eyes. The spiritual eyes of the witnesses were awakened as they saw this poor man's physical eyes opened for the first time in his life – all to the glory of the Father.

This blind man is a clear example of how sin lowers the human condition and strips away the dignity and honor intended for the crown of God's creation. In practically every major city around the world there are found the poor, the pitiful, blind, and lame – plus all those "poor in spirit" who are have lost their identity as children of God. Many of these people are reduced to nothing as they stay on the streets like human debris with no one to love or care for them. Once all hope is lost they wander the streets begging for enough to keep them alive just one more day. If Satan had his way, every human being would be reduced to this condition, but God in His mercy lifts out of the dust all those who put their trust in Him.

Jesus never explained why He chose to cover the blind man's eyes with spittle and clay: "It would seem as if the action of covering the eyes of the blind man with spittle-clay was better calculated to make a seeing man blind than to make a blind man see." Herbert Lockyer *All the Miracles of the Bible,* Zondervan, Grand Rapids, MI, © 1961, p.222.

"Jesus Heals a Blind Man."
By Maria Clara (Used by Permission)

One thing is known for sure: every move Jesus made was purposeful and calculated for maximum effect. The ancients believed a number of superstitions concerning saliva as a remedy for diseases of the eye. Saliva was used by faith healers and medicine men generally as a charm, applied with incantations. In Greek myth an old hag moistens her finger with spittle and applies it to the forehead and lip to keep away the evil eye. The Greek natural philosopher, Pliny the Elder, believed that by continually anointing each morning with fasting saliva, inflammation of the eyes is prevented. Still, no one had ever heard of a case where a man born blind was cured by one simple application of saliva. Certainly, Jesus would have been aware of this; but the making of the compound using clay and saliva was not intended to cure the man's blindness. Something more was being communicated here, but Jesus did not explain and John did not comment about it. Modern day Bible commentators point out that clay as symbolism is traced back to creation, and since Jesus was exercising creative power to restore the man's eyes, He was using the clay symbolically. Still other commentators speculate that the spittle-clay was a prop intended to create hope and expectation in the blind man that a cure was in process. The making of the spittle-clay may have been a deliberate act of defiance meant to provoke the religious leaders because all those who witnessed the act taught that no work was to be done on the Sabbath. Those who take a more mystical approach to interpreting this act argue that the clay symbolizes the Lord's humility and water represents the Holy Spirit. The spittle was seen by some other commentators to be a type of the waters of baptism. But whatever the reason was for the use of the clay, both the blind man and all those who stood by and witnessed the miracle could see that the actual power to heal was not in the spittle-clay, but was in Jesus alone.

The command to "go and wash" was a practical instruction since the clay would harden and make it difficult for the eyes of the man to function, but it took faith for the man to believe that by going and washing he would come back seeing. The place where he was to wash was called the Pool of Siloam, a term which literally meant "sent." Here there is found the first clue as to the whole purpose for the Lord's actions: the religious authorities had been challenging Jesus' claims all day long, and Jesus had been responding to them saying that He had the authority to do what He did and say what He said was because He was sent by His Father. The message was clear for all who had eyes to see: Jesus had the power to heal the man born blind because He was "The Sent One" from the Father.

The verses following the healing demonstrate the continued spiritual blindness of the Jewish authorities. They refused to see the truth of this miraculous sign that Jesus was "Sent" from God and instead focused upon their shortsighted traditions, concluding, "This man is not from God, because he does not keep the Sabbath." But something was stirring in the hearts of others who said, "How can a man who is a sinner do such signs?" Failing to reach consensus amongst the leadership, the most strident opponents of Jesus turned to the man who had been healed and attempted to intimidate him and his parents into renouncing Jesus and denying the miracle itself. Pressed for an answer, the man turns the tables on his prosecutors and boldly reminds them of their own teachings: "Now we know that God does not hear sinners; but if anyone is a worshiper of God and does His will, He hears him. Since the world began it has been unheard of that anyone opened the eyes of one who was born blind. If this Man were not from God, He could do nothing." The Pharisees and teachers of the law could not face the truth about Jesus and in the end had to declare "we do not know where He is from." In the end the ugly foot of pride was raised against the man who received his sight and he was kicked out of the Synagogue.

In verses 35-41 of this chapter, the story comes full circle. The man, in his blind condition was considered "unclean" and would have been excluded from the inner courts of the temple. Now seeing, this same man is cast out of the Temple area because those in charge of the Temple could not acknowledge the Lord of the Temple, Jesus Christ (John 2:13-21) had healed him and made him fit to enter and worship the God of their fathers. The disciples' question about "who sinned" is rendered totally irrelevant by the grace of God that healed the hopeless man – a man who did not know the identity of his Healer. The blind man, now seeing, believes and worships Jesus, the Living Temple of God. The Pharisees are exposed as faithless blind guides, "For judgment I have come into this world, that those who do not see may see, and that those who see may be made blind." The tables have been flipped in no less a dramatic way than the time that Jesus entered the Temple and overturned the tables of the money changers.

The real tragedy exposed was not the physical blindness of the poor beggar; it could be healed with a simple act of obedience in faith to Jesus Christ. The real tragedy was the spiritual blindness of the religious leaders. The blindness that judged them – of which they were guilty, and for which they alone were responsible – was the result of their deliberate disobedience and lack of faith. Therefore, not only their blindness, but also their sin remained. It would be a mistake to conclude from this healing miracle that Jesus healed only to show a sign of His Sonship, and at the same time, defy the Jewish authorities. If that were case, the poor, blind beggar would have been merely a pawn in a cosmic power play. Jesus saw the need and saw that the man had the faith to be healed and acted accordingly. The reactions of the disciples, the man's family, and the Jewish authorities were secondary to the intimate exchange that took place between Jesus and this man. The miracle had the desired effect in that it concluded with the healed man seeing and worshiping His Lord in spirit and truth. The Father alone received the glory, but the Son was not denied His honor in the process.

When faced with a genuine healing miracle, the modern observer is confronted with the same dilemmas as all of these witnesses. Too often when the poor, sick, and wretched dregs of society are encountered on the roadside, the reaction of the more fortunate passersby is to absolve themselves of any responsibility to help by judging and blaming the victim for whatever brought them to such a low estate. Jesus is unconcerned by the circumstances of birth or by sins committed; without prejudice, He comes and heals with a heart of compassion. The Jewish leaders of Jesus' day find their counterpart in the modern skeptics who deny the Lord has the heart or power to heal today. Religious, theological, or personal prejudices prevent them from seeing and believing. They would cast out of their presence anyone who challenges their set of beliefs before falling on their knees in faith and repentance before the Lord of all.

Jesus' healing on the Sabbath of a man with dropsy (Luke 14:1-6) is another fine example of the way Jesus would address the immediate physical need of a person near Him and at the same time address the broader spiritual implication of His action. From this account in Luke we have no indication that the sick man asked Jesus to heal him; there is no indication whatsoever that the sick man had the faith at that moment to receive a healing. Jesus did not even ask the man if he wanted to be healed; He simply healed him. Why? Because it was His good pleasure to heal him at that moment; as Jesus had said before, "Fear not, little flock, for it is your Father's good pleasure to give you the kingdom." Luke 12:32 (ESV)

Just before healing the man Jesus asked the lawyers and Pharisees sitting around him, "Is it lawful to heal on the Sabbath?" And hearing no answer, He healed the sick man. Immediately after the healing, Jesus was met with a stony silence from the crowd and answered that silence saying, "Which of you, having a donkey or an ox that has fallen into a pit, will not immediately pull him out on the Sabbath day?"

If the lawyers and Pharisees assembled that day said the Sabbath laws would not allow Jesus to heal, it would seem that they were suggesting that animals were more important than people. It is tragic that in some Asian cultures that exist today there are people who treat their animals with more care and respect than some members of their communities. In Western countries there are those who have more love for their pets than they do for their family members, their neighbors, or even for the lost souls who are dying without hope in Christ in this world.

The Pharisees were as upset that Jesus would heal on the Sabbath as they were upset with Him for exposing their false piety. Jesus forced them to face the truth that although they claimed to be defending God's Sabbath Laws, in reality they were denying God by the way they ignored the suffering of others and left them without hope in order to preserve their traditions. There are those in the church today who turn away those suffering and dying without hope, maintaining their traditional belief that the gifts of the Spirit – including healing miracles – ended with the Apostles almost 2,000 years ago. Denying the power of God to heal today is equal to suggesting that God does not care about the suffering of those who are sick and dying alone, and without hope in this present time. Jesus by His words and deeds of healing on the Sabbath demonstrated that there is a huge difference between preserving God's truth and promoting man's traditions; Christians of today need to beware that they are not doing the same.

Healing Various Sicknesses and Diseases

"And Jesus went about all Galilee, teaching in their synagogues, preaching the gospel of the kingdom, and healing all kinds of sickness and all kinds of disease among the people. Then His fame went throughout all Syria; and they brought to

Him all sick people who were afflicted with various diseases and torments, and those who were demon-possessed, epileptics, and paralytics; and He healed them." Matthew 4:23-24

The healing miracles of Jesus tell us much about Jesus' view of sickness, disease and death. He did not accept these things as part of a natural or necessary evolutionary process. Jesus looked upon sickness, disease, and death as sin's intrusions upon God's original plan for the human race (Note: John 9:1-3). Man was not created to experience decay and death. It was only after The Fall that the curse of decay and death was visited upon Adam's race and upon the rest of creation. Whenever Jesus encountered illness in a child of God He saw it as the consequence of sin. Because these things are sin's agents, Jesus saw them as conditions that needed to be confronted and banished, which He routinely did. For Jesus, sin was intricately woven into weft and weave of the fabric of every sickness and disease (Note: Matthew 9:1-8).

Because Jesus came as The Life, He was by nature able to restore life to all those who came into close personal contact with Him (Note: Matthew 9:20-22, the woman with the issue of blood). At the same time, Jesus as The Truth came as the Living Word. Therefore, we see in the Gospels how inseparable the depth and richness of His teaching ministry are from His healing miracles. The Word spoken in the Spirit and received in faith has power in and of itself to heal (Note: Matthew 8:5-10 & John 4:46-54). Jesus was sent into this world as the Word of God made flesh (John 1:14) fulfilling Isaiah 55:11 "So shall My word be that goes forth from My mouth; It shall not return to Me void, But it shall accomplish what I please, And it shall prosper in the thing for which I sent it" (NKJV).

The various healing miracles in the Gospels show Jesus as a man of great compassion for those who were hurting. Jesus described Himself not only as Truth and Life, but also the only Way to the Father (Luke 10:22 and John 14:6) who is full of mercy and compassion (Exodus 34:4-7). Motivated by love and compassion, Jesus demonstrated a spiritual insight that allowed him to see beyond the surface to address the real needs of those who sought his aid and comfort. Because He saw with spiritual eyes, Jesus was able to see into the afflicted souls and meet not only the outward physical ills of those who came to Him, but more importantly, the inward diseases caused by sin and spiritual death as well. It should never be forgotten that Jesus' spiritual insight was grounded in *agape* – the pure unconditional love of God that made no *quid pro quo* demands of obedience before He would act. His healing ministry was intended to restore in love that which was lost in those who were afflicted by living in this sin stained and fallen world. Thus, His miracles were intended to reveal God's character of love, and to show what man is intended to become in Jesus Christ.

EXAMPLES OF THE OF SICKNESS & DISEASE JESUS HEALED			
Physical Disorders	Cases	Nervous Disorders	Cases
Blindness	4	Demonical Possession	6
Leprosy	2	Paralysis	3
Fever	2	Spirit of Infirmity	1
Lameness	1		
Deafness & Dumbness	1		
Dropsy	1		
Issue of Blood	1		
Open Wound	1		

The fact that Jesus' healing methods were so diverse indicates that Jesus did not want to leave the impression with anyone that if His particular method of healing was followed anyone could heal. Using different methods to heal takes the focus off of the process and puts it squarely upon the divine Healer. When God heals He gets the glory – not the healer, the person being healed, or the methodology employed. Not everyone was immediately healed with the laying on of hands; Bartimaeus was healed simply by a word of healing spoken over him (Mark 10:46-52). Jesus applied His saliva to the eyes of the blind man of Siloam (Mark 8:22-26); it took two stages for the healing to become complete. Jesus demonstrated His power to heal whether present (as in Matthew 4:23) or absent (as in Matthew 8:13). Jesus could heal by word (Matthew 8:8, 13), by touch (Matthew 8:3), or application (John 9:6, 7). The method of healing was never the issue for Jews who were comfortable with the mysterious and were less concerned with the "how" of things than the "why." Regardless of the method used, Jesus' healing miracles shared three purposes that fit the overall cause for His Incarnation:

1. Provoke faith in Him as the Messiah/Savior/Lord by the person healed and all those who witnessed it
2. A higher spiritual purpose to reveal the present reality of the kingdom of God in the midst of the people
3. Glorify His Father

"Unlike magicians, he coerced no reluctant powers into his service and his activities were beneficent not malicious. Unlike the healing cults, distant and forbidden anyway to pious Jews, it appears not one returned from him uncured. In contrast to other Jewish exorcists, he required no aids in his exorcism, achieving effective results simply by word of command. It is unlikely then that the evangelist is exaggerating when we hear Jesus' spectators crying out in wonder, 'We never saw anything like this!' And Jesus is quickly compared with Elijah though, in the number and scope of miracles he is reported to have performed, he had no peer in antiquity." Andrew Daunton-Fear, *Healing in the Early Church*, Authentic Books, Secunderabad, India © 2011, pg. 36

Healings of the Blind, Deaf, and Dumb

"When Jesus departed from there, two blind men followed Him, crying out and saying, 'Son of David, have mercy on us!' And when He had come into the house, the blind men came to Him. And Jesus said to them, 'Do you believe that I am able to do this?' They said to Him, 'Yes, Lord.' Then He touched their eyes, saying, 'According to your faith let it be to you.' And their eyes were opened. And Jesus sternly warned them, saying, 'See that no one knows it.' But when they had departed, they spread the news about Him in all that country." Matthew 9:27-31

The miracle recorded in Matthew 9:27-31 is the earliest in the notable group of similar passages in the Gospels (Matthew 11:5; 12:22; 20:30; 21:14; Luke 7:21; John 9). The cries of the blind for Jesus, "Son of David" to heal them are significant because healing the blind was a literal fulfillment of the prophetic word concerning the ministry of the Messiah (Isaiah 29:18; and 35:5). When John the Baptist sent a delegation to Jesus asking confirmation that He was indeed the "Coming One" prophesied in Scripture, Jesus answered them, "…Go and tell John the things which you hear and see: The blind see and the lame walk; the lepers are cleansed and the deaf hear; the dead are raised up and the poor have the gospel preached to them" (Matthew 11:4b-5).

There is no indication of the cause or duration of the blindness of two men described in Matthew 9:27-31. The reasons for their condition were not the issue here; what is important in this story is that they saw and believed in Jesus' supernatural power to heal. They sought out Jesus and demonstrated their faith in His Messiahship in their declaration of Him to be "Son of David." This Messianic title of authority to reign (Note: Ezekiel 34:23, 24) was also used by the blind at Jericho. Their plea for mercy not only indicated their faith in Jesus' ability to heal, but also acknowledged that there was no reason for Him to heal except as an act of grace and mercy. There was no act of righteousness or religious rite these blind men could perform to pressure or entice God to heal them. Jesus asked them only one question: "Do you believe that I am able to do this?" Their simple and trusting response, "Yes, Lord" was all Jesus needed to hear to know they had come in faith and brokenness before Him.

Our study of the healing miracles of the Bible reveals that faith in Jesus' power to heal in the heart of the afflicted is often but not always the antecedent condition of a cure. Jesus' declaration to these blind men, "According to your faith let it be to you" should not be taken as a blanket statement making faith a prerequisite for healing; otherwise it would only take faith to heal. But it requires more than faith; it must incorporate the will of God in the presence of Jesus Christ for a healing to take place.

It is most certainly true that "…without faith it is impossible to please Him, for he who comes to God must believe that He is, and that He is a rewarder of those who diligently seek Him" (Hebrews 11:6). Faith often provides the spark that ignites the supernatural connection between the Divine Healer (Jesus Christ) and the one needing to be healed. In this case, the acknowledgement of Jesus as "Son of David" by these blind men caught Jesus' attention because the vast majority of the sighted that swirled around Jesus at that time could not see that He was indeed the long-awaited Messiah of the Jews (John 9:39-41). Jesus asked the question, "Do you believe that I am able to do this?" in order to get confirmation from the blind men that they knew and understood the authority the Son of David possessed. Having professed and affirmed their faith in Him as their Messiah, Jesus immediately, and generously honored their faith with the incalculable gift of sight.

It was not false humility that motivated Jesus to warn them not to tell anyone that He had healed them. It is important to remember the context. Jesus was being threatened by the Jewish authorities who had rejected any notion that He might be the Messiah. Everywhere Jesus went, the scribes, Pharisees, and keepers of the law followed Him trying to catch Him saying or doing something that they could use to charge Him and drag Him before the High Priest for trial. Jesus knew the time for that had not yet come; He still had work to do (John 7:30; 9:4). It was also for the protection of those men who were just healed. Openly professing Him to be the "Son of David" could get them banished from the synagogue of the Jews (John 9:13-34). So Jesus, not seeking His own glory in the first place, did not want to deliberately provoke the Jewish authorities or cause unnecessary trouble for those who had confessed His authority over the entire Jewish nation. Jesus was not looking for martyrs as followers. He knew the time would come when His followers would suffer (Matthew 24:9; John 15:18-21), but at that moment, He wanted those He had so graciously healed to go their way in peace and enjoy renewed lives.

"Then he returned from the region of Tyre and went through Sidon to the Sea of Galilee, in the region of the Decapolis. And they brought to him a man who was deaf and had a speech impediment, and they begged him to lay his hand on him. And taking him aside from the crowd privately, he put his fingers into his ears, and after spitting touched his tongue. And looking up to heaven, he sighed and said to him, 'Ephphatha,' that is, 'Be opened.' And his ears were opened, his tongue was released, and he spoke plainly. And Jesus charged them to tell no one. But the more he charged them, the more zealously they proclaimed it. And they were astonished beyond measure, saying, "He has done all things well. He even makes the deaf hear and the mute speak." Mark 7:31-37 (ESV)

When they brought the one who was deaf and had an impediment in his speech before Jesus, He did not immediately spring into action. He took him aside from the multitude, and away from the distractions that might inhibit His silent communication with the deaf man. "There are times in every man's life when God can only help him if he is alone and quiet. Many of us live in a crowd all our lives: we may be born as one of a big family, or we work in a big college or factory or office. Perhaps this is why we find it hard to 'hear' God." John Haregreaves, *A Guide to St. Mark's Gospel*, ISPCK, Dehli 2006, © 1965.

Once He had the deaf man's full attention, Jesus put His fingers in the man's ears, and He spat and touched his tongue. Two other occasions are recorded on which Christ made use of His spittle in the work of healing: with a blind man at Bethsaida (Mark 8:23), when He "spat upon his eyes"; and at Jerusalem (John 9:6-7) when He made clay of the spittle and anointed the eyes of one born blind. The Gospel writers never reveal to us why Jesus went through these particular motions when healing these men. It was a widespread belief that spittle, accompanied with magical formulas, possessed medicinal qualities (*Oil* possessed a similar virtue). In this case we can only speculate that it may have been that Jesus used something the deaf man could see and feel that was associated with healing to help him to understand what Jesus was about to do for Him.. Ultimately, the power that cured the man came from Jesus. So once his hearing and speech was restored to him, he believed in Jesus and could not help but to proclaim that belief to any who had ears to hear.

It is not unusual for the Lord to use ordinary things and common people to bless and heal. If we are always looking for the spectacular signs and wonders – the flash of lightening or the rolling thunder – to accompany a divine healing, we might miss the voice of the Living God speaking through the voice of a neighbor, or the answered prayer spoken in the solitude of a prayer closet. Jesus can heal us by means of an ordinary doctor's medicine (it is easy to forget that when we take medicine from the doctor, it is God who is healing us indirectly). It is also easy to forget that God designed and created our body to heal itself naturally. We can just as easily thank God for giving us this wonderful body that has the ability to fight off a multitude of sicknesses and diseases throughout our lifetime.

The many and varied examples of divine healing in the Gospels remind us that God treats each of us according to our own special needs and according to our individual level of faith. Because He knows each of us are different, He may choose to heal us through the application of medicines or the laying on of hands or any other means necessary. It is faith that gives us the eyes to see and the ears to hear the Lord's handiwork in and through the ordinary things and common people He often uses as healing agents.

"Jesus came to live in our world of wonder and was ever doing wonderful and seemingly impossible things while among men. The hidden yet mighty forces of the universe were as instruments ever ready at hand." Herbert Lockyer, *All the Miracles of the Bible*

FREDERICK OSBORN

Healing the Demon-possessed

"As they went out, behold, they brought to Him a man, mute and demon-possessed. And when the demon was cast out, the mute spoke. And the multitudes marveled, saying, 'It was never seen like this in Israel!' But the Pharisees said, 'He casts out demons by the ruler of the demons.'" Matthew 9:32-34 (NKJV)

There are two major errors inherent in the extreme positions on the subject of demons and demon-possession that people can fall into. The first extreme position is to attach demonic activity to every physical or psychological ailment that can affect human beings. Adhering to this extreme position, some people will go about casting out demons of the common cold, anxiety, and all the way up to cancer and congestive heart failure. No matter what the problem or symptom, they will see a demon behind it. The other extreme position is to take a purely rationalistic approach that seeks only natural, scientific explanations for everything. Adhering to this extreme position, some people attempt to explain away even the most evil and despicable acts as problems stemming from bad nature or poor nurture. Denying the existence of the supernatural, they think there must be a physical cause behind every bodily or mental disorder that can only be treated in a way that is acceptable to modern medical science.

C.S. Lewis in his work of genius on this subject, *The Screwtape Letters*, unmasked the strategy of Satan behind his attempts to keep his activities hidden from view. In the words of the senior devil, Screwtape to his nephew Wormwood: "Our policy, for the moment, is to conceal ourselves. Of course this has not always been so. We are really faced with a cruel dilemma. When the humans disbelieve in our existence we lose all the pleasing results of direct terrorism. And we make no magicians. On the other hand, when they believe in us, we cannot make them materialists, and skeptics. At least, not yet. I have great hopes that we shall learn in due time how to emotionalize and mythologize their science to such an extent that what is, in effect, a belief in us (though not under that name) will creep in while the human mind remains closed to belief in the Enemy. The 'Life Force,' the worship of sex, and some aspects of Psychoanalysis may here prove useful. If once we can produce our perfect work – the Materialist Magician, the man, not using, but veritably worshipping, what he vaguely calls 'Forces' while denying the existence of 'spirits' – then the end of the war will be in sight." C.S. Lewis, The Screwtape Letters, Bantam Books, Inc. N.Y., 1982, p. 19.

In the case of Matthew 9:32-34, the man had the physical condition of being unable to speak. This condition was not the result of any deformity or physical injury to his tongue or larynx (commonly called the "voice box"). It was only possible to identify the root cause of his condition by seeing beyond the physical realm and into the spiritual where dwell "the evil rulers of the unseen world, those mighty satanic beings and great evil princes of darkness who rule this world; and… huge numbers of wicked spirits in the spirit world…" (Ephesians 6:12b TLB). In this passage, the demoniac did not seem to be suffering from any obvious signs of mania or lunacy, making it all the more curious how they determined the man was demon-possessed. Matthew does not make it clear if it was Jesus who revealed the demon or if those who brought him to Jesus declared it to him. But either way, Jesus knew that the demon had to be cast out before the man could speak.

Although demonic possession may have the outward appearance of an ordinary, physical disease, it is far from ordinary. It takes the gift of discerning of spirits (1 Corinthians 12:10) to recognize those sicknesses and diseases which are not due to any functional or organic disorder. Jesus, of course, has the fullness of the Spirit within and when approached was able to see beyond the apparent physical malady, and go to the heart of the matter by casting out the demon that was preventing this man from speaking. It should be noted at this point that the Jews recognized the power of the spoken word; for them, words were not passive things used only to express thoughts and ideas, but the tongue has the power to produce both blessings and curses. The prophets possessed the power to bless or curse when they spoke the word of God. It was by the truth of His word that Christ gave us new lives and we became children of God (James 1:18). James continues and urges all believers to "lay aside all filthiness and overflow of wickedness, and receive with meekness the implanted word, which is able to save your souls" (1:21). Here, there is no action required on the part of the Lord to rid this man of the demon. Jesus simply speaks the word of command and the demon had to submit to His absolute authority and flee from the man, releasing his tongue so that he could speak. Although Matthew does not record for us the first words to come from the man's mouth, but it would not be difficult to imagine that his first words would have given all honor and glory to God for having healed him.

It is over the notion of demonic possession that the modern skeptics, materialists, and liberal theologians cross swords with those who take the Bible at its word. "Any open-minded, honest reader of the Bible cannot escape the conclusion that our Lord believed in the Devil and in demons and also their evil influence in, and over human beings. Had he not believed in the dreadful powers of darkness He would not have spoken as earnestly, profoundly, and courageously about these hideous forces as He did. He openly declared the manifestation of evil in the bodies and souls of men as coming from an evil source." Herbert Lockyer, All the Miracles of the Bible, Zondervan, Grand Rapids, Mich., © 1961, P. 187.

Atheists and materialistic non-believers need no rationale for rejecting the Bible passages that describe demonic activities. However, they often join with the liberal theologians who promote the theory that the accounts of demon possessions found in the gospels were in fact borrowed from the Babylonian and Persian religions that contained numerous references to malevolent spirits plaguing humans. The liberals argue that the Jews adopted these beliefs during their captivity and upon their return from exile incorporated them into their own religion. They argue that Jesus was only accommodating the superstitious of His day and giving lip-service to the beliefs of the Jews by commanding the supposed evil spirits to come out of the possessed who were in fact mentally ill. But the fact that demon possession and lunacy are expressly distinguished in the Scriptures (Note Matthew 4:24 for example), makes it incorrect to assume that demon possession is just another name for madness.

For the purpose of this study, a detailed discussion of demonology is not possible. Numerous books have been written on the subject from a variety of perspectives. However, what can be said here is what is generally agreed upon: that there exists a clear and distinctive theology in the Scriptures concerning the existence of a spirit realm and that the Devil and his fallen angels are real – although not physical – beings. Not having a material body, the Devil's power must be exercised in one of two ways:

1. Directly – by direct spiritual attack as in the case of Job and Jesus' temptation in the Wilderness.

Or
2. Indirectly - by his minions: the demons who are under the direct commands of their prince; or through human beings over whom he influences or possesses.

The Old Testament Scriptures establish Satan and his demons as fallen angelic beings that rebelled against their Creator in ancient pre-history and were expelled from heaven. Man's helplessness to Satan's power is the fruit of The Fall and is a terrible reality that all those who live on the Earth cannot escape. God and His guardian angels act on behalf of mankind to restrict Satan from completely destroying mankind. The New Testament cases of demon-possession show specific types of disorder – either physical or mental – that disrupt the normal function of the mind and/or body of the person possessed. They may have the same symptoms or characteristics as the person suffering from a physical sickness or disease, but unless the demon is revealed to the spiritually discerning, their presence remains concealed. Whenever a demon-possessed person came into close proximity to Jesus, the demons were immediately exposed and had to flee at His command. This same authority over demonic forces was given to Jesus' disciples (Mark 3:13-15; 6:12-13; 9:38-40; 16:15-18; and Luke 10:17). A careful study of all the healing miracles of Jesus will show that Jesus never treated the victims of demons differently from other victims of sickness or disease. All who came to Him were treated with equal compassion and care; and all were healed with a word of command or a touch of the Master's hands. "The whole atmosphere surrounding the narrative of these incidents is calm, lofty and pervaded with the spirit of Christ. When one remembers the manifold cruelties inspired by the unreasoning fear of demons,

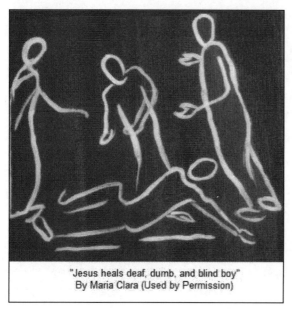

"Jesus heals deaf, dumb, and blind boy"
By Maria Clara (Used by Permission)

which make the annals of savage medicine a nightmare of unimaginable horrors, we cannot but feel the worldwide difference between the Biblical narratives and all others, both of ancient and modern times, with which we are acquainted." (From the *The International Standard Bible Encyclopedia*, James Orr, M.A., D.D., General Editor, Database © 2004 WORDsearch Corp.)

Demon-possession is defined as an invasion of the human personality by an evil, fallen spirit-being (or beings). It is an unwelcome intrusion into the human soul that has physical and supernatural consequences that manifest as physical sickness and disease, or mental discord and disharmony. In practically every case, the possessed either wittingly or unwittingly surrenders their will to the demonic spirit, giving them entrance to the soul. The old saying, "give the devil and inch and he'll take a mile," is appropriate here because when a person loses control over a certain part of their moral character, the evil spirits take the opportunity to enter into that person's soul and before they know it, they are overwhelmed. This is why moral depravity often precedes demon possession. Drugs, alcohol, prostitution, uncontrolled anger, unforgiveness, sexual promiscuity, idol worship, etc. weaken the soul, and drives it into the dark places where demonic spirits have their greatest advantage. Once the soul is a captive of the Devil, the person sinks into greater depravity and sensuality until they become totally devoted to gratifying their sinful appetites and lusts. Time and again, we witness the destruction of bodies through sickness and disease whose members have been given over to Satan's control.

Satan will stop at nothing to capture a human soul. His greatest weapon is the lie. In fact, Satan has no power over the Christian who has totally surrendered their life to Jesus Christ. Satan can and will attempt to torment, harass, and obstruct any Christian who is seeking to do God's will for their life, but he cannot possess once a person is "born again" because the Spirit of the living God has taken up residence in the new nature (Matthew 12:43-45). Satan's only power is to try and deceive the Christian and trick them into believing he has power over them when he does not. Those who are not "born again" have no defense against the devil's lies. Satan can easily say anything to persuade people to abandon the light and follow him. For Satan, any lie will do because he believes the ends always justifies the means. He will promise money, sex, and power for any who will surrender their will and fall down and worship him.

Satan offered Jesus all the kingdoms of the world knowing that once Jesus fell down and worshiped him, he would have the power to take them all back again. For every wealthy tycoon, famous movie star with adoring fans, or an absolute ruler that sold their soul to gain the whole world, Satan is able to draw in countless millions who have sold out for the false promises and have found themselves on the end of Satan's leash. Their lives will quickly spin out of control as they slavishly pursue the shallow dreams of fleeting fame and fortune in this world. "For what profit is it to a man," Jesus asked in Matthew 16:26, "if he gains the whole world, and loses his own soul? Or what will a man give in exchange for his soul?"

That the Bible teaches it is possible for evil spirits to take possession of men's bodies is not arguable. Sometimes men invited these spirits to do so and became friendly with them. The Scriptures call them "familiar spirits" (Leviticus 19:31; 20:6, 27). In modern terms mediumship, or channeling, is the practice of certain people – known as mediums – who allegedly mediate communication between spirits of the dead and other human beings. Attempts to contact the dead date back to Old Testament times, and has continued through today, mostly among primitive, animistic, and idolatrous people groups. However mediumship began to gain in popularity in modern Western countries during the 19th century, mostly as a reaction to the anti-supernatural materialism that prevailed in modern, industrialized nations. The sudden rise in popularity of spiritism led to scientific investigations during this period which revealed widespread fraud – with some practitioners employing techniques used by stage magicians and other props or tricks to deceive the gullible. The fad soon started to lose credibility and its popularity died out in the 20th century. But the practice still continues to this day in the West by a small group of self-identified witches, spiritists, and magicians.

The Lord commanded that any Israelite who attempted to communicate with the dead was to be put to death. The extreme measures were intended not only to make clear the seriousness with which the Lord saw the practice, but was also intended to protect the community of faith that would be damaged by the idolatry and moral depravity that usually precedes demon possession. That damage would most certainly spread once the demon-possessed settled into their midst (Psalm 106:36-39; Revelation 9:20). Sensuality and violence often becomes more pronounced in the demon possessed and would quickly involve others who were vulnerable to be seduced by "familiar spirits" looking for souls to inhabit that were weakened by sensuality. Once Satan enters and takes control of a person's soul, then surrender to his will is almost impossible to resist. The severe punishment of those who open the door to malevolent spirits was justifiable considering the physical, mental, and spiritual disorders are the inevitable result when evil spirits are present. It should also be noted that the Gospels never indicate that all disorders of the human mind and body are the result of demonic possession (Matthew 4:23, 24; 10:1; 11:5, for examples). It is true that insanity, epilepsy, blindness, dumbness, fevers, etc., are noted frequently as trappings and signs of demon possession (Matthew 12:22; 9:32; Mark 9:17; 25; Luke 11:4, 15, 16), but they were not necessarily identified with it in every case. Although all these disorders are not the direct result of demonic possession, often these conditions are aggravated by the presence of demonic powers. The Bible is not alone in the belief that such diseases could be due to a possession; other ancient beliefs shared the idea that demons had to be expelled from the patient before they could be healed.

As the reports of Jesus' miracles spread, sick people started coming to Him from near and far to be healed from whatever was causing them to be sick and suffering. If they were possessed by demons, were of unsound mind, traumatized by anxiety and fear, or broken in body He healed them all with equal compassion. Whether due to sin, natural, or supernatural causes, Jesus would meet and overcome whatever was presented to Him. This was His mission (Luke 4:17-21).

There were many exorcists among the Jews in the time of Jesus (Acts 19:13-14). They worked with elaborate incantations and methods; sometimes incorporating various spells or magical devices into their process. Jesus needed no such trappings; all He needed to do is speak one authoritative sentence and the exorcism was complete. Jesus taught His disciples to pray before they attempted to command any demon with authority because certain demonic spirits can only be cast out with prayer and fasting (Mark 9:29). Demonic spirits must always submit to the omnipotent authority of the Lord and His word. When dealing with demonic spirits, the believer must first be truly "born again" – meaning the Holy Spirit indwells them – and second must prayerfully approach the exorcism fully armed (Ephesians 6:10-20), and third, with the authority of Jesus Christ, speaking only the Word of God.

Mass Healings

"When the sun was setting, the people brought to Jesus all who had various kinds of sickness, and laying his hands on each one, he healed them. Moreover, demons came out of many people, shouting, 'You are the Son of God!' But he rebuked them and would not allow them to speak, because they knew he was the Christ." Luke 4:40-41 (NIV)

"When evening came, many who were demon-possessed were brought to him, and he drove out the spirits with a word and healed all the sick. This was to fulfill what was spoken through the prophet Isaiah: 'He took up our infirmities and carried our diseases.'" Matthew 8:16-17 (NIV)

"That evening after sunset the people brought to Jesus all the sick and demon-possessed. The whole town gathered at the door, and Jesus healed many who had various diseases. He also drove out many demons, but he would not let the demons speak because they knew who he was." Mark 1:32-34 (NIV)

Jesus preached the gospel – the Good News of salvation – to everyone who needed to hear it. The Old Testament prophets foretold a time when the Messiah would bring the Word of salvation and the Kingdom of Heaven. And when that time came, the Messiah would heal all of their infirmities and carry away all of their diseases. As proof that He was their long awaited Savior, Jesus healed, delivered, and restored to wholeness all that came to Him. Whenever anyone heals in Jesus' name, it is proof that God is with us (Luke 10:9), and that he cares for us. Christ can heal anyone who comes to Him – and not just of physical sickness, but of spiritual sickness as well. There's no sin or illness too great or too small for him to handle. Jesus' healings are always good news because they offer more than physical comfort; they bring freedom from sin and death, hope for the future, peace of heart, and eternal life with God. Every day, stories continue to pour in from around the world describing miraculous healings and deliverances in the name of Jesus Christ satisfying the prophecy of Isaiah that Jesus proclaimed "fulfilled" at His coming recorded in Luke 4:17-21.

Men can see the greatest miracles and miss the glory of God. What generation was ever favored with miracles as Jesus' generations was? Yet that generation crucified the Son of God!   Tom Wells – Christian: Take Heart!

Raising the Dead

By far, one of the best known of all of Jesus' miracles is the raising of Lazarus from the dead. The reason for its frequent mention has to do with the close relationship Jesus had with Lazarus and his sisters Martha and Mary. They are mentioned several times in the Gospels and seemed to have an important role in supporting Jesus' ministry. After Jesus raised him from the dead, Lazarus became a powerful witness for Jesus. When Jesus entered Jerusalem Lazarus was with Him, and John said that many who flocked to see Jesus also wanted to see Lazarus – the man Jesus brought back to life again. The chief priests plotted to kill Lazarus also because of him many of the Jews were deserting their leaders and believed in Jesus as their Messiah (John 12:9-11). But Lazarus was not the only one that Jesus raised from the dead during His earthly ministry. Luke 7:11-17 describes the raising of the son of a widow in the town of Nain. Matthew 9:18-26, Mark 5:35-43, and Luke 8:49-56 all describe the raising from the dead the daughter of a ruler of a synagogue in Galilee. It is very important to understand at this point that these "resurrections" from the dead were not identical to the future, general resurrection spoken of elsewhere in Scripture because in these cases those who were raised from death were raised in their natural bodies and not in their glorified bodies. Note the following paragraphs from my book, *The Gospel of Salvation: Our Complete Salvation in Body, Soul and Spirit*:

"Lazarus is raised from the dead by Jesus"
By Maria Clara (Used by Permission)

Glorification is the final step on the long journey to our complete salvation; it describes the Christian's ultimate and complete conformity into the image and likeness of God in Christ Jesus. Once the Holy Spirit is residing within the new creation that is born in the image and likeness of God, and once the soul is brought into perfect alignment with the Holy Spirit, our salvation is still incomplete (evidenced by the fact that the physical body of the believer is still under the power of sin and death). Glorification is the future and final work of God in the born again believer and is complete only after the Lord transforms their mortal, physical body into the eternal, imperishable, sinless body in which they will dwell in the presence of God forever (1 Corinthians 15:35-57). It is for glorification that the human race was created in the first place (Genesis 1:26), and it is for glorification that every person, predestined for salvation, was born again.

"For whom He foreknew, He also predestined to be conformed to the image of His Son, that He might be the firstborn among many brethren. Moreover whom He predestined, these He also called; whom He called, these He also justified; and whom He justified, these He also glorified." Romans 8:29-30

The Christian's glorification – the final transformation predestined for all those who have been saved – has been prepared by our heavenly Father since the foundation of the world. This is one of the many great mysteries of God that the human mind cannot comprehend: that God in His omniscient and eternal wisdom provided the means of our salvation long before the heavens and the earth were created (Revelation 13:8). The fullness of joy that will be experienced by those who enter into the kingdom of heaven was designed before time began (John 1:1-4); and those who will stand before the Lord, glorified (spotless and without blame) have been chosen from all eternity "…just as He chose us in Him before the foundation of the world, that we should be holy and without blame before Him in love" (Ephesians 1:4). Because God's great plan of salvation reaches from eternity past to eternity future, He will accomplish it perfectly. God's plan for our glorification is going to succeed because it depends upon God to accomplish it; the Christian does nothing to produce their glorified body. When that day and hour arrives, the "sons of God" (Luke 20:36) will be revealed: "for the earnest expectation of the creation eagerly waits for the revealing of the sons of God" (Romans 8:19).

Another mystery revealed in the gospel of our salvation in Christ Jesus is that there is always "the now and the yet to be" in regard to our salvation. Those who have been saved (justified), are being saved (sanctified), and will be saved (glorified). In Romans 8:29-30, the apostle Paul speaks of our salvation as a reality that has come and as a promise that is yet to come – both in the same tense. Those who have been justified from the beginning (eternity past) will discover in the end (eternity future) that they have been predestined to be sanctified. Those who have been justified and sanctified are predestined to be glorified with Christ in the sight of God, "knowing that He who raised up the Lord Jesus will also raise us up with Jesus, and will present us with you. For all things are for your sakes, that grace, having spread through the many, may cause thanksgiving to abound to the glory of God" (2 Corinthians 4:14-15). Paul's confidence in the future glorification of the saints was grounded in his understanding that it was not dependent upon man's work, but depends upon

God's work in the lives of those who have been saved: "For I am confident of this very thing, that He who began a good work in you will perfect it until the day of Christ Jesus" (Philippians 1:6).

In the great golden chain of salvation, not a single person is lost. Called, justified, glorified. Our glorification is so certain that in God's eyes it is as good as done. Wil Pounds

The reality of Jesus Christ's resurrection is what gives hope to every believer who puts his or her trust in Him. The election, effectual calling, and justification have already taken place in the believer's experience, but the glorification is yet to take place; it is still in the future. But the fact that Christ's tomb is empty confirms His promise for our future glorification.

Jesus came into this world to give life in abundance (John 10:10; Romans 5:18; and 1 Timothy 1:16). As *The Life,* Jesus came into this world and healed all manner of sicknesses and diseases; and as *The Resurrection,* Jesus raised the dead to life again. He did this in order to give hope to the living for the promise of the Great Resurrection that will surely come when He returns in glory. It is then that God the Father will receive the dead and the living in their glorified bodies and in Christ receive them to into His eternal kingdom. Until that time it is one of the deep mysteries of God that although Jesus loves us unconditionally, His perfect love (agape) permits pain, sickness, and death to continue until that moment predestined from eternity, when the new heaven and new earth will be revealed and there will be no more suffering, "And God will wipe away every tear from their eyes; there shall be no more death, nor sorrow, nor crying. There shall be no more pain, for the former things have passed away" (Revelation 21:4).

Each of these resurrection miracles are unique and reveal something different about Jesus' healing ministry. In Luke 7:11-17, Luke gives no indication that Jesus had any plan to bring that young man back to life. "Now it happened, the day after, that He went into a city called Nain…" is how Luke described it. Jesus and "many of His disciples" were accompanied by a large crowd. As this joyful crowd approached the city gate they were met with the approaching group of mourners carrying a dead man to be buried. "Up from the city close by came this 'great multitude' that followed the dead, with lamentations, wild chants of mourning women, accompanied by flutes and the melancholy tinkle of cymbals, perhaps by trumpets, amidst expressions of general sympathy. Along the road from Endor streamed the great multitude which followed the 'Prince of Life.' Here they met: Life and Death. The connecting link

"Jesus raises a dead man in Nain"
By Maria Clara (Used by Permission)

between them was the deep sorrow of the widowed mother." Alfred Edersheim, Jesus the Messiah (An Abridged Edition), Wm. B. Eerdmans Publishing Company, Grand Rapids, Michigan, Reprinted 1981, pp. 153-154.

Intimately familiar with the social customs of the Jews, Jesus quickly recognized the woman was a widow as she walked alone in front of the bier holding the body of her son she had brought into this life. She was totally unaware of Jesus as he approached the mournful group. Moved by compassion, and possibly projecting ahead thinking of His mother, Mary who one day would have to mourn the loss of her Son, Jesus catches this grieving mother's attention and urges her, "Do not weep." Jesus must have startled the crowd and stopped them in their tracks as He touched the bier. And without any prompting from anyone, does the totally unexpected, saying, "Young man, I say to you, arise." Immediately the dead man sat up and began to speak and Jesus offered him back to his mother. Then the fear of God came upon all who witnessed this great miracle "...and they glorified God, saying, 'A great prophet has risen up among us'; and, 'God has visited His people.'" Needless to say, the news of this miracle quickly spread throughout all of Judea and the surrounding regions.

Matthew, Mark, and Luke all describe the raising of the daughter of Jairus, the Ruler of the Synagogue at Capernaum. Luke helps us place this event after the miracle at Nain. Jesus and His disciples had just returned from a short journey across the Sea of Galilee to the region of Gadarenes, which is opposite Galilee. The expectant crowd sees Jesus and His disciples getting out of the boat and start pressing in all around them. One man pushes through the crowd and desperately urges Jesus to come to his home and heal his daughter who is at the point of death. Matthew speaks of her as dead at the time of the father's desperate plea to Jesus; the other two Gospels describe her as on the point of death, literally, "at death's door." A desperate father wanting to save his child will no doubt blur the lines between life and death if he believes there is the slightest hope of bringing that child back from the brink of death; which explains the different interpretations of his statement by the different Gospel writers. All acknowledged that awful moment when someone from the ruler's house came to him and in front of Jesus, tells him, "Your daughter is dead. Do not trouble the Teacher." To the grief-stricken father, Jesus' assurance "Do not be afraid, only believe, and she will be made well" was his last shred of hope that his daughter could be brought back from the threshold of death. When they reached the house the mourners were already wailing to the sounds of the flutes playing the tune of lament. All the same signs of death were there as at Nain, but Jesus already knew what He must do.

There is a striking difference between Nain and here. At Nain, Jesus' initial action is met with silent wonder and anticipation "what is this man about to do?" At Jairus' house, Jesus' attempt to calm and comfort the crowd by saying, "Do not weep; she is not dead, but sleeping." was met with scorn and ridicule. Here we are reminded of Jesus' earlier rebuke of the Pharisees and lawyers who refused to believe, "They are like children sitting in the marketplace and calling to one another, saying: 'We played the flute for you, and you did not dance; we mourned to you, and you did not weep'" (Luke 7:32). The mourners were so set upon mourning that they could not stop long enough to consider who was speaking to them. Taking inside only those necessary (no need for a large group crowding all around) Jesus permitted only Peter, James, and John, and the father and mother of the girl to accompany Him to where the little girl was laying. Jesus took her by the hand and called her just as if He was waking her in the morning from a deep sleep, saying, "Little girl, arise." Then He commanded that she be given something to eat just as if she was taking her morning breakfast. To the astonished parents, Jesus charged them not to tell anyone what had happened.

There is a calmness and naturalness about Jesus' miracles that runs counter to the modern-day, almost circus atmosphere of the evangelistic meetings that promise healings with signs and wonders following. Jesus never used the promise of healing miracles to draw a crowd. In fact at one point, He sent His disciples to the towns and villages ahead of Him and gave them the command and authority to heal when He was nowhere to be seen (Luke 10:1, 9). As far as Jesus was concerned, miracles were not for the masses, but were intended primarily for those immediately involved.

The crowds were superfluous to His activity; He did not crave nor seek the attention or adoration of the masses through His healing ministry. Jesus had passed that temptation already when Satan came to Him in the Wilderness and urged Him to make a dramatic entrance into Jerusalem by leaping from the pinnacle of the Temple and floating gracefully to the ground unharmed to the amazement of the crowds below (Matthew 4:5-7). Jesus had no problem with putting away the crowds and working this great miracle in the privacy of only those concerned.

John 11:1-45 presents an entirely different set of circumstances than the other two stories of Jesus raising the dead. Here, Jesus receives a message from Bethany. Mary and her sister Martha are urging Jesus to come and heal their brother Lazarus, one whom Jesus loved. John makes it clear in verse 5 that Jesus loved the sisters and Lazarus. But Jesus does a strange thing by any other normal human standard and remains two more days in the place where He was ministering. We know from other miracles that Jesus could have simply commanded the sickness to depart from His dear friend's body without ever walking a step in his direction. But Jesus has a greater purpose in mind, saying, "This sickness is not unto death, but for the glory of God, that the Son of God may be glorified through it." Once Jesus is aware that Lazarus is dead (verse 14), He is ready to return to Bethany. Jesus hints at a greater purpose for how this story is playing out when He says to His perplexed disciples, "I am glad for your sakes that I was not there, that you may believe."

Evidently, this was a wealthy and influential family because John tells us many Jews from the surrounding area (Bethany was only two miles down the road from Jerusalem) had come to comfort Martha and Mary and help them mourn the loss of their brother. As soon as Jesus came near to the house, Martha slips away from the crowd and goes to Him. It is obvious that she is confused and hurt, not knowing why Jesus did not come in time to save their brother and His friend. Still, Martha believes that anything is possible for the Lord. When Jesus tells her "Your brother will rise again." She acknowledges her belief in a future resurrection "at the last day." It is at this point that Jesus begins to reveal the true reason for His delay. He says to Martha, "I am the resurrection and the life. He who believes in Me, though he may die, he shall live. And whoever lives and believes in Me shall never die. Do you believe this?" Martha's response is what He came for: "She said to Him, 'Yes, Lord, I believe that You are the Christ, the Son of God, who is to come into the world'" which was as great a confession of faith as was Peter's in Mathew 16:16.

Martha then sends a private message to her sister that Jesus has arrived and is calling for her. Immediately Mary goes to the place where Jesus and Martha are waiting for her. Seeing her leave the house, the Jews who were there to comfort her followed her believing she was going to the tomb to weep and mourn for her brother there. When she came to Jesus, Mary falls down at His feet as hurt and confused as was Martha. In His humanity, Jesus was able to share their grief and wept openly, even though He knew the miracle that was predestined to take place.

The curious crowd wonders aloud why Jesus could not have saved someone He loved from dying: "Could not this Man, who opened the eyes of the blind, also have kept this man from dying?" To everyone's amazement, when they reach the tomb, Jesus orders the stone to be removed and the tomb opened. The offensive stench of death would be released when the tomb was opened, but nevertheless, at His command the stone was removed. Notice that in the natural, all the signs pointed in one direction, but Jesus is says, "Did I not say to you that if you would believe you would see the glory of God?" This is similar to how He worked His miracle of the large catch of fish when Peter saw and believed (Luke 5:4-11).

Volumes have been written detailing Jesus' words, "Lazarus, come forth!" and the miracle that followed. But the simplest commentary is found in Luke's own words, "Then many of the Jews who had come to Mary, and had seen the things Jesus did, believed in Him." All of Jesus' great miracles were intended for two purposes:
1. To bring glory to His Father
2. To so that those who were the beneficiaries and those who witnessed those miracles would see and believe in Jesus as the Son of God.

"Because of the great change in Lazarus, many people desired to see him, and his 'living witness' was used by God to bring people to salvation (John 12:9–11). There are no recorded words of Lazarus in the Gospels, but his daily walk is enough to convince people that Jesus is the Son of God. Because of his effective witness, Lazarus was persecuted by the religious leaders who wanted to kill him and get rid of the evidence." Warren W. Wiersbe, *The Wiersbe Bible Commentary: New Testament,* David C. Cook Publisher, Colorado Springs, CO, p.270

These purposes do not diminish the fact that Jesus acted out of compassion for those who were hurting and in need of physical, mental, emotional or spiritual salvation. But in the end, all of His great miracles could not convince anyone whose heart was not already open and willing to receive the truth. Note that Judas witnessed every miracle of Jesus, and many of the Jews saw them too, but in the end they rejected, betrayed, and crucified Him. If the sole purpose of His miracles were to convince people to believe and follow Him, then Jesus failed. And if modern-day evangelists believe that all they need to convince the masses are healing miracles with signs and wonders following, then they will fail as well. They may be able to attract the curious or those that are seeking a cure from whatever ails them, but miracles in and of themselves will not convince anyone to follow Jesus as the Lord of their life. It takes much more than miracles to accomplish that. "As with the previous miracles, the people were divided in their response. Some did believe and on 'Palm Sunday' gave witness of the miracle Jesus had performed (John 12:17-18). But others immediately went to the religious leaders and reported what had happened in Bethany. These 'informers' were so near the kingdom, yet there is no evidence that they believed. If the heart will not yield to truth, then the grace of God cannot bring salvation. These people could have experienced a spiritual resurrection in their own lives!" Warren W. Wiersbe, *The Wiersbe Bible Commentary: New Testament,* David C. Cook Publisher, Colorado Springs, CO, p.270

FREDERICK OSBORN

8.

"The King Enters Jerusalem"
The Events Leading up to Jesus' Final Hours

"Grand entry of Jesus into Jerusalem"
By Maria Clare (Used by Permission)

LESSON OUTLINE:

The purpose of this lesson is to describe the events leading up to the last week of Jesus' life.

- Events Leading to His Triumphal Entry Into Jerusalem from the Gospels

- Events of the Last Week from the Gospels

THE WAY, TRUTH, AND LIFE

EVENTS LEADING TO JERUSALEM

Matt. 16:21; 17:22-27; 20:17, 29-34
Mark 8:31, 10:1, 32, 46-52; 11:1-2
Luke 9:51-56, 10:38-42, 13:22; 18:31-42; 19:1-10, 28-35
John 12:1-8

"Now it came to pass, when the time had come for Him to be received up, that He steadfastly set His face to go to Jerusalem, and sent messengers before His face. And as they went, they entered a village of the Samaritans, to prepare for Him. But they did not receive Him, because His face was set for the journey to Jerusalem. And when His disciples James and John saw this, they said, 'Lord, do You want us to command fire to come down from heaven and consume them, just as Elijah did?' But He turned and rebuked them, and said, 'You do not know what manner of spirit you are of. For the Son of Man did not come to destroy men's lives but to save them.' And they went to another village." Luke 9:51-56 (NKJV)

When the "fullness of time had come" God sent forth His Son into this world with a specific mission to accomplish (Gal. 4:4-5). From the moment Jesus rose from the waters of John's baptism, marking the beginning of His public ministry, until this moment in Luke 9:51, everything the Son of Man did and said was intended to prepare His disciples and the nation for the events to take place in the final days and hours of His life on this earth.

Luke captures this moment. Jesus knew in His spirit that the time had finally come and neither His disciples nor the nation of Israel would be more prepared for His death, burial, and resurrection than they were at that time. So Jesus was resolute; and He "steadfastly set His face to go to Jerusalem" where everything was heading from the moment of His birth.

Luke's Gospel gives us the clearest and most detailed account of the events leading up to Jesus' arrival in Jerusalem for that last Passover (Luke 9:51 – 19:28). He begins his story of Jesus' final journey to Jerusalem with this encounter with the Samaritans – an encounter that will foreshadow His rejection by the Jews in Jerusalem. Unlike His earlier experience at Sychar (John 4), this time the Samaritans were unable to overcome their hostility towards the Jews in general and see that Jesus had come with the gift of Salvation for them and for anyone who would listen to Him. For centuries the Jews in Jerusalem had rejected the Samaritans and refused them entry to the city and the Temple during the Feasts. Because Jesus was now on His way to Jerusalem, the Samaritans could not overcome their prejudice and bitterness and refused hospitality to Jesus and His disciples. Knowing the rejection that was waiting for Him in Jerusalem, Jesus realized that His disciples would need to learn from this incident how to deal with strong opposition and outright rejection because of their preaching of the Gospel.

At first the disciples wanted to call down fire from heaven to punish those who abused them and rejected their Master. But Jesus would have none of it. Instead He rebukes His disciples for lashing out in anger against those who were spiritually blind and ignorant. The disciples would learn soon enough that following Jesus unconditionally and fulfilling the Great Commission would involve rejection and suffering. "Indeed, all who desire to live a godly life in Christ Jesus will be persecuted..." 2 Timothy 3:12 (ESV). Every disciple would die a martyr's death – except for Judas who would betray Him and John, the beloved disciple and Apostle who died of natural causes (but John had to endure a lifetime of suffering and persecution for His Lord and Master).

For more than three years now, Jesus had been preparing His core disciples – testing them and trying them in various situations – they were completely committed followers. But even these most dedicated followers would have their loyalty tested to the limits by what was waiting for their Master on the road ahead of them leading to Jerusalem and Golgotha. Every one of the gospel writers indicated that Judea was a dangerous place for Jesus; and especially Jerusalem because it was the epicenter of Judaism's religious and political elites that by now were all lined up against Him. Jesus' conflicts with the Scribes, Pharisees, Sadducees, and teachers of the Law had only intensified as time went on. The tension between Jesus and the religious rulers had reached a boiling point and the Jewish leaders intensified their plot to execute Jesus the next time He set foot in Jerusalem.

The first part of Luke 10 describes in detail the ministry of those Jesus sent ahead of Him on His journey towards Jerusalem. Jesus warned them that the gracious gospel His disciples were to announce would not be received by all. Those who believed and received would understand that the Kingdom of God had come near to them (verse 11). However, in another foreshadowing of the rejection to come Jesus gave them a

THE WAY, TRUTH, AND LIFE

prophetic warning of the final judgment coming to all nations when the great Day of the Lord arrives at the end of the age. Jesus said to those places where the Kingdom of God had come near, but rejected it: "Woe to you, Chorazin! Woe to you, Bethsaida! For if the mighty works done in you had been done in Tyre and Sidon, they would have repented long ago, sitting in sackcloth and ashes. But it will be more bearable in the judgment for Tyre and Sidon than for you. And you, Capernaum, will you be exalted to heaven? You shall be brought down to Hades. The one who hears you hears me, and the one who rejects you rejects me, and the one who rejects me rejects him who sent me." Luke 10:13-16 (ESV)

Jesus rejoiced with the disciples when they returned. Their mission had been successful, demonstrating their readiness to take the gospel of the kingdom beyond the walls of Jerusalem, to Judea, Samaria, and to the outermost regions of the world. "Rejected by the mass of the people, Jesus looked upon His humble followers and rejoiced in the Spirit, thanking the Father for His matchless wisdom. The seventy were not the wise and prudent men of this world. They were not the intellectuals or the scholars. They were mere babes! But they were babes with faith, devotion, and unquestioning obedience. The intellectuals were too wise, too knowing, too clever for their own good. Their pride blinded them to the true worth of God's beloved Son. It is through babes that God can work most effectively. Our Lord was happy for all those whom the Father had given to Him, and for this initial success of the seventy, which foretold the eventual downfall of Satan." William MacDonald, *Believer's Bible Commentary*, Thomas Nelson, Nashville, TN., © 1995, p.1409

Once Jesus had returned to His heavenly kingdom, His disciples would function as His ambassadors. They were not to rejoice in the power and authority that had been given to them over the forces of darkness (verses 17-20), but only in their salvation. Pride goes before a fall (verse 18) it was only their childlike faith that would commend them before God and these faithful few were privileged because "many prophets and kings longed to see what you see, but they didn't see it. And they longed to hear what you hear, but they didn't hear it."

As Jesus continues on His way to Jerusalem, the Jewish religious authorities continue their examination of Jesus' teachings along the way. We have the story of the "Good Samaritan" in answer to a question from a religious expert on the Law of Moses (10:25-37). It is here that Luke choses to insert the story of Martha and Mary (10:38-42).

Next, Luke recounts Jesus' instruction to His disciples on prayer (11:1-12) which is similar to the Sermon on the Mount recorded in Matthew's Gospel. This is followed by a parable about a man who asks a neighbor for bread to help feed his guests. Matthew's account of Jesus' teaching on the Lord's Prayer places the emphasis on the need for forgiveness (Matt. 6:14-15). Here, Jesus uses His teaching on prayer to illustrate the Father's desire to provide for those who ask Him.

"And as He said these things to them, the scribes and the Pharisees began to assail Him vehemently, and to cross-examine Him about many things, lying in wait for Him, and seeking to catch Him in something He might say, that they might accuse Him." Luke 11:53-54 (NKJV)

Luke's narrative describes how the crowds continue to ebb and flow around Jesus. The religious leaders are unrelenting in their desire to challenge Jesus, question His authority and power, and if possible trip Him up with His words so as to have an accusation against Him. The religious authorities are only looking for an excuse to put Jesus on trial when He reaches Jerusalem. In His words and actions Jesus demonstrated that He was not the Messiah they expected to ride into Jerusalem. They believed the Messiah would come riding on a stallion in front of a conquering army stained with the blood of their enemies. Instead, Jesus came to Jerusalem riding on a donkey with an army of disciples waving palm branches. And so their doubts and confusion over His true identity are keeping most in the crowds from fully committing to Him. Jesus' tactics at this point in time are clearly intended to weed out those "tares" that really do not believe. He is deliberately sifting out those who are uncommitted "hangers on" and testing the commitment of His loyal disciples. Jesus continued to warn the religious leaders and pronounced "woes" upon those hypocrites who placed burdens and obstacles upon those needing God's grace and mercy.

Jesus' teachings continue from chapter 12 through several more chapters leading up to His arrival in Jerusalem. As Jesus moves closer and closer to Jerusalem He is warned that the religious leaders are out to destroy Him. Jesus responds with another prophetic warning about the coming judgment:

THE WAY, TRUTH, AND LIFE

"On that very day some Pharisees came, saying to Him, 'Get out and depart from here, for Herod wants to kill You.' And He said to them,
'Go, tell that fox, "Behold, I cast out demons and perform cures today
and tomorrow, and the third day I shall be perfected." Nevertheless I must journey today, tomorrow, and the day following; for it cannot be that a prophet should perish outside of Jerusalem.'
'O Jerusalem, Jerusalem, the one who kills the prophets and stones those who are sent to her! How often I wanted to gather your children together, as a hen gathers her brood under her wings, but you were not willing!'
See! Your house is left to you desolate; and assuredly, I say to you, you shall not see Me until the time comes when you say, 'Blessed is He who comes in the name of the LORD!' "Luke 13:31-35 (NKJV)

In each chapter, Luke records more of Jesus' important teachings for the crowds. He describes the religious leaders opposing Him, and recounts Jesus' private teachings for His disciples. His teachings for the crowds are not generally understood or accepted. Whenever Jesus narrows His message to the true cost of following Him as a disciple, the crowds melt away. His teachings and ministry are being rejected with increased hostility by the the religious leaders. All the while, His disciples are struggling to keep pace with their Master and to understand His teachings. The disciples are trying to grasp the full implications of what is happening around them.

Luke chapters 12 - 18 describe more of Jesus' public teachings along the way to Jerusalem. It is important to note in Luke's Gospel the rising tensions between Jesus and the Jewish leaders the closer He gets to the city.

It is impossible to say exactly, but it seems to be approximately at this point (Luke 13:31-35) that John's narrative records the story of Jesus raising Lazarus from the dead (John 11:1-57). The elements of John's story make more sense when understood in context of Luke's part of this narrative. When the sisters sent word to Jesus that Lazarus was ill, He was already on the road coming to them (Bethany was on the way to Jerusalem and less than a day's journey from the city's gates.) But Jesus would not be diverted from the path He was taking and His plan to reach Jerusalem at the right moment during the Feast of Passover (11:6). By this point in time, the disciples knew of the plots to kill Jesus so they were reluctant to go (11:8), but when they understood Jesus' determination to go forward, Thomas says to his fellow disciples, "Let us also go, that we may die with him." When Jesus arrives at Martha's and Mary's home, He does not want to publically announce His presence. After raising Lazarus, the difference of opinions among the Jews over Jesus continues unabated (11:45-53). Jesus is now poised on the outskirts of Jerusalem waiting for the Passover to begin (11:54). The word about Jesus had spread far and wide and all were anxiously watching to see if He would dare come to Jerusalem knowing the Jewish leaders were ready to arrest Him (11:55-57).

JESUS' TEACHINGS IN LUKE: ON THE WAY TO JERUSALEM

- 12:1-12 - Jesus gives another warning to His disciples about the hypocrisy of the Pharisees. He encourages His disciples not to fear them (keep in mind Jesus' final confrontation with the Pharisees is just ahead of Him)
- 12:13-21 – In the parable of the Rich Fool, Jesus admonishes the crowds to not be consumed with material wealth
- 12:22-34 – Jesus teaches the people not to worry about material things, but to trust in God's provision
- 12:35-48 – Jesus speaks of His second coming; but not directly because the people are not yet ready to hear the details. He encourages them to be faithful and to watch a pray for His coming.
- 12:49-59 – Before His Second Coming there will be a time of division and crisis. They must remain steadfast and faithful to the end.
- 13:1-9 – Jesus calls upon the people to repent before the coming judgment upon Jerusalem
- 13:18-30 – Jesus teaches more parables on the Kingdom of God
- 13:31-35 – Jesus grieves over Jerusalem's rejection of their Savior
- 14:7-24 – Jesus teaches in parables about the great Marriage Feast of the Lamb to take place at the end of the age.
- 14:25-35 – Jesus teaches more on the high cost of discipleship
- 15:1-32 – Jesus teaches in parables about the saving grace of God in the "Lost Sheep," the "Lost Coin," and the "Prodigal Son"

THE WAY, TRUTH, AND LIFE

- 16:1-31 – Jesus confronts the Pharisees for their love of money and hard hearts in the Parables of the Shrew Manager and the Rich Man and Lazarus
- 17:1-10 – Jesus teaches His disciples about forgiveness and faith
- 17:20-37 – Jesus teaches about the coming kingdom of God at the end of the age
- 18:1-8 – Jesus teaches a parable about persistence in prayer
- 18:9-14 – Jesus teaches a parable about the right attitude in prayer
- 18:15-17 – Jesus teaches about the right attitude to enter the kingdom of God
- 18:18-30 – Jesus teaches rich young ruler about the cost of discipleship
- 18:31-33 – Jesus predicts His death and resurrection a third time
- 19:11-27 – Jesus teaches on Kingdom rewards and punishments at the end of the age in the Parable of the Ten Minas (19:28 JESUS ENTERS JERUSALEM)

"Jesus speaks to tax-collector Zacchaeus" By Maria Clara (Used by Permission)

"Then He took the twelve aside and said to them, 'Behold, we are going up to Jerusalem, and all things that are written by the prophets concerning the Son of Man will be accomplished. For He will be delivered to the Gentiles and will be mocked and insulted and spit upon. They will scourge Him and kill Him. And the third day He will rise again.' But they understood none of these things; this saying was hidden from them, and they did not know the things which were spoken." Luke 18:31-34 (NKJV)

Once again Jesus takes His disciples aside and tells them what is about to happen to Him, but Luke says they understood none of these things; it was hidden from them; and they did not know what Jesus was talking about. As He continued along the way to Jerusalem, Jesus was healing and teaching the people and was intensifying His teaching and training of His disciples. John never tells us what took place between Jesus and His disciples away from the crowds in the town of Ephraim, near the wilderness region (11:54). Jesus being away from the prying eyes of the religious leaders did not stop them from intensifying their efforts to arrest and execute Jesus as soon as He entered Jerusalem. By Luke chapter 19, Jesus has reached Jericho, the gateway to Jerusalem.

It is at this point that Luke records the conversion of Zaccheus. "Many, no doubt, were converted to the faith of Christ of whom no account is kept in the gospels; but the conversion of some, whose case had something in it extraordinary, is recorded, as this of Zaccheus. Christ passed through Jericho, v. 1. This city was built under a curse, yet Christ honoured it with his presence, for the gospel takes away the curse. Though it ought not to have been built, yet it was not therefore a sin to live in it when it was built. Christ was now going from the other side Jordan to Bethany near Jerusalem, to raise Lazarus to life; when he was going to do one good work he contrived to do many by the way. He did good both to the souls and to the bodies of people; we have here an instance of the former." *Matthew Henry's Commentary on the Whole Bible*

THE REBUILDING OF JERICHO

Then Joshua charged them at that time, saying, "Cursed be the man before the LORD who rises up and builds this city Jericho; he shall lay its foundation with his firstborn, and with his youngest he shall set up its gates." So the LORD was with Joshua, and his fame spread throughout all the country. Joshua 6:26-27 (NKJV)

In his days Hiel of Bethel built Jericho. He laid its foundation with Abiram his firstborn, and with his youngest son Segub he set up its gates, according to the word of the LORD, which He had spoken through Joshua the son of Nun. 1 Kings 16:34 (NKJV)

"How ill he sped. He built for his children, but God wrote him childless; his eldest son died when he began, the youngest when he finished, and all the rest (it is supposed) between. Note, Those whom God curses are cursed indeed; none ever hardened his heart against God and prospered. God keep us back from presumptuous sins, those great transgressions!" *Matthew Henry's Commentary on the Whole Bible*

| THE EVENTS OF PASSION WEEK |||||
DAY	MATT	MARK	LUKE	JOHN
SUNDAY (Palm Sunday) 1. Triumphal entry	21:1-9	11:1-10	19:28-44	12:12-19
2. To Temple and to Bethany	21:10-17	11:11	19:45-46	12:20-50
MONDAY 3. Jesus and fig tree	21:18-19	11:12-14	-	-
4. Temple Cleansed	-	11:15-19	19:45-48	-
TUESDAY 5. Return to Jerusalem	21:20-22	11:20-26	-	-
6. Jesus questioned	21:23-27	11:27-33	20:1-8	-
7. In the Temple	21:28-46; 22	12-1-37a	20:9-44	-
8. Condemnation by Scribes and Pharisees	23:1-36	12:37b-40	20:45-47	-
9. Temple Treasury		12:41-44	21:1-4	-
10. Prophetic Teachings	24:1-44	13:1-37	21:5-38	-
WEDNESDAY 11. Plot Against Jesus	26:1-5	14:1-2	22:1-2	-
12. Anointed at Bethany	26:6-13	14:1-9	-	12:2-8
13. Judas betrays Jesus	26:14-16	14:10-11	22:3-6	-

THURSDAY				
14. Last Supper preparation	26:17-19	14:12-16	22:7-13	-
15. Last Supper	26:20-29	14:17-25	22:14-38	13:1 – 18:1
16. Gethsemane	26:30-46	14:26-42	22:39-46	-
17. Arrest	26:47-50	14:43-52	22:47-53	18:2-12a
18. Jesus taken to Annas	-	-	-	18:12b-14, 19-23
19. Trial before Sanhedrin (Peter denies Jesus)	26:57-75	14:53-72	22:54-71	18:15-18, 24-27
FRIDAY				
20. Sent to Pilate	27:1-2	15:1-5	23:1-5	18:28-38
21. Judas' Suicide	27:3-10	-	-	-
22. Jesus to Herod	-	-	23:6-16	-
23. Death Sentence	27:11-26	15:6-15	23:17-25	18:39-40
24. Scourged, led to Golgotha	27:27-32	15:15-21	-	19:1-17
25. Crucifixion	27:27-32	15:22-41	23:33-49	19:18-30
26. Burial	27:57-61	15:42-47	23:50-56	19:31-42
SATURDAY In the Tomb	27:62-66	-	-	-
SUNDAY The Resurrection	28:1-10	68:1-8	24:1-12	20:1

JESUS IS NOW READY TO ENTER JERUSALEM FOR THE LAST TIME

Events of the Last Week

    Matt 21:1-19; 21:20-46; 22:1-46; 23:1-39; 26:1-19
    Mark 11:1-11; 11:19 – 12:44; 14:1-16
    Luke 19:29-44; 20:1-47; 21:1-4, 37-38; 22:1-13
    John 12:2-8, 12-50

Final Week - Day 1: Palm Sunday's Triumphal Entry

Beginning with "Palm Sunday," Jesus Christ starts the Week with a very public and dramatic entrance into the city. On the Sunday before his death, Jesus began his trip to Jerusalem, knowing that soon he would lay down his life for the sins of the world.

Nearing the village of Bethphage, he sent two of his disciples ahead to look for a donkey with its unbroken colt. Jesus instructed the disciples to untie the animals and bring them to him. Then Jesus sat on the young donkey and slowly, humbly, made his triumphal entry into Jerusalem, fulfilling the ancient prophecy in Zechariah: "Rejoice greatly, O daughter of Zion! Shout aloud, O daughter of Jerusalem! Behold, your king is coming to you; righteous and having salvation is he, humble and mounted on a donkey, on a colt, the foal of a donkey." Zechariah 9:9 (ESV)

The crowds welcomed him by waving palm branches in the air and shouting "Hosanna to the Son of David! Blessed is he who comes in the name of the Lord! Hosanna in the highest!"

On Palm Sunday, Jesus and his disciples spent the night in Bethany, a town about two miles east of Jerusalem. In all likelihood, Jesus stayed in the home of Mary, Martha, and Lazarus, whom Jesus had raised from the dead.

For Further Study:

Jesus' Triumphal Entry is recorded in Matthew 21:1-11, Mark 11:1-11, Luke 19:28-44, and John 12:12-19.

*(**Note:** The exact order of events during the Final Week is debated by Bible scholars. This timeline represents an approximate outline of major events.)*

FREDERICK OSBORN

The Final Week - Day 2: Monday Jesus Clears the Temple

"Jesus cleanses the temple of money-changers"
By Maria Clara (Used by Permission)

The Second Day of Jesus' final week traces the footsteps of Jesus from Bethany where He returned with his disciples the night before to Jerusalem. Along the way, Jesus cursed a fig tree because it had failed to bear fruit. Some scholars believe this cursing of the fig tree represented God's judgment on the spiritually dead religious leaders of Israel. Others believe the symbolism extended to all believers, demonstrating that genuine, living faith is more than just outward religiosity. What is unique about this miracle is that it is a sign of God's coming judgment. This parable contrasts with the parable of the barren fig tree in Luke 13:6-9 in that first parable, the fig tree is given one last chance. "And he answered him, 'Sir, let it alone this year also, until I dig around it and put on manure. Then if it should bear fruit next year, well and good; but if not, you can cut it down.'" Luke 13:8-9 (ESV)

Here, the "next year" has arrived and fruit is still not to be found. There is nothing left to do but cut it down. The imagery of this parable fits perfectly with Jesus' and John the Baptist's teachings on repentance (Matt. 3:10; Luke 3:9; John 15:6). The image also connects this judgment with the nation of Israel: "Like grapes in the wilderness, I found Israel. Like the first fruit on the fig tree in its first season, I saw your fathers. But they came to Baal-peor and consecrated themselves to the thing of shame, and became detestable like the thing they loved." Hosea 9:10 (ESV) True faith must bear spiritual fruit in the life of a nation or in a person's life.

When Jesus arrived at the Temple he found the courts full of corrupt money changers. He began overturning their tables and clearing the Temple, saying, "The Scriptures declare, 'My Temple will be a house of prayer,' but you have turned it into a den of thieves." (Luke 19:46) We will understand the full implications of Jesus' actions in the lesson on the trials of Jesus.

On Monday evening Jesus stayed in Bethany again, probably in the home of his friends, Mary, Martha, and Lazarus. Remember, once Jesus set out on His public ministry, He had no home of His own (Matt. 8:20). The only shelter He had was in the homes of others such as Martha, Mary, and Lazarus.

For Further Study:

> Monday's events are recorded in Matthew 21:12-22, Mark 11:15-19, Luke 19:45-48, and John 2:13-17.

*(**Note:** The exact order of events during the Final Week is debated by Bible scholars. This timeline represents an approximate outline of major events.)*

The Final Week - Day 3: Tuesday in Jerusalem, Mount of Olives

"Jesus talks to his disciples"
By Maria Clara (Used by Permission)

Tuesday, day three of Jesus' journey through His final week, He returns to the Temple in Jerusalem and then to the Mount of Olives. That morning, Jesus and his disciples returned to Jerusalem. As if to remind them of the reception Jesus would receive that day from the religious leaders of the Jews, they passed the withered fig tree on their way to the Temple. Matthew condenses the cursing of the fig tree to a single event and uses the opportunity to include the same message as Mark concerning what Jesus taught His disciples about faith.

Once Jesus and His disciples arrive at the Temple, the religious leaders aggressively challenged Jesus' authority, attempting to ambush him and create an opportunity for his arrest. Jesus responds to their threats with a series of Parables that have by now become His primary method of public discourse. In the parables of The Two Sons, The Wicked Farmers, and the Wedding Feast Jesus not only evaded their verbal traps, but at the same time pronounced harsh judgment on them:

- The Two Sons (Matthew 21:31-32) – Jesus exposed the disobedience of the Jewish leaders. Jesus declares that the corrupt tax collectors and prostitutes will get into the Kingdom of God before them.

- The Wicked Farmers (Matt. 21:33-46; Mark 12:1-12; Luke 20:9-19) – In telling this parable, it quickly became obvious that Jesus was speaking about the religious leaders who were plotting to kill Him. The imagery of this parable is a thinly veiled recounting of the long sad history of Israel's rebelliousness. The Landowner is God; the vineyard is Israel; the tenant farmers were the Jewish religious leaders; the servants of the Landowner were the faithful prophets and priests that preached to a rebellious nation; the son was Jesus Himself; and the other tenants were the Gentile nations.
- The Wedding Feast (22:1-14) – The Jews who were the chosen ones (the invited guests) refused the offer to come to the Lord's banquet in His kingdom. The others who were invited represented the Gentile nations. The leaders were terribly offended by this parable because it struck at the heart of their barrenness and at the same time prophesied the inclusion in the kingdom of the outcast nations.

In between these parables Jesus was having several direct confrontations with the Jews. The religious leaders were challenging Jesus' authority at every turn. They peppered Jesus with questions and demanded answers for controversial topics like paying taxes to Rome, Mosaic Law, and Jewish theology. At every turn Jesus stunned His prosecutors into silence with the wisdom of His answers. Jesus proved He could give better than He took and often threw the questions right back at His accusers. "Blind guides!" Jesus scolded them, "For you are like whitewashed tombs—beautiful on the outside but filled on the inside with dead people's bones and all sorts of impurity. Outwardly you look like righteous people, but inwardly your hearts are filled with hypocrisy and lawlessness...Snakes! Sons of vipers! How will you escape the judgment of hell?" Matthew 23:24-33 (NLT). By the time Jesus was finished, the religious leaders knew they had met more than their match from this upstart Rabbi from Galilee, but this made them more determined than ever to silence Him once and for all.

The Olivet discourse is the last of the Five Discourses of Matthew (see Appendix Five) and is given on Tuesday just before the narrative of Jesus' passion that begins in two of the Gospels with the Anointing of Jesus.

Tuesday afternoon Jesus left the Temple and the city and went with His disciples to the Mount of Olives, which overlooks Jerusalem due east of the Temple. Here Jesus gave the Olivet Discourse, an elaborate prophecy about the destruction of Jerusalem and the end of the age. He taught in parables using symbolic language about the End Times events, including his Second Coming and the final judgment (Matthew 24:1-51; Mark 13:1-37; Luke 21:5-38). These verses of Scripture are often called "The Little Apocalypse" of the Gospels and here we see Jesus' teachings on His Second Coming and the Last Days are clearly linked to the apocalyptic theology that shaped much of the Jewish beliefs concerning the great Day of the Lord. Jesus' teachings on the events surrounding His Second Coming addressed the expectations concerning specific events that were shaped in large part by Jewish scholars up until that time (See Appendix Six "The Little Apocalypse").

"As he sat on the Mount of Olives, the disciples came to him privately, saying, 'Tell us, when will these things be, and what will be the sign of your coming and of the end of the age?'" Matthew 24:3 (ESV). The disciples' questions indicate just how much impact apocalyptic thought had on the audience of Jesus' day. And that Jesus took these concerns seriously is indicated by His answers to the three burning questions being asked of Him by His disciples:

1. **WHEN WILL THE GREAT DAY ARRIVE? Matthew 24:15-35.** Jesus specifically mentions Daniel's "abomination of desolation" being set up in the Temple as a sign of His coming.

2. **WHAT WILL BE THE SIGNS OF ITS APPEARING? In Matthew 24:3-14; 24:27-35** and parallel verses in **Luke 21:7-19** Jesus lists a series of supernatural interventions into human history that will be signs of His Second Coming:
    - False christs
    - wars and rumors of wars
    - famines and earthquakes in various places
    - persecutions

    All are but the beginning of the birth pains....
    - His coming will be plain for all to see

- Astronomical signs: the sun and moon darkened, stars fall from heaven, and "the powers of the heavens will be shaken"
- The "sign of the Son of Man" will appear in the heavens "and then all the tribes of the earth will mourn, and they will see the Son of Man coming on the clouds of heaven with power and great glory." Title "Son of Man" is an apocalyptic term (cf. Daniel 7:13-14)
- The Lord will send out his angels with a loud trumpet call,
- Describes the eschatological ingathering of the elect at the cataclysmic end of history. His elect will be "gathered from the four winds, from one end of heaven to the other"

"Truly, I say to you, this generation will not pass away until all these things take place. Heaven and earth will pass away, but my words will not pass away." Matthew 24:34 – 35 (ESV)

3. **WHEN WILL GOD SET UP HIS KINGDOM?** Jesus said, "when you see all these things, you know that he is near, at the very gates." But He also made it clear that neither the day nor the hour would be known by men (note **Matthew 25:1-13** the Parable of the Wise and Foolish Virgins)

Jesus' Olivet discourse does not use the specific term "Day of the Lord." However, His descriptions of the events surrounding End Times or Last Days that culminate in His Second Coming are clearly apocalyptic (See Chart Below).

After a tiring day of confrontation and warnings about the future, once again, Jesus and the disciples stayed the night in Bethany. Scripture also indicates that Tuesday was the day the leading priests and elders were meeting at the residence of Caiaphas, the high priest, plotting in secret how to capture Jesus and kill Him away from the Passover crowds. "He went back to the peace of Bethany. Before he joined battle with the world, he sought the presence of God. It was only because each day he faced God that he could face the world's challenge with such courage. This brief passage (Mark 11:11) also shows us something about the Twelve. They were still with him. By this time it must have been quite plain to them that Jesus was committing suicide, as it seemed to them.

Matthew 24:6-7 9a, 29	Mark 13:7-9a 24 – 25	Luke 21:9-12a 25 – 26	Revelation 6:2-17; 7:1
1. Wars	1. Wars	1. Wars	Seal 1. Wars
2. International Strife	2. International Strife	2. International Strife	Seal 2. International Strife
3. Famines	3. Earthquakes	3. Earthquakes	Seal 3. Famine
1. Earthquakes	4. Famines	4. Famines	Seal 4. Pestilence (Death and Hades)
2. Persecutions	5. Persecutions	5. Pestilence	Seal 5. Persecutions
3. Eclipses of the sun and moon; falling of the stars; shaking of the powers of heaven	6. Eclipses of the sun and moon; falling of the stars; shaking of the powers of heaven	6. Persecutions	Seal 6. Earthquakes, eclipse of the sun, ensanguining of the moon (staining, smearing, or covering with blood)

Sometimes we criticize them for their lack of loyalty in the last days, but it says something for them, that, little as they understood what was happening, they still stood by him." William Barclay, *The Gospel of Mark*, Westminster John Knox Press, Louisville, KY, © 2001, pp. 312-313

For Further Study:

> The tumultuous events of Tuesday and the Olivet Discourse are recorded in Matthew 21:18 – 25:46; Mark 11:20-13:37; and Luke 20:1 – 21:38

*(**Note:** The exact order of events during the Final Week is debated by Bible scholars. This timeline represents an approximate outline of major events.)*

The Final Week - Day 4: Silent Wednesday

"A woman anoints the feet of Jesus with oil"
By Maria Clara (Used by Permission)

The Gospels have little to say what the Lord did on Wednesday of Passion Week.

1. Plot Against Jesus
2. Anointed at Bethany
3. Judas betrays Jesus

Scholars speculate that after two exhausting days in Jerusalem, Jesus and his disciples spent this day resting in Bethany in anticipation of the Passover.

Bethany was about two miles east of Jerusalem. Here is where Lazarus and his two sisters, Mary and Martha lived. They were close friends of Jesus, and probably hosted him and the disciples during these final days in Jerusalem.

Just a short time previously, Jesus had revealed to the disciples, and the world, that he had power over death by raising Lazarus from the grave. After seeing this incredible miracle, many people in Bethany believed that Jesus was the Son of God and put their faith in him. Also in Bethany just a few nights earlier, Lazarus' sister Mary had lovingly anointed the feet of Jesus with expensive perfume. It may or may not be that important to note that Matthew and Mark put this event just before the Last Supper, while John places this anointing just before the Triumphal Entry.

We cannot be absolutely certain, but it may be that John placed this event in the most likely chronological order. But since the main purpose of the all Gospel writers was to give an accurate record of Jesus' message, and not necessarily to present everything in an exact chronological order of his life, Matthew and Mark may have decided to place this event here to further contrast the complete devotion of Mary with the eminent betrayal of Jesus by Judas. "In dramatic fashion Mark (14:1, 2) sets the stage for what is coming. In two short verses he mentions the Passover, and then he mentions the religionist's plotting Jesus' death – two scenes as opposite from one another as can be imagined. The Passover was a feast, a joyous and festive occasion. It was a celebration of God's glorious deliverance of Israel from the bondage of Egypt. Yet during the very days of this joyous celebration, Jesus' murder was being plotted." *The Preacher's Outline & Sermon Bible ® Vol. 1;Matthew – John (New International Version)*, Authentic Books Logos, Secunderabad, India, Copyright © 2000 by Alpha-Omega Ministries. Inc. p.889

The Gospel writers respect the privacy of these final hours of peace and communion between Jesus and His dearest friends and disciples.

For Further Study:

Religious leaders plot to kill Jesus and Judas decides to betray Jesus (Matt. 26:1-5, 14-16; Mark 14:1,2, 10, 11; Luke 22:1-6). The disciples prepare for the Passover (Matt. 26:17-19; Mark 14:12-16; Luke 22:7-13).

*(**Note:** The exact order of events during the Final Week is debated by Bible scholars. This timeline represents an approximate outline of major events.)*

The Final Week - Day 5: Thursday's Passover, Last Supper and Jesus' Final Instructions to His Disciples

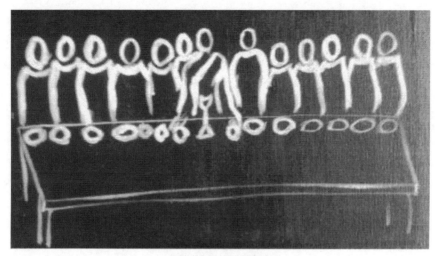

"The Last Supper"
By Maria Clara (Used by Permission)

Jesus' time on earth was about to come to an end. His disciples were still struggling to understand what was about to take place.

The final Passover meal with His disciples takes a somber turn as the fact He is about to be betrayed by one of His own is revealed. Jesus also causes His disciples to look forward in hope as He infuses the Passover celebration with new meanings.

From Bethany Jesus sent Peter and John ahead to the Upper Room in Jerusalem to make the preparations for the Passover Feast. That evening after sunset, Jesus washed the feet of his disciples as they prepared to share in the Passover. By performing this humble act of service, Jesus demonstrated by example how they were to love one another. (Today, many churches practice foot-washing ceremonies as a part of their Maundy Thursday services.)

Then Jesus shared the feast of Passover with his disciples saying, "I have been very eager to eat this Passover meal with you before my suffering begins. For I tell you now that I won't eat this meal again until its meaning is fulfilled in the Kingdom of God." (Luke 22:15-16, NLT)

As the Lamb of God, Jesus was about to fulfill the meaning of the Passover by giving his body to be broken and his blood to be shed in sacrifice, freeing us from sin and death. During this Last Supper, Jesus established the Lord's Supper, or Communion, instructing his followers to continually remember his sacrifice by sharing in the elements of bread and wine:

"And he took bread, and when he had given thanks, he broke it and gave it to them, saying, 'This is my body, which is given for you. Do this in remembrance of me.' And likewise the cup after they had eaten, saying, 'This cup that is poured out for you is the new covenant in my blood.'"(Luke 22:19-20, ESV)

The Final Teachings of Jesus in John's Gospel

John chapters 13 – 17 represent one of the longest passages of Jesus's teachings. These were His final words spoken to His disciples before His arrest, execution, and burial. The words are filled with emotion and urgency as Jesus knew they would be His last before He was taken away from His disciples. He knew the shock, terror, fear, and depression His disciples would face as they saw Him being abused, cursed, mocked, spat upon, and beaten almost to an unrecognizable condition. The disciples would not only have to be prepared for what was coming in the hours ahead, but they would have to be held together until they saw Him rise again. The words He spoke to them now would also have to sustain them and generations of disciples to come that would often face persecution and death. Jesus said in Luke 18:7-8 (NKJV) "And shall God not avenge His own elect who cry out day and night to Him, though He bears long with them? I tell you that He will avenge them speedily. Nevertheless, when the Son of Man comes, will He really find faith on the earth?"

The following is a synopsis of what Jesus taught His disciples in the hours before His arrest and trials.

- Jesus teaches the true meaning of servant leadership in word and deed. (13:1-17)
- Jesus announces that His departure from this world is at hand. 13:18-38
- Jesus comforts His disciples (14:1-4)
- Jesus affirms that the way to God is through Him alone: "I am the way and the truth and the life…" (14:5-14)
- Jesus promises the Holy Spirit to His disciples (14:15-26)

- Jesus is the source of His disciples' peace (14:27-31)
- Jesus teaches on the necessity for His disciples to bear spiritual fruit (15:1-8)
- Love is the basis of Jesus' relationship with Believers (15:9-17)
- Love is the basis of relationship between believers (15:12-17)
- Jesus teaches on the relationship of believers to the world. He warns of the world's hatred and of the Persecution that will come (15:18 – 16:6)
- Jesus teaches on the work of the Holy Spirit and His relationship with believers (16:7-15)
- Jesus teaches His disciples on the Resurrection and its results (16:16-22)
- Jesus teaches His disciples on prayer in His name (16:23-33)
- Jesus' final prayers with and for his disciples (17:1-26)

This completed all of Jesus' teaching and training of His disciples prior to his arrest, trial, and crucifixion.

After the meal was concluded and His teaching for the disciples completed, Jesus and the disciples left the Upper Room and went to the Garden of Gethsemane, where Jesus prayed in agony to God the Father. Luke's Gospel says "his sweat became like great drops of blood falling down to the ground." (Luke 22:44, ESV)

Late into that evening while still in Gethsemane, Jesus was betrayed with a kiss by Judas Iscariot and arrested by representatives of the Sanhedrin. He was taken to the home of Caiaphas, the High Priest, where the whole council had gathered to begin making their case against Jesus.

Meanwhile, in the early morning hours as Jesus' trial was getting underway, Peter denied knowing his Master three times before the rooster crowed.

For Further Study:

The events of the Last Supper (Matt. 26:20-30; Mark 14:17-26; Luke 22:14-38; John 13:1-38).

*(**Note:** The exact order of events during the Final Week is debated by Bible scholars. This timeline represents an approximate outline of major events.)*

FREDERICK OSBORN

The Final Week - Day 6: "Good Friday" The Trial, Crucifixion, Death, and Burial of Jesus Christ

This day is now known by Christians the world over as "Good Friday." It was the most difficult day of the Passion Week. Exactly as Jesus predicted all along the way to Jerusalem, His journey turned treacherous and acutely painful upon His arrest, through His trials, and to His final breath upon the cross. Jesus, the Lamb of God now had to face the full wrath and abuse of His enemies. The hatred that had been growing in intensity for the more than three years of His public ministry to the Jewish nation was unleashed upon the Son of Man. In these final hours leading to his death, Jesus would fulfill all prophecies concerning the suffering

Servant/Messiah that the Jews had no understanding of. Jesus came to be the atoning sacrifice – once for all mankind.

According to Scripture, Judas Iscariot, the disciple who had betrayed Jesus, was overcome with remorse and hanged himself early Friday morning. Meanwhile, before the third hour (9 a.m.), Jesus endured the shame of false accusations, condemnation, mockery, beatings, and abandonment. After multiple unlawful trials, he was sentenced to death by crucifixion, one of the most horrible and disgraceful methods of capital punishment.

Before Christ was led away, soldiers spit on him, tormented and mocked him, and pierced him with a crown of thorns. Then Jesus carried his own cross to Calvary where, again, he was mocked and insulted as Roman soldiers nailed him to the wooden cross. "Matthew describes the crucifixion simply and unemotionally. He does not indulge in dramatics, resort to sensational journalism, or dwell on sordid details, He simply states the fact: Then they crucified him. Yet eternity itself will not exhaust the depths of those words." William MacDonald, *The Believer's Commentary*, Thomas Nelson, Nashville, TN, © 1995, p.1308

Jesus spoke seven final statements from the cross. His first words were, "Father, forgive them, for they do not know what they are doing." (Luke 23:34, NIV). His last were, "Father, into your hands I commit my spirit." (Luke 23:46, NIV)

Then, about the ninth hour (3 p.m.), Jesus breathed his last and died. By 6 p.m. Friday evening, Nicodemus and Joseph of Arimathea, took Jesus' body down from the cross and laid it in a tomb.

For Further Study:

Friday's events are recorded in Matthew 27:1-62, Mark 15:1-47, Luke 22:63-23:56, and John 18:28-19:37.

*(**Note:** The exact order of events during the Final Week is debated by Bible scholars. This timeline represents an approximate outline of major events.)*

FREDERICK OSBORN

The Final Week - Day 7: Saturday in the Tomb

"The body of Jesus being taken for burial"
By Maria Clara (Used by permission)

  The veil that separated the Holy of Holies and that kept the Mercy Seat hidden from view was rent. The centurion, filled with awe and wonder at the signs in the sky above Golgotha and the signs from the quaking earth beneath his feat, had declared from the foot of the cross what the Jewish leaders could not: that Jesus was truly innocent. The few in the crowd that had remained until the bitter end had turned and returned home in deep sorrow. The women who waited and wept for Jesus had followed from a distance as Jesus' lifeless corpse was taken to the tomb. After every attempt by His followers failed to release Jesus in life from the clutches of evil men, Joseph of Arimathea and Nicodemus managed to negotiate for Jesus' lifeless body to be released for burial.

  Nicodemus, like Joseph of Arimathea, was a member of the Sanhedrin, the court which had condemned Jesus Christ to death. For a time, both men had lived as secret followers of Jesus, afraid to make a public profession of faith because of their prominent positions in the Jewish community. Similarly, both were deeply affected by Christ's death. They boldly came out of hiding, risking their reputations and their lives because they knew that Jesus was indeed the long-awaited Messiah. Together they cared for Jesus' body and removed it from the place of execution for burial.

Jesus' body was laid a rich man's tomb. The tomb was guarded by Roman soldiers throughout the day on Saturday, which was the Sabbath. Christ's body waited for the Sabbath to end at 6 p.m. so it could be properly and ceremonially treated for burial with spices purchased by Nicodemus. Joseph and Nicodemus brought about seventy-five pounds of perfumed ointment made from myrrh and aloes and hastily prepared Jesus' body. Following Jewish burial custom, they wrapped Jesus' body with the spices in long sheets of linen cloth," but there was no time for all the proper formalities because the Sabbath was rapidly approaching (John 19: 39-40, NLT). The rest would have to wait until after the Sabbath when the women could come and complete the process according to every Jewish custom.

While his physical body lay in the tomb, Jesus Christ paid the penalty for sin by offering the perfect, spotless sacrifice. He conquered death, both spiritually and physically, securing our eternal salvation: "For you know that God paid a ransom to save you from the empty life you inherited from your ancestors. And the ransom he paid was not mere gold or silver. He paid for you with the precious lifeblood of Christ, the sinless, spotless Lamb of God." (1 Peter 1:18-19, NLT)

"The kings and princes of this world set themselves to guard the sepulcher of the Son of God by sealing-wax and sentries. They might as well have endeavored to restrain the bursting life of spring. Said the King of Terrors to Captain Corruption, 'Take care to keep this Man's body fast.' But what did this avail, when it had been ordained that he should not stay in Hades, nor even see corruption? Whatever your foes may do against you will not avail, if only you wait patiently for God." F.B. Meyer

For further study:

Jesus is laid in the tomb (Matt. 27:57-66; Mark 15:42-47; Luke 23:50-56; John 19:38-42

*(**Note:** The exact order of events during the Final Week is debated by Bible scholars. This timeline represents an approximate outline of major events.)*

9.

Jesus on Trial

The Trials by the Sanhedrin, Pilate, and Herod

"Jesus before Pilate"
By Maria Clara (Used by Permission)

THE WAY, TRUTH, AND LIFE

LESSON OUTLINE:
   The purpose of this lesson is to examine the Six Major Trials of Jesus.
- First: the private trial before Annas.
- Second: the trial at the house of Caiaphas the high priest
- Third: His official trial before the entire Sanhedrin
- Fourth: the trial before Pilate the governor
- Fifth: the trial by King Herod
- Sixth: His second trial before Pilate (some commentaries divide this into two trials – the Seventh being the choice of Jesus or Barabbas by the crowds

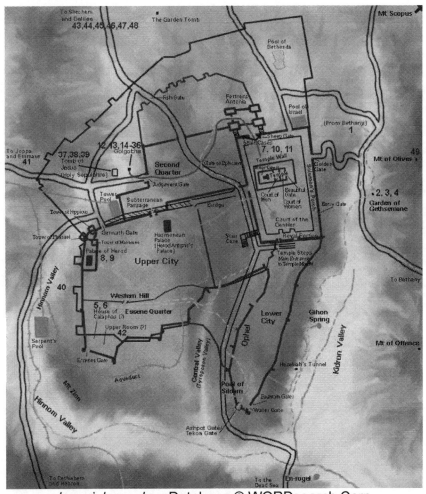

Jesus' Jerusalem Database © WORDsearch Corp.

Gethsemane
(Matt. 26:30-56; Mark 14:26-52; Luke 22:31-53; John 18:1-11)

The last Discourses had been spoken, the final prayers for Himself, His disciples, and all future believers had been offered; His disciples were as ready as they ever would be to see their beloved Messiah brutally taken from them. Now Jesus has to prepare Himself for the trials ahead of Him. He passes through the city gates and leads His disciples to the Mount of Olives. He crosses the Kidron Valley and stops at a lonely parcel of ground called the Garden of Gethsemane, "the 'Oil-press."

There, in the deep darkness of the night, surrounded by fruit trees and flowering shrubs, and a nearby, Olive press, Jesus would face His first major trial. This place is identified as the place where Jesus often gathered with His disciples when He visited Jerusalem. "It was a quiet resting-place, for retirement, prayer, perhaps sleep, and a trysting-place also where not only the Twelve, but others also, may have been wont to meet the Master. And as such it was known to Judas, and thither he led the armed band, when they found the Upper Chamber no longer occupied by Jesus and His disciples." Alfred Edersheim, *The Life and Times of Jesus the Messiah* (Unabridged), Database © 2012 WORDsearch Corp., p.1186

It is difficult for us to imagine the agony and loneliness the Savior felt that night, to understand the trial He had to face alone. Not in His transfigured state, but in His full humanity. The Son of Man would have to face the full force of Satan's wrath that night. Jesus longed for the company of His beloved disciples, but they quickly fell asleep. Jesus would be denied the company of even His closest disciples. It was His destiny to face this trial alone. If this trial was not faced in the weakness of His humanity, but in His glorified, transfigured state Jesus would never fully understand us:

"Since therefore the children share in flesh and blood, he himself likewise partook of the same things, that through death he might destroy the one who has the power of death, that is, the devil, and deliver all those who through fear of death were subject to lifelong slavery. For surely it is not angels that he helps, but he helps the offspring of Abraham. Therefore he had to be made like his brothers in every respect, so that he might become a merciful and faithful high priest in the service of God, to make propitiation for the sins of the people. For because he himself has

suffered when tempted, he is able to help those who are being tempted." Hebrews 2:14-18 (ESV)

Luke tells us that Jesus struggled through the night, "sweating great drops of blood" (Like 22:43-45). At the same time, He prayed for His disciples, and especially for Peter that his faith would not fail him in the morning. "Alone, as in His first conflict with the Evil One in the Temptation in the wilderness, must the Savior enter on the last contest. With what agony of soul He took upon Him now and there the sins of the world, and in taking expiated them, we may learn from this account of what passed, when, 'with strong crying and tears unto Him that was able to save Him from death,' He 'offered up prayers and supplications.' And - we anticipate it already - with these results: that He was heard; that He learned obedience by the things which He suffered; that He was made perfect; and that He became: to us the Author of Eternal Salvation, and before God, a High-Priest after the order of Melchizedek." Alfred Edersheim, *The Life and Times of Jesus the Messiah* (Unabridged), Database © 2012 WORDsearch Corp., p.1191

In His humanity, He prayed that the Cup of suffering and death would pass away from Him, but as the obedient Son of God, He prayed to His Father, "nevertheless, Thy will be done." Jesus passed through that terrible and extreme agony of soul the Garden. Just as in the Wilderness after forty days of fasting, Jesus reached the furthest point of human endurance without breaking. As the guards were reaching the outskirts of the Garden, "there appeared to him an angel from heaven, strengthening him." Luke 22:43 (ESV)

Jesus' first trial ended with the sound of the approaching guards sent to arrest Him. They were led by the traitor who would betray Him with a kiss. Pharisees and other religious leaders had given Judas a contingent of Roman soldiers and Temple guards to accompany him. Now with blazing torches and lanterns held high, and with weapons in hand, they arrived at the olive grove to bring to fruition the long anticipated dreams of Jesus' enemies to bring about His destruction. Jesus' stunned and sleepy-eyed disciples watched in horror as Judas stepped forward and kissed their Master, signaling His arrest. "Judas," Jesus asked, "would you betray the Son of Man with a kiss?" In the confusion of the moment the disciples wondered if they should fight or flee. It was then that the impulsive one, Peter lunged forward and struck the high priest's slave with his sword. Peter severed the servant's ear, but Jesus immediately healed him. The mood of the moment turned from stunned silence to awe-struck silence. Peter believed he was only trying to protect Jesus, but Jesus knowing that God's plan must unfold and be played out to the bitter end, ordered Peter to put away his weapon. "At times it is tempting to take matters into our own hands, to force the issue. Most often such moves lead to sin. Instead, we must trust God to work out his plan. Think of it—if Peter had had his way, Jesus would not have gone to the cross, and God's plan of redemption would have been thwarted." *Life Application Study Bible* note on John 18:10, 11.

Jesus turned to the elders and other authorities who had come with the soldiers to make sure the arrest went according to plan. "Then Jesus said to the chief priests and officers of the temple and elders, who had come out against him, 'Have you come out as against a robber, with swords and clubs? When I was with you day after day in the temple, you did not lay hands on me. But this is your hour, and the power of darkness.'" Luke 22:52-53 (ESV). If the conscience of any one of them was pricked, they did not show it. The disciples began to flee as Jesus was bound and dragged from the peace and seclusion of Gethsemane. This would be the last moment of freedom and dignity for the Son of God on the earth. It would be nothing but torture, humiliation, and death from here on.

No perfect chronological and complete accounting of Jesus' trials is contained within a single Gospel. However, from the four Gospel accounts we can piece together a fairly detailed account from the first moments after His arrest to His final trial before Pilate. What is important to know is that Jesus passed every test and was innocent of all wrong-doing. His first and greatest trial in the Garden was a deeply personal one between the Son and the Father.

"In the days of his flesh, Jesus offered up prayers and supplications, with loud cries and tears, to him who was able to save him from death, and he was heard because of his reverence. Although he was a son, he learned obedience through what he suffered. And being made perfect, he became the source of eternal salvation to all who obey him, being designated by God a high priest after the order of Melchizedek." Hebrews 5:7-10 (ESV)

If He failed this trial and was found with a single spot or blemish in His soul, He would have been rejected as the Lamb of God. This would have doomed mankind to an eternity of death and destruction. Instead, Jesus submitted himself to the humiliations of the mock trials to follow.

"For it was not to angels that God subjected the world to come, of which we are speaking. It has been testified somewhere, 'What is man, that you are mindful of him, or the son of man, that you care for him? You made him for a little while lower than the angels; you have crowned him with glory and honor, putting everything in subjection under his feet.' Now in putting everything in subjection to him, he left nothing outside his control. At present, we do not yet see everything in subjection to him." Hebrews 2:5-8 (ESV)

All heaven knew that the brutality of His death on the cross was now irrevocably and irreversibly ahead of the Son of God. Although this would be a time of tears and great sorrow upon the earth, was a time of rejoicing in heaven because the Son of God was about to receive His greatest victory and enter into His greatest glory. "But turning to them Jesus said, 'Daughters of Jerusalem, do not weep for me, but weep for yourselves and for your children.'" Luke 23:28 (ESV)

"One thing remains. Even when we have set the tragedy of the garden and the arrest at its blackest, its bitterest and its starkest, one indelible impression remains; and that is that in it and through it Jesus was always completely in control. He was never the helpless victim; he was always master of circumstance. Somehow even here there lie beneath the surface the first indications of the final triumph. The story never reads like the arrest of a criminal, unwillingly haled to judgment and to death; the story always reads like the willing sacrifice of one who of his own free will laid down his life for his friends." William Barclay, *The Mind of Jesus*, Harper San Francisco, CA, © 1960, 1961, p.220

THE SIX TRIALS OF JESUS

Some commentaries count six trials; some count seven. How they are counted also differs. In the timeline below you will note seven, but the

The 7 Trials of Jesus Timeline

	Time	Type	Authority	Scripture	Accusations	Legality	Results
1	2:00 AM	Jewish Preliminary examination	Annas, ex-high priest of Jews	John 18:13-23	Pre–trial trumped–up charges. General questioning, nothing specific	Illegal because it was unauthorized inquiry held at night at residence of Annas. Prejudice. No specific charges. Violent.	Purpose was to gain evidence for the trial. "Guilty" of irreverence. Taken to Caiaphas.
2	3:30 AM	Jewish	Caiaphas, current high priest, and members of Sanhedrin	Matt. 26:56-68; Mk. 14:53-65; Jn. 18:24	Blasphemy; claimed to be the Messiah, Son of God	Illegal because held at night at residence of Caiaphas. Perjured witnesses could not agree. Violence.	Guilty of blasphemy by common consent. Sent to the Sanhedrin
3	6:00 AM	Jewish	Sanhedrin (Jewish ruling authorities)	; Lk. 22:66-71	Charged with *blasphemy*; claimed to be Son of God. Rome not interested in blasphemy.	Formal trial to confirm capital sentence of the illegal night trial. Put Jesus under oath. Caiaphas made each member of Sanhedrin accredited witnesses.	Declared guilty of blasphemy by Sanhedrin. Sent to Roman Governor, Pilate, for legal sentence of death.
4	6:30 AM	Roman Civil Trial	Pilate, Governor of Judaea, at official residence (first time)	Matt. 27:1-2, 11-14; Mk. 15:2-5; Lk. 23:1-7; Jn. 18:28-38	Accused Him of *treason* which was worthy of capital punishment in Rome.	Illegal, yet held even though found innocent by Pilate. No defense attorney. Violent.	Innocent, Jn. 18:38. Should have ended trial, but sent to Herod Antipas. Mob overruled Pilate.
5	7:00 AM	Roman Civil Trial	Herod Antipas, Governor of Galilee	Lk. 23:8-12	No accusation. Mock trial. Mob violence.	Illegal because no grounds. Mockery in courtroom. Violence. No defense attorney.	Mistreated and mocked, returned to Pilate without decision by Herod
6	7:30 AM	Roman Civil Trial	Pilate (second time)	Matt. 27:15-26; Mk. 15:6-15; Lk. 23:13-25; Jn. 18:39-19:16	Treason. Bargain with mob, put on trial with Barabbas	Illegal because Pilate had no proof of guilt, allowed innocent man be condemned	Found innocent, but Pilate bowed to political pressure of Jews.
7	Today	Universal	You are the judge.	The whole Bible	Jesus Christ is Lord and Savior	This decision is legal and eternally binding	What did you do with Jesus?

SOURCE: http://www.bible.ca/doctrine-six-trials-of-jesus-3-jewish-guilty-3-roman-innocent.htm

seventh trial is called a "Universal" trial where each individual is placed in the judgment seat. Each person must weigh the evidence and decide for themselves if Jesus Christ is truly Lord and Savior. The trial of Jesus continues everywhere any time the Gospel is preached and a decision is asked for. The decision each "judge" makes over Jesus is legally and eternally binding, but not on Jesus Christ for the judgment we make is legally and eternally, binding on us. If we reject the Son of God now, judgment has already been passed before we stand before Jesus in eternity to be judged by Him.

Other commentaries split the final trial of Jesus before Pilate into two separate trials: the one where Pilate finds Jesus innocent of deserving any punishment; and the second where Jesus is presented to the Jewish nation. In this trial before the Jews, Jesus is thoroughly and finally rejected as the Messiah, and the guilty Barabbas is released as the "scapegoat" back into the world. "By giving the people the alternative of Christ or Barabbas, Pilate expected that they would certainly choose he former. To his dismay, this second effort to salve his conscience without endangering his reputation failed. So he drifted and sold his soul for power. Each of us has to choose between Christ and Barabbas, between the self-surrender of the cross and brutal selfishness." F.B. Meyer, Devotional Commentary, Tyndale House Pub., Wheaton, IL. 1989, p.452

In the next few hours Jesus will be brought before Annas, Caiaphas, Pilate, Herod, and then back to Pilate. In the end the Jewish nation as a whole would be represented by the assembled crowd. Every step of the way His own people passed judgment on Him and in so doing passed judgment upon themselves. As Jesus said, "Judge not, that you be not judged. For with the judgment you pronounce you will be judged, and with the measure you use it will be measured to you." Matthew 7:1-2 (ESV) And so the irony of these trials is that it was not Jesus who was on trial here, but it was the religious leaders who were on trial. They selfishly clung to their robes of self-righteousness as a means to power and self-aggrandizement and would not submit to the authority of the Son of Man, the true Lord of the Sabbath. It was Herod and his fellow aristocrats that valued the wealth and position of their earthly kingdoms more than the kingdom of heaven that Jesus ruled who were judged. It was Pilate and all the corrupt worldly powers that were on trial. They believed it was their might that justified their every act of cruelty and the enslavement of their fellow man; they never could understand the eternal power of the kingdom of God that ruled with justice, mercy, love, and set men free. The Romans came to enslave the nations; Jesus Christ came to set men free. And finally, it was the Jewish nation as a whole that was on trial. For centuries they had longed for and cried out for the Messiah to come and deliver them from bondage. They said they wanted no earthly king or Caesar to rule over them, but only God's chosen Messiah. But when the Messiah finally came, they rejected Him and had Him murdered. Why? Because He was not the kind of Messiah they wanted. They wanted a Savior that would save them from hunger, foreign powers, sickness and disease. They wanted a Messiah who would deliver to them a first century version of the "prosperity gospel." But they rejected the Messiah that came as the way, truth, and life. The kingdom Jesus offered was not the kingdom they wanted. So they refused Him. And having no need for His deliverance from sin and self-righteousness; having no desire for the bread of eternal life or the blood of atonement for sins, they judged Him a false Messiah and demanded His execution.

HISTORICAL BACKGROUND OF THE TRIALS

Before we can fully understand why Jesus was brought to Annas first and what that initial exchange was all about we need to examine a little of the historical background to this trial and the trials to follow. First it is important to keep in mind that at this time the Jews were ruled by the Roman Emperor. Therefore, they were subject to Roman civil law. As it was with all the Roman provinces, only Roman law could be applied for capital punishment. So in order to maintain a uniform code of justice throughout their diverse Empire, it was customary for local religious or tribal laws to be superseded by Roman law in the most serious cases.

Because the Jews were unable to legally put Jesus to death, they would have to somehow convince the Roman Governor that Jesus' crimes were serious enough for Roman law to intervene. If they could have executed Jesus without risking the intervention of the Romans on the one side or the wrath of the masses on the other, they would have immediately put Jesus to death. But because of His popularity with the people, they needed to separate Jesus from the crowds, and publically disgrace Him before handing Him over to Roman authorities to finish the job of killing Him by crucifying Him. Death by crucifixion was the most degrading and humiliating way the Jewish authorities could think of to destroy His popularity. After being crucified, the Jewish authorities believed no one would ever again want to identify themselves as a follower of Jesus.

The highest ruling body of the Jews while under Roman authority was a special religious council called the Sanhedrin. The Sanhedrin was a body of seventy men (there was a lesser Sanhedrin that had twenty-three men, but they only dealt with minor infractions of Jewish law). So, to get everyone's attention in Jerusalem, Jesus would have to be tried before the main body of the Sanhedrin, which meant He was in serious trouble.

If the Sanhedrin made a judgment against anyone that they believed was serious enough to be executed for, then they would bring their accusation to the Roman Governor. The Roman Governor would then decide if the person charged by the Sanhedrin deserved the death penalty under Roman law, not Jewish law. Of course, the Jews resented this situation. They wanted the right to punish those who broke Mosaic Law on the same level as the Romans punished those who broke Roman civil law. In some cases the Jews might get away with stoning someone to death (as in the case of the woman caught in adultery that Jesus saved, and in the case of Steven who was stoned to death by the Jews supposedly for telling believers they were not subject to the Laws of Moses). So that is why in the end Jesus was crucified for the official crime of high treason rather than being stoned for blasphemy.

This was the dilemma of the Jewish authorities: they could only find Jesus guilty of blasphemy in what everyone would know was a "show trial." If they ordered Him stoned to death, and the people objected and rioted, it would trigger a violent reaction from the Romans who would no doubt send out the soldiers into the streets and the Roman Governor could suspend the Sanhedrin. So Jesus' so-called crime against the religion of the Jews would have to be politicized, twisted, and turned into a crime of treason against Rome. Because as far as Rome was concerned, anyone found guilty of treason would instantly be put to death. You do not mess with Rome's power if you want to live very long.

Again, depending upon how they are counted, there were six or seven trials of Jesus throughout the night and most of the following morning. The shuffling back and forth between the religious authorities, the Roman Governor Pilate, and Herod represented the efforts of the

Jewish authorities to get someone to find Jesus guilty of something deserving of death.

- First there was a private trial before Annas.
- Second there was a trial at the house of Caiaphas the high priest, where the scribes and the elders were assembled
- Third, there was His official trial before the entire Sanhedrin.

All these were Jewish trials. Therefore, the whole question of treason is not even verbalized. The fourth trial was before Pilate the governor. This is where the charge of treason is first raised because now they were before a Roman Civil Court. After His arrest in Gethsemane, Jesus was immediately taken to the high priest's residence, even though this was the middle of the night (John 18:12, 13). This was totally against the rules of Jewish law (See Appendix Seven, "Laws Governing Criminal Trials."

There can be some confusion over the time and place of the first two trials for those unfamiliar with the historical background because both Annas and Caiaphas are named High Priest at a trial. However, once it is understood that both Annas and Caiaphas had been high priests, it is quickly cleared up. Annas was Israel's high priest from A.D. 6 to 15. He was deposed by Roman rulers for political reasons. However, Caiaphas, Annas' son-in-law, was then appointed high priest from A.D. 18 to 36/37. According to Jewish law, the office of high priest was held for life. Therefore, the Jews naturally considered Annas the high priest and still called him by that title, even though the title was unofficial. Although Annas retained considerable influence among the Jewish religious leaders, Caiaphas made the final decisions. (This is very similar to the United States where a former President is still addressed as "Mr. President," but the real power and authority of the government is with the current sitting President in the White House.)

Jesus was taken to the high priest Annas' house first for strictly political reasons. Annas still held considerable power and influence among the Jewish religious leaders. By bringing Jesus to him, it was a signal to the others that Jesus' arrest was not a rash action, but had been engineered and approved by the highest religious powers they had. There was another reason why Jesus was quickly brought to Annas' house in the middle of the night. Besides the concern for crowd reaction against the arrest, the religious leaders were in a hurry to have Jesus executed so as not to interfere with the Sabbath and the Passover celebrations that were coinciding with it. This residence was a palace whose outer walls enclosed a courtyard that would keep the crowds away and prevent anyone from witnessing their unfair examination of Jesus.

The first few hours after Jesus' arrest would be critical for the leaders of the Jews. If the crowds that just a few days before had hailed Jesus as their king and Messiah when He entered Jerusalem for the Passover, took offense and turned on their leaders it could be disastrous. If the Passover crowds rioted and demanded Jesus' release, it could mean Rome's intervention and they could be removed from power. The fact was both Caiaphas and Annas cared more about their political power and the wealth it brought them than they did about their religious duty to be spiritual leaders of the nation. They got into power and stayed there through bribery and deceit, not from any altruistic motives to be spiritual fathers to the nation. They did not know or care if Jesus was truly the Messiah the prophets promised would come. What they did care about was maintaining the status quo with them at the top. To stay on top meant eliminating all potential threats to their power and authority, even if that meant killing God's Son. Jesus knew very well who He was facing and what their motives were (Lk. 20:9-19).

ONE: The trial before Annas
John 18:12-27

"So the band of soldiers and their captain and the officers of the Jews arrested Jesus and bound him. First they led him to Annas, for he was the father-in-law of Caiaphas, who was high priest that year. It was Caiaphas who had advised the Jews that it would be expedient that one man should die for the people." John 18:12-14 (ESV)

"The high priest then questioned Jesus about his disciples and his teaching. Jesus answered him, 'I have spoken openly to the world. I have always taught in synagogues and in the temple, where all Jews come together. I have said nothing in secret. Why do you ask me? Ask those who have heard me what I said to them; they know what I said.'

When he had said these things, one of the officers standing by struck Jesus with his hand, saying, 'Is that how you answer the high priest?'
Jesus answered him, 'If what I said is wrong, bear witness about the wrong; but if what I said is right, why do you strike me?' Annas then sent him bound to Caiaphas the high priest." John 18:19-24 (ESV)

This first "official" trial of Jesus set the tone for all the other trials to follow.

Jesus, the sinless Son of God, stood before a man who represented all that was sinful and corrupt in this world. Annas was one of the most powerful men in Jerusalem. Because of his great wealth and power he exercised enormous influence over the religious and political elites of the Jews. He openly collaborated with the Romans and had no problem buying and selling influence whenever it was necessary. Annas had a lot of people in his pockets. If anyone crossed Annas, he had the ways and means to destroy them. (See Appendix Eight: Annas the High Priest)

He held the office of High Priest himself for a few years, and during that time he seized control of the money flowing in and out of the Temple treasury. He discovered it was more lucrative for him to be outside of the office of High Priest, but when he departed, he made sure that his family remained in charge. During Annas' lifetime the office of High Priest was held by no less than five of his sons, his son-in-law (Caiaphas), and by a grandson. "He enjoyed all the dignity of the office, and all its influence also, since he was able to promote to it those most closely connected with him. And, while they acted publicly, he really directed affairs, without either the responsibility or the restraints which the office imposed." Alfred Edersheim, *The Life and Times of Jesus the Messiah* (Unabridged), Database © 2012 WORDsearch Corp., p.1198

Since Annas was the father-in-law of Caiaphas, the High Priest, why was he examining the accused in his private residence at 2 o'clock in the morning when he is no longer an official of the court? It was Caiaphas's job to examine the prisoner. To understand this, it is necessary to go back to the times that Jesus put together some leather thongs to make a whip, went into the temple, and drove the moneychangers from the temple (Matthew 21:12, Mark 11:15; John 2:15). What Jesus did was more than a symbolic act. It was a direct provocation and challenge to the corrupt system that had profited Annas and his family for years.

Who was in charge of the system at the time, and who benefited financially from that place? Annas and his family – they were the High

Priests during Jesus' lifetime. His family had been in charge of the Temple for seventeen years. They had turned the activities surrounding the Temple sacrifices and worship into a commercial enterprise and benefited from all the buying and selling taking place in and around the Temple courts. Jesus threated that system by His actions and Annas was a major conspirator in Jesus' arrest, and now inevitable execution.

Annas was in effect the boss of the Jewish "Mafia" that controlled the religious activities of the Temple. He was not the official High Priest approved by the Roman governors, but was still respected as the High Priest by the Jews who considered the office "for life." Annas had Jesus brought to him to demonstrate to Jesus who was really in charge of the Temple – and it was not Jesus. Annas wanted to make an example of Jesus to show all of the Jews that anyone who challenged his power and control would be destroyed.

So when Jesus stood in front of Annas with his hands tied behind His back, He was indeed like a lamb being led to the slaughter. And like a sacrificial lamb, it was the one holding the knife who was the guilty party and the sacrifice would pay the price of their guilt. There are two things that Annas asked Jesus about:

- He wanted to know about His disciples, and
- He wanted to know about his teaching (John 18:19).

The question about His followers was intended to incriminate them also, but Jesus sidesteps the first question and instead addresses the second: "Jesus answered him, 'I spoke openly to the world. I always taught in synagogues and in the temple, where the Jews always meet, and in secret I have said nothing. Why do you ask Me? Ask those who have heard Me what I said to them. Indeed they know what I said.'" John 18:20-21 (NKJV)

With that answer, Jesus was struck by one of Annas' officers (verse 22). Jesus, in spite of the abuse, was in perfect control of Himself. He knew that his accusers were illegally attempting to get Him to incriminate himself, which was against the law. They would have to bring witnesses to testify against Him. So Jesus responded, "If I have spoken evil, bear witness of the evil; but if well, why do you strike Me?"

In the end Annas had no answer to Jesus' testimony. He did not have the answers he wanted out of Jesus – no confession – nothing that could be deemed blasphemous in front of witnesses. Annas himself was judged, not Christ. And so they sent him off to Caiaphas to prepare for a public "show trial" before the Sanhedrin.

The Six Stages of Jesus' Trial
John 18:12

Although Jesus' trial lasted less than 18 hours, he was taken to six different hearings.

Before Jewish Authorities	Preliminary Hearing before Annas (John 18:12-24)	Because the office of high priest was for life, Annas was still the "official" high priest in the eyes of the Jews, even though the Romans had appointed another. Thus, Annas still carried much weight in the high council.
	Hearing before Caiaphas (Matthew 26:57-68)	Like the hearing before Annas, this hearing was conducted at night in secrecy. It was full of illegalities that made a mockery of justice.
	Trial before the High Council (Matthew 27:1-2)	Just after daybreak, 70 members of the high council met to rubber-stamp their approval of the previous hearings to make them appear legal. The purpose of this trial was not to determine justice, but to justify their own preconceptions of Jesus' guilt.
Before Roman Authorities	First Hearing before Pilate (Luke 23:1-5)	The religious leaders had condemned Jesus to death on religious grounds, but only the Roman government could grant the death penalty. Thus, they took Jesus to Pilate, the Roman governor, and accused him of treason and rebellion, crimes for which the Roman government gave the death penalty. Pilate saw at once that Jesus was innocent, but he was afraid of the uproar being caused by the religious leaders.
	Hearing before Herod	Because Jesus' home was in the region of Galilee, Pilate sent Jesus

THE WAY, TRUTH, AND LIFE

	(Luke 23:6-12)	to Herod Antipas, the ruler of Galilee, who was in Jerusalem for the Passover celebration. Herod was eager to see Jesus do a miracle, but when Jesus remained silent, Herod wanted nothing to do with him and sent him back to Pilate.
	Last Hearing before Pilate (Luke 23:13-25)	Pilate didn't like the religious leaders. He wasn't interested in condemning Jesus because he knew Jesus was innocent. However, he knew that another uprising in his district might cost him his job. First he tried to compromise with the religious leaders by having Jesus beaten, an illegal action in itself. But finally he gave in and handed Jesus over to be executed. Pilate's self-interest was stronger than his sense of justice.

Tyndale Handbook of Bible Charts and Maps.

Two: The Trial Before Caiaphas

MT 26:57, 59-68 (NIV)	MK 14:53, 55-65 (NIV)	LK 22:54, 63-65 (NIV)	JN 18:24 (NIV)
Matthew	**Mark**	**Luke**	**John**
Those who had arrested Jesus took him to Caiaphas, the high priest, where the teachers of the law and the elders had assembled.	They took Jesus to the high priest, and all the chief priests, elders and teachers of the law came together.	Then seizing him, they led him away and took him into the house of the high priest. Peter followed at a distance.	Then Annas sent him, still bound, to Caiaphas the high priest.
The chief priests and the whole Sanhedrin were looking for false evidence against Jesus so that they could put him to death. But they did not find any, though many false witnesses came forward. Finally two	The chief priests and the whole Sanhedrin were looking for evidence against Jesus so that they could put him to death, but they did not find any. Many testified falsely against him, but their statements did not	The men who were guarding Jesus began mocking and beating him. They blindfolded him and demanded, "Prophesy! Who hit you?" And they said many other insulting things to him.	

came forward and declared, "This fellow said, 'I am able to destroy the temple of God and rebuild it in three days.'"
Then the high priest stood up and said to Jesus, "Are you not going to answer? What is this testimony that these men are bringing against you?"
But Jesus remained silent. The high priest said to him, "I charge you under oath by the living God: Tell us if you are the Christ, the Son of God."
"Yes, it is as you say," Jesus replied. "But I say to all of you: In the future you will see the Son of Man sitting at the right hand of the Mighty One and coming on the clouds of heaven."
Then the high priest tore his clothes and said, "He has spoken blasphemy! Why do we need any more witnesses? Look, now you have heard the blasphemy. What do you think?"
"He is worthy of death," they answered. Then they spit in his face and struck him with their fists. Others slapped him and said, "Prophesy to us, Christ. Who hit you?"

agree.
Then some stood up and gave this false testimony against him: "We heard him say, 'I will destroy this man-made temple and in three days will build another, not made by man.'" Yet even then their testimony did not agree.
Then the high priest stood up before them and asked Jesus, "Are you not going to answer? What is this testimony that these men are bringing against you?"
But Jesus remained silent and gave no answer. Again the high priest asked him, "Are you the Christ, the Son of the Blessed One?"
"I am," said Jesus. "And you will see the Son of Man sitting at the right hand of the Mighty One and coming on the clouds of heaven."
The high priest tore his clothes. "Why do we need any more witnesses?" he asked. "You have heard the blasphemy. What do you think?" They all condemned him as worthy of death.
Then some began to spit at him; they blindfolded him, struck him with their fists, and said, "Prophesy!" And the guards took him and beat him.

"And they led Jesus away to the high priest; and with him were assembled all the chief priests, the elders, and the scribes." Mark 14:53 (NKJV)

The High Priest, Caiaphas gathered together a group of high officials of the Sanhedrin at about 3:30 in the morning. This trial is illegal on several levels (see Appendix Seven Laws Governing Criminal Trials):
- It is in the dark of night Remember
- It is a preliminary hearing without the full body assembled
- It is illegal because they're in the wrong place, Caiaphas' house, not in the council chamber where official trials are supposed to be held.

Everything about this trial indicates that its sole intent is not to bring a just verdict, but is to find a reason to condemn Jesus whether is guilty of anything or not:

"Now the chief priests and all the council sought testimony against Jesus to put Him to death, but found none. For many bore false witness against Him, but their testimonies did not agree. Then some rose up and bore false witness against Him, saying, 'We heard Him say, "I will destroy this temple made with hands, and within three days I will build another made without hands."' But not even then did their testimony agree." Mark 14:55-59 (NKJV)

It quickly became obvious to all that were there that there was no case against Jesus:
- Witnesses had to be coerced or bribed to testify
- Others testified to gain favor with their leaders
- Witnesses were contradicting each other

Caiaphas knows that the Roman Governor will do them no favor by doing away with one of his rivals; so he has to get a strong capital case together before he marches Jesus off to Pilate. Caiaphas' father-in-law, Annas, who was the real power behind his appointment to the office of High Priest, wanted this man killed. Caiaphas wants Jesus out of the way as much as Annas, but he has no case for sedition. He has no legal avenue open to him so Caiaphas makes an illegal move and questions Jesus to try to force Him to incriminate himself. This is the reason for the exchange between the high priest and Jesus:

"And the high priest stood up in the midst and asked Jesus, saying, 'Do You answer nothing? What is it these men testify against You?' But He kept silent and answered nothing. Again the high priest asked Him, saying to Him, 'Are You the Christ, the Son of the Blessed?' Jesus said, 'I am. And you will see the Son of Man sitting at the right hand of the Power, and coming with the clouds of heaven.'" Mark 14:60-62 (NKJV)

In Matthew's gospel we get a further insight into why at this particular moment Jesus answered His accusers when legally He was not bound to do so. "But Jesus kept silent. And the high priest answered and said to Him, **'I put You under oath by the living God:** Tell us if You are the Christ, the Son of God!'" Matthew 26:63 (NKJV) When a pious Jew heard that, he was obliged to answer. Under oath to answer to God, he could not keep silent or be accused of lying to God – thus breaking the 9th commandment. "Jesus declared his royalty in no uncertain terms. In calling himself the Son of Man, Jesus was claiming to be the Messiah, as his listeners well knew. He knew this declaration would be his undoing, but he did not panic. He was calm, courageous, and determined." *Life Application Study Bible*

"Then the high priest tore his clothes and said, 'What further need do we have of witnesses? You have heard the blasphemy! What do you think?' And they all condemned Him to be deserving of death." Mark 14:63-64 (NKJV)

When Caiaphas grasped his robe and tore it, he was making the expression of ultimate grief and indignation. The Talmud required that when a mediator heard blasphemous words spoken under oath, he was to publicly express his total disagreement with the false testimony by tearing his garments. So Caiaphas' self-righteous indignation is on display in a deliberately staged show of revulsion. Everyone – including Jesus – knew that the moment Jesus was arrested and brought before Annas' corrupt circle of powerful elites the "fix" would be in and Jesus would have to be condemned to death. All of the trials were just going through the necessary motions to engineer His death. The veneer of religious piety came off and seeing Jesus' weakness and vulnerability before the powerful, vain, and evil men some standing near to Jesus began to abuse and humiliate Him. "Then some began to spit on Him, and to blindfold

Him, and to beat Him, and to say to Him, 'Prophesy!' And the officers struck Him with the palms of their hands." Mark 14:65 (NKJV)

While all of this abuse was taking place on the inside in the Palace of Caiaphas, just outside Peter is fulfilling another prophecy concerning the death of the Messiah of the Jews. Peter's denials were inevitable the moment the words passed Jesus' lips a few hours earlier that Peter's faith would fail him three times before he heard the rooster crow at dawn. "As [Peter] crossed the inner court to mingle again with the group around the fire, where he had formerly found safety, he was first accosted by one man, and then they all around the fire turned upon him, and each and all had the same thing to say, the same charge, that he was also one of the disciples of Jesus of Nazareth. But Peter's resolve was taken; he was quite sure it was right; and to each separately, and to all together, he gave the same denial, more brief now, for he was collected and determined, but more emphatic - even with an oath. And once more he silenced suspicion for a time." Alfred Edersheim, *The Life and Times of Jesus the Messiah* (Unabridged), Database © 2012 WORDsearch Corp., p.1203

Three: The Trial Before the Sanhedrin

MT 27:1	MK 15:1	LK 22:66-71
Matthew	**Mark**	**Luke**
When the morning was come, all the chief priests and elders of the people took counsel against Jesus to put him to death:	And straightway in the morning the chief priests held a consultation with the elders and scribes and the whole council, and bound Jesus, and carried him away, and delivered him to Pilate.	And as soon as it was day, the elders of the people and the chief priests and the scribes came together, and led him into their council, saying, Art thou the Christ? tell us. And he said unto them, If I tell you, ye will not believe: And if I also ask you, ye will not answer me, nor let me go. Hereafter shall the Son of man sit on the right hand of the power of God. Then said they all, Art thou then the Son of God? And he said unto them, Ye say that I am. And they said, What need we any further witness? for we ourselves have heard of his own mouth.

"Immediately, in the morning, the chief priests held a consultation with the elders and scribes and the whole council; and they bound Jesus, led Him away, and delivered Him to Pilate." Mark 15:1 (NKJV)

The sun was barely up over the Eastern horizon when Jesus was dragged bruised, battered, and bleeding before the hastily assembled main ruling body of the Sanhedrin. This should have been Jesus' first trial, but it was clear to see for all of those assembled that they were only there to give their official approval to a verdict that was already decided. Because the punishment of the accused had already begun it was useless to make any attempt to make a just and fair decision in this case. If any of the leaders assembled there were not happy with this obvious miscarriage of justice taking place in front of them, no one dared to express it – not even the few sympathizers in their midst, like Nicodemus, spoke up. Any doubts over the legality of the proceedings were suppressed by the expediency needed to finish the trial and return home for the approaching Passover Sabbath.

No doubt the members of the Sanhedrin were emboldened by the lack of popular support for Jesus. Annas' gambit had paid off. With Judas' help they were able to quietly arrest Jesus and seclude Him from the public while they swiftly, and without any chance for anyone to seriously question what was happening, condemned Jesus to death. The members of the Sanhedrin could look around them and ask themselves, "Where are the masses of Jesus' followers now? Why are they not protesting?" Life seemed normal around the city as all but a handful waiting for news of Jesus' trial were busy about their daily activities. The members of the Sanhedrin could comfort themselves with the thought that they all had overestimated Jesus' popular appeal. When it came shedding their blood for their Messiah even Jesus' closest followers ran away and hid.

Jesus, the Son of God and Messiah now stood before the supreme court of the Jews, the Sanhedrin. The one who is the Supreme Holy and Righteous Judge – the One who will judge the living and the dead at the end of the age – was now being judged by a room full of sinful, corrupt, and unrighteous judges. If the Son of God's judges could see beyond the moment and imagine themselves one day standing before the judgment seat of Christ, these men would have fallen on their faces and repented of evil and wicked schemes. But the god of this age blinds the minds of unbelievers so that they cannot see anything beyond their immediate circumstances. "In their case the god of this world has blinded the minds of the unbelievers, to keep them from seeing the light of the gospel of the glory of Christ, who is the image of God." 2 Corinthians 4:4 (ESV)

"As soon as it was day, the elders of the people, both chief priests and scribes, came together and led Him into their council, saying, 'If You are the Christ, tell us.' But He said to them, 'If I tell you, you will by no means believe. And if I also ask you, you will by no means answer Me or let Me go. Hereafter the Son of Man will sit on the right hand of the power of God.'
Then they all said, 'Are You then the Son of God?' So He said to them, 'You rightly say that I am.'
And they said, 'What further testimony do we need? For we have heard it ourselves from His own mouth.'" Luke 22:66-71 (NKJV)

"The claim of Jesus was understood, but the leaders rejected His claim. Jesus had both accepted and claimed the charge being made against Him. He was…
- The Messiah
- The Son of God
- The Son of Man

They had heard enough. In their obstinate unbelief, they condemned Him to death – condemned the Man who had come to save the word from its terrible plight of sin and death, from its desperate need for health and love and for salvation and life." *The Preacher's Outline & Sermon Bible ® Vol. 1;Matthew – John (New International Version)*, Authentic Books Logos, Secunderabad, India, Copyright © 2000 by Alpha-Omega Ministries. Inc., p.1386

These were the men that decided was became law for the Jews. There was no higher court for any Jew to appeal to in religious matters. Therefore, when the Sanhedrin met, and passed final judgment on anyone, it was absolute and irrevocable. Therefore, Jesus was destined for the cross. This third trial was the shortest of all the trials Jesus faced. There was only one question on the minds of Jesus' judges, jury, and executioners: Are you the Christ? It required a simple "yes" from Jesus' lips to seal His fate. Except for Nicodemus who stood silently in shock over the scene being played out in front of his eyes, all the members of the

Sanhedrin voted unanimously to condemn Jesus and deliver him to Roman justice for execution.

"Then the whole multitude of them arose and led Him to Pilate. And they began to accuse Him, saying, "We found this fellow perverting the nation, and forbidding to pay taxes to Caesar, saying that He Himself is Christ, a King." Luke 23:1-2 (NKJV)

The charge from the Sanhedrin was blasphemy, but that would not stand up in a Roman civil court. Therefore, plans were already in place to switch the accusation to sedition once they reached Pilate; their claim to Pilate was that Jesus was guilty of attempting to start a religious movement that would cause the people to make Jesus King of the Jews. This would result in an attempt by His followers to overthrow the Roman government in Palestine. But there were problems with this plan: (1) their charge against Jesus was completely false; and (2) there was no guarantee that the Roman Governor would believe any of it.

Four: The Trial Before Pilate

MT 27:2, 11-14 (NIV)	MK 15:1b-5 (NIV)	LK 23:1-5 (NIV)	JN 18:28-38 (NIV)
Matthew	**Mark**	**Luke**	**John**
They bound him, led him away and handed him over to Pilate, the governor. Meanwhile Jesus stood before the governor, and the governor asked him, "Are you the king of the Jews?" "Yes, it is as you say," Jesus replied. When he was accused by the chief priests and the elders, he gave no answer. Then Pilate asked him, "Don't you hear the testimony they are bringing against you?" But Jesus made no reply, not even to a single charge--to the	They bound Jesus, led him away and handed him over to Pilate. "Are you the king of the Jews?" asked Pilate. "Yes, it is as you say," Jesus replied. The chief priests accused him of many things. So again Pilate asked him, "Aren't you going to answer? See how many things they are accusing you of." But Jesus still made no reply, and Pilate was amazed.	Then the whole assembly rose and led him off to Pilate. And they began to accuse him, saying, "We have found this man subverting our nation. He opposes payment of taxes to Caesar and claims to be Christ, a king." So Pilate asked Jesus, "Are you the king of the Jews?" "Yes, it is as you say," Jesus replied. Then Pilate announced to the chief priests and the crowd, "I find no basis for a charge against this man." But they insisted, "He stirs up the people all over Judea by his	Then the Jews led Jesus from Caiaphas to the palace of the Roman governor. By now it was early morning, and to avoid ceremonial uncleanness the Jews did not enter the palace; they wanted to be able to eat the Passover. So Pilate came out to them and asked, "What charges are you bringing against this man?" "If he were not a criminal," they replied, "we would not have handed him over to you." Pilate said, "Take him yourselves and judge him by your own law."

THE WAY, TRUTH, AND LIFE

great amazement of the governor.

teaching. He started in Galilee and has come all the way here."

"But we have no right to execute anyone," the Jews objected.

This happened so that the words Jesus had spoken indicating the kind of death he was going to die would be fulfilled.

Pilate then went back inside the palace, summoned Jesus and asked him, "Are you the king of the Jews?"

"Is that your own idea," Jesus asked, "or did others talk to you about me?"

"Am I a Jew?" Pilate replied. "It was your people and your chief priests who handed you over to me. What is it you have done?"

Jesus said, "My kingdom is not of this world. If it were, my servants would fight to prevent my arrest by the Jews. But now my kingdom is from another place."

"You are a king, then!" said Pilate. Jesus answered, "You are right in saying I am a king. In fact, for this reason I was born, and for this I came into the world, to testify to the truth. Everyone on the side of truth listens to me."

"What is truth?" Pilate asked. With this he went out again to the Jews and said, "I find no basis for a charge

> against him. But it is your custom for me to release to you one prisoner at the time of the Passover. Do you want me to release 'the king of the Jews'?"

Once Jesus is brought before Pilate, the legal procedures of the Jews are no longer in place. Jesus is now under Roman jurisdiction. Although the Roman Code of Criminal Procedure included four steps that they must follow to keep the trial legitimate, these rules were only strictly applied to Roman citizens. Since Jesus was not considered a citizen of Rome, Pilate had considerable leeway on how to handle Jesus' case when it was brought before him. However, we will see from the Gospel narratives that right up to the last moment Pilate did all he could to assure a fair and just trial for Jesus. Note the following procedures:

- The first procedure of Roman criminal code was **accusation**
- The second procedure of Roman criminal code was after accusation came **interrogation** to probe and search for evidence against the accused
- The third process in the Roman code was **defense**. The accused have the right to defend themselves or to hire an attorney to defend them against all charges.
- The fourth step is a **verdict**. After accusation, interrogation, and defense, a verdict of guilt or innocence was required.

Pilate had been Governor of Roman Palestine for approximately four years and was well-informed about the Jewish religious legal system and their religious festivals. So when the Jewish high council came before him, dragging a beaten and bound prisoner, and requesting he be tried by Roman civil law, Pilate knew this was no ordinary case. Pilate was also well aware of the Jews' hatred for Rome and everything it stood for. Pilate and his soldiers were unwelcomed foreign occupiers who oppressed the Jews and extracted high taxes from them. The Romans did not like the Jews either. They were a troublesome lot – always complaining, often seditious – they resisted Rome's efforts to govern their Province without interference. So when Jesus was brought before him by His fellow Jews and accused of wanting to start an uprising against Rome, Pilate was suspicious to say the least.

It did not take a lot of effort for Pilate to figure out what was going on. It was obvious that these religious leaders hated Jesus and wanted Him executed, but Pilate did not want to be manipulated by these men to act as their executioner. Pilate also knew that the Jews often stoned people to death for blasphemy or other serious violations of Mosaic Law when they could do so without stirring up any trouble with Rome. The poor, the helpless, the unimportant or the outcasts of the Jews were ignored by Roman justice – Pilate would be involved only if the case involved a Roman citizen or if the case might so upset Roman peace and order in the region that Roman legions would have to be sent in to restore civility. Pilate's first question upon hearing the commotion over Jesus would have been "What does all of this have to do with Rome?"

The Jewish leaders were aware of the fact that only if Pilate could be convinced that executing Jesus was in Rome's best interest would he even consider putting Him to death. So once Jesus is presented to Pilate, He becomes a pawn in a political power play. At that moment, the Jews needed Roman law. Pilate wanted Jewish co-operation and improved relations with the Jews, but at what price? Did the Jews want this man executed badly enough to acquiesce to Rome's authority? Would Pilate go so far as to put to death an innocent man just to improve relations with the Jews? These questions would be answered before this day was finished.

Pontius Pilate was man under a lot of pressure. There were a lot of easier assignments for a Roman official than the province of Judea, but he was put in charge of this administrative district and he was determined to succeed. The Jews were a rebellious and obstinate people, and unlike most of the small city states that were absorbed into the Empire, the majority of Jews did not want Rome's peace or protection. Like other Governors before him, Pilate's relationship with the Jews had been a troublesome one. Pilate had made the same mistake that most foreign rulers of the Jews made: he believed a quick show of force and a heavy-handed administration would subdue the Jewish subjects of the Empire.

His militaristic training caused him to reject compromises and act decisively to put down any trouble. This led on several occasions for Pilate to make matters worse, often offending the religious leaders of the Jews and causing Herod to keep a safe distance from Rome. His mistakes on several occasions resulted riots and chaos that sent his soldiers into the streets to quell the violence and restore order.

It is only speculation, but it is quite possible that Pilate felt at times that he was in over his head – especially on this day when a group of Jewish leaders came and pounded on his door demanding he execute someone who clearly was innocent of doing anything seriously wrong. Pilate was being asked to make a judgment on something that he could not understand.

Pilate gave Jesus every opportunity to defend Himself and declare His innocence. The Gospel narratives make it clear that there was never any doubt in Pilate's mind that Jesus was innocent; three separate times in Jesus' trial, Pilate pronounced Him innocent. Why then did these people want Jesus killed in such a brutal fashion? But the more Pilate resisted condemning Jesus, the more insistent the Jews became that Jesus was to be crucified.

Pilate must have been mystified by all this hostility to Jesus; and his interrogations of Jesus reflected his bewilderment. Pilate could see that Jesus was unlike anyone he encountered before. But he could not risk another riot – especially when the city was filled to overflowing with pilgrims for the Passover Feast. Pilate could have a serious situation on his hands in a matter of moments if he did not handle this trial correctly.

Every attempt to set Jesus free would only push Pilate deeper into a political corner. He had is duty to Rome to maintain law and order in the province on the one side, and the pressure from the Jews on the other. He had been given an opportunity to win the favor of the Jews and a declaration of loyalty to Rome from the Jews who never respected Roman authority before. How could Pilate explain to the Emperor that he let this opportunity slip through his fingers, causing an ensuing riot all because he would not order the death of some unknown, Jewish rabbi from an outlying province that the crowds were demanding he execute?

So faced with the alternatives, Pilate chose his duty to Rome over his moral obligation to save an innocent man. For the Roman citizen, truth, justice, and mercy were nice ideals, but they had to be subject to the enforcement of Roman law and order. "What is truth?" Pilate asked Jesus, rhetorically. Might is what makes right – and might was the only real truth Pilate acknowledged.

John's gospel gives a clear account of this stage of Jesus' trial. The time was around 6:30 to 7 o'clock in the morning. (John 18:28) Because it was the eve of the Sabbath of the important Jewish Feast of Passover, the

Jewish leaders would not enter the *Praetorium* (judgment hall of the governor's palace) that they might not be defiled (become ceremonially unclean). No unclean person would be fit to participate in the Passover celebrations. The Talmud stated that no Jew could enter a Gentile court on Passover, or he would be defiled. So they stayed out of the court itself, and Pilate came out to meet them (John 18:29, "Pilate then went out unto them..."). This is why John describes Pilate coming out and going back in several times during his examination of Jesus.

The hypocrisy of the scribes, Pharisees, and religious elders of the Jews was on display here. Outwardly they were extremely legal in their religion, but inwardly they were criminal in the attitude of their hearts.

In John 18:29-30 we see the first principle of the Roman judicial code taking place: **accusation**. "Pilate then went out to them and said, 'What accusation do you bring against this Man?' They answered and said to him, "If He were not an evildoer, we would not have delivered Him up to you." John 18:29-30 (NKJV)

The Jewish response was sarcastic and did not answer Pilate's question. They were saying in essence, "If he was not guilty of something serious, we wouldn't be here, Pilate!" Since no real accusation was announced that would require Jesus to be tried by Rome, Pilate told them that if it was a problem in their law, then they should take him and judge him.

"Then Pilate said to them, 'You take Him and judge Him according to your law.' Therefore the Jews said to him, 'It is not lawful for us to put anyone to death,' that the saying of Jesus might be fulfilled which He spoke, signifying by what death He would die." John 18:31-32 (NKJV)

The Synoptic gospels make it clear that at this point in the trial the Jews are accusing Jesus of high crimes against the Roman government, including declaring himself a king (Caesar), stirring up the people against Rome, and opposing payment of taxes to Caesar. This immediately changes the whole trial from a minor concern over points of Jewish religious law to a trial for treason against Rome. The plotting of Annas and Caiaphas seems to be working as Pilate enters the Praetorium a second time to question Jesus.

Now that the charges have been clearly made, Pilate follows the second code of Roman justice and follows the accusation with interrogation (John 18:33-35): "Are you the King of the Jews?" Jesus answered, "My kingdom is not of this world. If My kingdom were of this world, My servants would fight, so that I should not be delivered to the Jews; but now My kingdom is not from here." John 18:36 (NKJV) In the brief interrogation that follows, Jesus makes it clear that (1) He is a king, but (2) His kingdom is not an earthly kingdom; and (3) He was not in the process of overthrowing the Roman government in Palestine.

Jesus pointed out the obvious fact that if He wanted to overthrow the government, his servants would be fighting, carrying on a revolution, taking lives, storming this Roman trial, and ruining the entire procedure. So it was obvious to Pilate that Jesus spoke the truth because he did not see any of Jesus followers anywhere. So the third process in the Roman code, **defense**, was working in Jesus' favor. And in John 18:37, Pilate starts to see Jesus' side of the story. Pilate looks at it from Jesus' point of view: "So you're a king!" and understands that Jesus is talking about a spiritual kingdom and not an earthly one. Jesus pushes Pilate even further: "You are right in saying I am a king. In fact, for this reason I was born, and for this I came into the world, to testify to the truth. Everyone on the side of truth listens to me."

By now Pilate is convinced that this case has nothing to do with Rome; it only concerns a heavenly kingdom and Rome claims no jurisdiction over that. So the only crime Jesus might be guilty of is a crime of Jewish law, which would not be anything deserving death.

Pilate's personal weaknesses and mistakes are being exposed by His inability to acknowledge any objective, transcendent truth even when it was standing right in front of him in the person of Jesus Christ. Pilate said to Him, "What is truth?" And when he had said this, he went out again to the Jews, and said to them, "I find no fault in Him at all. John 18:38 (NKJV) Jesus' fate would not be decided by whether or not the charges against Him were true, His fate would be decided by what was expedient at that moment. This would mean His death because the Jews had already decided He must die and will go to any lengths to secure it.

After his examination of the accused, Pilate fulfills the fourth step in the Roman judicial process: **verdict**. But to the Jews' total surprise, Pilate says he finds no guilt! All he finds is that Jesus believes Himself to be the king of some spiritual kingdom that is not going to threaten Rome's authority in any way. So Jesus is found not guilty of treason.

At this point, John skips over the next trials and goes straight to the last one. But Luke, wanting a more complete picture in his narrative, includes what happened next:

"So Pilate said to the chief priests and the crowd, 'I find no fault in this Man.' But they were the more fierce, saying, 'He stirs up the people, teaching throughout all Judea, beginning from Galilee to this place.' When Pilate heard of Galilee, he asked if the Man were a Galilean. And as soon as he knew that He belonged to Herod's jurisdiction, he sent Him to Herod, who was also in Jerusalem at that time." Luke 23:4-7 (NKJV**)**

Pilate could have released Jesus at that moment and sent his soldiers to disperse the crowd, but it was obvious that it would not appease the anger of those who brought Jesus to him. But as soon as Pilate heard the word "Galilee," he had an ingenious idea. Technically speaking, Galilee really was not under Rome direct jurisdiction, and since he wanted nothing else to do with this case, he decided to find somebody else to try Jesus.

Herod was made the king of the Jews by Rome; he was kept in power by Rome and served at Rome's pleasure. If Herod did not have any objections to Jesus claiming to be some kind of heavenly king, than certainly Rome would have no objections. Herod had already proven he was bloodthirsty and had no problem executing anyone he felt was a threat to his power. He had recently beheaded John the Baptist for a song and a dance (Matt. 14:3-11). So Herod might be the answer to Pilate's dilemma.

Five: The Trial Before Herod

LUKE 23:6-12 NIV
On hearing this, Pilate asked if the man was a Galilean. When he learned that Jesus was under Herod's jurisdiction, he sent him to Herod, who was also in Jerusalem at that time. When Herod saw Jesus, he was greatly pleased, because for a long time he had been wanting to see him. From what he had heard about him, he hoped to see him perform some miracle. He plied him with many questions, but Jesus gave him no answer. The chief priests and the teachers of the law were standing there, vehemently accusing him. Then Herod and his soldiers ridiculed and mocked him. Dressing him in an elegant robe, they sent him back to Pilate.
That day Herod and Pilate became friends – before this they had been enemies.

When Pilate heard Galilee mentioned, he asked if the prisoner was a Galilean. And as soon as he knew that Jesus was from there and therefore belonged to Herod's jurisdiction, Pilate sent Him to Herod. Being the Passover, Herod was also in Jerusalem at that time.

The Herodian family ruled over the Palestinian territory from 40 B.C. until around A.D. 100. Herod Antipas, like his father before him, owed his position to Rome's power. His brother Herod Archelaus was removed from power because his excessive cruelty led to continued civil unrest. His removal left Herod Antipas tetrarch of Galilee and Perea – places where Jesus and John the Baptist concentrated their ministries. The Herodians were persons of influence who were aligned with the ruling family and were friendly with the Romans.

Herod's friendship with Rome was an uneasy one. He knew that he could be removed from power any time and for any reason. Therefore, he must appease Rome and side with them in any dispute with the Jews. On the other side, Herod had to keep his Jewish subjects happy, which was not easy. Herod was there to act as a buffer between Rome and their Jewish subjects.

Naturally, the Herodians were life-long enemies of Jesus because reports had reached Herod that people were starting to call Him Messiah and King of the Jews. He feared an uprising, but was shrewd enough to know that if he acted rashly against Jesus and His followers it could trigger another revolt which could lead to his removal from office.

The Roman governor and Herod viewed each other with suspicion and saw each other as rivals for dominant political power over the region. Because the Herodians had a well-deserved reputation for abuse of power and for ruling over their subjects with vicious cruelty, one of Pilate's main responsibilities was to keep an eye on Herod and keep him in control. Herod could only tolerate the Roman governor's interference and control, but could do nothing about it.

By sending Jesus to Herod Antipas, Pilate freed himself from involvement in what he saw as a strictly Jewish matter. At the same time, Pilate was giving Herod an opportunity to demonstrate his authority as king of the Jews by handling something Rome claimed no jurisdiction over. Herod's delight at seeing Jesus was also because he had heard about him for so long and had been hoping to see him perform one of his miracles for him.

Herod's Hellenistic educational background led him to seek rational answers from Jesus concerning His ministry. Herod had stopped John the Baptist's movement by throwing him in prison. Herod's people had already made it known that he wanted to kill Jesus (Luke 13:31-33) and Jesus responded defiantly, sending a message to "that fox" that He intended to continue his ministry of casting out demons and healing until He was ready to face Herod in Jerusalem. Scholars can only speculate why Luke is the only gospel writer that includes this face-to-face encounter with Herod; it just may be the case that it was of little or no interest to other gospel writers because it changed nothing about the exchanges between the Jewish religious leaders and Pilate where the real drama is taking place.

Still, Herod's exchange with Jesus is noteworthy because Jesus wanted nothing to do with the Hellenists. They were only interested debating and intellectual arguments that in the end, only confused the issue. The time would come when Jesus' followers would reach the very heart of Hellenism, but Jesus' earthly ministry was to the Jewish nation first. So Luke's narrative conforms to what we would expect Herod to do and how we would expect Jesus to respond.

Luke's account is also noteworthy for the presence of the leading priests and the teachers of religious law who followed Jesus under guard to Herod's palace. They were there to make sure Herod did not interfere with their plans to have Jesus executed. So they stood by the entire time shouting their accusations against Jesus and insisting Herod send Jesus back to Pilate for execution.

Herod must have been a very superstitious man. At first he refused to execute John the Baptist for fear of him. John was recognized as a prophet of God and Herod did not want to come under God's curse. It took his lust for a woman to deceive him and order the prophet's beheading (Matt. 14:1-12). So Herod wanted a sign from Jesus before doing anything that might bring God's wrath upon himself. It is possible that if Jesus performed a great miracle for Herod that he would have feared Jesus and released him. So when Jesus refused to perform any sign for Herod, he tried another tactic and started asking Jesus questions. We do not know what Herod asked, but we can speculate that having been instructed by the best Greek tutors, his intent was to get Jesus to debate with him, which Jesus refused to do. If Herod was going to believe, he would have to do it by faith unseen alone.

This "trial" was quickly turning into a farce. After getting no response from Jesus, the Herodians mocked him and bullied him and sent him back to Pilate. It was his way of saying to Pilate, "I don't care what you do with this man. He is of no concern to me." Herod and Pilate, who had been enemies before, gained a new respect for each other by the way they handled this controversial trial and became friends from that day.

So Herod quickly tired of Jesus and his soldiers began mocking and ridiculing Jesus. They put a royal robe on him and sent him back to Pilate. This time the Jewish religious leaders would push Pilate to make a purely political decision for the execution of Jesus.

Six & Seven: The Second Trial Before Pilate & the Jews Condemn Jesus to Death and Choose to Release Barabbas

MT 27:15-23 (NIV)	MK 15:6-14 (NIV)	LK 23:13-22 (NIV)	JN 18:39-19:6 (NIV)
Matthew	**Mark**	**Luke**	**John**
Now it was the governor's custom at the Feast to release a prisoner chosen by the crowd. At that time they had a notorious prisoner, called Barabbas. So when the crowd had gathered, Pilate asked them, "Which one do you want me to release to you: Barabbas, or Jesus who is called Christ?" For he knew it was out of envy that they had handed Jesus over to him. While Pilate was sitting on the judge's seat, his wife sent him this message: "Don't have anything to do with that innocent man, for I have suffered a great	Now it was the custom at the Feast to release a prisoner whom the people requested. A man called Barabbas was in prison with the insurrectionists who had committed murder in the uprising. The crowd came up and asked Pilate to do for them what he usually did. "Do you want me to release to you the king of the Jews?" asked Pilate, knowing it was out of envy that the chief priests had handed Jesus over to him. But the chief priests stirred up the crowd to have Pilate release Barabbas instead. "What shall I do, then,	Pilate called together the chief priests, the rulers and the people, and said to them, "You brought me this man as one who was inciting the people to rebellion. I have examined him in your presence and have found no basis for your charges against him. Neither has Herod, for he sent him back to us; as you can see, he has done nothing to deserve death. Therefore, I will punish him and then release him. "With one voice they cried out, "Away with this man! Release Barabbas to us!" (Barabbas had been thrown into prison for an insurrection in the	But it is your custom for me to release to you one prisoner at the time of the Passover. Do you want me to release 'the king of the Jews'?" They shouted back, "No, not him! Give us Barabbas!" Now Barabbas had taken part in a rebellion. Then Pilate took Jesus and had him flogged. The soldiers twisted together a crown of thorns and put it on his head. They clothed him in a purple robe and went up to him again and again, saying, "Hail, king of the Jews!" And they struck him in the face. Once more Pilate came

THE WAY, TRUTH, AND LIFE

deal today in a dream because of him."
But the chief priests and the elders persuaded the crowd to ask for Barabbas and to have Jesus executed. "Which of the two do you want me to release to you?" asked the governor. "Barabbas," they answered.
"What shall I do, then, with Jesus who is called Christ?" Pilate asked. They all answered, "Crucify him!"
"Why? What crime has he committed?" asked Pilate. But they shouted all the louder, "Crucify him!"

with the one you call the king of the Jews?" Pilate asked them. "Crucify him!" they shouted.
"Why? What crime has he committed?" asked Pilate. But they shouted all the louder, "Crucify him!"

city, and for murder.) Wanting to release Jesus, Pilate appealed to them again.
But they kept shouting, "Crucify him! Crucify him!"
For the third time he spoke to them: "Why? What crime has this man committed? I have found in him no grounds for the death penalty. Therefore I will have him punished and then release him."

out and said to the Jews, "Look, I am bringing him out to you to let you know that I find no basis for a charge against him."
When Jesus came out wearing the crown of thorns and the purple robe, Pilate said to them, "Here is the man!"
As soon as the chief priests and their officials saw him, they shouted, "Crucify! Crucify!" But Pilate answered, "You take him and crucify him. As for me, I find no basis for a charge against him."

MT 27:24-31 (NIV)	MK 15:15-20 (NIV)	LK 23:23-25 (NIV)	JN 19:7-16 (NIV)
Matthew	**Mark**	**Luke**	**John**
Then the governor's soldiers took Jesus into the Praetorium and gathered the whole company of soldiers around him. They stripped him and put a scarlet robe on him, and then twisted together a crown of thorns and set it on his head. They put a staff in his right hand and knelt in front of him and mocked him. "Hail, king of the Jews!" they	Wanting to satisfy the crowd, Pilate released Barabbas to them. He had Jesus flogged, and handed him over to be crucified. The soldiers led Jesus away into the palace (that is, the Praetorium) and called together the whole company of soldiers. They put a purple robe on him, then twisted together a crown of thorns and set it on him.	But with loud shouts they insistently demanded that he be crucified, and their shouts prevailed. So Pilate decided to grant their demand. He released the man who had been thrown into prison for insurrection and murder, the one they asked for, and surrendered Jesus to their will.	The Jews insisted, "We have a law, and according to that law he must die, because he claimed to be the Son of God."
When Pilate heard this, he was even more afraid, and he went back inside the palace. "Where do you come from?" he asked Jesus, but Jesus gave him no answer.
"Do you refuse to speak to me?" Pilate said.

said.
They spit on him, and took the staff and struck him on the head again and again.
After they had mocked him, they took off the robe and put his own clothes on him. Then they led him away to crucify him.
And they began to call out to him, "Hail, king of the Jews!"
Again and again they struck him on the head with a staff and spit on him. Falling on their knees, they paid homage to him.
And when they had mocked him, they took off the purple robe and put his own clothes on him. Then they led him out to crucify him.

"Don't you realize I have power either to free you or to crucify you?"
Jesus answered, "You would have no power over me if it were not given to you from above. Therefore the one who handed me over to you is guilty of a greater sin."
From then on, Pilate tried to set Jesus free, but the Jews kept shouting, "If you let this man go, you are no friend of Caesar. Anyone who claims to be a king opposes Caesar."
When Pilate heard this, he brought Jesus out and sat down on the judge's seat at a place known as the Stone Pavement (which in Aramaic is Gabbatha). It was the day of Preparation of Passover Week, about the sixth hour. "Here is your king," Pilate said to the Jews.
But they shouted, "Take him away! Take him away! Crucify him!" "Shall I crucify your king?" Pilate asked. "We have no king but Caesar," the chief priests answered.

6ᵗʰ & 7ᵗʰ SEVENTH TRIALS – Before Pilate (2) and Barabbas

Depending upon how it is presented, the final minutes of Jesus' trials can be considered one or two trials.

Like the Ark of the Covenant in Philistine hands, Jesus becomes an unwelcomed prize being shuffled back and forth between the different powers represented in Jerusalem because no one wants to bear the ultimate responsibility for ordering the death of someone that in their heart of hearts they know is truly innocent of any wrong-doing and should not be touched. And so Pilate, thinking he is once and for all rid of this strange prophet from a strange land suddenly finds the prisoner Jesus standing at his door once more.

Luke says that the common problem of what to do with Jesus becomes the means for overcoming the animosity between Herod and Pilate for one another and they become friends from this time forward. Any peace between Rome and the religious zealots of the Jews is short-lived at best.

By this point in time Jesus had been tried by the former High Priest Annas, the current High Priest Caiaphas, the full Sanhedrin, Pilate, and Herod. None of these trials were legal, and none of them could find Jesus guilty of anything worthy of execution by crucifixion. Jesus had already been tried once by Pilate and found not guilty. Pilate was not about to reverse himself now and declare Jesus "guilty" in a second illegal trial just to appease the religious leaders of the Jews that hated Rome and everything about it.

The Jews had never accepted Rome's authority over them or anything to do with their religion. Now Pilate is embroiled in what he perceived to be a dispute over a despised religion. Pilate tried several avenues to get out of sentencing Jesus to be crucified; by now it was obvious that he resented these Jews using Roman law as the means to solve this particular problem when they resisted Roman law at every other turn. From his exchanges with Jesus and his attempts to release Him, it seems that Pilate at the very least pitied Jesus, but on some level may have respected His integrity and refusal to compromise one bit to save Himself.

So Jesus was not going to give Pilate any help. He would not beg for mercy and He would not plead His innocence. Pilate saw that the Jewish religious leaders wanted blood – Jesus' blood. They did not want Him neutralized; they wanted Him totally humiliated and crucified as an example to anyone who dared cross them or challenge their supreme authority over the religious matters of the Jewish nation in the future. Pilate hoped to appease the crowd by offering to publically chastise Jesus by beating Him and then offer to release him.

After mocking Jesus "the king of the Jews" by placing a crown of thorns upon His head and a purple robe on His shoulders, the soldiers mercilessly scourged His body. Pilate presents Jesus' broken and battered body to the assembled crowd pronouncing His innocence and saying to them, "Behold the Man!" If Pilate had any illusions that the Jews would look upon Jesus with pity and sympathy – that they would cry out for mercy upon Jesus at this point – his illusions were quickly shattered. Their thirst for blood and vengeance boiled over and they cried out "*Crucify Him, crucify Him!*" Pilate said to them, "You take Him and crucify *Him*, for I find no fault in Him."

No doubt, the word of Jesus' arrest for blasphemy and sedition had spread like a wildfire throughout the city. The members of the Sanhedrin took no chances with the crowds assembled for the Passover and sent their representatives throughout the city to spread their propaganda that Jesus threatened to destroy the Temple, had spoken against Rome and had falsely claimed to be the Son of God.

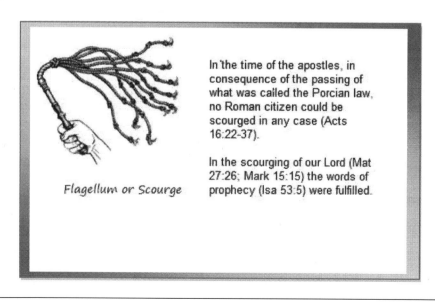

Flagellum or Scourge

In the time of the apostles, in consequence of the passing of what was called the Porcian law, no Roman citizen could be scourged in any case (Acts 16:22-37).

In the scourging of our Lord (Mat 27:26; Mark 15:15) the words of prophecy (Isa 53:5) were fulfilled.

Once the Sun was up, there is little doubt that some of the crowds on the Temple Mount would have seen Jesus, bound and bruised, being dragged under guard from the council chambers of the Sanhedrin, to the Praetorium, from the Praetorium to Herod's Palace, and then back to the Praetorium. In a time when there were no TV or radio broadcasts to flash the news, people depended upon word of mouth to spread the news. All but a small handful of Jesus' most devoted followers were nowhere to be found. And those few that had not scattered followed Jesus under guard in the desperate hope that He might be released to them.

The representatives of the Sanhedrin made sure that the people heard that one of Jesus' own disciples had betrayed Him and turned Him over to the authorities. One of Jesus' chosen disciples with curses on his lips had denied knowing Him, and the rest had abandoned their Master. The Jewish authorities spread out over the city and quieted the doubtful and calmed the fearful. Their scribes, Pharisees, teachers of the Law, and Sadducees were all in agreement that Jesus must pay for His crimes against the nation. The one the crowds had proclaimed Messiah and king of the Jews only a few days before had been exposed as a false Messiah and the masses must go along with their leaders' judgment.

So by the time Jesus is finally presented by Pilate to the crowd of Jewish onlookers, the Jews were in no mood for mercy, "We have a law, and according to our law He ought to die, because He made Himself the Son of God."

When Pilate heard that saying, he was the more afraid, "Besides, while he was sitting on the judgment seat, his wife sent word to him, 'Have nothing to do with that righteous man, for I have suffered much because of him today in a dream.'" Matthew 27:19 (ESV) Pilate was struggling on a personal level because he did not know who to believe. In one last desperate attempt to save Jesus He asked Him, "Where are You from?" When Jesus does finally answer Pilate, he knows the Man he is judging is no ordinary Man. "From then on Pilate sought to release Him, but the Jews cried out, saying, 'If you let this Man go, you are not Caesar's friend. Whoever makes himself a king, speaks against Caesar.'"

The Final Trial

Having failed to persuade the religious leaders of the Jews that Jesus was undeserving of death, Pilate turned to the crowds had gathered around to watch the trial of Jesus unfold.

A large mass of people was in Jerusalem for the Feast of Passover, by now the word had spread throughout the city that the prophet from Galilee, the rabbi Jesus had been arrested in the night and was now on trial at the Roman Governor's palace.

Those who believed Jesus was the promised Messiah were falling away by the minute. The Jewish propagandists made sure the crowds were informed that Jesus had been tried and found guilty of blaspheme. The crowd had only heard their leaders' side of events. Jesus made no public statements, offered no defense, asked no one to speak on His behalf. It was at this point that Pilate tried one last tactic to release Jesus but the verdict of the crowd was a foregone conclusion.

Romans had the option to employ the custom of releasing a prisoner on the Passover. He asked the crowd, "Do you therefore want me to release to you the King of the Jews?" They asked for Barabbas instead. Very little is known for sure about Barabbas. We know that Barabbas never led a successful revolution, and was only notorious as a bandit. The people may have considered him some kind of patriot in their ongoing struggle against their Roman occupiers. But all of that is speculation.

All we know from the biblical account is that High Priest sent Jesus to Pilate to be crucified. Pilate tried to find a way to get around using Roman law to murder Jesus just to appease the Jews. Pilate was not doing this because he wanted to be noble; Pilate did not rise to power by being noble, he rose by being ruthless. And he kept Roman law and order with an iron fist and a sword if necessary. But the one thing that held the Roman Empire together besides their many legions was Roman law; and according to Roman law and procedure, Jesus of Nazareth had done nothing to deserve the death penalty. In fact, Jesus never should have been on trial before Roman law in the first place. But Pilate knew his duty was to keep the peace of Rome at any cost. And if the unjust trial and execution of one Jewish rabbi was need to keep the peace, then Jesus would have to be sacrificed.

But there was also a spiritual dimension to all of these events that neither Rome nor the Jews could control. The day on which all of this is taking place is the Passover. Passover is a special Feast that commemorates the Liberation of the Hebrew people from the Egyptians. For many years the Jews had been hoping and praying for independence and liberation from the Babylonians, then the Persians, then the Seleucids, and now the Romans. On the Passover the priests were responsible for helping the people make atonement for sins.

The atonement on the Passover, like the sacrifice on the great Day of Atonement, was arranged by the High Priest. And just as on the great Day of Atonement when the High Priest selected the sacrifice, and determined which one was to be sacrificed to God and which was to be released into the wilderness, so too on that first "Good Friday," the High Priest was responsible for arranging the sacrifice of Jesus, while releasing the other (Barabbas) out into the wilderness never to be seen or heard of again. Here, as on the great Day of Atonement, there are two grand spiritual ideas of the Savior being presented: the idea of Christ the Lamb of God sacrificed for the sins of the world, and the idea Christ the Lamb of God who took our guilt and shame upon Him to set sinners free – represented by Barabbas who was the human choice for liberation made in place of Christ.

The high priest and the people made their choice and sacrificed Jesus because Barabbas was as guilty as they were. They chose a man of violence, murder, destruction, hate, and fear. Barabbas' kingdom was of this world; by choosing him, they were in essence choosing their own kingdoms over the kingdom of heaven that Jesus reigned and ruled over. By choosing to sacrifice Jesus to atone for the sins of the world, Barabbas becomes the scapegoat who carries the sins of the people out into the wilderness, "as far as the east is from the west, so far does he remove our transgressions from us." Psalm 103:12 (ESV)

The Jews who cried out for Jesus to be crucified that day chose to sacrifice the King of love, compassion, forgiveness, justice, and peace because deep down inside those things are offensive to sinful human beings. Pilate found no fault in Jesus, but what was more important is that the Father found no fault in the Son of God. Pilate may have believed that brutally beating Jesus would be enough to cause the crowds to cry out for mercy on Him. But beating Jesus was not enough. Peter could not save Jesus in Gethsemane because Jesus did not need saving. Pilate could not save Jesus because Jesus did not need saving. Jesus was not asking anyone to save Him; that was not what He came for. He came to die so that all men would be saved. In the end, Pilate succumbed to public pressure and added his name to the long list of those guilty of executing the innocent Lamb of God, "For there is no distinction: for all have sinned and fall short of the glory of God..."

REVIEW OF THE TRIALS:

A. The Six Trials of Jesus:
1. Jesus had six trials: Three religious (Jewish), and three civil (Romans).

2. All these six trials were carried out in eight hours on Friday, from 2 AM to 10 AM

B. Three Jewish religious trials where Jesus was unlawfully convicted for Blasphemy:

1. First Religious Trial: Annas (John 18:12-14) where the Decision was made to go ahead and execute Jesus.

2. Second Religious Trial: Caiaphas (Matt.26:57-68) where the death sentence for the charge of blasphemy was given because Jesus proclaimed himself the Messiah and God the Son.

3. Third Religious Trial: Sanhedrin (Matt. 27:1-2, Luke 22:63-71) where the final death sentence is given

C. Three Civic trials where Jesus was proclaimed innocent (twice by Pilate and once by King Herod).

1. First Roman Civil Trial (John.18:28-38). Pilate finds Jesus Not guilty.

2. Second Civil Trial by King Herod (Luke 23:6-12) Herod dismisses Jesus with no decision of guilt

3. Third Civil Trial – Second trial by Pilate (John 18:39-19:6). Pilate again finds Jesus not guilty, but turns Jesus over to the Jews to be crucified anyway (Matt. 27:26).

THE WAY, TRUTH, AND LIFE

10. "Mission Accomplished"

The Death, Burial, and Resurrection of Jesus

"Jesus Christ crucified on the cross at Golgotha"
By Marie Clara (Used by Permission)

LESSON OUTLINE:

The purpose of this lesson is to describe the events from the Resurrection to the Ascension of Jesus Christ.

FREDERICK OSBORN

Praise be to the God and Father of our Lord Jesus Christ! In his great mercy he has given us new birth into a living hope through the resurrection of Jesus Christ from the dead, and into an inheritance that can never perish, spoil or fade – kept in heaven for you, who through faith are shielded by God's power until the coming of the salvation that is ready to be revealed in the last time. 1 Peter 1:3-5

The Empty Tomb: Mission Accomplished

"**He has risen!** Since the creation of the world, there has never been another event as important as the rising of Christ from the dead. If Christ had not risen from the dead, there would be no Christian religion, no Christians. There would be no salvation for man (1 Corinthians 15:17-19). The whole course of history would have been totally different. Because, by rising from the dead, Jesus gave final and absolute proof that He was indeed God's own Son. God Himself came to earth and overcame the last enemy, death (2 Timothy 1:10), and showed men and women the way to heaven." From: *The Applied New Testament Commentary* on Mark 16:8, © 1996 by Thomas Hale and Steven Thorson)

1. **God the Father chose Jesus to be on mission with Him to reconcile a lost world to Himself.**

From the circumstances of His birth to His death, resurrection, and beyond, everything about Jesus' life was foretold. From the moment Jesus' public ministry began, until the last revelation we see of Him in John's Revelation, He was declared "The Lamb of God" who came to take away the sins of the World. Jesus Christ was a man on a mission to fulfill that divine destiny foretold by the Old Testament prophets. Therefore, His mission would not be complete and He could not ascend to His heavenly throne until He endured the cross – despising its shame – and was placed in the tomb to await His resurrection all according to the mission He was sent to accomplish.

"Then I saw a Lamb, looking as if it had been slain, standing in the center of the throne, encircled by the four living creatures and the elders. He had seven horns and seven eyes, which are the seven spirits of God sent out into all the earth. He came and took the scroll from the right hand of him who sat on the throne. And when he had taken it, the four living creatures and the twenty-four elders fell down before the Lamb. Each one had a harp and they were holding golden bowls full of incense, which are the prayers of the saints.

And they sang a new song: 'You are worthy to take the scroll and to open its seals, because you were slain, and with your blood you purchased men for God from every tribe and language and people and nation.
You have made them to be a kingdom and priests to serve our God, and they will reign on the earth.'
Then I looked and heard the voice of many angels, numbering thousands upon thousands, and ten thousand times ten thousand. They encircled the throne and the living creatures and the elders.
In a loud voice they sang: 'Worthy is the Lamb, who was slain, to receive power and wealth and wisdom and strength and honor and glory and praise!'
Then I heard every creature in heaven and on earth and under the earth and on the sea, and all that is in them, singing: 'To him who sits on the throne and to the Lamb be praise and honor and glory and power, for ever and ever!'" Revelation 5:6-13 (NIV)

2. God the Father called Jesus and accompanied Him on His mission.

The Father's calling of Jesus is an essential element of the Gospel message. It also raises the whole mystery of the incarnation and the relationship between the Father, Son and Holy Spirit. A thorough study of the doctrine of the Trinity, which must include the theology and history of the doctrine, is not suited to this lesson, but is best included in a study of Systematic Theology. But I will include this statement on the Christian doctrine of the Trinity from Kerry D. McRoberts, M.A., M.C.S., Assistant Professor of Bible and Theology at Trinity Bible College:

"Historically, the Church formulated its doctrine of the Trinity following great debate concerning the Christological problem of the relationship of Jesus of Nazareth to the Father. Three distinct Persons – the Father, the Son, and the Holy Spirit – are manifest in Scripture as God, while at the same time the entirety of the Bible tenaciously holds to the Jewish *Sh'ma*: 'Hear, O Israel: The LORD our God, the LORD is one' (Deut. 6:4). The conclusion derived from the biblical data is that the God of the Bible is…'one God in Trinity and Trinity in Unity.'" *Systematic Theology*, Logion Press, Springfield, IL, © 1994, 1995, p.146

The calling of Jesus by the Father is established early on. Even as a child, long before He officially entered His earthly ministry, the Scripture says:

THE WAY, TRUTH, AND LIFE

So [Joseph] got up, took the child and his mother during the night and left for Egypt, where he stayed until the death of Herod. And so was fulfilled what the Lord had said through the prophet: "Out of Egypt I called my son." Matthew 2:14-15.

Later, Luke describes a time when the boy Jesus is at the Temple. And sensing the Father's call, even at the tender age of 12, He declared to His parents, "I must be about My Father's business" (Luke 2:49). Again Jesus heard God's call confirmed at His baptism:

"When all the people were being baptized, Jesus was baptized too. And as he was praying, heaven was opened and the Holy Spirit descended on him in bodily form like a dove. And a voice came from heaven: 'You are my Son, whom I love; with you I am well pleased.'" Luke 3:21-22 (NIV)

And throughout His ministry, Jesus of Nazareth understood that He had a special relationship with His Father. He had the acute sense that He must do only what His Father was doing and work only when His Father worked:

Matthew 11:27; 26:39

Luke 9:26; 10:22; 23:46; 24:49

John 4:23; 5:17-27; 5:36-38; 6:27, 32-33, 37, 44-46, 57, 65; 8:16-19, 28-29, 54; 10:14-18, 25-38; 11:41-42; 12:26-28, 49-50; 13:3; 14:6-31; 15:1, 9, 15-16, 23-27; 16:10, 15, 23, 25-28, 32; 17:1, 5, 11, 21, 24-25; 18:11; 20:17, 21

Near the end of His life, He declared to Philip and the rest of His disciples:

"Jesus answered: 'Don't you know me, Philip, even after I have been among you such a long time? Anyone who has seen me has seen the Father. How can you say, 'Show us the Father'? Don't you believe that I am in the Father, and that the Father is in me? The words I say to you are not just my own. Rather, it is the Father, living in me, who is doing his *work. Believe me when I say that I am in the Father and the Father is in me; or at least believe on the evidence of the miracles themselves. I tell you the truth, anyone who has faith in me will do what I have been doing. He will do even greater things than these, because I am going to the Father."* John 14:9-12 (NIV)

3. The God of Israel initiated a covenant of promise and obedience with Abraham and His descendants – a covenant that Jesus fulfilled.

Jesus obeyed His Father even to the point of the ultimate sacrifice of Himself on the cross. The night of His arrest, Jesus wrestled with being obedient to His Father – His will was to live, but "nonetheless," Jesus said, "not My will but Yours be done." Jesus' obedience is not only an example for us all, but because of His obedience, we have been saved:

"During the days of Jesus' life on earth, he offered up prayers and petitions with loud cries and tears to the one who could save him from death, and he was heard because of his reverent submission. Although he was a son, he learned obedience from what he suffered and, once made perfect, he became the source of eternal salvation for all who obey him." Hebrews 5:7-9 (NIV)

4. God the Father prepared Jesus of Nazareth for His mission.

At the moment of His baptism, the Holy Spirit descended upon Jesus like a dove, and the Father's presence is expressed in His voice declaring, *"You are My beloved Son; in You I am well pleased "* (Luke 3:22). Jesus would need the Spirit of the Living God and His Father's presence to empower Him and equip Him for the journey He would take to Calvary and beyond. But even before the moment of His baptism, God prepared a home for Jesus, with a loving mother, Mary, and a strong stepfather, Joseph. Jesus' parents, brothers, sisters, teachers, and many others would help Him along the way as He grew in wisdom and stature, and in favor with God and men (Luke 2:52 NIV).

None of the Gospel writers were led by the Holy Spirit to include any of the details of the years Jesus spent growing up in Nazareth. Cult groups have often speculated on these years and have come up with some wild and fanciful tales of the young Jesus' supposed miracles and travels to places as far away as the Himalayan Mountains of Tibet. But there is nothing to indicate that Jesus did any of that. Except for His sinless nature,

Jesus' life was not extraordinary in any way before the moment when He stepped into public ministry and the Holy Spirit descended upon Him at His baptism. And this would fit with the Messianic prophecies of Isaiah:

"There shall come forth a shoot from the stump of Jesse, and a branch from his roots shall bear fruit." 11:1 (ESV)

"For he grew up before him like a young plant, and like a root out of dry ground; he had no form or majesty that we should look at him, and no beauty that we should desire him." 53:2 (ESV)

5. God the Father sent Jesus where He could best work through Him to accomplish His mission.

In order to fulfill His mission, Jesus had to totally identify with humanity; therefore, He had to live among the people. His mission required Jesus to come as the humble Servant and Son of God clothed in humanity.

"Aware of this, Jesus withdrew from that place. Many followed him, and he healed all their sick, warning them not to tell who he was. This was to fulfill what was spoken through the prophet Isaiah: 'Here is my servant whom I have chosen, the one I love, in whom I delight; I will put my Spirit on him, and he will proclaim justice to the nations. He will not quarrel or cry out; no one will hear his voice in the streets. A bruised reed he will not break, and a smoldering wick he will not snuff out, till he leads justice to victory. In his name the nations will put their hope.'" Matthew 12:15-21 (NIV)

The time will come when Jesus will arrive in all His glory with the hosts of heaven – as was also prophesied; but before that time, Jesus had a specific mission to fulfill, and that mission required Him to relate to the Jews, God's chosen people, first:

"These twelve Jesus sent out and commanded them, saying: 'Do not go into the way of the Gentiles, and do not enter a city of the Samaritans. But go rather to the lost sheep of the house of Israel.'" Matthew 10:5-6 (NKJV)

"But He answered and said, 'I was not sent except to the lost sheep of the house of Israel.'" Matthew 15:24 (NKJV)

"Therefore let all the house of Israel know assuredly that God has made this Jesus, whom you crucified, both Lord and Christ." Acts 2:36 (NKJV)

6. God the Father guided Jesus, the obedient Son, who joins His Father on His mission to redeem mankind.

Jesus often went alone to pray and commune with His Father. He never failed to seek God's guidance and to operate within the parameters the Father gave Him:

"Jesus gave them this answer: 'I tell you the truth, the Son can do nothing by himself; he can do only what he sees his Father doing, because whatever the Father does the Son also does. For the Father loves the Son and shows him all he does. Yes, to your amazement he will show him even greater things than these.'" John 5:19-20 (NIV)

Non-Trinitarians often cite Jesus' submissive role to the Father as their reason for rejecting the doctrine of the Trinity. How can Jesus be "submitted" to the Father and yet be equal to the Father? The writers of the New Testament addressed this apparent contradiction by understanding that Jesus' earthly ministry was accomplishing a far greater eternal purpose:

"During the days of Jesus' life on earth, he offered up prayers and petitions with loud cries and tears to the one who could save him from death, and he was heard because of his reverent submission. Although he was a son, he learned obedience from what he suffered and, once made perfect, he became the source of eternal salvation for all who obey him." Hebrews 5:7-9 (NIV)

"For just as through the disobedience of the one man the many were made sinners, so also through the obedience of the one man the many will be made righteous." Romans 5:19 (NIV)

Another important reason for Jesus being submitted to the Father is the example of perfect servanthood He modeled for all those who must follow in His footsteps:

"Your attitude should be the same as that of Christ Jesus: who, being in very nature God, did not consider equality with God something to be grasped, but made himself nothing, taking the very nature of a servant, being made in human likeness.
And being found in appearance as a man, he humbled himself and became obedient to death-- even death on a cross!
Therefore God exalted him to the highest place and gave him the name that is above every name, that at the name of Jesus every knee should bow, in heaven and on earth and under the earth, and every tongue confess that Jesus Christ is Lord, to the glory of God the Father." Philippians 2:5-11 (NIV)

7. God the Father used Son to bring glory to His name through Jesus' mission.

"After Jesus said this, he looked toward heaven and prayed: 'Father, the time has come. Glorify your Son, that your Son may glorify you. For you granted him authority over all people that he might give eternal life to all those you have given him. Now this is eternal life: that they may know you, the only true God, and Jesus Christ, whom you have sent. I have brought you glory on earth by completing the work you gave me to do. And now, Father, glorify me in your presence with the glory I had with you before the world began.'" John 17:1-5 (NIV)

Jesus had the assurance of knowing that He was completing the work His Father gave Him to do. The Father delighted in the Son every day of His ministry, knowing that the Son, in every way, revealed His nature and glory to the world. This was Jesus' ultimate mission: to glorify the Father. It is difficult for us to understand how the horrible and humiliating death of Jesus upon the cross would bring glory to God, but that is exactly how Jesus spoke of it:

"Jesus replied, 'The hour has come for the Son of Man to be glorified. I tell you the truth, unless a kernel of wheat falls to the ground and dies, it remains only a

single seed. But if it dies, it produces many seeds. The man who loves his life will lose it, while the man who hates his life in this world will keep it for eternal life. Whoever serves me must follow me; and where I am, my servant also will be. My Father will honor the one who serves me. Now my heart is troubled, and what shall I say? 'Father, save me from this hour'? No, it was for this very reason I came to this hour. Father, glorify your name!'
Then a voice came from heaven, 'I have glorified it, and will glorify it again.'"
John 12:23-28 (NIV)

"Jesus had 'steadfastly set His face to go to Jerusalem' (Luke 9:51), knowing full well what would happen to Him there; and how those events were about to occur. They were appointments, not accidents, for they had been determined by the Father and written centuries ago in the Old Testament Scriptures (Luke 24:26-27). We cannot but admire our Savior and love Him more as we see Him courageously enter into this time of suffering and eventual death. We must remember that He did it for us." Warren Wiersbe, *The Wiersbe Bible Commentary*, David C. Cook Publisher, Colorado Springs, CO, © 2007, p.212

In the end, Jesus fulfilled His mission and went all the way to the cross for us. But His death was not the end. He rose from the tomb and from the other side of that empty tomb; we now clearly see the glory of God in the resurrection, and our part in that:

"I want to know Christ and the power of his resurrection and the fellowship of sharing in his sufferings, becoming like him in his death, and so, somehow, to attain to the resurrection from the dead. Not that I have already obtained all this, or have already been made perfect, but I press on to take hold of that for which Christ Jesus took hold of me.
Brothers, I do not consider myself yet to have taken hold of it. But one thing I do: Forgetting what is behind and straining toward what is ahead, I press on toward the goal to win the prize for which God has called me heavenward in Christ Jesus." Philippians 3:10-14 (NIV)

FROM THE TOMB TO THE THRONE
Matthew 28:1 – 20; Mark 16:1 – 20; Luke 24:1 – 53; John 20:1 – 21:25

The Resurrection of Jesus Christ from the tomb on the first Easter Morning is one of the most significant events in all of human history. In fact Paul said that if the resurrection had not taken place, "then our preaching is empty and your faith is also empty. Yes, and we are found false witnesses of God, because we have testified that He raised up Christ..." (1 Corinthians 15:14, 15) "And if Christ has not been raised, your faith is futile; you are still in your sins." 1 Corinthians 15:17 (NIV); and yet not one of the Gospels gives us a complete account of all the events that took place the morning Jesus rose from the tomb.

On the one hand, it seems odd that the Holy Spirit would not have directed at least one, if not all of the Gospel writers to record all that happened not only that morning but also for the weeks following that event all the way to the Ascension of Our Lord. But we are told almost nothing of what Jesus taught His disciples during that period between the Resurrection and His Ascension.

We are told that after the resurrection Jesus appeared numerous times to His disciples and that over five hundred people saw Him at one time (1 Cor. 15:3-8). Keep in mind that fact that we have four different witnesses to the same event, much like a modern courtroom drama where each witness contributes a part of the picture, but the whole picture does not emerge until the end when all the witness have testified. In the same way, the four different Gospels bear witness to the same event, but the whole picture will not emerge until the end.

The four Gospels taken collectively do not tell us all we would *like* to know about the resurrection, but they do tell us all we *need* to know:

1. that Jesus did indeed rise from the dead as He said He would and according to the Scriptures; and
2. that His resurrection was a physical resurrection and not a figurative or mystical experience seen only by a few.
3. Jesus proved without a doubt, to those who saw Him (and afterwards to those who did not see but believed their testimonies) that He was, is, and forever shall be Lord and Christ.

Some critics of the New Testament have argued that the Gospel reports are incompatible, and in some places contradictory. A surface reading of the four accounts would seem to support their claims because it is difficult to put the events into a strict timeline (the Holy Spirit did not lead any of the Gospel writers to narrate the story like a blow-by-blow newspaper account). Although different reference materials may place the events of the early morning of the resurrection in a slightly different order, if we approach the Gospel accounts like a good detective and piece together the testimonies of those who were there, we will have a good understanding of every essential thing that happed that morning and the days following up to the Ascension of Jesus.

"The resurrection of Jesus"
By Maria Clara (Used by Permission)

The Morning of the Resurrection
(Matthew 28:1-15; Mark 16:1-11; Luke 24:1-7; John 20:1-18)

Everything happened exactly as Jesus predicted it would. Mark records three times when Jesus specifically warned His disciples that after entering Jerusalem the last time, He would be arrested, beaten, and crucified, but on the third day He would rise from the dead. It was clear however, that all those who heard those words were still unable to grasp the truth of them; they could not take them literally. The significance of the Jewish prophecies concerning the suffering servant Messiah had yet to be revealed to them. It would not be until the day of His resurrection that the truth and reality of these prophecies would begin to unfold for them.

On Sunday morning after the Sabbath had ended, while it was still dark, some women who had come with Jesus and the disciples from Galilee got up and started for to the tomb where Jesus was laid. Joseph and Nicodemus hastily prepared Jesus' body before sunset Friday when the Sabbath would begin. These women took with them the spices that they had prepared to anoint Jesus' body and complete the final preparations of the body according to Jewish burial customs. The women who were identified to undertake this task are Mary Magdalene, the other Mary (the mother of James), Joanna, and Salome. But Luke adds in his Gospel that "certain other women" (Luke 24:1) not named, went there as well.

The women arrived at the tomb still very early in the morning, but after the sun had risen. And they were uncertain who would be there to help roll away the stone from the door of the tomb for them, but trusting they would find assistance [note that when Mary first sees Jesus, before recognizing Him, she believed He was an attendant of the cemetery (John 20:15)]. But when they looked and saw the tomb, they realized that the stone had already been rolled away. Matthew fills in the details of what happened just before the women arrived at the tomb:

"Now after the Sabbath, toward the dawn of the first day of the week, Mary Magdalene and the other Mary went to see the tomb. And behold, there was a great earthquake, for an angel of the Lord descended from heaven and came and rolled back the stone and sat on it. His appearance was like lightning, and his clothing white as snow. And for fear of him the guards trembled and became like dead men." Matthew 28:1-4 (ESV)

Placing the accounts side-by-side it becomes clear that sometime after the women left home to go to the tomb, but before they arrived at the tomb an angel of the Lord descended from heaven, came and rolled back the stone from the door – causing a great earthquake – and sat on it. The rumbling of the earth and the sudden appearance of the angel in full radiance startled the guards who were at the tomb, causing them to quake with fear of him, and faint. After they regained their composure, they fled

"Mary Magdalene meets the resurrected Lord"
By Maria Clara (Used by Permission)

from the tomb. So when the women arrived sometime later they found the tomb opened and unguarded.

Upon entering the tomb, the women saw an angel that looked like a young man clothed in a long white robe sitting on the right side of the place where Jesus' body was placed. (Note that Luke mentions there were "two men" – obviously angels – but Matthew and John chose to only mention the one angel that actually did the speaking.) At first the women were alarmed. But he said to them, "Do not be afraid. I know you seek Jesus of Nazareth, who was crucified. Why do you seek the living among the dead? He is not here, for He has risen as He said to you while He was still in Galilee: 'The Son of Man must be delivered into the hands of sinful men, and be crucified, and the third day rise again.' See the place where they laid Him. But go, tell His disciples – and Peter – that He is risen from the dead, and indeed He is going before you into Galilee; there you will see Him again, as He told you." Matthew 28:5-7 (NIV) In Mark's Gospel the angel specifically mentions Peter in the angel's instructions.

Once the women fully grasped what had happened, they quickly left the tomb and with fear and great joy; they said nothing to anyone they encountered along the way and ran to bring His disciples word of what happened. When the women returned to the place where they were staying, told the eleven and to all who were with them what had happened at the tomb, and what the angels had told them, no one believed them. In desperation Mary Magdalene said to Peter and John, "They have taken away the Lord out of the tomb, and we do not know where they have laid Him" it dawned upon them that even if they did not believe the supernatural part of the women's story, the body of Jesus went missing. So they got up and ran to the tomb. Mary and some other unidentified women followed after them.

John arrived at the tomb just ahead of Peter, looked in and saw the linen cloths lying there, but he did not go in. Peter arrived at that moment and went into the tomb. He saw the linen cloths lying there, and the handkerchief that had been around Jesus' head. The handkerchief was not lying with the linen cloths, but was folded together in a place by itself. John followed Peter into the tomb. At that moment he saw the empty tomb for himself and believed what the women had said. In spite of all that Jesus told them, what the Scriptures said, and seeing the empty tomb, Peter and John were still struggling to understand the full implications of what they were witnessing.

They exited the tomb and departed again to the place where they were staying. No doubt, they were contemplating the Scriptures Jesus shared with them that said He must rise again from the dead. The words Jesus spoke when He stood in front of the Temple in Jerusalem ("Destroy this temple, and I will raise it again in three days." John 2:19) were starting to be understood.

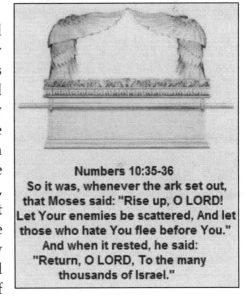

Numbers 10:35-36
So it was, whenever the ark set out, that Moses said: "Rise up, O LORD! Let Your enemies be scattered, And let those who hate You flee before You." And when it rested, he said: "Return, O LORD, To the many thousands of Israel."

About this time Mary arrived back at the tomb. She stood outside by entrance of the tomb weeping, and as she wept she bent down and looked into the tomb. Inside the tomb she saw two angels in white (no doubt the same two angels Luke reported they saw on their first visit to the tomb) sitting, one at the head and the other at the feet, where Jesus' body had been. (Note that on the Ark of the Covenant in the Temple two angels surround the Mercy Seat where the blood of the sacrificial lamb was sprinkled on the Day of Atonement).

The angels said to her, "Woman, why are you weeping?" She said to them, "Because they have taken away my Lord, and I do not know where they have laid Him." As she was saying this, she turned around and saw someone standing there, but did not know that it was Jesus. Jesus said to her, "Woman, why are you weeping? Whom are you seeking?" Assuming Him to be the gardener, Mary said to Him, "Sir, if you have carried Him away, tell me where you have laid Him, and I will take Him away."

Jesus said to her, "Mary!"

Realizing it was Jesus, she said to Him, "Teacher!"

Jesus said to her, "Do not cling to Me, for I have not yet ascended to My Father; but go to My brethren and say to them, 'I am ascending to My Father and your Father, and to My God and your God."

At this moment the other women who followed Mary to the tomb arrived. Jesus greeted them, saying, "Rejoice!" So they bowed down and held Him by the feet and worshipped Him. Then Jesus said to them, "Do not be afraid. Go and tell my disciples to go to Galilee, and there they will see Me." Mary Magdalene and the women went and told the disciples that they had actually seen the Lord, and that He had spoken to them, but again they did not believe them.

Now while the women were at the tomb early in the morning, the guards who fled from the angel came into the city and reported to the chief priests all the things that had happened. The chief priests quickly assembled with the elders and consulted together. They decided to deny the report that Jesus had risen from the dead and gave a large sum of money to the soldiers, instructing them to tell anyone who asked what happened, that His disciples came at night and stole away His body while they slept. "And if it comes to the governor's ears," they promised, "we will appease him and make you secure." So the guards took the money and did as they were instructed.

The Afternoon and Evening of the Resurrection
(Mark 16:12-13; Luke 24:13-43; John 20:19-25)

The day of the resurrection, Luke gives us the best account of the encounter with Jesus by two disciples who were traveling to a village called Emmaus, seven miles from Jerusalem. As they walked, it was only natural that they would talk with one another about all the things that had happened earlier that morning. While they were talking and trying to make sense of what happened, Jesus Himself drew near and walked with them. But their eyes were kept from recognizing Him, and so they did not know it was Jesus walking with them. Jesus asked them about conversation they were having and why they were sad as they walked and talked together.

The one named Cleopas answered him, "Are you the only visitor to Jerusalem who does not know the things that have happened there in these days?" Ironically, Jesus is the *only* one so far who truly knew what had happened and knew the full implications of those events. But Jesus goes along with the conversation of the moment and asks them, "What things?" And the two said to him, "Concerning Jesus of Nazareth, a man who was a prophet mighty in deed and word before God and all the people." They go on and tell how the chief priests and rulers delivered Jesus to be crucified. "But we had hoped that he was the one to redeem Israel."

"The risen Jesus reveals himself to two disciples on the road to Emmaus" By Maria Clara (Used by Permission)

They continue with their story and tell the stranger of the events of the day; how it was now the third day since His death, and how the women went to the tomb and found Jesus missing. They told of the angelic vision informing the women that Jesus was alive and how others had gone to the tomb and found it empty as the women had said. Jesus responded to their confusion, "Foolish ones, and slow of heart to believe in all that the prophets have spoken! Ought not the Christ to have suffered these things and to enter into His glory? And beginning at Moses and all the Prophets, He expounded to them in all the Scriptures the things concerning Himself." Luke 24:25-27 (NKJV)

As they drew near to the village they were going to they urged Him to say with them a while longer. Jesus sat at the table to eat with them and when He took some bread, blessed it, broke it and gave it to them, they suddenly saw that it was Jesus with them all along. And as soon as they recognized Him, He disappeared from their sight. Immediately they got up and returned to Jerusalem to report what had happened.

As soon as they arrived back in the city, they found the disciples and those who were with them. Before they could tell them their story about their journey, those who were gathered together told Cleopas and his traveling companion that "The Lord has risen indeed, and has appeared to Simon!" The two disciples related their story to the others and how they knew it was Jesus in the breaking of the bread.

(NOTE: Only Luke's Gospel mentions that the Lord appeared to Simon Peter that morning, but Luke gives us no more information than the fact that it happened. Paul also mentions the testimony that Jesus appeared to Peter before He appeared to the other disciples in 1 Corinthians 15:5).

In Jerusalem

While the disciples were discussing all the things that had happened that day in Jerusalem and on the road to Emmaus, Jesus Himself appeared and stood in the midst of them, and said "Peace be with you." and He said to them, "Why are you troubled? And why do doubts arise in your hearts? Behold My hands and My feet, that it is I Myself. Handle Me and see, for a spirit does not have flesh and bones as you see I have."

After He said this, He showed them His hands, feet, and side. But they still could not believe it was Him in the flesh, even while they rejoiced and marveled that He had appeared to them. He asked them if they had any food with them. And they gave Him a piece of broiled fish and some honeycomb, which He took and ate in their presence. Again, Jesus said, "Peace to you!" Then continued, as the Father has sent Me, I also send you.

Another miraculous and mysterious thing happens when Jesus breathed on them, and said to them. "Receive the Holy Spirit." Then He said, something else mysterious: "If you forgive the sins of any, they are forgiven them; if you retain the sins of any, they are retained." Some have mistakenly taken this to mean that believers have the power to forgive sins, but no man has that power. Only God can forgive sins. Believers can "proclaim" or "declare" that a person's sins are forgiven in Christ (John 1:12) and they are not forgiven if they reject Christ. We also have the power to forgive those who trespass (sin) against us. If we forgive them, then they are forgiven, but not eternally. That level of forgiveness is for those who repent and turn to God for salvation. If we refuse to forgive, shame on us. How can we expect God to forgive us (Matt. 6:14-15)? "There is only one Mediator between God and man, the Man Christ Jesus (1 Tim. 2:5-6). No other man has ever been worthy to give His life as a ransom for others. No other ransom has ever been acceptable to God. Christ Jesus alone is worthy and acceptable to die as a ransom for someone else. He alone is the Perfect Man. Therefore only Christ can forgive and judge sins." *The Preacher's Outline & Sermon Bible ® Vol. 1;Matthew – John (New International Version)*, Authentic Books Logos, Secunderabad, India, Copyright © 2000 by Alpha-Omega Ministries. Inc., p.1771

One of the eleven remaining disciples, Thomas, was not with them when Jesus came. As soon as he returned, the other disciples told him, "We have seen the Lord." But Thomas said, "Unless I see in His hands the print of the nails, and put my finger into the print of the nails, and put my hand into His side, I will not believe." Some have labeled Thomas as "Doubting." But the truth is that when all accounts are put together, all of the disciples doubted and it took some real convincing on the Lord's part to get them to believe. Thomas may have been the last one to believe, but he was no more or less doubting than the others.

This Ends the Account of All That Happened On the Day Jesus Rose From the Tomb.

Appearances of Jesus After the First Day
(Matthew 28:16-20; Mark 16:14-20; Luke 24:44-52; John 20:26 – 21:25; Acts 1:4-11)

Eight days after the resurrection, the disciples were still in Jerusalem. Once again they are inside the house with the doors shut, and Thomas was with them. Jesus suddenly came into the room, stood in their midst, and said, "Peace to you!" Then He said to Thomas, "Reach your finger here, and look at My hands; and reach your hand here, and put it into My side. Do not be unbelieving, but believing." John 20:26

Thomas answered Jesus saying, "My Lord and my God!"
Then Jesus said to him, "Thomas, because you have seen Me, you have believed. Blessed are those who have not seen and yet have believed." (John 20:29)

"The risen Jesus meets his disciples when they go fishing"
By Maria Clara (Used by Permission)

The disciples followed Jesus' instructions to go to Galilee (Matthew 28:10) where He would meet with them by the sea. Simon Peter, Thomas, Nathanael, the sons of Zebedee (James and John), and two other disciples not named were together near the Sea of Galilee. They decided to go fishing. They went out in a boat and fished all night but caught nothing. When the morning came, Jesus was standing on the shore (the disciples did not know it was Jesus). Then Jesus asked them, "Children, have you any food?" They answered, "No."

And He said to them, "Cast your net on the right side of the boat, and you will find some." They followed the instructions and now they were not able to draw in the net because of the large amount of fish. John said to Peter, "It is the Lord!" Peter understood that it was the Lord, and immediately put on his outer garment (for he had removed it), and jumped into the sea to swim ashore where Jesus was standing.

The other disciples followed in the boat, dragging the net with fish behind. As soon as they reached the land, they saw a fire with cooked fish laid on it, and bread. Jesus said to them, "Bring some of the fish which you have just caught." Simon Peter went to help the others drag the net full of fish to land. And although there were one hundred and fifty-three fish, the net did not break.

Jesus invited them to come and eat breakfast. They all thought it was Jesus, but them disciples dared asked His identity. Jesus then took the bread and gave it to them, and likewise ate the fish. (John notes that this was now the third time Jesus showed Himself to His disciples after the resurrection.) After they had eaten breakfast, Jesus has an exchange with Peter that is intended to restore him after his dismal failure and denying

THE WAY, TRUTH, AND LIFE

Him three times the morning Jesus was arrested. Three times Jesus asked Simon Peter if he loved Him. And three times Peter answered affirmatively. Three times Jesus tells Peter to feed or tend His lambs. When Jesus asked Peter the third time, "Simon, son of Jonah, Do you love Me?" Peter was grieved because Jesus asked him again and again, "Do you love Me?" Peter finally responds, "Lord, You know all things; You know that I love You."

Then Jesus spoke to Peter, signifying that by his death he would glorify God. And when He had spoken this, He said to him, "Follow Me." Jesus has powerfully restored Peter after his fall. For each word of denial that dreadful night, Peter has spoken a word affirming His love for Jesus. Peter could not die for his Lord that night, but only Jesus was destined to die that night. Jesus was now saying to Peter that the time would come when he would have to lay down his life for the Lord, and on that day Peter's death would glorify God. But for now, Peter had an important role to fulfill: to take care of Jesus' sheep.

Peter, turned around, saw John following, and asked, "But Lord, what about this man?" Jesus' response was intended to put Peter's mind back on track. Jesus was saying in essence, "Peter, it's none of your business what happens to John, you follow me."

Next the disciples went to a mountain in Galilee where Jesus told them they would see Him. When they saw Him there, they worshiped Him. But in spite of all Jesus had done, some doubted. This is understandable since nothing like this had ever happened before. We have had some 2,000 years to process all of this, but at that time, many disciples were still trying to mentally process what was going on.

Jesus spoke to them at that time, saying, "All authority has been given to Me in heaven and earth. Go therefore and make disciples of all nations, baptizing them in the name of the Father and of the Son and of the Holy Spirit, teaching them to observe all things that I have commanded you; and lo, I am with you always, even to the end of the age." This is the "Great Commission" passed on to the church from generation to generation up to today and on to tomorrow.

The final scene in the Gospels takes place back in Jerusalem where it all started with the announcement of the birth of the forerunner, John. Jesus instructs His disciples, "These are the words which I spoke to you while I was still with you, that all things must be fulfilled which were written in the Law of Moses and the Prophets and the Psalms concerning Me." And He opened their understanding, that they might comprehend the Scriptures." Luke 24:44-45 (NKJV)

Jesus then gives them the foundational gospel message that has now been preached to the ends of the world. "This it is written, and thus it was necessary for the Christ to suffer and to rise from the dead the third day, and that repentance and remission of sins should be preached in His name to all nations, beginning at Jerusalem. And you are witnesses of these things. Behold, I send the Promise of My Father upon you, which you have heard from Me; for John baptized with water, but you shall be baptized with the Holy Spirit not many days from now. But tarry in the city of Jerusalem until you are endued with power from on high." Luke 24:46-49

Acts 1:1-11 is actually as much the end of the Gospel of Luke as it is the beginning of the book of Acts. Everything was accomplished. Jesus had done all He was commissioned to do. Now He led His core group of disciples that He personally chose and trained to become His first Apostles and led them out as far as Bethany. Still they expected Jesus to establish His kingdom at this time. The church age was still hidden from their view. The times or seasons for the close of this age and when the kingdom will be restored to Israel is still unknown. That is in Father's hands. But Jesus said until that time, His church shall receive power from the Holy Spirit. And until that time His disciples shall be witnesses to Him in Jerusalem, all Judea, and Samaria, and to the ends of the earth.

Jesus lifted His hands and gave then one final blessing from this earthly realm. And while He blessed them, He ascended into the heavens. The disciples continued to look intently toward heaven as He went up. No doubt they were looking for Him to immediately return. But two angels in human form appeared next to them in white apparel and said, "Men of Galilee, why do you stand gazing up into heaven? This same Jesus, who was taken up from you into heaven, will so come in like manner as you saw Him go into heaven." (Acts 1:11) And they worshiped Him, and returned to Jerusalem with great joy, and were continually in the temple praising and blessing God. Luke 24:52-53

"Jesus ascends into heaven"
By Maria Clara (Used by Permission)

POSTSCRIPT

"And truly Jesus did many other signs in the presence of His disciples, which are not written in this book; but these are written that you may believe and that Jesus is the Christ, the Son of God, and that believing you may have life in His name."
John 20:30, 31 (NKJV)

FREDERICK OSBORN

Final Thoughts

The Gospels tell the story of an ordinary man born out of extraordinary circumstances and destined to live an extraordinary life. On one level, we see a humble Jewish Rabbi with a mother, brothers, sisters and a small band of dedicated followers. Jesus was brought up no differently than any other Jewish boy of His time. There was nothing about Him that would indicate to all that knew Him that He was destined to change the world forever.

Then comes that fateful day – when the fullness of time arrives and Jesus emerges from the water of John's baptism ready to step onto the world stage as the long-awaited Messiah and Savior of the world. There is a brief interlude where Jesus is led by the Spirit for forty days to test His endurance. He passes through the fiery furnace of temptation and emerges on the other side the "new Adam" spotless and without sin.

Slowly and prayerfully, Jesus selects a core group of disciples and begins the hard work of molding them and shaping them to be like their Master. At the same time Jesus presents Himself to the nation of Israel as their promised Messiah. But John's baptism might have made them ready for Jesus' arrival, but clearly the hopes, dreams and expectations of the Jews were far apart from the reality of Jesus Christ and His kingdom.

The Jews had their own ideas about the kingdom of God and the King who would sit on David's throne. They were looking for a conquering King who would smite all of their enemies with the edge of His sword and lead a glorious army of the ceremonially pure Jewish warriors. The publicans, sinners, and tax collectors would not be allowed entrance to this kingdom unless they submitted to the laws of Moses as the Pharisees and teachers of the Law defined them. The Jews had built strong barriers between themselves and the unrighteous and there was no way they would allow this upstart rabbi from the backwaters beyond the Sea of Galilee to pass Himself off as their Lord.

The religious leaders did not care how many miracles Jesus performed, or how amazing were His teachings, they were not going to allow Him to overturn their traditions and strip them of their power. Judea was only big enough for one kingdom and the Sanhedrin, the Herodians, and the Romans had already carved it up and were in complete control – there was no room left for the Messiah and His kingdom.

Once it became clear to Jesus that by rejecting Him the Jews had squandered their last chance to fulfill their destiny to be a light to the nations and a banner of Salvation above the world, He concentrated His efforts on preparing His disciples for the time when their Lord would be viciously torn from them and laid in a tomb. We see Jesus shifting His teaching from openly and plainly proclaiming the kingdom of God had arrived and Jesus was its King, to speaking in parables to hide the glorious mysteries of His kingdom from those whose hearts were too hard, too stony, and too thorny to receive the word of His kingdom and multiply it.

The time comes when Jesus is ready to turn towards Jerusalem for the last time. The teaching and training of His disciples intensified while His conflicts over the Sabbath and the traditions of men with the religious elites of the Jews boil over. By the time Jesus is triumphantly welcomed through the city of Jerusalem's gates, the Scribes, Pharisees, and the priestly classes are lying in wait for him and ready to pounce on Him at the first opportunity. The opportunity is handed to them on silver platter when Judas Iscariot, one of Jesus' own turns and betrays Him. Jesus is sold out and after a final night of teaching them the true meaning and purpose for His coming, He prays for them that their faith will not fail them in the hours and days to come.

Jesus in His humanity struggled alone through the long night to remain faithful to the end. His prayers are interrupted by the soldiers' footsteps and a traitor's kiss. This sets in motion the final hours of Jesus' earthly life and ministry. In those final hours Jesus is put through the humiliation of a series of mock trials. He is abused, spit upon, pummeled by His tormentors, beaten to within an inch of His life and then forced to drag a heavy cross through the streets of Jerusalem on His bloodied back.

Jesus' earthly ministry is finished when He breathes His last breath from the cross. "It is finished."

Then there came the silence of the tomb followed by the miraculous resurrection. Something that Jesus foretold all along, but none could understand it.

It is not until that resurrection morning that everything is transformed and the ultimate plan and purpose for Jesus' life, death, and resurrection becomes crystal clear. It is the resurrection that proves beyond any shadow of a doubt that Jesus is the way to the Father and eternal life. The resurrection proves that throughout His lifetime, Jesus did more than teach the truth – He was the living embodiment of the truth. And it is the resurrection that reveals to the world that Jesus Christ is eternal life for all those who believe.

So in the end, Jesus' life is revealed to be an extraordinary life from start to finish. He is:

The Lamb of God who takes away the sins of the world
The Son of David the promised Messiah of the Jewish nation
He is the Servant of God
The Good Shepherd who lays down his life for the sheep
He is the Divine Physician who has the cure for every human disorder
He is the Savior of the world
The Prophet
King of Kings
The Stone that the builders rejected
The Bridegroom of the church
The Bread of Life
The Light of the World
The Door and the true Vine
The Resurrection and the Life
The Judge of the living and the dead
The Scapegoat
The Mediator of a better covenant
The Logos
Our great High Priest
The Beloved, Only, and Chosen One
The Just One
He that should come
The Amen
The Alpha and the Omega, the beginning and the end
The Head of the church
The Image of God
The Firstborn of all creation
The Bright Morning Star

By the time we finish studying the teachings and ministry of Jesus Christ, we realize that He is nothing less than Everything.

APPENDICES

Appendix One

THE SIGNIFICANCE OF JOHN'S BAPTISM
From the Article on John the Baptist

The symbolic rite of baptism was such an essential part of the work of John that it not only gave him his distinctive title of "the Baptist" (ὁ βαπτιστής, *ho baptistés*), but also caused his message to be styled "preaching the baptism of repentance." That a special virtue was ascribed to this rite, and that it was regarded as a necessary part of the preparation for the coming of the Messiah, are shown by its important place in John's preaching, and by the eagerness with which it was sought by the multitudes. Its significance may best be understood by giving attention to its historical antecedents, for while John gave the rite new significance, it certainly appealed to ideas already familiar to the Jews.

(1) Lustrations Required by the Levitical Law.
The divers washings required by the law (Leviticus 11-15) have, without doubt, arcligious import. This is shown by the requirement of sacrifices in connection with the cleansing, especially the sin offering (Leviticus 14:8-9, 19-20; compare Mark 1:44; Luke 2:22). The designation of John's baptism by the word βαπτίζειν, *baptízein*, which by New Testament times was used of ceremonial purification, also indicates some historical connection (compare Sirach 34:25).

(2) Anticipation of Messianic Lustrations Foretold by Prophets.
John understood that his baptism was a preparation for the Messianic baptism anticipated by the prophets, who saw that for a true cleansing the nation must wait until God should open in Israel a fountain for cleansing (Zech. 13:1), and should sprinkle His people with clean water and give them a new heart and a new spirit (Ezekiel 36:25-26; Jeremiah 33:8). His baptism was at once a preparation and a promise of the spiritual cleansing which the Messiah would bestow. "I indeed baptize you with water unto repentance: but he that cometh after me .... shall baptize you with the Holy Spirit and with fire" (Matthew 3:11 margin).

(3) Proselyte Baptism.

According to the teaching of later Judaism, a stranger who desired to be adopted into the family of Israel was required, along with circumcision, to receive the rite of baptism as a means of cleansing from the ceremonial uncleanness attributed to him as a Gentile. While it is not possible to prove the priority of this practice of proselyte baptism to the baptism of John, there can be no doubt of the fact, for it is inconceivable, in view of Jewish prejudice, that it would be borrowed from John or after this time.

While it seems clear that in the use of the rite of baptism John was influenced by the Jewish customs of ceremonial washings and proselyte baptism, his baptism differed very essentially from these. The Levitical washings restored an unclean person to his former condition, but baptism was a preparation for a new condition. On the other hand, proselyte baptism was administered only to Gentiles, while John required baptism of all Jews. At the same time his baptism was very different from Christian baptism, as he himself declared (Luke 3:16). His was a baptism of water only; a preparation for the baptism "in the Spirit" which was to follow. It is also to be observed that it was a rite complete in itself, and that it was offered to the nation as a preparation for a specific event, the advent of the Messiah.

We may say, then, that as a "baptism of repentance" it meant a renunciation of the past life; as a cleansing it symbolized the forgiveness of sins (Mark 1:4), and as preparation it implied a promise of loyalty to the kingdom of the Messiah. We have no reason to believe that Jesus experienced any sense of sin or felt any need of repentance or forgiveness; but as a Divinely appointed preparation for the Messianic kingdom His submission to it was appropriate.

The International Standard Bible Encyclopedia

(Refer to Page 82)

Appendix Two

Why Are There Different Genealogies For Jesus In Matthew 1 And Luke 3?

https://carm.org/why-are-there-different-genealogies-jesus-matthew-1-and-luke-3

Matthew 1:16 - Luke 3:23

Both Matthew 1 and Luke 3 contain genealogies of Jesus. But there is one problem--they are different. Luke's genealogy starts at **Adam** and goes to **David**. Matthew's genealogy starts at **Abraham** and goes to **David**. When the genealogies arrive at David, they split with David's sons: **Nathan** (Mary's side?) and **Solomon** (Joseph's side).

There are differences of opinion with two main options being offered. The first is that one genealogy is for Mary and the other is for Joseph. It was customary to mention the genealogy through the father even though it was clearly known that it was through Mary.

"The second thing is that this genealogy differs in significant ways from the genealogy in Matthew. Why? Most Bible scholars believe that Luke gives the genealogy of Mary (who was also of the royal Davidic line), while Matthew traces the family of Joseph. Thus by both His mother and His earthly father, Jesus had a right to the throne of Israel."[1]

"Luke paused from his narrative to give Christ's genealogy. While Matthew traced Christ's lineage through Joseph, his legal father (see Matt. 1:1–17), Luke traced it through Mary, beginning with Mary's father, Heli. (Men in ancient times often regarded their sons-in-law as their own sons.) The lineages of Mary and Joseph converge at King David (compare 3:31 with Matt. 1:6).[2]

"Those who take the latter opinion, that we have here the line of Mary, as in Matthew that of Joseph—here His real, there His reputed line—explain the statement about Joseph, that he was "the son of Heli," to mean that he was his son-in-law, as the husband of his daughter Mary (as in Ru 1:11, 12), and believe that Joseph's name is only introduced instead of Mary's, in conformity with the

Jewish custom in such tables. Perhaps this view is attended with fewest difficulties, as it certainly is the best supported." [3]

Some critics may not accept this explanation and it is not without its problems.

"The theory that Luke really gives us the family tree of Mary rather than of Joseph is improbable. The theory with least difficulties is that Matthew gives the descendants of David down the royal line (i.e. who was heir to the throne at any given time), but Luke gives the particular line to which Joseph belonged."[4]

The Bible should be interpreted in the context of its literary style, culture, and history. Breaking up genealogies into male and female representations was acceptable in the ancient Near East culture since it was often impolite to speak of women without proper conditions being met: male presence, etc. Therefore, one genealogy might be of Mary and the other of Joseph--even though both mention Joseph. In other words, the Mary genealogy was counted "in" Joseph and under his headship.

I find it difficult to accept that those who collected the books of the New Testament, and who believed it was inerrant, were unaware of this blatant differentiation in genealogies. They must have understood what the historical/cultural context was and had no problem with it. Even though we cannot ascertain at this time a precise explanation does not mean one isn't forthcoming. After all, archaeological discovers clear up Bible "difficulties" on a regular basis. But, back to our discussion.

Notice that Luke starts with Mary and goes backwards to Adam. Matthew starts with Abraham and goes forward to Joseph. The intents of the genealogies were obviously different which is clearly seen in their styles. Luke was not written to the Jews, Matthew was. Therefore, Matthew would carry the legal line (from Abraham through David) and Luke the biological one (from Adam through David). Also, notice that Luke's first three chapters mention Mary eleven times; hence, the genealogy from her. Fourth, notice Luke 3:23, "And when He began His ministry, Jesus Himself was about thirty years of age, being supposedly the son of Joseph, the son of Eli," This designation "supposedly" seems to signify the Marian genealogy since it seems to indicate that Jesus is not the biological son of Joseph.

Finally, in the Joseph genealogy is a man named Jeconiah. God cursed Jeconiah (also called Coniah), stating that no descendant of his would ever sit on the throne of David, "For no man of his descendants will prosper sitting on the throne of David or ruling again in Judah," (Jer. 22:30). But Jesus, of course, will sit on the throne in the heavenly kingdom. The point is that Jesus is not a biological descendant of Jeconiah, but through the other lineage -- that of Mary. Hence, the prophetic curse upon Jeconiah stands inviolate. But, the legal adoption of Jesus by Joseph reckoned the legal rights of Joseph to Jesus as a son, not the biological curse. This is why we need two genealogies: one of Mary (the actually biological line according to prophecy), and the legal line through Joseph.

LUKE - Adam, the father of Seth, the father of Enosh, the father of Cainan, the father of Mahaleleel, the father of Jared, the father of Enoch, the father of Methuselah, the father of Lamech, the father of Noah, the father of Shem, the father of Arphaxad, the father of Cainan, the father of Shelah, the father of Heber, the father of Peleg, the father of Reu, the father of Serug, the father of Nahor, the father of Terah, the father of

MATTHEW - Abraham, the father of Isaac, the father of Jacob, the father of Judah, the father of Perez, the father of Hezron, the father of Ram, the father of Admin, the father of Amminadab, the father of Nahshon, the father of Salmon, the father of Boaz, the father of Obed, the father of Jesse -- the father of

(Mary) LUKE David, father of (Joseph) MATTHEW

Nathan	**Solomon**
Mattatha	Rehoboam
Menna	Abijah
Melea	Asa
Eliakim	Jehoshaphat
Jonam	Joram
Joseph	Uzziah
Judah	Jotham
Simeon	Ahaz
Levi	Hezekiah
Matthat	Manasseh
Jorim	Amon
Eliezer	Josiah
Joshua	Jeconiah
Er	Shealtiel
Elmadam	Zerubbabel
Cosam	Abihud

FREDERICK OSBORN

Addi	Eliakim
Melchi	Azor
Neri	Zadok
Shealtiel	Achim
Zerubbabel	Eliud
Rhesa	Eleazar
Joanan	Matthan
Joda	Jacob
Josech	Joseph
Semein	
Mattathias	
Maath	
Naggai	
Hesli	
Nahum	
Amos	Joseph Adopted Jesus
Mattathias	as his own son giving him
Joseph	all legal rights involving heirship.
Jannai	
Melchi	
Levi	
Matthat	
Eli	

supposedly of Joseph (Mary)

JESUS

- 1. Richards, L., & Richards, L. O. (1987). *The teacher's commentary*. Includes index. (650). Wheaton, Ill.: Victor Books.
- 2. Willmington, H. L. (1997). *Willmington's Bible handbook* (582). Wheaton, Ill.: Tyndale House Publishers.
- 3. Jamieson, R., Fausset, A. R., Fausset, A. R., Brown, D., & Brown, D. (1997). A commentary, critical and explanatory, on the Old and New Testaments (Lk 3:23). Oak Harbor, WA: Logos Research Systems, Inc.
- 4. Carson, D. A. (1994). New Bible commentary : 21st century edition (4th ed.) (Lk 3:23–38). Leicester, England; Downers Grove, Ill., USA: Inter-Varsity Press

(Refer to page 86)

Appendix Three

The Seventy Sent Forth (Luke 10:1-16)
William MacDonald, *The Believer's Commentary,* Thomas Nelson, Nashville, TN, © 1995 pp.1407 – 1408

This is the only account in the Gospels of the Lord's sending out the seventy disciples. It closely resembles the commissioning of the twelve in Matthew 10. However, there the disciples were sent into the northern areas, whereas the seventy are now being sent to the south along the route the Lord was following to Jerusalem. This mission was seemingly intended to prepare the way for the Lord in His journey from Caesarea Philippi in the north, through Galilee and Samaria, across the Jordan, south through Perea, then back across the Jordan to Jerusalem.

While the ministry and the office of the seventy was only temporary, nevertheless our Lord's instruction to these men suggest many life principles which apply to Christians in every age.

Some of these principles may be summarized as follows:

1. He sent them out **two by two** (v. 1). This suggests competent testimony. "In the mouth of two or three witnesses every word shall be established" (2 Cor. 13:1).
2. The Lord's servant should constantly **pray** that He will **send out laborers into His harvest** field (v. 2). The need is always greater than the supply of workers. In praying for **laborers**, we must be willing to **go** ourselves, obviously. Notice **pray** (v. 2), **go** (v.3).
3. The disciples of Jesus are sent forth into a hostile environment (v. 3). They are, to outward appearances, like **defenseless lambs among wolves**. They cannot expect to be treated royally by the world, but rather to be persecuted and even killed.
4. Considerations of personal comfort are not to be permitted (v. 4a). **"Carry neither money bag, knapsack, nor sandals."** The **money bag** speaks of financial reserves. The **knapsack** suggests food reserves. The **sandals** may refer either to an extra pair, or to footgear affording extra comfort. All three speak of the poverty which, though having nothing, yet possess all things and makes many rich (2 Cor. 6:10).
5. **"Greet no one along the road"** (v. 4b). Christ's servants are not to waste time on long, ceremonious greetings, such as were common in

the East. While they should be courteous and civil, they must utilize their time in the glorious proclamation of the gospel rather than in profitless talk. There is not rime for needless delays.

6. They should accept hospitality wherever it is offered to them (vv. 5, 6). If their initial greeting is favorably received, then the host is **a son of peace**. He is a man characterized by **peace**, and one who receives the message of peace. If the disciples are refused, they should not be discouraged; their peace **will return to** them again, that is, there has been no waste or loss, and others will receive it.
7. The disciples should **remain in the same house** that first offers lodging (v. 7). To move **from house to house** might characterize them as those who are shopping for the most luxurious accommodations, whereas they should live simply and gratefully.
8. They should not hesitate to eat whatever food and drink are offered to them (v. 7). As servants of the Lord they are entitled to their upkeep.
9. Cities and towns take a positon either for or against the Lord, just as individuals do (vv. 8, 9). If an area is receptive to the message, the disciples should preach there, accept its hospitality, and bring the blessings of the gospel to it. Christ servants should **eat such things as are set before them,** not being fastidious about their food or causing inconvenience in the home. After all, food is not the main thing in their lives. Towns which receive the Lord's messengers still have their sin-sick inhabitants healed. Also the King draws very near to them (v. 9).
10. A town may reject the gospel and then be denied the privilege of hearing it again (vv. 10-12). There comes a time in God's dealings when the message is heard for the last time. Men should not trifle with the gospel, because it may be withdrawn forever. Light rejected is light denied. Towns and villages which are privileged to hear the good news and which refuse it will be judged more severely than the city of Sodom. The greater the privilege, the greater the responsibility.

(Refer to Page 110)

Appendix Four

THE PARABLES OF JESUS		
"All these things Jesus spoke to the multitude in parables; and without a parable He did not speak to them, that it might be fulfilled which was spoken by the prophet, saying: 'I will open My mouth in parables; I will utter things kept secret from the foundation of the world.'" Matthew 13:34, 35		
PARABLE	THEME	SCRIPTURE
1. The Sower	A Key Parable (Mark 4:13); Individual responses to the Word	Matt. 13:3-8; 18-23 Mark 4:3-8; Luke 8:5-8
2. The Wheat & Tares	Sons of the Kingdom & Sons of the evil one	Matt. 13:24-30
3. The Mustard Seed	The Kingdom begins insignificantly but grows to greatness	Matt. 13:31, 32; Mark 4:30-32; Luke 13:18, 19
4. The Leaven	Inner transformation of citizens of the kingdom	Matt. 13:33; Luke 13:20, 21
5. The Hidden Treasure	Value/cost of the kingdom	Matt. 13:44
6. The Pearl	Value/cost of the kingdom	Matt. 13:45, 46
7. The Dragnet	Wicked separated from the righteous at the end of the age	Matt. 13:47-50
8. The Unforgiving Servant	Kingdom forgiveness	Matt. 18:23-35
9. The Landowner	Grace (Unmerited favor) of God Extended to citizens of the kingdom	Matt. 20:1-16
10. The Two sons	Kingdom obedience	Matt. 21:28-32
11. The Wicked Tenants	Kingdom rejected	Matt. 21:33-46; Mark 12:1-12; Luke 20:9-19
12. The Marriage Feast	Invitation rejected & extended; God clothes those who respond	Matt. 22:1-14
13. The Wise and Foolish Virgins	Watch for the arrival of the Bridegroom	Matt. 25:1-13
14. The Talents	Kingdom stewardship	Matt. 25:14-30

15. The Growing Seed	God produces the growth	Mark 4:26:29
16. The Two Debtors	He who is forgiven little loves little	Luke 7:41-43
17. The Good Samaritan	True religion of the Kingdom	Luke 10:25-37
18. The Friend in Need	Persistence in the Kingdom	Luke 11:5-8
19. The Rich Fool	Inadequacy of earthly wealth	Luke 12:16-21(Note: Luke 12:22-34)
20. The Fruitless Fig Tree	Period of Grace will come to an end	Luke 13:6-9
21. Kingdom Lessons	The way up is the way down; Invite those who cannot repay (Note:16-24 Prov. 19:17); those who refuse God's Invitation will be excluded	Luke 14:7-11; 12-14;16-24
22. The Lost Sheep	God's love for the lost	Matt. 18:12-14; Luke 15:4-7
23. The Lost Coin	God's love for the lost	Luke 15:8-10
24. The Lost (Prodigal) Son	God's love for the lost	Luke 15:11-32
25. The Shrewd Steward	God and Mammon	Luke 16:1-9
26. Rich Man & Lazarus	Our actions in this life have eternal consequences	Luke 16:19-31
27. The Unworthy Slaves	Faith or Obedience	Luke 17:1-10
28. The Unrighteous Judge	Contrast with god's justice for His Elect	Luke 18:1-8
29. The Pharisee and The Tax Collector	Self-righteous are not justified	Luke 18:10-14
30. The Ten Minas	Use what God has given or lose it	Luke 19:12-27
31. The Sheep and Goats	The Last Judgment	Matt. 31:46

(Refer to page 173)

Appendix Five

The Five Discourses of Matthew

Bible scholars use the term **"Five Discourses of Matthew"** to refer to five specific passages of Matthew's Gospel that contain discourses by Jesus. The five discourses have been identified:

- The *Sermon on the Mount* (5:1 – 7:29)
- The *Missionary Discourse* (10:5-42)
- The *Parabolic Discourse* (13:3-52)
- The *Discourse on the Church* (18:1-35)
- The *Discourse on End Times* (24:1 – 25:46)

"Jesus talks about heaven"
By Maria Clara (Used by Permission)

The discourses in Matthew are marked by the closing phrase "when Jesus had finished" speaking, saying, or instructing certain things (7:28; 11:1; 13:53; 19:1; 26:1), referring to the teachings immediately preceding that statement. Some scholars include chapter 23 in the final discourse, but others consider the final discourse to be only two chapters (24 and 25).

Each of these discourses can be found in shorter forms in the Gospels Mark or Luke. The *Sermon on the Mount Discourse* relates to Luke 6:20-49. The second or *Missionary Discourse* relates to Mark 6:7-13; Luke 9:1-6 and 10:1-12. The so-called *Parabolic Discourse* corresponds to Mark 4:3-34; and 9:35-48. The *End Times Discourse* relates to the final discourses in Luke 21:5-36 and Mark 13:5-37.

Some scholars attempt to closely relate the five discourses to the five books Moses, but it requires a lot of Scriptural gymnastics to accomplish more than a casual parallel between them. Very few contemporary scholars accept the idea of an intentional parallel between Matthew's discourses and the Pentateuch. So it is best to take the Gospel discourses of Matthew on their own terms in context of the other Gospel discourses.

The first discourse

The first discourse (Matthew 5-7) is known as the *Sermon on the Mount.* This sermon by Jesus is possibly one of the best known and most quoted parts of all the Gospels. It starts with the Beatitudes and includes the Lord's Prayer. The *Sermon on the Mount* contains many of the central doctrines of Christianity. The "blessings" or Beatitudes are a key to this sermon because they express the inward attitude of the heart that all followers of Jesus must possess. The entire Sermon is intended to correct the Pharisaical distortions of Mosaic Law that exacted a slavish keeping of the traditions of men as the means to fulfill the Law. Jesus presented a fulfillment of the Law that was from the heart; keeping the Law required love, mercy, humility, and compassion.

The second discourse

In the second or *Missionary Discourse* of Matthew 10, Jesus provides instructions to the Twelve Apostles (named in 10:2-3) for making a missionary journey. Jesus tells them how they should travel from city to city; they should carry no belongings and to preach only to Israelite communities. He warns them to watch out for opposition to their mission, but they should have no fear because the Holy Spirit will lead them in what to say and how they should defend themselves when that time arises, "For it is not you who speak, but the Spirit of your Father speaking through you..." Matthew 10:20 (ESV)

The third discourse

The third discourse of Matthew (13:1-53), also known as the *Parabolic Discourse,* introduces several parables describing the mysteries of the Kingdom of Heaven that Jesus says are only for His followers to know and understand, "To you it has been given to know the secrets of the kingdom of heaven, but to them it has not been given."

The first part of this discourse takes place outside when Jesus leaves the house where He and His disciples are staying and sits near the shore of the Sea of Galilee to address His disciples as well as the multitudes of people who have gathered to hear His teachings. This part includes the parables of The Sower, The Tares, The Mustard Seed and The Leaven. The second part takes place when Jesus goes back inside the house and addresses the disciples in private to give them the meanings of the parables. This part of the discourse also includes the parables of The Hidden Treasure, The Pearl, and the Dragnet.

The fourth discourse

The *Discourse on the Church* is the fourth discourse in Matthew. Chapter 18 is significant because it also includes the Kingdom parables of The Lost Sheep and The Unforgiving Servant. This discourse is in response to the disciples' question about greatness in the kingdom of heaven. Jesus' response to that question provides insight for the role His disciples will play in the future Messianic kingdom all were anticipating to arrive soon. The discourse also provides instructions for all those in the future community of disciples on how to conduct themselves and how to treat one another. Jesus' disciples are to conduct themselves in piety and humility; they are not to condemn others, but forgive them and gently restore to the community of believers those who repent and change their ways. The discourse stands in stark contrast to the teachings of the Pharisees because emphasizes the importance of humility over pride, and self-sacrifice over social prominence and power. This discourse expresses the highest virtues of those seeking greatness in the kingdom of God which are a childlike faith in humility and love.

The fifth discourse

This final discourse is usually taken to include Matthew 24 and 25 and sometimes includes chapter 23. The discourse is given in response to related questions the disciples ask about the "end of the age." Matthew 24 is usually called the "Olivet Discourse" because it was given on the Mount of Olives overlooking the Temple Mount in Jerusalem. It is also often referred to as the *Discourse on the End Times* because of its subject matter. The discourse, which has corresponding sections in Mark 13 and Luke 21, is mostly about judgment and rewards to be handed out at the great Day of the Lord that the Jews expected upon the arrival of the Messiah, King of the Jews. Jesus, informed His disciples of the need for vigilance and steadfast faith in the time of the coming judgment. This discourse provides important insights to Jewish and early Christian eschatology (the study of the End times and beginning of the world to come which would be ruled by the Son of God). Here Jesus gives His most detailed treatment of the apocalyptic theology that heavily influenced Jewish expectations of the Messiah and his coming kingdom. In this discourse, Jesus refers the coming destruction of the Temple in Jerusalem, the End Times, and His Second Coming of Christ.

(Refer to page 247)

Appendix Six

The "Little Apocalypse" in Matthew

The Gospels of Matthew and Mark, described Jesus speaking this discourse to his disciples privately on the Mount of Olives, opposite the Temple Mount in Jerusalem. Luke's Gospel indicates that Jesus was teaching at the Temple that day, and in the evening he stopped at the Mount of Olives with His disciples on His way back to Bethany.

This discourse is widely believed by scholars to contain material delivered on a variety of occasions. (Remember that Jesus often repeated the same message in different settings to different groups. So it is reasonable to believe He addressed the End of the Age at other times.) However, the setting on the Mount of Olives provides the Gospel writers with the most dramatic and memorable setting because it takes place just before Jesus' arrest and trial. Jesus prophetic words echo a passage in the Book of Zechariah which refers to this location as the place where a final battle would occur between the Jewish Messiah and His opponents: "And in that day His feet will stand on the Mount of Olives, which faces Jerusalem on the east. And the Mount of Olives shall be split in two, from east to west, making a very large valley; half of the mountain shall move toward the north and half of it toward the south." Zechariah 14:4 (NKJV)

Jesus' teaching on the **destruction of the Temple is** a response to the remarks of an anonymous disciple on the greatness of Herod's Temple, which is said to have been a beautifully crafted building adorned with gold, silver, and other precious materials. Jesus responded that not one of those stones would remain intact in the building. In fact, the whole structure would be reduced to rubble (this prophecy is fulfilled in 70 AD with the burning and looting of the city and the total destruction of the Temple by the Roman Legions under the cruel leadership of the General and soon-to-be Emperor of Rome, Titus).

The disciples were like so many of the Jews of the time. They wanted to know what would be the sign they should look for; they asked Jesus three questions in one, "When will this happen, and what will be the sign of your coming and of the end of the age?"

Being Jewish in the first century meant believing that the Messiah would come someday soon, and that his arrival would mean the fulfillment of all the glorious prophecies of a golden messianic age they hoped for. They believed that the Temple would play a large role in this, which fueled the Jewish pride in the Temple. The disciple's boasting about the Temple's construction was in alignment with the Jewish expectations of the Messiah and His kingdom. Jesus' prophecy concerning the Temple's destruction must have been a shock to His disciples; it was contrary to their belief system. Throughout His ministry Jesus sought to correct the false impressions of the Jews concerning the Messianic kingdom to come. The Jews believed it would be an exclusively Jewish kingdom, ruled by a warrior king like David, and that the Gentiles and other unrighteous sinners would be excluded. Jesus reversed those expectations by affirming from Old Testament prophecy and in His parables that the all nations would be included. He added that He had come as the Sacrificial Lamb to save men's lives and not to destroy them. He taught that His kingdom was a spiritual kingdom and that the entrance to His kingdom was by being born again of the Spirit and not by blood relation to Abraham. All those who repented of their sins in humility, seeking the grace of God would be saved. He leveled the pride of the Jewish elites who believed in their invincibility because of their Jewish birthright by first prophesying the destruction of the coming Roman invasion (Matt. 24:4–34); and then by commenting on His Second Coming to render an apocalyptic universal judgment on Jew and Gentile alike (24:35–51).

Jesus' warnings to them about the things that would happen in the End Times follow the accepted apocalyptic theology of the time:
- Some would claim to be Christ, but would be in fact Antichrist. It was a general belief among the Jews that if the Messiah arrived in Jerusalem, it would mean that the Kingdom of Heaven was imminent.
- There would be wars and rumors of wars as part of the overall societal upheavals to take place.

Jesus identifies "the beginnings of birth pangs" (a metaphor for false alarms that will cause many to believe the End Times are upon them):
- Nations will rise up against nations, and kingdoms against kingdoms
- Earthquakes
- Famines
- Pestilence
- Dreadful events

Next he described more birth pangs which would precede the coming of His Kingdom:
- False prophets
- Apostasy
- Persecution of the followers of Jesus
- The spread of Jesus' message (the gospel) around the world

Jesus then warned the disciples about the Abomination of Desolation "standing where it does not belong" prophesied in Daniel's apocalypse. The Gospels of Matthew and Mark add "let the reader understand..." which is generally understood to be a reference to two passages from the Book of Daniel (9:27 and 11:31).

A key element in Jesus' discourse concerns the parable of the fig tree (already discussed in the lesson on Jesus' miracles is the symbolism of cursing the fig tree.) This parable is intended to connect the two parts of the questions and answers concerning the destruction of the Temple and Jesus' Second Coming. The disciples had connected the destruction of the Temple with the Second Coming; however, Jesus reveals they are two separate events that will "bookend" the age to come. It will begin with "this generation" that would see the fulfillment of the destruction of the Temple, but the opposite end that marks the return of the Lord and the fulfillment of all End Times prophecies "No man knows" when it will be.

Great Tribulation

Jesus cites the part of the prophecy from the Book of Daniel about the "abomination that causes desolation." Given to Daniel by Gabriel during the Babylonian captivity, Jesus uses it to warn the people of Judea to quickly flee to the mountains when it appears. The judgment will be so swift and so destructive that they will not have time to return home from their fields or businesses and gather things from their homes. Jesus also warned that it would be particularly hard on people if the end of the world events happened in winter or on the Sabbath. Jesus said it would be a time of "Great Tribulation" and worse than anything anyone had experienced before.

The apocalyptic vision of Jesus is a confirmation and affirmation of the prophetic words of the Old Testament concerning the End of the Age. Jesus states in apocalyptic terms that immediately after the time of tribulation people would see a sign: "the sun will be darkened, and the moon will not give its light; the stars will fall from the sky, and the heavenly bodies will be shaken". (Matt. 24:29–30). The statements about the sun and moon turning dark fit the apocalyptic visions of the Old Testament; this particular quote comes from a prophecy of Isaiah (13:10). Descriptions of the sun, moon and stars going dark is also described by the prophet Joel; he wrote that astronomical disturbances would be a sign before the great and dreadful Day of the Lord (2:30–31). As would be expected, the Book of Revelation also mentions the sun and moon turning dark. John describes the opening of seal number six of the seven seals, but with far more detail than the Old Testament prophecies mentioned (Rev. 6:12–17).

"Immediately after the tribulation of those days the sun will be darkened, and the moon will not give its light, and the stars will fall from heaven, and the powers of the heavens will be shaken. Then will appear in heaven the sign of the Son of Man, and then all the tribes of the earth will mourn, and they will see the Son of Man coming on the clouds of heaven with power and great glory. And he will

send out his angels with a loud trumpet call, and they will gather his elect from the four winds, from one end of heaven to the other." Matthew 24:29-31 (ESV)

    As His "Little Apocalypse" draws to a close, Jesus stated that after the appointed time of tribulation and great cosmic distress, the Son of Man would be seen arriving in the clouds with "power and great glory." The Son of Man will be accompanied by the angels. At the trumpet call the angels would gather the elect (God's chosen) from the heavens and the four winds of the earth (Matthew 24:31).

    In modern times, a popular opinion is that Jesus is using the apocalyptic language in the Olivet Discourse as merely *symbolic* language that is not to be understood as referring to any actual historical events as did many Jewish apocalyptic writers. But when taken within context of everything the Bible teaches us about the End of the Age, there is little doubt that although Jesus is speaking in symbolic language, He is describing historical events that would take place in the future.

    Bible scholars have settled on four major, but quite different, interpretations of apocalyptic writings in the Bible. These interpretations of Revelation in particular and of Matthew 24 are Futurist and Preterist, Idealist, and Historicist each of these interpretations have their proponents as well as their detractors. The Futurism of modern day evangelicals dominates the more conservative eschatology. However, if one studies them closely, elements of all four interpretations can be discovered at points. But what is most important to remember is that Jesus will indeed come again, just as He promised He would.

(Refer to page 248)

Appendix Seven

LAWS GOVERNING CRIMINAL TRIALS

Much has been written about the illegalities of all of Jesus' trials. It is clear from the beginning that Jesus was innocent of any wrong-doing (and certainly innocent of anything deserving crucifixion). Jesus' Jewish accusers never considered Jesus "not guilty until proven guilty" by a court of law, but had already been tried, convicted, and sentenced to death by them before He was dragged before them in the dark of night. The presumption of innocence sometimes referred to by the Latin expression ***Ei incumbit probatio qui dicit, non qui negat*** (the burden of proof is on the one who declares, not on one who denies), is the principle that one is considered innocent unless proven guilty. Here are some of the illegalities of the Jewish trials pointed out by scholars.

(SOURCE http://www.ecclesia.org/truth/trial-jesus.html)

1. If a man was arrested for a capital crime, he was not to be arrested at night. It had to be in broad daylight. Since Jesus' arrest took place between 1 and 2 o'clock at night, it was not legal.

2. If a man was arrested for a capital crime, no one cooperating in the arrest could be in any way connected to the one who is accused. To assure that impure motives were not the cause of any accusation, no arrest for a capital crime could be made based upon information given by a follower or colleague of the accused. Authorities believed that if the accused was guilty so were his followers and that no follower could "turn state's evidence" to spare themselves of complicity. Since the entire plot to arrest and accuse Jesus revolved around Judas, one of the followers, this law was blatantly and openly ignored. Not only that, but after Jesus' arrest, Judas renounced his involvement in the arrest and fled the scene, and overcome with guilt and remorse committed suicide.

3. No Jewish trial could ever be held at night. The law stated that it must be held in the daytime. Quoting directly from the code in the Jewish Talmud: "The members of the court may not alertly and intelligently hear the testimony against the accused during the hours of darkness." The Gospels clearly show that both trials before Annas and before Caiaphas were held in darkness.

4. The members of the Jewish court, after hearing the testimony of witnesses in a capital crime, could not immediately act and judge. There had to be a period for reflection and careful consideration of the evidence they heard. They were to go home and remain alone and separate from one another for at the least, one full day and think about the testimonies they had heard. Once they are rested and refreshed, they once again return and hear the testimony against the accused. Then, and only then, should they render a vote. Once more we see from the writers of the Gospel that they did not follow Jewish law. They Jewish court never left the presence of Caiaphas before making an immediate judgment that Jesus was guilty.

5. Jewish law specified the method of voting guilt or innocence in capital cases. They were not to take an "all in favor say I, all opposed say no" kind of a voice vote. Their vote was supposed to be taken starting from the youngest to the oldest so that the youngest would be intimidated or improperly influenced by the older votes. This kind of vote was never taken after any of Jesus' trials before the Jews.

6. Trials were supposed to be held before more than one judge, and never without a defense attorney to argue on behalf of the accused. Those requirements were overlooked; the haste of the trials and the need to hold them as far away from the public eyes as possible meant that all legal formalities had to be blatantly and willfully ignored. Even though the Jewish leaders prided themselves for doing everything by the book, Jesus constantly exposed their hypocrisies and exposed the fact that they didn't follow their own rules when it suited them. Jesus' arrest and trials proved once more that the religious leaders of the Jews were "white washed tombs full of dead men's bones" when it came to living by the rules they made for everyone but themselves to follow.

(Refer to page 270)

FREDERICK OSBORN

Appendix Eight

Annas the High Priest

Je http://www.bible-history.com/HighPriests/NTHIGHPRIESTSAnnas.htmwish Spiritual Leaders

Annas, whose name means "The grace of Jehovah" was the son of Seth and appointed high priest of the Jews in 6 A.D in his 37th year. He was high priest from 6 to 15 A.D. but as long as he lived he was the virtual head of the priestly party in Jerusalem. He was chosen to the high priesthood by Quirinius, the imperial governor of Syria; obliged to give way to Ismael by Valerius Gratus, procurator of Judaea, in the beginning of Tiberius' reign, 14 A.D. Eleazar, the son of Annas, followed Ismael; then Simon; then Joseph Caiaphas, son-in-law of Annas (John 18:13).

In the time of Christ high priests were appointed and removed at the command of the Roman governors. Although removed from office, Annas' power and influence was so great that five of his sons, as well as his son-in-law Caiaphas and his grandson Matthias, also became high priests. Years afterward he lost the high priesthood, but even then he was popularly considered as still in office and was called "high priest"; even after Pentecost his name appears first in the list of priestly leaders:

Acts 4:5-7 "And it came to pass, on the next day, that their rulers, elders, and scribes, as well as Annas the high priest, Caiaphas, John, and Alexander, and as many as were of the family of the high priest, were gathered together at Jerusalem. "

In John 18:19, 22 the high priest is undoubtedly Annas, although in vs. 13 and 24 Caiaphas is mentioned as the high priest. Annas is referred to in connection with the beginning of John the Baptist's ministry, which took place *"in the high-priesthood of Annas and Caiaphas"* (Luke 3:2), as though father and son-in-law were joint holders of the office.

It seems clear that due to his ability and force of character he was virtually high priest, although Caiaphas had the title. When Jesus was arrested, He was first brought before Annas (John 18:13). It was apparently Annas who questioned Him about His disciples and His teaching, and who gave orders to one of the officers standing by to strike Jesus with his hand (18:19-22). After the questioning, he sent Jesus "bound" to Caiaphas.

John 18:19-24 "The high priest then asked Jesus about His disciples and His doctrine. Jesus answered him, "I spoke openly to the world. I always taught in synagogues and in the temple, where the Jews always meet, and in secret I have said nothing. Why do you

THE WAY, TRUTH, AND LIFE

ask Me? Ask those who have heard Me what I said to them. Indeed they know what I said." And when He had said these things, one of the officers who stood by struck Jesus with the palm of his hand, saying, "Do You answer the high priest like that?" Jesus answered him, "If I have spoken evil, bear witness of the evil; but if well, why do you strike Me?" Then Annas sent Him bound to Caiaphas the high priest."

He was undoubtedly the ruling voice in the council that condemned Jesus, although nothing is said about his part in the proceedings that followed the preliminary questioning. He was present at the meeting of the Sanhedrin before which Peter and John defended themselves for preaching the Gospel of the Resurrection (Acts 4:6).

Annas is called "high priest," Caiaphas, John, and Alexander are called "of his kindred." He lived to old age, and he had five sons apointed as high priests.

Also see Josephus, *The Antiquities of the Jews, XVIII. ii. 1, 2; XX. ix. 1*

(Refer to page 272)

Bibliography

Barclay, William, *Jesus As They Saw Him*, William B. Eerdmans Publishing Company, Grand Rapids, MI, © 1962

Barclay, William, *The New Daily Study Bible: The Gospel of Luke*, Theological Publications India, Bangalore, 2010

Barclay, William, *The Mind of Jesus*, Harper San Francisco, CA, © 1960, 1961,

Barclay, William, *The Parables of Jesus*, Westminster John Knox Press, Louisville, KY, © 1970

Barclay, William, *The New Daily Study Bible: The Gospel of Mark*, Westminster John Knox Press, Louisville, KY, © 1975, 2001

Barker, Kenneth L, Kohlenberger, John R., III, *The Expositor's Bible Commentary*, Abridged Edition, Zondervan, Grand Rapids, MI, © 1994

Broadus, John A., *Commentary on the Gospel of Matthew*, Database © 2006 WORDsearch Corp.

Butler, Trent C., *The Holman New Testament Commentary: Luke*, Broadman & Holman Publishers, Nashville, TN, © 2000

Cadman, S. Parks, *The Parables of Jesus*, Testament Books, New York, NY, © 1999

Daunton-Fear, Andrew, *Healing in the Early Church*, Authentic Books, Secunderabad, India © 2011

Dictionary of Jesus and the Gospels, Joel B. Green; Scott McKnight; I. Howard Marshall, Editors InterVarsity Press, Downers Grove, ILL, © 1992

Green, Michael, *The Message of Matthew*, InterVarsity Press, Downer Grove, IL, © 1988, 2000

Hale, Thomas and Thorson, Stephen, *The Applied New Testament Commentary*, CCMI and OM Books, Secunderabad, India 2004

Haregreaves, John, *A Guide to St. Mark's Gospel*, ISPCK, Dehli 2006, © 1965

Henry, Matthew, *Matthew Henry's Commentary on the Whole Bible*, Database © 2014 WORD*search*.

Josephus, Flavius, *The Works of Flavius Josephus,* Translated by William Whiston, Database © 2007 WORD*search* Corp

Kendall, R. T., *The Complete Guide to the Parables*, Chosen Books, Grand Rapids, MI, © 2004

Kistemaker, Simon J., *The Parables: Understanding the Stories Jesus Told*, Baker Books, Grand Rapids, MI, © 1980

Life Application Study Bible Notes, Copyright © 1988, 1989, 1990, 1991, 1993, 1996, 2004, 2007 by Tyndale House Foundation, Database © 2014 WORDsearch

Lockyer, Herbert, *All the Parables of the Bible,* Zondervan, Grand Rapids, MI, © 1963

MacArthur, John F. Jr., *God with Us: The Miracle of Christmas*, Zondervan Books, Grand Rapids, MI, © 1969

MacDonald, William, *The Believer's Commentary,* Thomas Nelson, Nashville, TN, © 1995

Meyer, F.B., *Devotional Commentary*, Tyndale House Pub., Wheaton, IL, 1989

Osborn, Frederick, *This Gospel of the Kingdom,* BfA Books, USA, © 2011, 2014, 2017)

Osborn, Frederick, *Exploring the New Testament,* BfA Books, USA, © 2010, 2015

Osborn, Frederick, *Our Jehovah Rapha,* BfA Books, USA, © 2014

Pentecost, J. Dwight, *The Parables of Jesus: Lessons in Life from The Master Teacher*, Kregel Publications, Grand Rapids, MI, © 1982

Pheiffer, Charles F., *Between the Testaments*, Baker Book House, Grand Rapids, MI, © 1959

Pink, Arthur W., *The Gospel of John (Arthur Pink Collection Book 29),* Prisbrary Publishing; ASIN: B009CM52AQ, 1 edition (June 18, 2012), Kindle Edition
The International Standard Bible Encyclopedia, James Orr, M.A., D.D., General Editor, Database © 2004 WORDsearch Corp.

The Preacher's Outline & Sermon Bible ® Vol. 1; Matthew – John (New International Version), Authentic Books Logos, Secunderabad, India, Copyright © 2000 by Alpha-Omega Ministries. Inc.

The Ultimate Commentary On Mark: A Collective Wisdom On the Bible
Albert Barnes; John Calvin; Adam Clarke; Matthew Henry; Charles H. Spurgeon; John Wesley, ASIN: B01BFHF218, Kindle Edition

The Ultimate Commentary On Matthew: A Collective Wisdom On the Bible,
Albert Barnes; John Calvin; Adam Clarke; Matthew Henry; Charles H. Spurgeon; John Wesley, ASIN:B01AOMP9WC, Kindle Edition

Wiersbe, Warren W., *The Wiersbe Bible Commentary*, David C. Cook Publisher, Colorado Springs, CO, © 2007

Wilson, Walter L., *A Dictionary of Bible Types*, Hendrickson Publishers, Peabody, MA, © 1999

BIBLE TRANSLATIONS
The New King James Version Bible (NKJV)
Copyright © 1982 by Thomas Nelson, Inc. All Rights Reserved.
Database © 2008 WORDsearch Corp.

English Standard Version (ESV)
© 2001 by Crossway Bible, a division of Good News Publishers.
Database © 2015 WORDsearch

New International Version of the Bible (NIV)
© 1973, 1978, 1984, International Bible Society, Database© 2007 WORDsearch

Holy Bible, New Living Translation, Second Edition (NLT)
© 1996, 2004 by Tyndale Charitable Trust. All rights reserved. Database © 2013 WORDsearch.

Biography

Dr. Frederick Osborn travels the world teaching and preaching the Word of God. His first trip to South Asia was in 2001, and since 2005 he has been fully involved in ministry. From 2009 – 2017 he served as the India Field Director for *Bibles for All Ministries* and traveled around the country as a lecturer, distributing Bibles and biblical resources to pastors, evangelists and ministry leaders. His books and study guides have been used by hundreds of students and have been translated into several languages. He earned his M.Div. from Andhra Christian Theological College in Hyderabad and completed his D.Min. in Theology from Covenant Bible College & Seminary in Madison, FLA in 2017. He now lives in Atlanta, Georgia with his wife, Lakshmalla Deena Benjamin.

Several of his books and study guides have been translated into the local languages of South Asia and hundreds of village pastors, ministry leaders, and lay leaders completed one or more of his courses on *This Gospel of the Kingdom, Exploring the New Testament, Legacy of Women in the Bible, Kingdom Discipleship, and Disciple to Disciple.* In addition to the books and study guides, he has delivered countless seminars and sermons relating to one or more of these subjects. These lessons have been shared and are being shared today with literally thousands of believers in India. He does all of this free of cost to those who have benefitted from these teaching materials. He has been able to distribute thousands of Bibles, Bible study books, and commentaries also free of cost to those in need throughout South Asia. He believes it is his calling to teach the unvarnished truth of the Word of God to those who have little or no opportunity to study God's Word on their own.

FREDERICK OSBORN

Books Written By Frederick Osborn

1. *Building Wealth 2: Kingdom Economics in the 21st Century*
2. *Church Planting Movements - India*
3. *Deceived! Overcoming the Age of Mass Deception*
4. *Disciple-to-Disciple: Making Disciples Like Jesus*
5. *Disciple- to-Disciple: Making Disciples Like Jesus, Study Guide*
6. *Exploring the New Testament*
7. *Exploring the Old Testament: Vol. One – The Pentateuch*
8. *Following Christ on the Indian Road: A Missionary's Story of Discipleship*
9. *From Genesis to Revelation: Interpreting the Book of Revelation Through the Old Testament Scriptures*
10. *Jesus Over India: A 52 Week Spiritual Journey Through the Heart of India*
11. *Judges: A 21st Century Prophetic Commentary*
12. *Kingdom Discipleship: Becoming Like Jesus*
13. *Kingdom Discipleship: Becoming a Disciple Like Jesus, Study Guide*
14. *One Holy Passion: A Daily Devotional Guide for 40 Days of Prayer and Fasting for the 1040 Nations*
15. *Our Jehovah Rapha: A Christ Centered Holistic Approach to Wellness*
16. *Reviving A Nation*
17. *The Book of Acts: The Holy Spirit's Handbook for Church Planting Movements*
18. *The Church in Crisis: Four Essays on Contemporary Issues for Christians in the 21st Century*
19. *The Gospel of Salvation*
20. *The Gospel of Salvation: Study Guide*
21. *The Healthy Heart*
22. *The Holy Spirit in You: Nourishing the Life of Holiness and power in You*
23. *The Legacy of Women in the Bible – Study Guide*
24. *The New Reformation: An Assessment of the New Apostolic Reformation from Toronto to Redding*
25. *The Physics of Heaven: The Theology of the New Apostolic Reformation*
26. *The Spirit of Religion*
27. *This Gospel of the Kingdom*
28. *This Gospel of the Kingdom – Study Guide*

BACK COVER

"I am the way, the truth, and the life. No one can come to the Father except through me."

Beginning with Luke's inspired account numerous books have been written that attempt to describe the life of Jesus of Nazareth in an orderly fashion. However, one of the great challenges for the modern commentator is the fact that the Gospel writers were not historians by contemporary standards. Matthew, Mark, Luke, and John were first and foremost, missionaries; and the stories they told had one primary purpose: to convince their readers that what they testified about Jesus Christ was faithful and true.

Frederick Osborn has spent the last twelve years on the mission fields of South Asia preaching and teaching the Gospel in cross-cultural settings. Relying upon the texts of Matthew, Mark, Luke and John, his goal is to make convincing arguments to communicate the idea that through His life, death, and resurrection Jesus of Nazareth is indeed Lord and Christ for all who believe.

This study on the life of Christ is topical not chronological. It does not completely ignore the Gospels' sequence of events, but the topics overlap at times and at times the chronology is not precise. The topics will at least touch on every major event, and will only go into details when those details are necessary to give greater depth and understanding to the particular topic of that lesson. This volume is a wide-ranging study of the words and ministry of Jesus of Nazareth. In the end it will be thorough and complete.

Made in the USA
Columbia, SC
02 January 2018